D0828439

Whose FBI?

Whose FBI?

Edited by
Richard O. Wright

Open Court · La Salle, Illinois

Copyright © 1974 by Open Court Publishers

All rights reserved. Printed in the United States of America. No part of this publication may be reproduced, stored in a retrieval system, or transmitted, in any form or by any means, electronic, mechanical, photocopying, recording, or otherwise, without the prior written permission of the publisher, The Open Court Publishing Co., Box 599, La Salle, Illinois 61301.

Printed in the United States of America

Library of Congress Cataloging in Publication Data
Wright, Richard O   1942-
  Whose FBI?
  Includes bibliographical references.
  1. United States. Federal Bureau of Investigation.
I. Title.
HV8138.W73   364.12'06'173   74-60
ISBN 0-87548-148-5

Contents

Foreword
Clark R. Mollenhoff

Freedom demands that a society police itself. When it does so fairly, a direct relationship exists between the effectiveness of the police system and the survival of civil rights, personal property rights, and political rights that is the essence of real freedom. It can be said without fear of contradiction that an honest and fair-minded cop is the best defender of civil rights.

While recognizing the need for a society to police itself in order to safeguard the civil rights and property rights of its citizens, there must also be recognition that any police power can be abused and can become a constant menace to the freedom of every citizen.

The power to police is actually less important in a democratic society than an understanding of the need to limit that power. Restraint in the exercise of that power is important to every citizen. The limitations on police power must assure basic procedural rights to every militant civil rights demonstrator, no matter how irresponsible; every Mafia member, no matter how despicable his alleged crimes; and every member of the Ku Klux Klan, no matter how hate-filled his rhetoric.

Too often, discussions of the FBI have tended to inflame participants with the rhetoric of extremism that has left little room for persuasion and reason to bring agreement on the middle ground.

Proper balance in the police function is difficult to achieve in any society. Too often, overreaction to the chaos resulting from excesses in the pursuit of liberty has resulted in the establishment of a police state.

The well-documented abuses of police power revealed in the hearings on the Watergate incident and related matters make the publication of this book of particular importance at the present time, when there is a real possibility of citizen and legislative overreaction to the excesses of the executive branch.

It is well to remember that the abuses of police power as disclosed during the Watergate hearings would have been greater if the late J. Edgar Hoover, then director of the Federal Bureau of Investigation, had not rejected a 1970 White House plan for intelligence gathering that approved burglary. Certainly, the politicizing of the FBI under Acting Director L. Patrick Gray III gives us a look at the manner in which politics can quickly distort and destroy even the best disciplined law enforcement agency.

This book presents, in a balanced and objective manner, a clear picture of the FBI as a necessary American institution, even as it strips away the myths of infallibility. It demonstrates to the critics of the agency how the late J. Edgar Hoover was the greatest single obstacle to expansion of federal police powers, contrary to the uninformed rhetoric that has often clouded his name.

Critics on both sides of the political spectrum will do well to examine the facts recorded in this book and then attempt to punch holes in the ideas presented. In doing so, it is likely that any serious reader will find his way to the balanced middle ground.

The editors have done a particularly good job, presenting again and again examples of why the rule of law must apply in the same manner to the Ku Klux Klan, the Mafia, or to militant civil rights groups. The various writers point out with surprisingly uniform balance that the FBI cannot be allowed to assume the mythical character upon which the most ardent defenders and most vocal critics dwell.

The oversimplifications of television and the movies have convinced the great majority of Americans and many of its staunchest supporters that the FBI is a super-crusade bureau that deals harshly, but efficiently, with the enemies of a free society, both foreign and domestic. Many well-intentioned critics, and some cynical FBI haters, have viewed the FBI in the ghostly counter-myth of an Orwellian Big Brother or Gestapo force.

Throughout this book, the authors clear the air of the nonsensical rhetoric used by the extreme civil libertarian critics and the blind defenders. They analyze through examples and explanation the specific duties and responsibility assigned by the Congress to the FBI, as well as the external and self-imposed restraints placed on the activities of the bureau.

Whether it involves the espionage activities of left-wing or right-wing governments, or deals with extremists on the domestic scene, the ever-present theme of this book is to persuade conscientious civil libertarians and conscientious advocates of law and order that the limitations placed upon the FBI must apply equally in all instances. It is demonstrated that these limitations are not set as obstacles to the attainment of either civil rights or proper law and order, but that they are a necessary control to prevent abuses of legitimate police powers.

Time after time dramatic examples are offered of how the late J. Edgar Hoover shunned additional powers. We are reminded that he was opposed to court-authorized wiretapping for years, and only reluctantly allowed it. He consistently opposed injecting the FBI into such sensitive matters as investigation of labor leaders, enforcement of laws dealing with the financing of elections, or political scandals. He always fought off the well-intentioned proposals that would make the FBI a national police force.

The FBI has a large enough duty to perform under the federal laws in just obtaining the facts on matters called to its attention through the proper governmental channels without taking on the vague carte blanche job of seeking to "uphold the Constitution" while applying its own judgments.

This book should be must reading for anyone who really wishes to understand how the FBI operates, the limitations on its power, why those limitations exist, and why the critics should think long and hard before removing those limitations.

It is in the best interest of this nation that every citizen understand a little better the power of the FBI and the limitations on that power that are so important to keeping it the fine organization that it became under J. Edgar Hoover. It is well to remember that order in a society is dependent upon an effective police force that makes it reasonably certain that those who violate the laws and the rights of other citizens will pay for their law violations. However, by the same token, there is always a likelihood that police powers will be abused by men who are malicious or impatient with procedures that must protect criminals as well as the innocent.

It will be difficult for any extremist of the right or left to read this book without becoming a little more tolerant. For those who tread the middle of the road, it is a documented fortification for judgments that balanced thinking always supports firm, but fair, enforcement methods.

Acknowledgment

The editors wish to acknowledge the diligent research work of Professor Dwight D. Murphey, Wichita State University, Professor Olan B. Lowrey, Temple University Law School, William Stanmeyer, on leave from Georgetown University Law Center, Attorney Fred Gambino, University of Chicago law students Donald and Sue Schwartz, and journalist Alice Widener.

This book is the result of a study conducted by Americans for Effective Law Enforcement, Inc., under the direction of the editor, assisted by William K. Lambie, also of the AELE staff.

Source materials were made available by the FBI on the same basis as the bureau provides materials for all bona fide researchers. The editors acknowledge the valuable counsel of former bureau officials Louis Nichols, Stan Tracy, and William Sullivan; and former agents Russell White and Jack Shaw. The study was made possible by a grant from the Friends of the FBI, Inc. The opinions expressed here are those of the individual authors and editors.

RICHARD O. WRIGHT, *staff*
Americans for Effective
Law Enforcement
Evanston, Illinois 60201

1. This Is the FBI
Editors

In the post-World War II years, conflict convulsed the world of government and politics in America. The wartime unity at home gave way to hostile debates and angry campaigns. Much of this turmoil was part of a larger world conflict, the "Cold War" with Communist nations and organizations. The Federal Bureau of Investigation gained a new reputation in this "cold" but real war.

Government in Washington, not without great anxiety, was tightening its security. Loyalty boards reviewed the records of employees, some of whom were found to be risks to the national security; the Communist Party of America was on trial; and new laws were being passed to strengthen the government's position against domestic Communists. All these things brought the FBI, as an investigatory arm of the federal government, more and more into the field of internal security.

In 1950, a New York attorney-author, Max Lowenthal, published *The Federal Bureau of Investigation,** a book which purported to be a documented examination of the FBI from its beginnings in 1908. Only a few chapters dealt with the total bureau, however; the remainder constituted an attack on the internal security functions of the agency. To Lowenthal, the FBI was an organization which investigated opinions and beliefs, involved itself in labor disputes (on the side of management), raided radical headquarters and homes, compiled "dossiers" on suspected radicals, and prepared the way for the "red-baiting" of the post-war period. Whatever investigations the FBI conducted in criminal law enforcement Lowenthal characterized as secondary to the real aim of the bureau, which was, in his belief, to war against radicals.

*New York: William Sloan Associates, 1950.

1

Lowenthal's book reduced to print the suspicious attitude of many with regard to the bureau's internal security function. Many others hotly disputed his contentions (Walter Winchell labeled the book "a vicious one-sided attack on J. Edgar Hoover").

On a morning in July 1951, however, the Kansas City, Missouri office of the FBI had things other than the Cold War to contend with. The office had received a telephone call from a worried businessman in Columbia, Missouri. The caller was a coal and building materials retailer, and his family was rather well-to-do. He had received a threatening letter in the morning mail and immediately called the FBI.

Whoever wrote the letter demanded $10,000 in cash by 3:00 P.M. the following day and said "I'll kill you like a frog" unless the demand was met.

FBI agents at the Kansas City office went to work quickly, opening an extortion investigation and giving it "major case" status. The special agent in charge (SAC) immediately telephoned bureau headquarters in Washington, the usual practice for major cases. Headquarters ordered the field office to teletype daily reports to Washington throughout the active phase of the investigation.

At the same time, the assistant SAC contacted an agent then working in Columbia and ordered him to the extortion victim's office. Within the hour eleven other agents left for Columbia in cars equipped with two-way radios and supplied with additional communications equipment.

In Columbia, the agent interviewed the intended victim and obtained the extortion note. He hoped to develop leads to a suspect. Perhaps a disgruntled employee or former employee, a competitor or others potentially hostile to the businessman had written the note. But in a town like Columbia, the lumber dealer was known to everyone, and would be an easy target for anyone who wanted to try his hand at extortion. The extortion note itself was the only good clue.

The note appeared to be deadly serious. It was a two page, hand-printed letter which described in great detail how the victim or a family member could easily be seen and shot through a large picture window. This clearly indicated that the writer had seen the home, located in a remote wooded area south of Columbia and having the sort of picture window and surroundings described in the letter.

The letter also contained detailed instructions on the preparation of the package of money, and when and where it was to be left. The money, in old bills, was to be placed in a large coffee can and left by the side of what was then a rather remote road south of the University of Missouri football stadium and not far from the victim's residence.

The note also stated that no one was to notify the Columbia Police Department. The writer claimed that he had friends in the department and that he would find out if such a report were made.

The note was sent to the FBI Laboratory, but there was no time to wait for the results. The agents had to be ready at the site of the cash drop, and they made plans for the preparation and drop of a package the following day.

In the meantime, it was decided not to notify the Columbia Police Department because of the demand made in the note. The intended victim had not done so himself, and despite the fact that the case also constituted a violation of the criminal laws of the State of Missouri, the FBI agents were instructed not to make any disclosures to the Columbia Police Department —an unusual procedure in a criminal case, particularly since the local police were well regarded and the chief and chief of detectives were both graduates of the FBI National Academy.

Agents talked over this matter with the victim, for it was his safety at stake. The agents also discussed with him whether he should pay the cash as demanded. This was his decision to make.

The agents followed the usual FBI procedure in this. Except in unusual circumstances, the FBI's primary consideration is the safety of the threatened person. Here, however, the extortionist held no hostage, and the FBI recommended that a dummy package be placed at the scene of the pickup.

It was his option, and he knew the risk, but the Columbia

businessman agreed to have the FBI prepare a dummy package. It followed the instructions in the letter but contained cut-up newspaper with a few actual bills on top, instead of the full sum of $10,000. This was the bait. The FBI would attempt to apprehend the extortionist at the time and place of the pickup.

This decision together with a report of the results of the day's investigations were communicated to the bureau by teletype on the first evening of the investigation. In addition, agents sent a copy of the extortion letter by airplane to the FBI Laboratory with a request for a complete laboratory examination. This included testing for latent fingerprints, a full examination of the common notepaper and a preliminary examination of the hand printing for comparison with samples in the laboratory's files.

Also that day, some of the twelve assigned agents began a discreet physical observation of the pickup area, in hopes that the suspect might appear to check the situation. No suspect turned up.

In fact, the agents had little hope of identifying their suspect before the pickup time, but they tried in any case. Some of the twelve agents began quietly checking the background of employees, former employees and associates of the victim. The results of these checks were negative. No suspect was developed.

On the following day, while background investigation continued, several of the agents prepared for the deposit and pickup of the package. A few hours before the appointed time other agents stationed themselves in underbrush and in concealed locations near the designated location. Since it was an undeveloped area with a relatively unused road for access, the FBI autos were kept out of sight and communications were maintained by using two-way radios. Other agents concealed an "extortion switch," a simple battery-operated metal contact underneath the dummy package, and they then concealed wires to a location where two agents were hidden.

Well before the deadline hour the Columbia businessman

drove alone in his own car to the designated spot. There he dropped a red, two-pound coffee can as prepared, and quickly left. The trap was set.

Watching patiently, the agents waited for the extortion switch to signal that the package had been moved. Soon the light went out, and like a guerrilla band hitting a road, the agents swarmed out of the bushes to confront a young man, carrying a small caliber rifle, kicking the coffee can, still sealed and full, along the shoulder of the road.

"This is the FBI," exclaimed an agent. The young man was overwhelmed by the army he faced and offered no resistance. Agents disarmed and physically searched him but did not formally place him under arrest at this time.

Since the local police department had not been advised of the case, the agents were using rooms in a local hotel as their headquarters rather than the local police facility. Agents took the subject to one of the rooms, and though he was not formally under arrest, they advised him of his rights. Two agents then interviewed him extensively.

He wanted to talk. The suspect furnished complete background data, telling the agents that he was a local resident, married with one child, a student at the university and the son of a local real estate dealer and attorney. He denied any knowledge of or participation in the extortion attempt. He claimed that he had been out in the woods hunting for squirrels, had walked along the road and, seeing the can, had simply kicked it along the shoulder of the road as any small boy might do. He also voluntarily furnished extensive handwriting and hand printing samples including the text of the extortion letter, in his own hand printing. The suspect wanted to appear cooperative, but he apparently did not know what experts could do by examining his handwriting sample.

During this initial interview, a number of inconsistencies appeared in his statements. A visual comparison of the handprinted samples with the extortion letter, both of which contained misspellings of many of the same words, together with the inconsistencies and his general demeanor, all tended to convince the interviewing agents that he was indeed the person who had written and sent the letter. However, in view of his denials and the somewhat unusual circumstances of the pickup, prosecution was not authorized at that time. All of the above was communicated to bureau headquarters by telephone and the subject was released and returned to his home.

The FBI had its man, they were certain, but their work was just begun. Now, they had to make a case. They sent his handwriting and printing samples to the FBI Laboratory for comparison with the extortion letter, and they began a loose (covert) physical surveillance on the subject. At the same time, agents began an intensive background investigation, interviewing all the suspect's known associates and contacts in an effort to learn all that could be learned about him. This included a search of his locker at the university, consented to by appropriate university authorities, and a search of his residence, consented to by the subject.

During the course of the background investigation, the FBI learned that the subject was doing poorly in his university studies, that his marriage had not been approved by his parents, and that he was in financial difficulty. It was further learned that his favorite hobby was "frog gigging." Twice in the extortion letter the writer had used the phrase, "I'll kill you like a frog." But that, of course, was not enough to make a case.

The surveillance and background investigation continued through that week, with daily teletyped summaries of the progress of the case being sent to Washington. However, when no significant new information was developed, the agents suspended the surveillance.

On Sunday the FBI Laboratory telephoned the Kansas City assistant SAC. A comparison of the subject's known hand printing samples with the hand printing on the extortion letter had resulted in a positive identification of the subject as the writer of the letter. The laboratory examination had revealed no other physical evidence. The assistant SAC relayed this information to the United States attorney, who, on the basis of the laboratory examination, authorized prosecution on the extortion charge.

At the same time, agents resumed their physical surveillance of the subject, this time around the clock. It was a Sunday, so a warrant for arrest was not obtainable; but the FBI had no intention of losing its man.

An agent contacted the nearest United States commissioner in Jefferson City, Missouri, who agreed to be in his office at 7:00 A.M. on Monday to issue the arrest warrant, and the agents on the case were instructed that the arrest was to be made when the subject left his home for an 8:00 A.M. class.

However, the suspect appeared to be preparing to escape. Late on Sunday morning, he left his residence by car and took a short ride. FBI agents followed. The suspect began making sudden increases and decreases in speed and engaged in a number of maneuvers designed to determine whether or not he was being followed. He made no stops until he returned to his home. Early in the afternoon, with his wife and child, he again left in his car and drove to the residence of a friend several miles out in the country. After several more brief auto trips, he traveled finally to a farm near his friend's parents. There, he and his friend picked up a four wheel drive jeep vehicle, drove in the jeep a short distance, turning from the paved road onto a dirt road that had been under water until a few days before and which, though negotiable by the jeep, could not be safely entered by the bureau cars without risk of bogging down. The agents did not enter but quickly learned that the road dead-ended at a farm about a mile away. After a reasonable time, when the jeep did not return, agents in one bureau car returned to the friend's house and sought the assistance of an additional surveillance car. At these premises the subject's friend was observed returning on foot. Stepping to the man, "This is the FBI," an agent explained and questioned him about the whereabouts of the suspect. He was hostile but he admitted that the subject and he had parked the jeep and walked cross-country back to the house, apparently in an effort to elude the surveillance.

The agents figured the time had come to end the little game. Telephoning the assistant director in charge of the General Investigative Division in Washington, they requested the authority to arrest the subject without a warrant in light of his efforts to escape the surveillance. In the meantime the subject and his family returned to their home, remained there briefly and then drove to the local swimming pool.

After approximately two hours, headquarters advised that, upon consultation with the Department of Justice, authority had been granted to arrest the subject prior to the issuance of a warrant. At the swimming pool late Sunday afternoon agents again approached the suspect, flashed their identification and said, "This is the FBI, you're under arrest." He did not resist and was immediately transported to the county jail at Jefferson City where he was locked up over night. Again, the subject was formally advised of his rights immediately upon his arrest and arraignment was set to take place before the United States commissioner at Jefferson City at 9:00 A.M. on Monday, the beginning of his regular office hours.

During the 30 mile trip to Jefferson City, the subject steadfastly maintained his innocence, although he made several casual comments that seemed to hint at his guilt.

With his parents and his attorney present in the office of the United States commissioner at 9:00 A.M. on Monday, the suspected extortionist, still maintaining his innocence, was formally charged with the crime of extortion through the use of the U.S. mail. The commissioner granted bond in the amount of $50,000 and he was released.

Following the suspect's arraignment and release, the case still was not closed as far as the FBI was concerned. Agents began writing investigative reports and a trial summary report for the United States attorney. Other agents completed remaining background investigation.

The bureau had made its case. When the suspect later came

to trial, he entered a plea of guilty to the extortion charge. He was convicted, and as a first offender, he received a probationary sentence of five years.

"This is the FBI," was a statement which meant something quite different in Columbia, Missouri, than what it meant for Max Lowenthal and for those who fought the Cold War battles. No weighty matters of the Cold War were being investigated here, no radicals were under surveillance, nor was anyone greatly concerned either before or after the case as to whether the FBI was acting properly—none of the momentous issues of the times seemed to have bearing on this FBI case. Instead, an attempt at extortion was made by an amateur, a student whose hardships, he thought, could be 'erased by a small part of the wealth of another, his victim. The Federal Bureau of Investigation—were they ignorant of the greater issues?—spared no effort, and nipped the crime in the bud.

Indeed this is the FBI. A "major case" involving only $10,000 but in which a family was endangered, was the object of investigation by twelve FBI agents, working long hours, amounting to a total of over 700 man hours in the initial six-day period of the investigation. Additionally, the case was a major concern to officials at the Washington headquarters of the bureau, and at the FBI Laboratory, where more effort was expended.

As it turned out, the case was routine, although extortion cases are treated as major cases by the bureau. These and similar routine cases, however, are by far the main work of the FBI. And whatever issues are involved are limited, submerged in the daily work of law enforcement in this country.

Agents made certain judgments in this case, which, had the same sort of discretion been exercised in less routine investigations, could have embroiled the FBI in heated controversy. For example, there was the matter of the arrest warrant. Because the agents feared the suspect's escape, they arrested him prior to obtaining a warrant. Even then, permission was requested from higher authority, evidencing a high degree of caution. Imagine another case, where the same attempts to elude the

FBI were made, but the suspect, rather than an extortionist, was one whose alleged law violation was in the internal security field, thus touching the sensibilities of those who debate the issues of the Cold War. In the latter instance, anti-FBI forces would very probably have raised a hue and cry about the arrest. Then what was the practical judgment of the FBI would have been damned as intimidation. But no one made an issue of it on behalf of an extortionist. Instead, in this case, only the matter of the FBI's relationship with the Columbia Police Department was an issue, and this in private.

As indicated previously, the local police were not notified of the reported extortion threat or of the FBI activity in the case in spite of the fact that extortion is a violation of state as well as federal law, thus, the local authorities had concurrent jurisdiction. Under ordinary circumstances this would have been a routine procedure and normally the local authorities will defer to the FBI, asking only to be kept advised of progress. Because of the statement in the extortion letter, however, a judgment was made, either by the special agent in charge of the Kansas City office or by a bureau official (but necessarily concurred in by headquarters in any event) that the Columbia police not be advised. However, with active surveillance being conducted, the local police were aware of the presence of bureau personnel in Columbia and generally aware of the bureau's activity. This they presumed to be connected with an internal security investigation. Indeed, surveillances being what they are, in a relatively small community, the police had received calls from concerned citizens reporting the presence of the FBI cars. The police reassured them, not wishing to interfere with whatever investigation the bureau was performing.

Unfortunately, a state Highway Patrol lieutenant who had learned of the case during a visit to the Kansas City office earlier in the week, made a casual remark about the case to the Columbia police chief on the Saturday after the letter was received. The chief, a graduate of the FBI's National Academy and a highly respected police official, was angered and complained bitterly to the Kansas City FBI office. It was then suggested that he be invited to take part in the arrest of the subject, a courtesy that would have been extended routinely under more usual circumstances. In this case, however, the chief, still smarting from what he regarded as a professional discourtesy as well as an affront to his personal and departmental integrity, declined. The bureau, convinced of the correctness of its original decision, made no effort to apologize to the chief although a number of the individual agents made subsequent personal apologies (thereby risking official censure). Official relations between the FBI and the local police, which had been extremely cordial and cooperative, cooled considerably, although overall efficiency was not impaired because the informal, personal relationships remained good.

The bureau is usually convinced of its rightness; it is an organization of agents doing a tough job in the best way they can. They are cautious and thorough, and they seldom get caught making mistakes. Their work is systematized to the point that most of it is routine—few cases have any more drama than the one just narrated. Arrests and investigations are perfunctory, most often; *French Connection* scenes are lacking.

The point is, this is the FBI, and the real FBI story is hardly the stuff of thrilling novels and gripping true stories (although any police agency has them to tell). Why then do people write books about the bureau? Why did Max Lowenthal tell his tale of intimidation and woe thrust upon us by the agents of the Federal Bureau of Investigation? Why do the contributors to the present book spend so much effort at developing perspectives on the FBI?

The answer lies in the fact that occasionally—only in certain functions—the FBI's investigative work is intertwined with the great issues of the century. Its investigations are routine, but the objects of some of them are inexorably a part of a protracted conflict between tyranny and freedom. Certain of the bureau's assignments involve it as a frontline force in this war.

Thus it is that a book on the FBI is really a discussion of

the broader issues of the conflict. Even in this perspective, however, it should be remembered always that the Federal Bureau of Investigation is an agency built to do its job in a quiet, efficient way. The larger issues are inflamed and vital, but *this* is the FBI.

2. Myth and Counter-Myth
Editors*

John Doar, as an assistant attorney general, headed the Justice Department's civil rights campaign in the Kennedy administration. He is a fine gentleman and lawyer, and an uncommon idealist—just the sort of man Robert Kennedy wanted to charge into the South on behalf of civil rights. Charge he did indeed, leading a regular crusade for Negro voting rights in the South.

In the years 1961-63, Doar's Justice Department attorneys journeyed into the deep South to investigate registration records, registration officials, and registration patterns in dozens of southern state counties, and federal law suits were prepared against some of the counties and even some states. The entrenched officials of the South thought it was an invasion.

Justice Department lawyers, however, were too few to mount a full scale offensive. Knowing this, Doar wanted the FBI to join his crusade. In this hope, he was largely disappointed.

Not that the bureau did not participate—the assistant attorney general employed hundreds of FBI agents for conducting thousands of interviews, copying thousands of registration records and other investigations related to federal civil rights suits. Doar wanted more, however. He wanted the FBI agents to become soldiers in a war against the "caste system" of the South.

---

*The editors are indebted to Charles Rice, professor of law at Notre Dame University, for a basic draft of a major part of this chapter.

The assistant attorney general was chagrined at the lack of bureau preparation for the Civil Rights Division's southern foray, and he was unhappy with the fact that the FBI agents, although spending countless man-hours, did no more than what was specifically requested by division attorneys. His most persistent complaint was that investigative reports from FBI agents were no more than raw data. Analysis remained the job of the Justice Department division. He had all these criticisms, but they reduce to one irritant: that the bureau investigations were confoundedly neutral. The FBI just was not trying to show that discrimination existed, in John Doar's view.

Being fair minded, Doar does not charge, as have others, that the FBI was populated by southerners interested in protecting the invidious "caste system." He recognizes that after 1964, when the nation awoke to the civil rights cause, the bureau changed, and undertook civil rights investigations with the same "thoroughness, persistence, and toughmindedness" for which it had become famous.

What Doar does not recognize, however, are the nuances of the niche carved out in America's federal system for the Federal Bureau of Investigation. He does not quite understand— although he and others in the Kennedy Justice Department struggled with it—the bureau's independence from essentially political decision-making in Washington, including its independence from the same within the Justice Department. He cannot understand the FBI's reluctance to expand its efforts into a crusade which might plow over long and well-defined jurisdictional barriers. He does not understand these things and as a result he does not know what the FBI is all about.

What Doar thought were "superficial" investigations by FBI agents in the early civil rights offensive by the Justice Department, in actuality were the efforts of a bureau force trained to operate within its lawful authority. What Doar viewed as a lack of interest and preparation, in actuality was an attitude of FBI agents determined to do their duty in a professional manner, neutral in the sense that they only enforced the law and did not make the law. Yet, to have expected anything else of the FBI, is to have believed in a mythical agency, an FBI which grew up in the public mind, but has never actually existed. Civil rights crusaders have not been the only Americans to accept the myth. Indeed, the common impression is that the FBI is the country's frontline force, ready to do anything in its relentless battle to eradicate evil and dispense justice. When a law enforcement problem of national concern arises, the first thought is to send for the FBI, and the bureau is expected to rush in with all the considerable forces at its disposal. This was the case when concern arose about the pervasive and deadening influence of organized crime—a job for the FBI they said. But the crusaders (this time they were crusaders against syndicated crime) expected a mythical FBI to respond to their demand, quickly, forcefully and persistently until organized crime was eradicated from shore to shore. The real FBI, however, waited for the lead of Attorney General Robert Kennedy, and then Attorney General John Mitchell, as well as Congress, before joining the crusade.

To be sure, the real FBI is a frontline force in the battle for justice. It is not, however, an agency which rushes in to do whatever job needs done, nor can America permit it to take that character. The FBI should be and is an investigative agency having very limited powers. Instead of a police unit which charges into every legal crusade, it properly remains a bureau which operates cautiously, ever watchful of its proper authority and the traditional restraints on federal power. This is the real FBI, the FBI studied in detail by the contributors to this book.

Understanding the FBI, unfortunately, has been made even more difficult by another phenomenon, the belief in another non-existent FBI, the FBI of a counter-myth. Like the myth of a super-crusader bureau, the counter-myth is also ignorant of the true character of the FBI.

The counter-myth has many complicated external shapes, but its heart is simple: the desire to dispel the "legend" of the FBI. Knowing that the American public holds the bureau in very high esteem, the perpetrators of the counter-myth seek to destroy that public favor, and to do so they themselves create legends. Among these are: the legend of the police state-FBI (which opposes all radical change), and the legend of the rigid bureaucratic-FBI (which is not capable of adapting new priorities). These are the legends created by the critics who respond to the more commonly believed legend of the super action agency FBI.

Both views of the bureau are wrong. Both exaggerate the position of the FBI in the American system, and in so exaggerating, both views are dangerous to the continued propriety of federal investigative work.

The simple fact is, the Federal Bureau of Investigation is a creature of the United States Constitution and federal statutory law. It is no more than what has been established as its jurisdiction and power; or if it is more, it has grown beyond its proper limits.

This latter point cannot be overemphasized. There are several areas in which it has been charged that FBI investigations invade personal liberties, exceed the bureau's jurisdiction, or encroach on the powers of the state. Most often, however, these complaints are expressed in generalities and are not based on the constitutional and statutory powers of the FBI. Yet, the legal legitimacy of the FBI's operations can be understood only in terms of the statutory framework of its jurisdiction in the context of constitutional division of powers between state and federal governments. This is a consideration somewhat separate from a discussion of whether the FBI invades personal liberties, a subject undertaken later in this book.

The FBI is bound to observe what was once generally understood: that the U.S. Constitution divides governmental powers between federal and state governments, and that the federal government has only such powers as are delegated to it, all others being reserved to the states or the people. FBI investigations observe this division of powers even in cases which are of obvious importance to the federal government. An example is the recent assassination attempt against Governor George Wallace. Arthur Bremer, who had stalked political targets for months, finally caught the presidential candidate at a rally in a Laurel, Maryland shopping center. Pushing toward his victim Bremer began shooting, seriously wounding the governor and also hitting a campaign worker, a Secret Service agent and an Alabama State Police captain.

Bremer, of course, had no chance of escaping and was wrestled to the ground immediately after firing the shots. Nevertheless, an investigation was necessary to determine the facts on which Bremer could be prosecuted to the fullest extent. The FBI quickly opened an investigation on the Wallace shootings, but its role was limited to preparing a case under the federal statutes involved. State of Maryland authorities also opened an investigation but approached the problem primarily as a case of attempted murder, which is in its jurisdiction. The FBI's authority in the Wallace case, on the other hand, had to be based on a specific federal statute, in this case the prohibition against violating the civil rights of a presidential candidate.

An illustration of the jurisdictional situation came eight days later, when Bremer was indicted by both state and federal grand juries. Maryland charged him with attempted murder, assault and battery, assault with intent to murder, assault with intent to maim, and violation of Maryland's hand gun control law. On the same day, the federal grand jury, based on evidence collected by the FBI, indicted Bremer for assaulting a presidential candidate (a federal civil rights violation), assaulting a federal officer (Secret Service agent), illegally transporting the gun from Wisconsin to Maryland, and using the weapon to commit a felony.*

As illustrated, the FBI is an arm of the federal government and has only limited powers to investigate certain cases. The general power to investigate murders and similar crimes is a

*New York Times, Tuesday, May 24, 1972 p. 35; U.S. News & World Report May 29, 1972 p. 13.

power belonging to the states, and the FBI had to restrict its investigations of Arthur Bremer to the alleged violation of federal law.

This made little difference in the Bremer investigation, because the FBI had effective jurisdiction. But it happens in some cases that the FBI's investigation uncovers facts which require it to withdraw from the case. This was the situation a few years ago when a Negro church in a southern state was burned in circumstances indicating that this may have been intended to intimidate Negroes from registering to vote, a violation of federal law at the time. The FBI investigated, within 24 hours determining that the persons responsible for the fire were in no way preventing Negroes from registering. The FBI was compelled to withdraw from the case, since at the time federal jurisdiction turned on the intent to violate the voter registration law, not on the occurrence of other acts against Negroes. The four arsonists were, in any case, convicted in local court and received substantial sentences.*

It happens that in other cases, particularly in the civil rights area, when the FBI withdraws or does not open a case, there is no assurance that local authorities or a local jury will bring the violators to justice because of prejudice or some other reason. However, this is no fault of the FBI. Those who are too impatient to understand the limitations on the FBI may think its agent is in league with the local authorities in such a situation. However, should the FBI step out of its bounds, even for such a laudable purpose as to right a wrong, it would do violence to the other important rights which are dependent on the checks and balances of the American federal system. The FBI is not, and should not become, a national police force. It does not have general authority to investigate violations of the Fourteenth Amendment or other civil rights violations. It has jurisdiction only as granted by the statutory law of the

---

*FBI Release, *The FBI and Civil Rights* (August, 1971).

United States, the directives of the president, and the direct orders of the attorney general.

The governing statutes provide the broad outlines of the FBI's investigative jurisdiction, and the detailed applications of that jurisdiction are determined administratively. It is important to note that the FBI does not have the power to determine its responsibilities on its own initiative. That is not its job, nor should it be, and the FBI is quite aware of this. The late director, J. Edgar Hoover, commented on this point in a letter to Professor Duane Lockard of Princeton University;

> We frequently are the targets of personal abuse, of the most vile invectives at the command of both the totalitarian right and the totalitarian left. Yet neither these nor those who appear to sympathize with them seem willing to publicly admit the basic and obvious fact that our investigative duties are not of our own choosing. They were delivered to us, with the requirement that we take all necessary action, by laws passed by the Congress and by rules and regulations laid down by the President and the attorney general.*

The Congress of the United States created the Federal Bureau of Investigation by statute** and it has also defined the general duties of the FBI. The Congress provided that the attorney general may appoint officials (1) to detect and prosecute crimes against the United States; (2) to assist in the protection of the President; and (3) to conduct such other investigations regarding official matters under the control of the Department of Justice and the Department of State as may be directed by the attorney general.*** But the Congress provided also that the FBI was not to be an exclusive federal police for it said also that the authority given the FBI did not limit the authority of departments and agencies other than the Justice Department to investigate crimes against the United States when jurisdiction has been assigned by law to such other departments and agencies. An example of this in practice is the Treasury

*Letter from J. Edgar Hoover to Duane Lockard, September 28, 1971.
**Chapter 33 of Title 28 of the United States Code, Section 531.
***Section 533 of Chapter 33 Title 28 of the United States Code.

Department's enforcement of the internal revenue laws, which is conducted by a division of the Treasury, the Internal Revenue Service.

Yet, these general provisions by themselves do not empower the FBI to investigate federal violations generally. The bureau is further limited in that it can investigate only those activities which are substantive violations of the United States Code. These are mainly the substantive crimes against the United States defined in Title 18 of the U.S. Code, covering such varied subjects as arson, civil rights, lotteries, perjury, racketeering, subversive activities, and others.

With respect to violations of most of these provisions, the FBI has a general investigative responsibility. With others, such as assassination of the President, investigative responsibility is expressly conferred on the FBI.*

An idea of how the American people, through the Congress, has vested investigative powers in the FBI can best be seen by examining a few of the 185 matters which are now substantive violations within the jurisdiction of the bureau. Some of the FBI's duties would surprise the casual viewer of Efrem Zimbalist's TV series, "The FBI."

For example, Indians and horses are a concern of the federal law. Congress banned the use of aircraft or motor vehicles in hunting any wild unbranded horses or burros on public land or ranges with the purpose of capturing or killing those animals. A law passed in 1960 makes it unlawful to destroy, deface, or remove certain boundary markers on Indian reservations, and to trespass on Indian reservations to hunt, fish, or trap. The FBI must investigate these matters.

More commonly known violations under the FBI's jurisdiction include interstate transportation of stolen goods, and interstate transportation in aid of racketeering, two obvious federal concerns.

Kidnapping is a famous concern of the bureau. After the

*18 U.S.C. 1751.

Lindbergh case, Congress authorized the FBI to initiate investigation of any kidnapping in which the victim has not been released within a certain time (now 24 hours) after a kidnapping. This is based on a "presumption" that the kidnappers have crossed state lines after that time. Otherwise the criminal act would be a state law enforcement concern.

Some of the FBI's jurisdiction relates to internal security. For instance, Public Law 88-290 (1964) amended the Internal Security Act of 1950 (McCarran Act) to provide that no person shall be employed in, detailed or assigned to, or continued to be employed, etc., in the National Security Agency unless he has been the subject of a full field investigation by the FBI (with certain exceptions).

Other provisions relate to violence and civil rights violations but the FBI can investigate those actions only as specifically defined by Congress, rather than the "do everything" version most often expressed by orators. For instance, the Civil Rights Act of 1968 established criminal penalties for interstate activities relating to riots; and for teaching or demonstrating the use of firearms, explosives, or incendiary devices, knowing these items will be used unlawfully in connection with a civil disorder. Additionally civil penalties are provided for discrimination in housing transactions. The FBI must depend on these and other statutes for jurisdiction in this area.

Sometimes the FBI gets jurisdiction as an afterthought. When President Kennedy was assassinated, many people assumed quite naturally that the FBI would enter the case. In fact, because of the national emergency the bureau did, but under the law, the assassination was a murder which vested jurisdiction only in the Texas authorities. Realizing this, Congress in 1965 passed a law providing penalties for killing, assaulting, or kidnapping the President, Vice President, and certain other officials. "Violations of this section shall be investigated by the Federal Bureau of Investigation," the act proclaimed.

A similar law is Public Law 91-614 (1971). This amends the Omnibus Crime Control and Safe Streets Act of 1968 to make it a federal violation to assassinate, kidnap, or assault a member of Congress or a member of Congress-elect. The FBI is specifically given investigative responsibility under this statute, as well.

Other areas of jurisdiction include aircraft hijacking, a problem of great importance in the past few years. This criminal activity was defined in an act passed in 1961, and other aircraft laws add to the FBI's duties, such as a 1962 act which authorizes the Civil Aeronautics Board to avail itself of the FBI's assistance in investigating the activities of any person in connection with a civil aircraft accident.

The fact that much of the FBI's work is far from the exciting pursuit of arch-enemies of the public, is illustrated by a few of many provisions relating to more mundane criminals. For example, the Federal Cigarette Labeling and Advertising Act makes it unlawful to manufacture, import, or package for sale or distribution within the United States any cigarette in a package which fails to bear a health caution statement. The FBI enforces this. Burning paper can result in FBI arrests, after Congress deemed it an offense knowingly to destroy or mutilate a Selective Service registration card. If instead of the draft card, the individual burns the American flag, he is in trouble pursuant to Public Law 90-381 (1968), which prohibits contemptuous public mutilating, defacing, burning or trampling of the flag of the United States.

This list does not begin to exhaust the statutory grants of investigative jurisdiction to the FBI. But the list does illustrate the variety and complexity of the FBI's responsibilities.

It illustrates also that in the main what the FBI does is rather specifically defined by the U.S. Congress. The bureau cannot simply initiate investigations of criminal activity. It must first be sure it has jurisdiction, and this is provided by its superiors in the executive and legislative branches.

Finally, the FBI's operations are limited in scope and method by constitutional requirements. These are often controversial matters and will be illustrated by an example.

The "civil rights" area of violations has become an important responsibility of the FBI. It was not always so. Prior to 1960, the federal criminal statutes relating to civil rights were quite narrow and the bureau's jurisdiction was correspondingly limited. The FBI could not merely rush about enforcing the Constitution. It needed specific statutory authority.

Returning to our beginning story, John Doar and his Civil Rights Division were too sophisticated not to recognize that the FBI, and the Justice Department overall, needed specific statutory authority to pursue the civil rights question in the South. The tendency in his department, however, was to take a broad view of what could be done under existing law. The FBI was not so prone to that view.

At the time of the Justice Department-FBI campaign in the South in the early 1960s, the broadest authority derived from two old statutes passed in the days of Reconstruction and violent Ku Klux Klan activities against Negroes.* These provided some criminal sanctions for violations such as holding persons in involuntary servitude, restricting a person's right to travel interstate, and discriminating against Negroes in voting. Any deprivation of rights secured or protected by the Constitution was subject to these criminal sanctions, but only those acting "under color of law" or acting in conspiracy with those who under color of law were violating civil rights.

This "under color of law" provision was a severe limitation. Private persons, not acting with state authority, were not violating constitutional rights, according to court interpretations of the act. The FBI, of course was compelled to respect this limitation. It could investigate only those civil rights matters which seemed to involve state and local authority.

Gradually, the interpretation was broadened by the Supreme Court, and as this happened, the FBI obtained more power to investigate matters of discrimination. In 1966, for instance,

---

*18 U.S.C. 241 and 242. Expanded power of the attorney general (and the FBI) to seek judicial relief was provided by the civil rights acts of 1957 and 1960.

the Supreme Court held that a person need not be a public official to be acting "under color of law."* Now, the FBI could cover persons who acted in willful joint activity with state agents.

This was the case in which the FBI investigated, by way of a massive manhunt, the murder of three civil rights workers in Mississippi, Michael Schwerner, James Chaney, and Andrew Goodman. The murders involved a sheriff, his deputy, and a local police officer of Meridian and Philadelphia, Mississippi. The others were private persons (and Klansmen). All were subject to the investigation, all were convicted of civil rights violations and the Supreme Court ultimately upheld the convictions. Without the new, broader interpretation of the law, the FBI would not have had adequate jurisdiction.

Jurisdiction in civil rights matters expanded rapidly in the 1960s. More remedies for voting right violations were provided in acts of 1957, 1960 and 1964, and 1965. The 1964 act covered also discrimination in education, employment, public accommodations and federally assisted programs. Finally in the Civil Rights Act of 1968, a comprehensive list of federally protected rights was placed in the investigative jurisdiction of the FBI.

Thus, while today the civil rights law is so broad that it would be an unusual case where some basis for federal prosecution could not be found, in the past the FBI could act in only very limited situations. It could not itself broaden its jurisdiction. That was for the Congress, the executive branch and courts. The FBI is bound to exercise whatever jurisdiction is conferred on it by those institutions, its superiors, and no more.

This is the FBI which exists in the American system of federalism, and checks and balances. Its limitations had best be carefully observed, even by the crusaders, if America is to avoid the abuse of legitimate police powers.

United States vs. *Price* 383 U.S. 787 (1966).

3. The FBI as a Libertarian Institution
M. Stanton Evans

Attacks on the Federal Bureau of Investigation have increased in vigor and frequency in the past few years, reaching a crescendo of sorts in the period since 1968. As noted elsewhere in this volume, the specific character of these complaints will vary from case to case, depending on the outlook of the particular critic and the nature of the FBI activity which is up for discussion. The driving theme of nearly all such comment, however, is essentially the same—the allegation that the bureau is a ganglion of arbitrary, unchecked power, implacably hostile to American freedoms.

A characteristic statement of this view is given by journalist Hank Messick, in a biographical slam at J. Edgar Hoover.* This author asserts that, in the course of his tenure at the bureau, Director Hoover "built a secret organization subject to his will, or whim, alone. Neither Congress nor President has dared demand a review of FBI activities. Consequently, Hoover has not only been above the law but able to put his agency above it, too. Mistakes, abuses of power and special privileges have been concealed behind a curtain of one-way glass while an active propaganda machine created a popular legend about Hoover and the G-Men."

A similar picture is offered by Fred J. Cook, in a more systematic denunciation of the agency called *The FBI Nobody Knows.*** Cook argues that the actions of the FBI and its relative

---

* New York: David McKay Company, Inc., 1972
** New York: Macmillan, 1964

immunity from criticism are leading us into a "police state atmosphere" destructive of our freedoms. This process, he says, "has already gone far. Hoover's enormous and unchecked power—the clandestine wiretapping, mail checking, and surveillance; the gossip, the rumor, the damaging truth and half-truth that repose in the secret dossiers of the FBI—has served to intimidate the highest officials in government and to repress debate."

Other examples might be multiplied at length from recent discourse, each portraying the bureau as a despotic institution. Anyone who has given more than cursory attention to the drift of political debate is doubtless familiar with many of these. By arguments of this type, we are instructed to view the FBI as the anti-libertarian agency *par excellence* —tapper of telephones, keeper of dossiers, relentless enemy of dissent. The critics themselves, in implicit or open contrast, assume the mantle of indignant libertarians. So steadily have these contrasting images been projected, it is likely a number of Americans have come to accept them as accurate descriptions of reality.

Closer examination of the subject, however, may suggest another set of conclusions. We have available to us, after all, a considerable body of literature which defines the goals and methods of libertarian statecraft in some detail. In this literature we may discover criteria by which the actions of government agencies should be ruled, the proper relationship of public authority to private right, and the specific powers appropriate to a corps of national police. So libertarian guidelines by which to gauge the performance of the bureau—or any other arm of government—are rather easily accessible.

In addition, we have a considerable body of evidence concerning the FBI itself—the public record of its development, the major cases in which it has been involved, a growing body of books and articles. In the nature of things, of course, there is much we do not know, and a good deal more we think we know that is demonstrably false. Yet the record is there, and will yield its secrets under patient inquiry. If we sort through this mass of fact and allegation, we can winnow out the essential data. And if we compare these data with the acknowledged guidelines of libertarian government, we may be prompted to opinions quite different from those expressed by Messrs. Cook and Messick.

For purposes of the immediate discussion we may distinguish three separate levels of libertarian affirmation. The first of these is the *philosophical* conception of a libertarian state, propounded in the writings of Locke, Jefferson, Mill, Spencer, Sumner and numerous other spokesmen for maximum individual liberty. In the simplest terms, this libertarian view conceives the state as an agency for *neutralizing the aggressive use of force.* It defines liberty as that condition in which people may do as they wish so long as they do not interfere with the similar rights of others. It is to prevent such interference that government is conceived by these spokesmen as necessary, its essential functions being to defend the society from foreign enemies, and to suppress the outbreak of domestic crime.

The second level of libertarian definition important to Americans is the *constitutional.* Here we move from the theoretical clouds to the more solid earth of historical reality. The United States is supposed to be a free society, and it has an extensive literature defining the ends of libertarian government as our founders conceived them. With some exceptions, these ends are very much in keeping with the view of government entertained in libertarian philosophy. Our founders believed the principal business of government was to superintend the affairs of society so as to maximize the liberty of the person, to maintain conditions in which people could go peacefully about their business without coercive interference.

To attain this objective, the founders came to believe a central government was necessary. In two departments especially, they felt the lack of such a government during the period of Confederation, and sought to remedy things with the new authority created in Philadelphia. A principal deficiency was in the field of foreign affairs; the separate states were not very effective in this realm, and the impoverished central government of the time could do little to uphold their several interests abroad. A second major evil was contention among the states themselves, which treated one another very much as foreign powers. The new government was conceived as an agency to handle internal tasks of government which the states could not encompass tasks authentically national in scope.*

The third level of definition necessary to a libertarian understanding of the state we may define as the *legal*. This may be looked upon as a product of both the philosophical and constitutional definitions sketched above, since it was the general belief of both the libertarian theorists and the writers of America's Constitution that governments should be made to conduct themselves according to rules of law. This view holds that government agencies should act only in obedience to maxims of conduct laid down beforehand, and not invent conditions under which their power may be extended. This meant in the first instance deference to the rules of the Constitution, but it meant as well adherence to statute law, obedience to the rulings of the courts and due subordination of agencies to their constitutional superiors.

On that reading, the duties of the United States government

---

*Thus *Federalist* No. 15: "We may indeed with propriety be said to have reached the last stage of national humiliation. There is scarcely anything that can wound the pride or degrade the character of an independent nation which we do not experience...Are we in a condition to resent or repel [an] aggression? We have neither troops, nor treasury, nor government. Are we even in a position to remonstrate with dignity?...Is respectability in the eyes of foreign powers a safeguard against foreign encroachments? The imbecility of our government even forbids them to treat with us. Our ambassadors abroad are the mere pageants of mimic sovereignty."

The apportionment of powers aimed at in the Constitution was spelled out in the convention by Roger Sherman of Connecticut: "The objects of the Union, he thought, were few: 1. defense against foreign danger; 2. against internal disputes and resort to force; 3. treaties with foreign nations; 4. regulating foreign commerce and drawing revenues from it. These and perhaps a few lesser objects alone rendered a confederation of the states necessary." The resemblance to the paradigmatic-function views of the libertarians is apparent.

were to be quite limited and the deployment of its power subject to numerous constraints—which means, *a fortiori,* any police agency working as a subdivision of that government will be subject to all the same generic restraints plus others specific to its own position within the larger structure. Needless to remark, this severely limited interpretation of federal powers has been the subject of intense debate in modern America. In particular, it is disparaged by members of the liberal-left political communities, who have worked long and successfully to substitute for this constricted view of government a much broader interpretation of federal responsibilities.

Whatever one may think of these criteria, they define the libertarian's view of government, and they set a standard of governmental behavior far *more* limiting in most respects than those preferred by the usual critics of the FBI. It would be simple enough, perhaps, to justify the behavior of this agency by adopting the standards of "loose construction," which these same critics apply to other governmental powers, citing as they are prone to do problems or purposes the founders had never conceived, and so on. Indeed, it is hard to conjure up any form of government activity which may not be sanctified by such arguments. The limitations of our libertarian definition, on the other hand, set a much more rigorous standard of performance.

Libertarian government would, then, require that the United States government have a federal police agency at its disposal, but that such an agency be subject to the limitations enumerated. The object of such an agency must be, not to manipulate the peaceful activities of the people, but to neutralize the aggressive use of force. Where the American federal government is concerned, this means above all defense against foreign enemies of the United States, which was the principal end and object of our founders in devising the Constitution and establishing the central government. In domestic matters its purpose should also be to limit the aggressive use of force, but to do so subject to the proviso that original authority in such matters is reserved by the terms of the constitutional balance to the states and local communities. Finally, such an agency should operate in strict obedience to the law as promulgated by statute, the courts, and its own civilian superiors. It is against these libertarian precepts that the performance of the Federal Bureau of Investigation should be measured.

To read the growing literature in denunciation of the FBI, one could only suppose the agency had violated each and every one of our libertarian guidelines, and then some. On the presentation of his critics, J. Edgar Hoover was avaricious for authority, oblivious of constitutional restraint, and zealous in opposition to the most elementary precepts of civil liberties. In the critical literature he is routinely portrayed as demanding more men, more funds, and more worlds of innocent radical opinion to conquer, and in cases where he did not receive approval from a complacent Congress, simply going ahead and seizing whatever power he wanted. In particular, say the critics, he was eager to steal the spotlight from other federal agencies, muscle in on local police, and expand the already sweeping jurisdiction of his bureau.

If this hair-raising portrayal were true, then indeed the FBI is an "American Gestapo" and Hoover was its Heinrich Himmler. All our libertarian precepts would be violated at a swoop, and we might end our discussion forthwith. Inspection of the record, however, suggests that it isn't true—that, indeed, it is almost an exact inversion of the truth. Far from being enormous and infinitely expandable, the jurisdiction of the FBI has been and continues to be subject to very serious limitations. From the outset of Hoover's service, it has been conceived in terms quite similar to those propounded by the philosophers of libertarian government—as an order-keeping agency whose principal function is to defend the nation from foreign enemies and to handle internal order-keeping tasks which were authentically national in character. Stress has continually been placed on the need for keeping the bureau limited in this fashion, and for leaving normal law enforcement functions to the states and local communities. There is little evidence of Hoover's or the bureau's setting out to expand FBI power at the expense of other agencies or the states, or to use the authority of the FBI to trample on the liberties of private citizens. The material before us on each and all these points is precisely to the opposite effect.

Hoover's estimate of the bureau's proper role can be gleaned from numerous statements down through the years, e.g., "There have been efforts to draw the bureau into the investigation of local crime, which efforts I have consistently resisted" (1950). "America's compact network of local law enforcement agencies has traditionally been the nation's first line of defense against crime. Nothing could be more dangerous to our democratic ideals than the establishment of an all-powerful police agency on the federal scene" (1960). "I am against, and have been for years, the growth of the FBI. I think we are entirely too big today, bigger than we should be. I would have liked to see the FBI remain small; but that has been impossible because Congress has yearly enacted legislation expanding the investigative jurisdiction of the bureau" (1965).

Mere rhetoric? The record suggests otherwise. These statements were fully supported across the years by Hoover's rejection of proposals that the bureau assume increasing power at the expense of other agencies. We have this on the testimony not only of Hoover himself but of various highly situated witnesses. In 1940, for example, Attorney General Robert Jackson conveyed to Hoover a suggestion for consolidating federal intelligence functions proposed by President Roosevelt. Under this formula, Hoover would have had control of all federal investigative and intelligence agencies, but he dissuaded the attorney general. Jackson recounted the episode by commenting that "it is something of a gift in men to see beyond today and see what the tomorrows will bring . . . The director has been able to take a long-term view of some things and I was impressed by it this afternoon. I laid before him a little matter which would have resulted in his having had some additional power—and most men in Washington are supposed to be reaching for that—and he said to me, 'General, that plan would be very good for today, but over the years it would be a mistake.'"

Hoover also took the unheard-of step of requesting, in the early 1950s, that the bureau be divested of authority it already possessed—that of conducting investigations on a wide variety of federal job applications. He contended that this work was not directly relevant to the task of law enforcement and therefore should be transferred to some other agency. Pursuant to his request, most of these investigations were handed over to the Civil Service Commission. Also, he repeatedly negated proposals that the FBI encroach on areas covered by the Secret Service and the Bureau of Narcotics and Dangerous Drugs. Concerning a proposal that the FBI take over enforcement of narcotics laws, Hoover observed that this task should remain with the Narcotics Bureau because it had the necessary expertise and "has done a very good job under very great difficulties."

The hostility toward absorption of indiscriminate powers suggested by these episodes is reflected as well in the aggregate growth of the bureau. It is plain enough on the record that the agency has moved into new jurisdictional fields precisely as Hoover suggested in 1965—at the behest of Congress and the orders of the executive. What seems not generally to be understood about the FBI—although the bureau's learned critics are of course aware of it—is that it enters *no* area of responsibility on its own initiative. The FBI is in some areas the enforcement arm of the federal government, and as such its task is to carry into effect the laws and directives which proceed from superior authority. Thus, if the President issues an executive order relative to national security and directs the FBI to do thus and so concerning it, the FBI must carry that order into effect. If the Justice Department brings an action in the federal courts, then the FBI must gather the evidence upon which that action is based. If Congress passes a law concerning civil rights, or truth in lending, or airline hijacking, then, unless explicitly provided otherwise, the FBI has the duty of monitoring these laws, apprehending violators, and gathering evidence for prosecution.

One may quarrel with the wisdom of such orders and laws in whole or part or even suggest that Congress and the federal government have overstepped the bounds appropriate to them —which, gauged by our theoretical model of limited government, they most certainly have. Yet to focus blame for this phenomenon *on the FBI* is an absurdity; its job is not to promulgate laws or to evaluate them as right or wrong, but to enforce them. And on libertarian principles concerning the rule of law and subordination of police agencies to representative institutions, it could properly be held to account if it did *not* enforce them, whatever their abstract merits. That possibility conjures up a rather frightening and non-libertarian prospect of a police agency which defies the will of the elected legislature and its own civilian superiors, a prospect about which we shall have more to say momentarily.

Obviously, if one is concerned about an excessive level of federal law *enforcement* under our system of government, then the evident and only answer is to cut back on the level of federal law *enactment.* This thought is seldom stressed by the FBI's liberal critics, however, for very good reason—since the general level of federal power that has been created in the past 40 years and much of the specific legislation which constitutes that power have been the handiwork of the liberals themselves. Above all, the intrusion of federal police power into areas once reserved by the Constitution to the states has been the work of the liberals, most notably Franklin D. Roosevelt. It was under Roosevelt that the federal government got into the act on crimes like kidnapping which once were left to local law enforcement agencies. This occurred as part of the general expansion of federal power.

Among the critics of the bureau, Fred J. Cook is the most forthright in noting that Roosevelt and the New Deal were the principal causes of jurisdictional expansion by the bureau. He observes that in 1934, "the administration further broadened the scope of federal police powers. It added the death penalty to the Lindbergh law. And it put a whole host of new crimes under federal jurisdiction for the first time: the robbing of a national bank, the flight of a defendant or a witness across state lines to avoid prosecution or giving testimony, the transmission of threats by any means whatsoever; racketeering practiced on businessmen engaged in interstate commerce; transporting stolen property across a state line; resisting a federal officer."

The self-evident truth of the matter is that, beginning with the New Deal, the president and Congress have been engaged in a vast expansion of federal powers, and in the course of this have piled more and more responsibilities on the FBI. It is clear that Hoover himself often wished it otherwise, and within the bounds of propriety said so. The result of the federal expansion has been a staggering workload for the bureau, the end of which is nowhere yet in sight, with 185 jurisdictional responsibilities of varied sorts, from internal security intelligence to organized gambling to antitrust investigations.

It can well be argued that the FBI under Hoover's direction did an amazing job of absorbing these responsibilities with a minimal increase of funding and personnel—certainly without the hint of anything that looks like empire-building. The FBI's employment tables show the only really explosive growth of the agency occurred during World War II, with its challenge of enemy espionage and sabotage, when the number of special agents grew from 996 to 4,853, largely due to plant security work, and total personnel including clerks went from 2,489 to 14,290. In Hoover's final budget request a generation later (fiscal 1973), the requested force level, *in toto* was 19,857, with 8,631 listed as agents and 11,266 as clerks. What other government agency anywhere in the United States is within shouting distance of the force levels it had in 1945?

There was concededly a general reduction in government functions in the immediate post-war period, well below the levels attained at the height of hostilities. This being so, we may make the maximum case for FBI expansion by comparing present figures to those attained in 1950, when the total personnel amounted to 9,873. Using that bench-mark, the FBI has roughly doubled in numbers in the past 23 years. Considering the constantly escalating burdens on the agency, and the performance of other government bureaus, this is a modest record indeed. We need only note in this respect the record of the Department of Health, Education, and Welfare, which began with 36,000 employees in 1953 and boasts no less than 108,000 today, a growth record of 200 percent. If the liberal critics of the FBI are really concerned about empire-building, why don't they zero in on the activities of the HEW?

What is especially ironic about many attacks on the FBI is the manner in which the critics berate it for "empire-building" but are themselves completely negligent of any limited-government model by which its activities might be subject to appropriate restraint. While complaining of this or that specific action and declaiming on the need for abridgment of its powers, they have with few exceptions little or nothing to say against the general build-up of federal activity that determines the level of FBI performance and a good deal more besides. Comparison of Hoover's views concerning such matters as the state-federal balance reveals that he was much more cognizant than they of the need for generic limitations on the reach of governmental power.

Indeed, Hoover's limited-government stand, and his unwillingness to over-reach the proper bounds of federal power, are on occasion acknowledged by the critics—but these, too, by a kind of curious inversion, are alleged as failings of the bureau. The same people who denounce the FBI for "empire-building" and doing *too much* will turn about in another context and berate it for doing *too little*. Hank Messick, for example, blasts the agency for involving itself in a kidnapping case, asserting "the FBI had no business being involved in the case at all since the drama was confined to Dade County." In view of that assertion, one would suppose Messick's view of the proper course of conduct for the FBI was to leave such matters to the locals until proper federal jurisdiction was established. Not so, however, for when the narrative reaches a Hoover statement that direction of the Lindbergh kidnapping case should have been left to New Jersey officials, that too invites a slam: "The assignment was a hot potato—and Hoover felt he might be burned."

This yin and yang of purported error may be found in nearly every major criticism of the FBI. If the bureau becomes involved in some particular sector of law enforcement, it is grabbing too much power and trampling the rights of state and local police. If it does *not* become involved in some particular sector of law enforcement, then it is sloughing off its duty and is probably doing so for unspeakable reasons. This back and forth criticism is particularly notable in Cook, who argues strongly that the FBI has muscled in on local police—the Dillinger case being cited as an especially flagrant example. And, as noted, Cook is particularly voluble about the bureau's alleged threat to personal liberty and its supposed stand "above the law."

Yet Cook also derides the agency for not jumping into the fray over "organized crime," criticizes Hoover for not demanding more power in this area, and takes him to task for "this stickling for ultra-fine points of law." He cites as an example of effective work by another law enforcement agency the indictments brought against the "Appalachian" group which met at the home of Joseph Barbara in 1957. The FBI and the Justice Department had found that the meeting, whatever the character of the people attending it, violated no known federal law. A Special Group on Organized Crime, however, managed to get indictments on the grounds that the very secrecy of the meeting itself was actionable, a course which, understandably enough, the FBI had not pursued. The court of appeals threw out the convictions on the grounds that the government's case was "a shotgun conspiracy charge aimed at everyone who gave an explanation inconsistent with the government's suspicion of the purpose of the meeting." This is the official example which, according to Cook, the FBI should have followed!

These backings and fillings, which appear to place the FBI and its critics first on one side of the libertarian line and then the other, are more consistent than they seem. In the FBI's case, the consistency is a matter of adherence to statute law; in the areas where the bureau has moved, it has moved in obedience to acts of Congress and the jurisdiction legally defined for it. Where it has *not* moved, its restraint is traceable to the fact that either statutory authority or the practical legal tools have not existed permitting it to do the job. The consistency of the critics is the mirror-image of the agency's: They do not want the FBI to act in certain areas, even though it is legally mandated to do so; and they *do* want the FBI to act in other areas, even though it is *not* mandated to do so. The whys and wherefores of this peculiar argument we shall examine in the concluding section of our analysis.

If the charge of empire-building is false, the charge of indifference to civil liberties seems equally so. Certainly, judged by law enforcement standards known anywhere, FBI procedures and respect for individual liberties are legendary for fairness. It is worth recalling in this context that Hoover was first appointed to his position as head of the bureau by Harlan Fiske Stone, noted as a liberal and defender of civil liberties. Stone never ceased to praise Hoover's conduct of the bureau, asserting that the director had removed every agent about whose character there was any suspicion, refused to submit to political pressures on the bureau, "withdrew it wholly from extra-legal activities and made it an efficient organization combatting criminal offenses against the United States."

Stone's verdict has been sustained by other civil libertarians who have no conceivable axe to grind in behalf of the FBI. Two well-known liberals, Harry and Bonaro Overstreet, devoted an entire book to this subject a few years back and gave the bureau highest civil liberties marks across the board.* Hoover's performance won kudos from so unlikely a source

*The FBI in Our Open Society, New York, W. W. Norton, 1969.

as Roger Baldwin of the ACLU, while civil libertarian Morris Ernst conducted a lengthy analysis of the bureau's practices and concluded that "a real smear campaign has been carried on against Hoover's work. The FBI is unique... It has a magnificent record of respect for individual freedom." Even its severest critics, like Cook and Thomas I. Emerson, are compelled to acknowledge the bureau's exemplary performance in various civil liberties areas.

Such encomia do not, of course, settle the argument about the FBI's general record, which can be determined only by getting down to specifics. Before examining the typical charges made against the agency, however, it may be useful to recall a particular episode which fully supports these favorable civil liberties conclusions and in addition speaks volumes about the contrasting attitudes of Hoover and certain prominent liberals on essential matters of personal freedom. This was the case of more than 100,000 Japanese who were rounded up and herded into concentration camps at the outset of World War II, a step demanded by the Treasury Department, columnist Walter Lippmann, and California Attorney General Earl Warren, among others. Hoover opposed the action, pointing out that it served no security purpose, despite the clamor of such as Lippmann that the Pacific Coast was a "combat zone" and that "nobody's constitutional rights include the right to reside and do business on a battlefield."

That hysterical outcry ignored the fact that the vast majority of the people rounded up were American citizens against whom there was not the slightest evidence of disloyalty, and that the FBI had already arrested those enemy aliens on whom it had carefully collected data suggesting potential harm to the national security. Hoover described the Warren-Lippmann demand as a capitulation to "public hysteria" and told Secretary Morgenthau arrests should not be made "unless there were sufficient facts upon which to justify the cases of the persons arrested." He said the rights of American citizens should be protected and disparaged such "dragnet" procedures. He was overridden—but the episode clearly demonstrated his concern for civil liberties at a time when popularity was easily courted by trampling on the rights of defenseless Japanese-Americans, even as many of the Nisei were serving with distinction in the American armed services.

Undoubtedly the most controverted aspect of FBI activity over the years is the accumulation of data by what are sometimes clandestine means, and the question of the uses to which these data are put. These means include wiretapping, electronic eavesdropping, the use of confidential informants and undercover agents, and compilation of files of derogatory data. This constellation of devices is usually presented by FBI opponents as Exhibit A in the argument that the agency is "an American Gestapo." It is suggested that the FBI is bugging or tapping everybody, has secret "dossiers" to keep recalcitrants in line, and in general pries and snoops in such a fashion as to threaten the freedom and privacy of Americans.

The issues raised in this discussion are real ones, and the prospect of diminished liberty and privacy through the use of wiretaps, for example, is one which should deeply concern the American people. There *is* a tendency in some circles to accept any measure as good if it is proposed in the name of combating crime, without due reflection on the result such measures might have on popular freedoms. Indiscriminate use of wiretaps or other such means is a matter which should engage the interest of every authentic libertarian, whether his politics on other matters be left, right, or middle of the road. Saying this, however, is quite different from saying the FBI has been guilty of the charges lodged against it, or that the FBI has been oblivious of the dangers of which we speak.

As ever in examining such matters it is well to state at the outset the ground rules which must govern the discussion. In cases of wiretapping, the relevant constitutional provision is that contained in the Fourth Amendment, which states that "the right of the people to be secure in their persons, houses, papers and effects, against unreasonable searches and seizures, shall not be violated, and no warrants shall issue but upon probable cause, supported by oath or affirmation, and particularly describing the place to be searched, and the person or things to be seized."

While the possibility of wiretaps and electronic eavesdropping did not exist at the time this language was drafted, it seems perfectly proper, in view of the practices our founders wanted to control, to construe the language as applicable to electronic eavesdropping, and the courts have so construed it. Indeed, a good case can be made that electronic eavesdropping is even more hazardous to freedom than physical invasion for at least two reasons. Whereas a physical search is aimed at securing certain given objects, a wiretap may encompass anything that happens to be said over the instrument that is tapped. Second, the individual whose premises are physically searched is generally aware of it; the individual whose conversations are tapped most generally is not. For these reasons and others, it may be plausibly argued that wiretaps should be even more limited than are physical searches.

This said, the fact remains that the Fourth Amendment prohibition is not *absolute;* rather than preventing searches altogether, it establishes conditions under which they may occur. Obviously there are some situations in law enforcement in which a search is necessary, and the amendment prescribes the guidelines that should be followed in such situations. In most cases, a warrant must be secured; probable cause established; the nature of the item or information sought must be stated beforehand. Without entering here into all the complexities of wiretapping, under Fourth Amendment ground rules it appears that similar standards should apply to electronic "searches"—with the proviso noted above that this use should be even more jealously limited than physical entry.

While statute law and judicial opinion on this subject have been and continue to be in flux, it can be asserted that, so far as the record discloses, the practice of the FBI is in keeping with the guidelines set forward above. It is theoretically *possible,* of course, that the FBI has engaged in countless wiretaps of which there is no record, which is, indeed, the charge of the critics. For that matter, given the existing technology in such instances, it is *possible* that almost anybody is wiretapping almost everybody. In the nature of things such claims are almost incapable of proof or disproof. The best we can do is to examine the evidence that is on the record, and extrapolate from the things we can see to the things we cannot. If we conduct our inquiry in this fashion, we find the available evidence refutes the usual wiretap charges against the bureau. It reveals: (1) a general reluctance on the part of Director Hoover to employ wiretaps, even when other government agencies were known to be using them; (2) a strict insistence that all taps be authorized, in writing, by the attorney general and not by the director himself; and (3) a concentration when taps have been employed on a limited species of cases—principally those involving national security.

Hoover was known to believe that wiretapping was a "lazy man's" method of law enforcement. In the early years of the FBI, for example, one of his standard regulations read: "Wiretapping will not be tolerated in the bureau." In 1931, at the insistence of Attorney General William Mitchell, the regulation was changed to read: "...telephone or telegraph wires shall not be tapped unless prior authorization of the director of the bureau has been secured." At Hoover's request, however, the power to authorize wiretaps was subsequently placed in the hands of the attorney general and not the director. Since that time, all taps have been authorized, in writing, by the attorney general.

In 1939, Hoover asked the attorney general to oppose a law which would have given the FBI wide-ranging wiretap powers. "I do not wish," he said, "to be the head of an organization of political blackmailers." It was this request which aroused the interest of Morris Ernst, counsel for the American Civil Liberties Union, and led him to deliver his encomium in behalf of the bureau. As demonstrated by the Overstreets, most of the charges against the FBI in the matter of wiretapping are false. The record shows a consistent effort by Hoover not only to oppose taps but when they were authorized from above, to limit their use to a few cases—kidnap, national security, and, of late, organized crime.*

It is possible to quarrel with the extent of wiretapping even on these grounds, but the available data suggest that those who would pursue that quarrel should take it up with Congress and the Department of Justice, whose will the FBI has executed in such matters against a background of general reluctance to employ the taps. Congress has legislated on wiretaps in the Omnibus Crime Control Act of 1968—and in so doing established standards far more latitudinarian than those traditionally favored by the FBI. And it is in Congress that the battle should be fought.

Second only to wiretaps as a source of civil libertarian horror is the use of secret informants—most typically, agents (not special agents) within the Communist Party and in various new left groups. (The FBI has also used informants inside the Ku Klux Klan, but this particular usage has not aroused much civil liberties outcry.) This is an issue which has been hashed over a great deal in public debate, not only with respect to the FBI but also with respect to congressional investigating committees. One civil libertarian goes so far as to contend that protection against informants, like protection against wiretaps, should be included in a broadened interpretation of the Fourth Amendment safeguard against "searches and seizures."

The short answer to these assertions is that police agencies have used informants from time immemorial, particularly when their criminal adversaries were conspiratorial in nature. By hypothesis, a criminal conspiracy which seeks to mask the nature of its actions from public observation can be broken only by those with access to inside data. The relevant question with respect to secret informants, then, is whether the organi-

*See Chapter Nine of *The FBI in Our Open Society,* op. cit.

zation being thereby penetrated is in fact engaged in criminal activity. If the answer is yes—and we shall examine that answer presently—then the use of secret informants can hardly be considered a deprivation of constitutional privilege.

As for the argument that the Fourth Amendment language now applied to wiretaps should also be applied to informants, the two situations are not at all analogous. Wiretapping was something the founders could not have conceived when they drafted the Fourth Amendment, and it is reasonable to suppose in the light of what we know about their intentions that they would have wanted to limit this particular species of intrusion just as they sought to limit physical searches. But the use of confidential informants was something they surely knew very well, since this is a police technique of venerable pedigree requiring no employment of modern technology. If the founders had meant to ban this type of activity it would have been included in the language of the amendment. It isn't, so obviously they didn't.

A related issue is that of surveillance, more accurately termed "intelligence coverage," which some critics of the FBI hold to be as bad as wiretapping. This topic came forcibly to light in the spring of 1971 when Senator Edmund Muskie of Maine denounced the FBI for conducting surveillance of an "Earth Day" rally he had addressed. "If anti-pollution rallies are a subject of intelligence concern," said Muskie, "is anything immune? Is there any citizen involved in politics who is not a potential subject for an FBI dossier?" This and similar complaints about intelligence coverage have blended into the uproar over wiretapping, the result being a composite picture of the FBI securing data on innocent citizens by every available method. That picture is faulty, however, for a number of reasons—the first being the fact that wiretapping and physical surveillance are very different things.

Wiretapping, after all, is a *clandestine* method of gathering information, its principal demerit being an intrusion upon privacy and the fact that the person intruded upon is not aware

of its occurrence. On the scene surveillance is quite the opposite in several respects; the instances complained of by Muskie
and others who have raised the issue involved *public* meetings,
not private conversations. The Earth Day rally which was the
focus of Muskie's complaint took place in downtown Washington, D.C., before an audience of 2,000 people. Anyone speaking
there or attending that rally was engaged in a public act in a public
place, and anyone who wished to observe what occurred there
had every right to do so. Where the right of privacy is being discussed, the distinction is of the utmost importance.

It is extremely rare, however, for that distinction to make
much difference to critics of the FBI. In the usual case, where
physical surveillance is distinguished from wiretaps, the critic
continues to berate the bureau, but merely changes his
grounds for doing so. Consider, for example, the argument of
Yale law professor Thomas I. Emerson, who moves without a
hitch from the standard complaint that it is wrong to scrutinize
someone without his knowledge to the additional complaint
that it is equally wrong to scrutinize someone *with* his knowledge. Emerson says awareness "that the government is watching and recording one's political thoughts and moves is for
most people a shattering experience," and he argues that the
FBI should be prevented from "photographing peaceful demonstrations, recording license numbers of people attending a
meeting, *ostentatious surveillance of a public gathering,* or similar
blanket collection of data on persons not engaged in criminal
activities."* (Italics added.)

Such open surveillance, Emerson says, has a "chilling effect"
upon those investigated, and is therefore in violation of the First
Amendment guarantee of free speech. We confront, again, the
civil liberties Catch-22: If the FBI gathers data by clandestine
methods, then it is engaged in police-state tactics invading the
right of privacy; but if it gathers data through open surveillance
in a public place, such activity has a "chilling effect," and that

*Emerson, at the October, 1971, Princeton Conference on the FBI.

is a police-state method too. The net result of such argumentation is, obviously, that the FBI should not be able to gather any data at all, which is in fact exactly what Emerson and others like him are arguing. At first glance he appears to offer an exception in the case of commission of a specific crime, but that, as we shall see, is not the case.

It may be doubted that the knowledge of being scrutinized by government in the course of one's political activities is quite so shattering as Emerson alleges—especially when these activities are undertaken in a public place before a mass audience. It seems apparent, in particular, that protest rallies and mass demonstrations are intended in considerable measure to *be* observed by government, as well as by the public. Why else do demonstrators assemble in Washington, picket the White House, present petitions, march on Congress, and the like? The whole point of such activity is to have government made aware of one's position. So the mere fact of being observed by government agents is hardly the psychic crusher that Emerson makes it out to be.

Nonetheless, it may be granted that a chilling effect occurs in certain circumstances—if one believes, specifically, that a government agent is observing him in order to undertake some punitive action. If a motorist is cruising along the highway and paying little attention to his speed, for example, he may indeed be "chilled" to see a highway patrolman in his rearview mirror with his red light flashing. So much is self-evident but nothing to the purpose. For if such reconnaissance has a chilling effect on those who have reason to fear arrest and punitive action, how much greater is the chilling effect of being arrested, tried, and convicted! Indeed, if "chilling effect" *per se* is to be considered a decisive argument against police actions, then there would be no police actions whatever.

Obviously, the question that needs answering is not whether somebody is "chilled" by police surveillance, or other activity, but whether that activity is necessary to the performance of the agency's proper functions. If the activity is necessary and proper, then "chilling effect" is irrelevant—is, indeed, a gigantic red herring, obscuring the substantive point at issue. The real question, quite simply, is whether the FBI should be engaged in surveillance of certain types of individuals in certain areas of national concern. The critics say "no." The elementary facts of crime, defense, and national survival say "yes."

Consideration of this issue moves us closer to the heart of the liberal-left attack on the FBI, and reveals quite plainly the philosophical revolution which is being smuggled into political discourse under the name of "civil liberties." For what is in essence being proposed in this particular type of criticism is a society which is on principle defenseless against subversion and violence so long as these crimes are committed by the revolutionary left. This is made crystal clear by the activity which the critics want us to look upon as privileged, and by the theoretical arguments they devise in support of their position. In this respect the views of Professor Emerson may be taken as the liberal model.

In essence, Emerson argues that both clandestine methods and open surveillance are wrong because the thing investigated should be immune to official scrutiny. What the bureau is focusing on, he says, is "political conduct," which under our constitutional system is privileged. He contends that the FBI has been engaged in monitoring of ideas, free speech, and political association, thereby suppressing an intellectual position with which it disagrees. The bureau allegedly sees the principal threat to our security as coming from "alien ideologies," and attempts to protect Americans from "false ideas, and those who propose or work toward serious change in the established order [and thereby give] aid and comfort to the enemy."*

This style of argument underlies nearly every major criticism of the FBI for alleged indifference to civil liberties. It is therefore useful to note from Emerson's chosen sources just what it is he proposes to pass off as "political" association and free

*Emerson, Princeton Conference, loc. cit.

speech. In attempting to document the nature of FBI procedures, he relies on two sources of FBI material in which confidential agency files were made public without the consent of the bureau. Both are treated as coruscating revelations of FBI encroachment on civil liberties and hostility toward unfamiliar "ideas" and "dissent." The most cursory examination will suggest to less partisan readers a slightly different interpretation.

The first cache of documents concerns the case of Judith Coplon, arrested in 1949, tried, and convicted of trying to pass secret data to a Soviet agent, Valentin Gubitchev. Miss Coplon's conviction was overturned by Judge Learned Hand—who said he had no doubt about her flagrant guilt—because she had been arrested without a warrant, an action taken at the orders of Attorney General Tom Clark on the belief it was necessary to forestall her escape. It was also established that the FBI had conducted a wiretap of Miss Coplon's phone, again at the written authorization of the attorney general, and Hand ruled that the wiretap evidence should have been available to the defense.

In connection with the points raised previously, it is worth repeating that throughout the Coplon case the FBI followed the procedures mandated by the attorney general, and thus behaved according to the appropriate guidelines. However, the case took a sudden turn which violated those guidelines when a federal judge demanded that the "raw files" compiled by the agency be introduced into the open record. Such files contain all sorts of information worked up in the course of normal investigative procedure, and are not intended for public dissemination. They were placed in the open record only over the vehement objections of Hoover, since disclosure could blow the "covers" of many FBI sources, and the names of many people who were not considered guilty of anything but who had turned up in various remote or irrelevant connections would be melded into the general public flap over Coplon and Gubitchev.

Emerson ignores this background entirely. Omitting factual discussion of the Coplon case, he moves directly into the file material and confines his discussion to the marginal data therein contained. His purpose is to fix attention on this ancillary material, to show that "innocent" political activities were officially recorded to the detriment of the people named. One could scarcely infer from his discussion the real point of the episode—the fact that an employee of the American government was engaged in passing secret data to an agent of the Soviet Union, and that the "raw file" existed as a general information pool from which the facts of Communist espionage could be winnowed. Substantive discussion of Miss Coplon's crime, of course, might obscure Emerson's point about political innocents confined to secret dossiers for seeking "political change."

Clearly, the passing of government secrets to a Soviet agent is not a privileged exercise in free speech or political dissent. It is criminal espionage, and in certain legal circumstances, treason. If the United States government may not conduct investigations concerning *this* subject, and gather materials from which to make its case, then that government is incapable of performing its most bedrock function. A society which could not conduct the kind of inquiry involved in the Coplon case would be incapable of insuring its own survival. The attempt to fob off the events surrounding *l'affaire* Coplon as something merely "political" tells us volumes about the critics of the FBI.

Indeed, even the incidental materials from the raw files tracing out to remote individuals are hardly so innocent as Emerson would have us believe. Among the subjects of FBI reports contained in the Coplon documents, which Emerson lists as though they were self-evidently absurd, are such items as reports on affiliations with the Henry Wallace Progressive Party (controlled by the Communist Party), a report on one person who expressed admiration for the Soviet army during World War II, on another who participated in a 1955 skit about the battles of Leningrad and Stalingrad, and a report on the visit of a "music student" to his mother at Communist Party headquarters in New Jersey. On Emerson's presentation, such data are apparently matters of privileged "political" opinion. On any informed reading of the Cold War record—particularly against the substantive backdrop of the Coplon case—these are hardly matters of which the FBI should have been oblivious.

Fred Cook is fairer than this, since he acknowledges the nature of Miss Coplon's crime, Judge Hand's assertion that her "guilt is plain," and the implausibility of her substantive defense.* However, he does not record that the arrest without a warrant and the taps of Miss Coplon's various telephones, of which he makes a great deal, both occurred at the orders of the attorney general. He attributes these actions to the FBI alone, and indeed attempts to make it seem in his discussion of the Coplon case that the Justice Department was being victimized by the bureau. The facts of record are precisely the opposite.

The point made manifest in the Coplon case is applicable to many other instances of alleged persecution by the FBI. In the usual argument, membership in and cooperation with the Communist Party is described as a "political" matter, so that the FBI in its continual battlings with the Communists is depicted as trampling the rights of opinion, speech, and political association. This scenario invites us to accept the Communist Party at its own evaluation—as a political party like the Democrats, Republicans, or Vegetarians, and therefore entitled to unlimited privilege in pursuit of its activities. As the most cursory inspection of the record will reveal, this picture has not the slightest connection with reality. The Coplon case provides us with a vivid example of what the reality *is,* but it is only one of numerous examples. The historical record is literally stuffed with other instances of exactly the same import—all going to show that the Communist "party" is not a political party at all, but a criminal conspiracy in service to a hostile foreign power.

This fact has been established on the empirical record and

*Cook, op. cit.

in courts of law on countless occasions, affirmed by statute, and acknowledge even by such liberal spokesmen as William O. Douglas and Robert Kennedy. In all its actions, the objective of the Communist Party is to betray and subvert the United States in behalf of its principal, the Soviet Union. So much is elementary fact, denied by no one who can be brought to focus attention on the matter for more than a fleeting instant. And since it is the duty of the federal government to protect American citizens from such foreign enemies, so it is the duty of that government to protect us from the machinations of their stooges in our midst. To the extent that it *fails* to offer that protection, it is defaulting the minimal order-keeping tasks of government.

There is a modulation of this argument which might be pursued still further if the foreign-agent issue were not decisive. This is the question of whether the First Amendment guarantee of liberated speech is "absolute"—whether, that is, it permits the exercise of advocacy and opinion which are by hypothesis destructive of society. No such constitutional guarantee could be valid, if the hypothesis were correct, since such a view involves the logical contradiction of destroying the freedom protected in the general ruin of all our freedoms. I hasten to add, however, that I do not consider this to be the real issue before us, although the civil libertarians by their rhetoric and a number of anti-Communists by their responses have among them conspired to make it seem so.

It is not the issue, first of all, because the normative liberal position is really *not* that the First Amendment is absolute up to and including the destruction of the society—but rather that free speech under even the most aggravating conditions somehow *strengthens* the society. The justification offered therefore is not in fact absolute, but utilitarian, and it is worth recording that this defense is offered both by Mill and by our friend Prof. Emerson.* It is not the issue, in the second place, because if

---

*See, in this connection, Emerson's book, *Toward a General Theory of the First Amendment,* passim.

such a threat did in fact exist through "speech," the proper remedy for it could be obtained under the most rigid rules of strict construction rather than through improvisation—namely, by amending the Constitution to cover the contingency in question.

Finally, I consider the debate over First Amendment rights as "absolute" to be a distraction because it serves to obscure the real danger presented by members of the American Communist Party. That danger, to repeat, has little to do with what the Communists *say* but a great deal to do with their generic commitment to the Soviet Union and their status as agents of a hostile foreign power functioning in our midst. It is this status which above all renders the CPUSA an object of legislative concern and of inquiry by the agents of the federal police power. The repeated suggestion that the debate is over "speech" enforces the Communists' self-serving description of their activities, and therefore darkens counsel on the measures appropriate to dealing with them.

On this analysis, the FBI has not merely the right but the imperative duty to monitor the performance of the CPUSA. Congress has repeatedly legislated in this area, not only with respect to espionage and sabotage, but with respect to the broader threat to the nation presented by the "party" in its dimension as a conspiracy and agent of a foreign power. And while courts and civil libertarians may quarrel as they will about the legal sanctions imposed by such statutes, there has yet to be the slightest factual challenge to the assertion that the CPUSA is precisely such an instrument, or that in this guise it is at a minimum deserving of the consistent scrutiny of federal bodies, which for the moment is the principal issue at stake.

On examination, the demand that the CPUSA be exempted from inquiry and observation as a matter of constitutional privilege is tantamount to saying there is *a constitutional right to betray one's country to a foreign enemy and to be exempted from scrutiny while doing so.* A country which acknowledged any such "right" would not be in existence for very long, nor would its citizens enjoy for any extended period any kind of constitutional rights whatever. Needless to remark, the United States Constitution contains no such provision.* And if it did it would violate the first principle of libertarian government—provision of the national defense.

Similar reflections arise upon examination of Emerson's second set of documents—the files which were stolen in 1971 from the FBI office in Media, Pennsylvania. Again we are invited to react with horror at bureau infringement on dissent, and again the reaction of the more conventional reader will be otherwise. Emerson sets forward the type of people who, according to the Media files, were monitored by the FBI. Among them are "antiwar activists," black militants or those who could shed some light on their activities, campus agitators, academicians inviting "controversial speakers without permission," and so on. We get a picture, in sum, of the FBI keeping tabs on various aspects of militant activity among the denizens of the "new left"—a picture which to Emerson's mind suggests the bureau is once more misusing its power in purely "political" areas. But what, again, are the relevant facts?

That question may be answered by reference to the January, 1971, issue of *Scanlan's,* a left-oriented magazine then published in Canada. In a feature entitled "Suppressed Issue: Guerrilla War in the U.S.A.," this journal listed some 1,300 acts of political violence that had occurred in this country in the years 1965-70. Included in this unhappy inventory was a breakdown of events in a single month (March, 1970): dynamitings of Post Offices and other government buildings in Seattle, Champaign,

---

*Quite the contrary. Article III, Section 3 defines the crime of treason as "adhering to" or giving "aid and comfort" to the enemies of the United States. That definition is obviously applicable to American Communists and others who have done everything in their power, to assist not only the Soviet Union but also North Vietnam, with whom we were engaged in a shooting war for the past decade. This continuing aid and comfort is a compelling argument for congressional declarations of war, which would clearly define such actions as treason and make them punishable accordingly.

Illinois, and Cambridge, Maryland; firebombings of selective service offices in Urbana, Illinois, Colorado Springs and Boulder, Colorado; time-bombs planted in army installations at Oakland, Brooklyn, and Portland; arson and firebombings at numerous colleges and high schools and attacks on buildings and personnel at others, guerrilla attacks on police in various cities, 17 bombing attacks against corporations and banks, etc. etc. All of this, mind you, in a *single month*—and 1,300 such actions in a span of six years.

Scanlan's concluded from all this that "the now quite visible wave of bombings is not the work of some isolated terrorist nuts, but part of an overall guerrilla war which has been waged in hot pursuit of American institutions for at least the last three years without anyone, most of all Attorney General John Mitchell, declaring or recognizing it as such. . .The current left-wing terrorism in the United States is modeled on strategies developed during guerrilla struggles in other nations. . .It is now getting to the point. . .where it won't require the services of a computer to project a war out of the rapidly multiplying attacks of guerrilla terrorism and sabotage."

These are assertions, I repeat, of a *left*-wing magazine—the point of them being, apparently, that the complacent view of Americans who believe "it can't happen here" is mistaken, and that the escalation of violence, according to Editor Warren Hinckle, is a kind of reproach to America in general and the Nixon administration in particular ("responsible for the perverse maintenance of imbalances in society without which there would be no popular base or support for guerrilla acts"). Whatever one thinks of that explanation (not much, in my own case), the brute empirical fact of *Scanlan's* documentation can hardly be ignored. And the picture of bombings, arson, sniping, vandalism and physical assault set forward by the magazine is rather different from the sketch of innocent politics and cherubic "dissent" presented to us by Professor Emerson. Also different is the *Scanlan's* version of government efforts to forestall and punish the acts of these "guerrillas," as follows:

> The government's research in this area is appallingly insufficient, although we suspect the administration knows more than it allows, since to admit what is to follow here would be to admit its inability to cope with it. . . With all the resources at their disposal to monitor and supervise reputed revolutionaries, it must be a matter of considerable professional and political embarrassment that the combined law enforcement, military, security, and spy establishment of the United States has been unable to catch even a literal handful of the thousands of underground revolutionaries who, now as a matter of daily benediction, harass the government with sniper fire or bombs. *Guerrillas interviewed in the course of preparing this issue found it a matter of exultant amusement that the government's intelligence system has turned out to be such a basket case . . .* [Italics added.]

That rendering of left-wing action and government counter-action hardly sounds like good old-fashioned dissent being crushed by a police state. It sounds instead like what it is; a gang of violence-prone revolutionaries raising havoc in the country and thumbing their noses at law-enforcement agencies —a fact which *Scanlan's* lays to the incompetence of those agencies and the guerrillas suppose is traceable to the justness of their cause. A more likely explanation is that such guerrillas invariably can call on professional verbalizers and certain civil libertarians to cover up the nature of their actions, or pin the blame on somebody else. (Hinckle: "We cannot blame the guerrillas for the process which has brought this society to such a crisis condition that astonishing number of people are forsaking the ballot for the bomb," etc. His co-editor, Sidney Zion, condemned the violence in no uncertain terms, sans copout.) In any event, the *Scanlan's* presentation makes it plain that gov-was not being nearly effective *enough* in coping with it.

The same conclusion emerges, indeed, from Emerson's own treatment of the Media files. In one passage, he invites us to ponder the plight of an individual under FBI surveillance as follows: "The Swarthmore philosophy professor, referred to previously, was checked on the possibility that it might lead to the *apprehension of two women alleged to have participated in a bank robbery and murder engineered by a radical political group.* The bureau's agents made contact with the college security officer, a neighbor, the switchboard operator, the local chief of police who lived two doors away, and the postmaster, all of whom gave information and promised to keep the professor, his telephone calls, his mail, and his other doings under close surveillance. *These side-effects of a bureau investigation cannot be ignored."* (Italics added.)

If this passage says anything, it says the FBI should *not* investigate possible connections of the professor to a bank robbery-murder because such an investigation has unpleasant side-effects. (Emerson nowhere suggests the FBI was *mistaken* in thinking it might develop leads in this fashion.) Precisely the same thing might be said concerning investigation of an axe-murder, rape, mugging, or gangland shoot-out. In every case investigation of possible leads would have "side-effects" unpleasant to those investigated. And while there has been a general deterioration of thought on the subject of law enforcement in this country, no one has yet suggested these latter actions be privileged against investigation. Evidently it is because the bank robbery-murder in the Media file was alleged to the account of a "radical" group and the professor being examined was himself a leftist that this particular investigation is considered *ipso facto* outrageous, a formula which opens up some interesting new vistas of criminality. All one need do is label himself as "radical" or "revolutionary" and he may commit murder and robbery *ad libitum,* confident that inquiry into possible leads will be halted on grounds of political infringement.

Consider also in this connection the complaint of Senator Muskie—in which the FBI was allegedly culpable for conducting surveillance of an innocent "anti-pollution rally." What really happened at this gathering in behalf of the most sacred of secular causes was something rather different. This particular "anti-pollution rally" was addressed by numerous individuals, few of whom had much of anything to say about pollution. Speaking to the assembled multitude, for example, was one Rennie Davis, a radical leader who had been involved in the disorders at the 1968 Chicago convention at which Muskie himself had been nominated for vice president. And Rennie Davis chose the occasion to tell his audience that, rather than exercising themselves about pollution, they should have been on their way to New Haven, Connecticut, to "stop" the murder trial of Black Panther leader Bobby Seale.

It was, in sum, hardly the ingenuous episode that Senator Muskie would have us believe. And hardly *ultra vires* of the FBI to be keeping its eye on a radical leader whose avowed intention was to create a revolution in America and who had already achieved a considerable notoriety for his attempts to realize that goal. If it is seriously to be argued that the FBI should not keep watch on such as Rennie Davis then it is argued that the United States should stand defenseless before those who seek to destroy it and who have already taken action to do so. The argument is particularly ludicrous in view of the double fact (a) that large gatherings of this type have erupted into violence on previous occasions, and (b) that nobody's constitutional rights are violated an iota by the FBI's observing such massive public meetings and reporting what occurs there. The self-evident absurdity of the argument does not, however, prevent a number of influential people from parroting it—which is a measure of our national distress.

We may note the case of another leftist who became the object of FBI inquiry and who committed two established acts of political violence—Lee Harvey Oswald. The bureau had a file on Oswald as a result of his defection to the Soviet Union, his activities with the Castro-financed Fair Play for Cuba Committee (a now-defunct forerunner of the new left), and an attempt to go to Cuba. Yet it did not put the finger on Oswald as a dangerous character prior to President John F. Kennedy's visit to Dallas. In the light of the foregoing, what comment should we expect from bureau critics on the left? The answer, once again, is Catch-22: The bureau is blasted for not being thorough *enough* in predicating restrictive actions on its investigations. Messick, for example, attacks the bureau for having information on Oswald but doing nothing about it, commenting that "Hoover as usual defended the failure of his agency by denying it had failed."*

Similar allegations have been made by the late Drew Pearson, ex-FBI agent turned critic William Turner,** writer Harold Feldman and numerous other spokesmen for the liberal-left. Noting these commentaries, the Overstreets raise the obvious and telling questions: "What stand would Pearson, Feldman, and Turner have taken if Oswald had protested that the FBI had branded him as a potential assassin and initiated an infringement of his rights just because he was a defector, had been court-martialed, had distributed Fair Play for Cuba leaflets without a permit, was a Marxist, and had tried to visit Cuba? Would these critics of the FBI have told Oswald flatly that, in view of his record, the bureau had done what was obviously called for? Or would they have taken up his cause—as that of a dissenter persecuted by the FBI?"***

Considering the recent uproar of the Muskies, Emersons, and others about the evils of FBI "surveillance" and the terrible uses of "secret dossiers," we *know* what would have happened if the FBI, before any overt act had been committed, had taken Oswald into custody, or put him under surveillance tight enough to alter his course of action. Quite plainly, Oswald would have been "chilled" by any such performance, the overt act against Kennedy would not have been committed, and there would have been no crime demonstrable in a court of

*Messick, op. cit.
**William Turner, *Saga* Magazine, March, 1964.
****The FBI in Our Open Society*, op. cit.

law. In that event a platoon of civil liberties lawyers led by Professor Emerson would have been camped on his doorstep, ready to take the matter to the highest court in the land. And under the circumstances, they might well have won their case.

That hypothesis, however, stirs a further interesting thought: If it is true that tighter FBI surveillance could have prevented Oswald from murdering President Kennedy, it may well be that FBI surveillance on *other* leftist radicals, also with accompanying chill, has prevented an unknown number of other such actions in the intervening years. If the Kennedy assassination proves anything, it is that there should indeed be emphasis on screening activities of the more fanatical new leftists, where the syndrome of Marxist violence and irrationality displayed by Oswald is all too common. It is astonishing to note, indeed, the similarities between Oswald and Sirhan B. Sirhan, another self-professed Communist and political radical, who murdered Senator Robert F. Kennedy in June of 1968. The assassination evidence fits all too grimly with the other data before us.

None of this, however, tells us *why* the FBI and Secret Service didn't zero in on Oswald before the President's trip to Dallas. The record here is rather plain: the feds weren't looking for potential assassins on the left because, in obedience to the spirit of the times, the relevant agencies were looking for potential assassins *on the right.* The Kennedy administration was agitated about the supposed menace of the radical right, and in fact the President was on his way to deliver a speech concerning this topic when he was murdered. These fears were underscored by a demonstration which had occurred in Dallas a month before in protest of a visit by Adlai Stevenson. The Secret Service obtained pictures of some of the people involved in that demonstration and, according to the Warren Commission Report: *"On November 22 a Secret Service agent stood at the entrance to the Trade Mart, where the President was scheduled to speak, with copies of these photographs. Dallas detectives in the lobby of the Trade Mart and in the luncheon area also had copies of these photographs. A number of people who resembled some of those in the photograph were placed under surveillance at the Trade Mart."* (Italics added.)

Thus while a Communist lurked in waiting to kill the President, the Secret Service and the police were standing around keeping an eye on Texas right-wingers. The mind-set that produced this performance was that of the Kennedy administration itself. We are told that members of the Kennedy entourage agonized endlessly over the conservative character of Dallas and the possible dangers to the President from right-wingers if he visited there. William Manchester, in his authorized account of the assassination, covers this in detail, and in fact treats the Kennedy murder (despite the fact that Oswald's Communist connections were fully known at the time Manchester was writing), as if it were somehow related to Dallas' conservatism. Numerous other commentators have done the same thing, of course, and continue to do so.

Given an ideological outlook which perceives the Kennedy assassination as the result of "right-wing" tendencies even after it has been shown the President was killed by a Communist, it is hardly surprising the FBI and Secret Service were not placed on the alert for Oswald *before* the assassination occurred. That the watch was on for conservatives and not for Communists is indeed a grotesque and horrible irony, but it is not the sort of irony of which the FBI, absent counter-programming from above, is likely to be guilty. That the very liberals who cry up the "danger on the right" and dismiss internal communism as a manifestation of "dissent" should denounce the FBI for not uncovering Oswald before the fact is ludicrous.

The case of Oswald is additionally interesting because it tells us something about the nature of FBI "dossiers," so frequently depicted as an instrument of repression. As noted, the mere existence of a file on someone, or the mention of someone's name in such a file, in no way means the FBI considers that person guilty of anything, Oswald being an obvious example. Files are compiled in security investigations, check-ups on applications for employment, and files are kept on individuals who might be considered threats to the President or other federal officials. In each of these instances, the job of the bureau is not to determine that X is guilty of any particular crime, but rather to act as a receiver of information, collecting all data and passing them on to relevant authorities who are then to make the appropriate evaluation.*

While some evaluation work is required of the FBI (e.g., in deciding under the now-revised criteria what data to pass along to the Secret Service in cases of presidential security), the bureau's essential job is to investigate, not to make judgments of guilt or innocence. This means its files necessarily contain a great deal of non-incriminating information, of marginal relevance to any final decision, or in some cases information which is flatly untrue (as in the case of a contact who for reasons of malice or misinformation purveys false gossip about an individual under investigation). The FBI neither "clears" nor "convicts"; it carries out its investigatory duties as assigned by law. If it should attempt to screen out data from its files once an investigation is under way, then it would be usurping the evaluating role and overstepping its proper bounds.

What is true of precautionary intelligence investigations is even more true, obviously, of investigations pursuant to the violation of federal law—as in the case referred to from the Media files. Such information as the possible contact of the professor with the bank robbery-murder developed through perfectly normal and proper police procedure, in which the investigating agency seeks out all possible data relating to an alleged law violation. (In this case, the FBI was seeking fugitives and needed the information for its own use.) In the course of this undertaking it is necessary to gather up a good deal of information about people who are *not* criminals, or who have only a potential relationship to some criminal act, but whose exact relevance to the proceeding can be determined only *after* the

---

*See Warren Commission testimony of FBI official Alan Belmont.

facts are in. The Swarthmore professor's name was entered in the file because agents keep reports, not because he was a radical.

To suggest that the FBI or other police agencies investigate criminal actions by limiting their inquiry only to the individuals ultimately found guilty by the courts (and this has in effect been proposed, almost in as many words) is manifestly inane. Among other difficulties, such a suggestion presupposes that the problem of the investigation—who is guilty, and what is the evidence going to prove it—has been solved before the inquiry begins. If the FBI or other police agency knew beforehand exactly who was guilty and so could limit inquiry to that individual and no other, there would be no need for investigation. Indeed, armed with such infallible radar, we would have no need of courts or juries or the rest of our legal paraphernalia because only those who are guilty would have been under investigation to begin with. Since we have no such radar and must proceed by the normal rules of human inquiry, any police investigation will have to cast a considerable net to assemble potentially relevant data for a criminal investigation.

The alleged menace of the "dossiers" is thus cut down to size, along with wiretapping, informants, and surveillance. In all three cases, there is precious little evidence that the bureau has used its powers to persecute dissidents, silence anybody's opinion, or harass innocent liberals. There *is* a powerful body of evidence, however, to show that it has battled against Communists, new left revolutionaries, and criminals, as well it might. It can be argued that it might do better in one respect or another, although its efficiency, fairness, and thoroughness are without discernible parallel in the annals of American government. But whatever improvements might be made in its procedures (as in the Oswald case), the liberal critics are hardly the people to consult concerning them. On almost every count the arguments of these critics would make the agency *less* effective where it needs to be, and therefore less serviceable in defending the nation against foreign enemies and domestic criminals.

From our brief empirical review, it is possible to see that the FBI is far more libertarian than its critics suggest and indeed more libertarian than the critics themselves. In matters of fundamental philosophy, constitutional balance, and obedience to the rule of law, the bureau by statement and action has demonstrated a rather close adherence to the standards of libertarian statecraft. The normative FBI opinion has been, exactly, that its function is to neutralize the aggressive use of force, and that to this end its principal functions are (a) to protect the nation from foreign enemies, and (b) to protect the nation from criminal acts authentically national in character. In both these tasks, so far as the record discloses, it has proceeded with due regard for constitutional safeguards, the restrictions inherent in the federal character of our system, the will of Congress as expressed by statute, and the orders of the executive branch of which it is a subordinate agency.

It may be truly alleged that the FBI is involved in zones of activity outside the range of federal power as conceived by the nation's founders, but as observed this is the result of the continual build-up of federal power generally. Although the agency has shown acute awareness of states' responsibilities and rights and Director Hoover had repeatedly stressed the nature of the federal balance, the FBI could not nullify the legislated expansion of central government authority if it would. To do so would be to violate the rule of law and usurp authority within the federal chain of command. The proper corrective for the presently expanded level of federal power is not be berate the FBI, but to move by legislation to roll back the intrusions of the central government upon the states.

Finally, there is the bureau's insistence on following the course of statute law, of accepting jurisdiction where it is granted and of refusing to range afield where it has been withheld. "This stickling for ultra-fine points of law," as Fred Cook described it, is a major strength of the FBI, and one of the reasons it has withstood so long the batterings of its enemies. It is also, as noted, a policy in full alignment with the third of our libertarian principles, which asserts that government agencies should be bound by the rule of law, and should not attempt to improvise occasions for the absorption of power.

Contrast this with the positions adopted by its detractors. There is to begin with the fact that these critics, by covering with the mantle of "politics" and "dissent" the actions of the Communist Party, and demanding that such actions be privileged against the scrutiny of the FBI, are saying our government should neglect a major part of its responsibility to the people —that of protecting them from agents of a hostile foreign power seeking to bring about their destruction. This is in effect a demand that government default an essential aspect of the national defense function, *not* deploy its energies *vis-à-vis* the Soviet Union to neutralize the aggressive use of force.

In similar fashion, the critics would have the FBI curtail its surveillance of new-left activists, also supposedly privileged by virtue of their "political" designation. But as we have seen these allegedly "political" dissenters have produced an amazing number of acts of violence and terror, and some among them have stated their intention of producing still more in the future. The demand that the FBI not cover such people in its investigations, or not follow-up on leads connected with the new left-oriented violence, is a demand that the agency abandon the battle against a particularly vicious species of domestic crime—and thus default on the domestic front as well the most minimal order-keeping tasks of government.

On this point, therefore, the FBI is clearly more libertarian than its critics, since it seeks to perform the tasks which in the libertarian theory are essential to a regime of freedom, while the critics want those tasks abandoned. And the anti-libertarian consequences of that default are more than theoretical, since according to our model this deficiency would permit the reign of coercion by foreign enemies and domestic criminals. The citizens the government is supposed to be protecting are thereby submitted to the rule of force. A deficiency of law enforcement properly defined is as injurious to freedom as the excess of it—a point which is seldom raised in modern debate but is properly recognized in the libertarian literature of the West, from the *Vindiciae Contra Tyrannos* to Locke to Mill.* A rampage of 1,300 acts of left-wing terror is hardly congenial to the liberty of those subjected to such violence—nor is a supposedly "libertarian" philosophy which would curtail investigation of such acts because they have political ramifications.

Insistence on covering riot, arson, and bombing with the mantle of "dissent" involves another disservice to freedom as well. By blurring the distinction between violence and mere spoken or printed words, it destroys the very distinction upon which freedom of speech and opinion have been protected. The point of free opinion is that it does not impinge on the rights of others; the point of new-left violence and disruption is, precisely, that it does. In a system of constitutional liberty the first should be privileged, the second should not. Those who insist on confusing the difference between these modes of behavior are anything but libertarian.

On matters of general constitutional interpretation, we have said enough to make the distinction between the bureau and its critics tolerably plain. In place of Hoover's demand that the FBI be kept on a limited basis and that original law enforcement powers be left with the states, the liberals would give us an amorphous and spreading FBI with no certain bounda-

---

The Vindiciae, for example, states: "...because life is a thing precious, and to be favored, peradventure it will be demanded whether the king may not pardon and absolve those whom the law has condemned? I answer, no. Otherwise, this cruel pity would maintain thieves, robbers, murderers, ravishers, poisoners, sorcerers, and other plagues of mankind, as we may read tyrants have done heretofore in many places...and therefore, the stopping of law in this kind will, by impunity, much increase the number of offenders...certainly that shepherd is much more pitiful who kills the wolf, than he who lets him escape; the clemency of the king is more commendable who commits the malefactor to the hangman, than he who delivers him; by putting to death the murderer many innocents are delivered from danger; whereas by suffering him to escape, both he and others through hope of like impunity are made more audacious to perpetrate further mischief, so that the immediate act of saving the delinquent arms many hands to murder diverse innocents."

ries to its jurisdiction. It has, of course, been the liberals them-selves who have promoted the general accretion of federal power and the rising level of federal law, which in turn estab-lishes the agency's enforcement responsibilities. The critics are as indifferent to the character of the federal balance as Hoover was sensitive to it—and are as deficient on libertarian grounds in this respect as they are in matters of basic philosophy.

In our final category, the rule of law, the contrast between the agency and its detractors is equally clear. The view of the critics has been suggested only implicitly, but the manner in which they chide the bureau both for doing *too much* and *too little,* according to the ideological content of the actions in ques-tion, points us toward a more explicit formulation. In essence, the guidelines of FBI activity preferred by the critics are no guidelines at all, but merely extensions of their own naked will. Where FBI performance has offended their ideological sensi-bilities, they want its activities stifled, irrespective of congres-sional enactments. As noted, these *verboten* areas have to do with internal security, subversion, and—of late—domestic dis-order. By the same token, these same critics want the FBI to be *more* involved in areas where their ideological sympathies are engaged, again irrespective of whether legislative authority has granted the appropriate power. The most frequently cited examples here, of course, are civil rights and organized crime.

In each case—less involvement or more involvement—the criterion is not law, or constitutional mandate, or even the gen-eral imperatives of civil order, but the ideological fervor of the critic, however subtly rationalized. The reader may judge for himself the libertarian implications of such an approach. Speaking for myself, it is hard to imagine anything which could more certainly turn the FBI into a *real* "American Gestapo" than the attitude of its more adamant critics. A federal police agency which conducted itself on principles of ideological pas-sion would be perpetually out of bounds and indeed there would be no bounds by which to compass it. A government of men and not of laws is bad in any event; a national police agency conducted on such premises is ideally suited to the uses of dictatorship. When its ideological passions were not engaged, such an agency would refuse to enforce duly enacted legislation; when they were enflamed it would act as it pleased, even in the absence of legislative authority. Here is a perfect formula, if ever there was one, for the destruction of our liberties.

We are fortunate that J. Edgar Hoover and the agency he built took a different view of the matter. With Hoover's passing and the insistent pressure of the liberal critics, the danger we confront is that the bureau will by degrees be shifted over to the *modus operandi* demanded by the left. When that occurs, and only then, will the FBI become a menace to American freedoms.

4. Coping with Anti-Democrats in a Democracy
Ernest van den Haag
with the Editors

The Editors

The law enforcement-criminal justice system is supposed to protect citizens from dangerous persons in our midst, and as a part of this system the challenge is presented to the FBI as well. It is this question which underlies the problems in the FBI's future: will the system protect the people?

The people of one community, at least, must now wonder about the answer. Paul Corbett, an insurance executive, and his family lived in Barrington Hills, Illinois, a fashionable community northwest of Chicago. On August 4, 1972, his wife Marion; her sister, Mrs. Dorothy Derry; and Marion's daughter, Barbara Boand, were visiting in the Corbett home, going about their family business in the usual way, quite content in their surroundings and their lives, and only vaguely aware of the trouble afflicting the world.

That evening, however, a dreadful sample of the terror, the senseless brutality, the hateful vengeance of the world also visited the Corbett home, and the family lay dead, "executed" by the guns of a marauding band of male Negro criminals, a terror squad of a group called De Mau Mau. The terror squad consisted of only a few men, about ten, but a list found by authorities contained the code names of 150 more Mau Mau. Some of the ten have at this writing, been charged with eight similar execution-murders, all of white persons, all executed without ever understanding why they were singled out as victims.

Examine for a moment the situation of the Mau Mau murders. A challenge is presented. The threat to a free civilization which the situation portends is the one, in Professor van den Haag's analysis, to which American institutions including the FBI must have the power to respond.

The Mau Mau are racist, but that is not the important factor. Racism does not explain the actions of the small Mau Mau terror squad. The brutality was too specific, a war against white people too distant in relation.

No, these executions were not just racist—they were barbarous. Certain human qualities are missing in anyone who would do what was done in the Corbett home. The murders were wanton; the murderers can only be directionless, marauding barbarians.

Consider also the reaction to the Mau Mau when they were found out in October, 1972. There was anger, but it was detachedly expressed, as one shakes one's head when a senseless tragic drama unfolds on a TV screen. And there were those who worried more about the reaction than the events. In an October 18 editorial of the *Chicago Today*, for instance, the paper cautioned against demands for strong action. *Chicago Today* is concerned that the public will react too harshly, instead of clamoring for dealing "intelligently" with "the forces that created it" (the Mau Mau). Thinking likewise, some Negro spokesmen worried aloud about the damage public reaction to the Mau Mau would do their cause, but only one publicly denounced the killings, Dr. Charles Hurst, the outspoken former president of Chicago's Malcolm X College. Then, of course, the local ACLU leadership expressed its peculiar concern, blasting the Sheriff's Department for possible civil rights violations visited on the six Mau Mau who were held in jail without arraignment while the sheriff searched for the remaining four.*

Something is awry here. None of the above spokesmen would mean to condone terrorism. But they do. They do because their understandings of societal needs have not the capacity to consider more than particular interests. To *Chicago Today,* it is the social environment which creates the Mau Mau. To the black leaders, it is their cause. To the ACLU, it is that instrument of abstract justice—the technical procedural limitations on the police. In the name of these interests, they tolerate terror. Who among them really grieves for the Corbett family?

Where the concern for other interests tends to unconcern for the victims of even senseless, terror murders, then the pendulum has indeed swung far toward one side. The criminal justice system may be incapable of dispensing justice when it cannot adequately deal with the barbarians in our midst. The government may no longer serve its people, where it is defenseless to protect the civilized values which are the precondition to its citizens' peace and freedom.

The Mau Mau are but one—the most terrifying—illustration of the situation which challenges American institutions. American society is besieged by other barbarians: the criminals who rob, rape, and kill, the street radicals who "mau mau" the universities and the government in their own way, and the gangsters and narcotics pushers who hook their customers to satisfy their own greed. Are not these elements barbarians, and is not that portion of society uncivilized which cannot assure peaceful persons the use of their city parks and preserves, their streets, their public transportation, or their educational institutions without fear of brutal assault or poorly disguised intimidation?

We do not wish to exaggerate the threat. Obviously, the barbarians have not directly attacked most of us as the uncivilized horde ran amuck in an earlier dark age. However, it is equally as obvious that the present horde at least threatens the continued progress toward a free society.

Chicago Tribune, October 16, 1972, p. 2.

To be sure, "freedom" must mean something else where in its name a significant part of the population is destined to live in fear. And individual rights must be no more than abstractions where others must suffer injustice at the hands of those who are free because of the concept in practice. A free society which is not a mere abstraction must not permit the barbarians to prey on their victims.

The proper function of the FBI, as well as law enforcement generally, must be examined in this light. In a truly free society, the government must have at least the power to uphold that free society, and law enforcement should fit that mold. Surely, American society has strayed from this precept when its law enforcement system has been disabled from dealing properly with criminal elements which threaten the continued peace and freedom of society.

It is balance which is missing. The quest for the civil rights of individuals has evolved into something quite different. The pendulum has to swing back; the imbalance in American institutions which serves to tolerate this sort of uncivilized situation must be restored to an equilibrium where the broad interest in the protection for individuals does not disable the law enforcement—criminal justice system's response to disorder. Professor van den Haag more specifically points out that the privacy and protection of suspects is an interest which must be balanced against the need for adequate police powers. There must be a balance struck in the system of justice such that law enforcement agencies may respond to the situation, and barbarians are no longer tolerated.

The present imbalance, of course, affects more than the FBI, since the bureau is not responsible in the first instance for keeping peace in our communities. The bureau is, however, charged with a primary duty of protecting the constitutional form of government, and in performance of this function, the imbalance is even more pronounced. The point is made elsewhere in this book that the internal security laws have been decimated by the courts, all in the name of liberty.

Professor van den Haag's analysis should be applied. The

function of the FBI in the internal security area should be determined by balancing, with the desirable limitations on the agency measured by the threat to democratic government. He makes the point that ultimately democratic principles permit suppression of totalitarian forces, thus requiring that change in governments be the function of the vote, and that change itself not endanger the democracy. Perhaps, the present situation does not merit suppression of some radical forces, but if not, it should be understood that if the power is denied to the FBI, then it is the result of the American people's forbearance, not their inability in principle.

This is a concept not generally recognized by the American institutions—particularly the courts—which enforce the limitations on the power of the FBI. In fact, the situation in effect denies to the bureau any power against totalitarians other than the one of restricting them to peaceful activities, without regard to the danger to democracy and the free society. The Communist Party for instance is in effect free to participate in democratic processes, even though the party avowedly would destroy the same for the rest of us. More on that later; here the point is, the FBI has been restricted in a way that disables it from providing full protection to a free society.

Not only have the courts been tolerant of late of the existence of totalitarian movements, but even the criminal violence perpetrated by the movements is in effect tolerated. Seemingly, the political motivation of the violent, where the act is not too severe, has mitigated the consequences to the perpetrator. For instance, the protester-vandal is handled more gently than the burglar, even though both do the same damage.

In another sense, the conspirators who plan to victimize a city with an illegal demonstration are treated to rights which make them nearly immune from the consequences of their advocacy. Their protest, it is said, is an expression of opinion protected by the First Amendment. Can this be the case? Must free speech be protected to the extent that protesters can, with relative impunity, victimize society?

An imbalance is apparent here too. Civilized discourse on

change in society is endangered by the barbaric actions of radicals in the streets. Yet, no distinction is made between their form of "political" action and democratic action. The barbarians are as free to perform as are the democratic politicians, and are free to prey on the very political system which is meant to preserve a free society. The ideas are out of balance, the result of overdevelopment of abstract notions about freedom of expression and democratic tolerance, and neglect of countervailing considerations.

It is in this context that the internal security functions of the FBI should be reconsidered. The pendulum must swing back to a reasonable equilibrium. Authoritarian measures must be applied against the totalitarian radicals who threaten free society, and limitations must be regarded on the powers of the FBI such that the authoritarian powers do not themselves do disservice to a free society.

One cannot simply apply one consideration in the absence of the other. An FBI which is too limited in power is as much a danger to freedom as an agency which treats its targets as in a police state; the freedom of action of free citizens is victimized as much by totalitarians who subvert democratic processes and discourse as it is victimized by a Gestapo. It is in the interest of freedom that both be controlled.

These concepts must be reintroduced into the life of our country before the challenge to freedom can be met, and before the FBI can perform its proper functions. Instead of stubbornly pursuing, as has been done, protection only for individual privacy and freedom, some consideration must be given also the needs for an FBI which is empowered to contend adequately with certain of the barbarians who take advantage of the increasing tolerance.

It is in this perspective that the following chapters explore the relation of FBI functions to individual freedom, and assess the agency's performance.

A Free Society's Need / Ernest van den Haag

What degree of suspicion of what kind of crime or what other justification is required to permit law enforcement agencies to spy on suspects? What means of spying (electronic surveillance, wiretaps, informants, etc.) should be permissible, when, if ever? How far should local police or the FBI be allowed to go in their never ending war with suspected criminals?

To balance the right of protection from violations of privacy against other rights is to decide, *inter alia*, how much law enforcement agencies should be allowed to infringe on the privacy of suspects in order to protect the privacy (and all the rights) of other citizens—above all the right not to be victimized by lawbreakers such as burglars or murderers. The same question arises with respect to politically motivated suspects.

Each violation of a criminal statute injures the social order and thereby all members of society in addition to injuring in some cases specific victims. Nothing follows about the wisdom of specific laws. Perhaps prostitution should be allowed. But as long as the citizens do keep the laws prohibiting it, to violate them is to victimize the social order, which must be defended if it is to remain enforceable. In principle then, the police should have the same latitude in investigating any suspected crime. But there is nothing wrong in exercising such latitude wisely and with discretion, using it to the hilt where heinous crimes are suspected, and in moderation when the crime is regarded as comparatively trivial. Wherefore prosecutors and police have always had considerable discretion. There is nothing wrong with legally limiting particularly unpleasant investigative means used by law enforcement agencies (e.g., electronic surveillance) to persons suspected of particularly grave crimes.

Although the law determines the rights and duties of law enforcement agencies the courts have often had to decide when to superordinate their claims to those of suspects and when to subordinate them. Courts decide by interpreting laws and (to decide upon the validity of laws) constitutional principles. The apparent effect is to establish a permanent order of priorities.

This however is a legal fiction. The order of priorities changes quite frequently through changed interpretations—even though the constitutional provisions interpreted do not.

Thus, in the past twenty years the courts have found that the Constitution grants certain (hitherto undiscovered) rights to suspects and defendants. Evidence previously admitted in court no longer is. Convictions to that extent have become harder to obtain. (This is not necessarily reflected in the recorded disposal of cases by the courts. Lack of admissible evidence may prevent prosecution, or lead to the acceptance of guilty pleas to lesser offenses. Minor burglaries, shopliftings, and muggings, may not even lead to police investigation.) Punishment of the convicted also has become less and less harsh with new interpretations of the Constitution. For example, what constitutes "cruel and unusual" punishment or capricious infliction of it was reinterpreted in 1972 in the Supreme Court dealth penalty ruling.

At present, changes of interpretation are quite independent of the factors on which they ought depend. In time of social danger—for example, in time of war, or when the crime rate is high or rising—measures of social defense should be strengthened. Individual rights should be subordinated to social defense to a greater degree than is desirable when the social danger recedes. The rights of suspects in their relation to the rights and duties of law enforcement agencies should not be treated as fixed forever. On the contrary, these rights should be enlarged when the need for social defense diminishes and restricted when the need increases. At present the pattern of change is not related in any rational way to changes in the need for social defense—and there is no provision to insure a rational relationship.

The courts have always balanced rights against each other, and the balance, although it appears to be fixed by the Constitution, has been shifted often—but perversely. While crime rates have risen steadily in the past twenty years, the courts have chosen to enlarge the rights and immunities of suspects and defendants and to restrict law enforcement agencies. Similarly, in practical terms the criminal justice system has reduced the severity and frequency of penalties, whether via plea bargaining, the enforcement of rules of evidence, or other help to defendants. Obviously changes in the social need for protection from crime are not rationally reflected in the present tendency of the criminal justice system.

Perhaps legal provisions could be made to reflect such changes automatically and rationally. Rights might be automatically restricted (or enlarged) and penalties increased (or decreased) within broad constitutional limits, in response to increases (or decreases) in social danger just as, for instance, the penalty for espionage automatically increases in wartime, and decreases when the nation is at peace. Some countries, in times of political danger, declare "martial law" or use other emergency legal devices to arrest and try suspects without the usual procedural safeguards of their rights. This goes far beyond what is needed in this country. Yet an automatic shifting of the balance in response to shifting needs would be quite desirable, and the law could well provide for such automatic shifts within our constitutional limits.

Expenditures on defense and police forces usually are changed with circumstances, and new legislation is passed in response to changes of conditions and attitudes. Yet the legal balance between the right of suspects to privacy and the investigative duties of law enforcement agencies is not systematically shifted in accordance with circumstances. The conflicting claims are treated as though their priority were determined exclusively and permanently by constitutional principles. However, if wiretapping by law enforcement agencies is always a threat to privacy, so is crime, which threatens privacy no less than people or property. Citizens want protection from both threats. And at any time more protection should be provided against what is more threatening at that time. It follows that the protection of the privacy of suspects is to be reduced where it impedes law enforcement (needed for the protection of the privacy and of the other rights of victims) when the crime rate is high; and to be increased when the crime rate is low.

There is no reason for the law not to satisfy this standard. The rights to be balanced are permanent. The order of priorities need not be; it should depend on fluctuating quantities or urgencies. A general legal rule could automatically increase or (decrease) police surveillance powers (and change related matters) as the crime rate (determined by official authority) increases (or decreases) beyond certain predetermined points. (A constitutional interpretation permitting as much is not beyond the ingenuity of the Supreme Court.) At present, because neither the law nor its interpreters acknowledge the need to meet quantitative changes by shifting the priorities of rights, we often find the powers of law enforcement curtailed when they should be expanded, and vice versa—for the judicial dynamics which determine the interpretation of the Constitution seem, if anything, negatively correlated to social needs. At any rate they are not systematically and rationally correlated and adjusted to these social needs.

It is such an adjustment that must be made whenever it is to be decided whether or not an FBI operation ought to be permitted. The potential harm to privacy must be weighed against the necessity for police action in the context of the social needs of the time; to the extent only one or the other interest is considered to the exclusion of the other, the result is irrational. And whenever such irrationality continues for a period, in either direction, the nation tends to tyranny, that of anarchy on the one side or that of the police state on the other.

This balancing approach simply is beyond many of the FBI's critics. It is often urged that subordination of the privacy (and of the many other rights) which suspects retain, to the claimed needs of law enforcement agencies is a "police state method," which should not be countenanced in a democracy under any circumstances. "Police state" here probably means a state in which the rulers enforce their wishes by using the police, without sufficiently limiting the means available to it.

There are nearly pure instances of "police states" extant at the present time in the Communist world and somewhat less pure ones in Africa, South America, the Caribbean, the Near East, and the Iberian Peninsula. One cannot reasonably identify the political system of the United States with that of any of these "police states." Clearly we have effective and legal opposition parties and civil liberties, conspicuously lacking in police states. However protesters probably intend to stress that the American "police state methods" protested bear an uncomfortable resemblance to some of those generally applied in actual "police states." If this be so, it is of little relevance to the evaluation of the methods in question. Occasional resemblance does not imply essential similarity or identity in those matters which actually distinguish police states from others which are not. There is no indication of a planned or actual introduction of a "police state" in the U.S.—no party plans or advocates anything like the Soviet or Nazi regime. Even the Communists deny that they do. Here the famous Marxist proverb "quantity becomes quality" might make sense: a "police state" is one which systematically deprives all suspects of all defenses, and gives the police overwhelming power. However, to give the police in a democracy some of the powers it also holds in a dictatorship—but not all powers, nor the most important ones—would not be to transform a democracy into a police state.

It may also be suggested that the "police state methods" protested, rather than merely resembling those of a police state, ultimately will lead to a "police state," or even to indicate that we are on the way to becoming one. This would be a factual observation or prediction. As far as past experience goes, it is incorrect. The known "police states"—including Nazi Germany and Fascist Italy, as well as those mentioned before—have all been preceded by either a period of spotty and lax law enforcement and general social disorder (with or without civil war, revolution, or coup d'etat) or by a period in which the means available proved unequal to the task of enforcing the law and were not sufficiently improved in time. If one disregards "police states" which became such as a result of conquest, no "police state" has ever followed a timely enlargement of the powers of law enforcement by a democracy, let alone grown from, or been caused, by it. In other words, no "police state" has ever been the effect of "police state methods."

A good case may be made—although it shall not be made here—for the contrary contention: whenever there is a rise of general crime and of activity directed against a democratic system, severe laws, strictly enforced, and increased power for law enforcement agencies, even at the cost of temporarily reducing the privacy and protection of suspects, serve to prevent a "police state"; insistence on the right to privacy at all costs does not.

Overreacting police agencies would appear to hardly be the problem today. The tendency is in the other direction—toward imbalance in favor of the rights of suspects. Illustrating this, in the famous case *Miranda* vs. *Arizona,* the Supreme Court found that, beyond heeding a request for counsel by a suspect in custody, the police must, even if unrequested, offer him counsel and notify the suspect that he need not make any statements. The decision helps suspects to avoid disclosing information they might not want to disclose when advised by counsel.* If heeded fully, *Miranda* could possibly eliminate altogether confessions to the police, and other revealing statements; counsel seldom will advise a client to talk when doing so might help the police. In any case, the court here shifted the balance radically in favor of suspects.

The decision is usually justified by arguments aptly expressed by Joseph W. Bishop, Jr., Ely Professor of Law at Yale University: "*Miranda* gave the poor, unskilled criminals what mafiosi...had all along—the means to exercise their constitutional right to keep silent and talk to a lawyer...Rich, sophisticated

---

*For a defense of *Miranda* and protection of privacy see R. S. Gerstein, "Privacy and Self-Incrimination," *Ethics* 80 (Jan. 1970) pp. 87-99.

criminals [do not] deserve a better chance than poor, ignorant criminals."* Thus, the argument for *Miranda* is that since "rich, sophisticated criminals" may escape conviction by not confessing on advice of counsel, "poor, ignorant criminals" also must be enabled to escape conviction by not confessing on advice of counsel. If one group of (rich) criminals escapes conviction, another group of (poor) criminals ought to be helped to do likewise.

The equality between the two groups is regarded as more important than the conviction of those criminals who are "ignorant" enough to confess their guilt. It would seem, then, that the purpose of court action is no longer to protect the innocent and punish the guilty, but to make sure that the guilty rich and the guilty poor get an equal chance to escape conviction. Shouldn't we correct the inequality between rich and poor criminals by making sure that the guilty rich will not escape conviction, rather than by helping the guilty poor to escape because the rich might? And should it prove impossible to prevent the rich from escaping conviction—which I doubt— should we really help one group of criminals to escape conviction because another might or did? Suppose all redheaded people had the miraculous ability to avoid apprehension and conviction for any crime. Should we suspend law enforcement for people of any other hair color?

The case for *Miranda* is not improved much if, unlike Professor Bishop and most supporters, one assumes the suspect to be innocent. Even in the absence of counsel most suspects are unlikely to confess to what they have not done. But should they confess, owing to confusion, or pressure, and should trial counsel be unable to show the confession to have been extracted by illegitimate means (and thus inadmissible), defendants can always repudiate their confession in court. The jury would then have to determine whether the confession was extracted by overeager police or the repudiation was engineered by overzea-

New York Times Magazine, Sept. 7, 1969.

lous defense counsel. I do not see how a repudiated confession, unless corroborated by convincing independent evidence, would greatly influence the jury. On the other hand, failure to confess on advice of counsel might indeed help as many "poor, ignorant criminals" to escape conviction as it does help "rich, sophisticated criminals" to do so. And that would be a calamity.*

That much about dealing with suspects in general. Something more specific must be said about dealing with revolutionaries.

The right to forbid incitement to revolution is inherent in the lawful authority which all governments claim, in legitimacy *per se.* But democratic principle regards only governments which issue from the freely expressed wishes of the majority as morally legitimate. Therefore incitement to revolution is not only unlawful in a democracy as it is in any system, but also immoral, i.e., contrary to the substantive moral principles on which the democratic law rests. Because opponents are legally free to urge the ouster of the government and, if they grow into a majority, to replace it by a peaceful vote, democratic governments cannot stay in power when opposed by a majority. Because it stays in power by the consent of the majority and allows its own ouster when the majority so wills, revolution against democratic government would necessarily aim at defeating the wishes of the majority that keeps the government in power. That much is acknowledged at least by some. Thus, one of the more old fashioned and naive theoreticians of Marxism, Herbert Marcuse, insists throughout his work that a "dictatorship of the elite over the people"** is needed, since capitalism prevents the people—who do not know any better—from realizing, voting, or acting according to their true interests which only dedicated Marxists (such as Marcuse)—the elite—understand.

Indeed since democratic government rests on majority consent, only groups despairing of persuasion and resolved to

---

*The Bazelon-Katzenbach letters (*The Journal of Criminal Law,* "Criminology and Political Science," Dec., 1965) are pertinent here.
**A *Critique of Pure Tolerance,* p. 100 and passim.

conquer power in spite of the wishes of the majority need urge violence. But in a democratic system, governments have the duty to safeguard the effective franchise of both the majority and the minority. Thus, while other governments may have the authority, democratic governments also have the moral obligation to ban incitement to revolution. To permit it is to permit preparation for the "dictatorship of the elite over the people."

Perhaps the majority is only lukewarm, and democracy though fulfilling their wishes does not satisfy their wants. But what government does? At least democracy does not allow the government to decide what the citizens want by disregarding the wishes they express, or by forestalling expression. God reads our hearts' desire better than we do. But it is unlikely that governments will. And they might misread their desires into our muted hearts.

Indeed the logic of democratic principles leaves no place in a democratic system for parties which propose to abolish democracy even by a peaceful vote, for such parties necessarily wish to bring in a dictatorship, and this purpose remains illegitimate whether it is to be accomplished by vote or violence. At present organized attempts to persuade citizens to bring anti-democratic groups to power by the ballot are lawful. This writer does not think that such presently lawful conduct should remain so; it should be outlawed, as violence is.

Even though the facts have sadly disproved his optimism, many democrats will continue to quote Jefferson to the effect that enemies of our system should be left "undisturbed as monuments of the safety with which error of opinion may be tolerated where reason is left free to combat it." Yet in John Stuart Mill's words:

> It is a piece of idle sentimentality that truth merely as truth has an inherent power denied error... Men are not more zealous for truth than they often are for error, and a sufficient application of legal or even of social penalties will generally succeed in stopping propaganda of either.

Where there are no "penalties" truth may not be suppressed.

But there is nothing to bear out Jefferson that it will win. And one would have to share Jefferson's natural law metaphysics—which seem absurd—to share his confidence that the "right" values will prevail. They certainly have not in the past unless the prevailing standards are simply defined as *eo ipso* the right values.

Many people will insist, however, that antidemocratic groups could never hope to sway us peacefully and that the dangers of suppressing them outweigh the danger of not doing so. This cannot be so. Hitler came to power largely by persuasion. And we were (rightly) worried about the outcome of some peaceful postwar votes in Italy and France. We are not certain that communism might not win free elections in some parts of Asia now. I submit, then, that the voters of no nation are naturally immune to antidemocratic persuasion—particularly if they suffer from national misfortunes.

But is there such a thing as peaceful antidemocratic persuasion? As a matter of fact, Communists at least never come to power without using or threatening violence even if they argue that they are only readying themselves for the violence anticipated from the opponents they hope to defeat at the polls. Stalin, in describing the overthrow of the short-lived democratic government of Russia, implied that this is argued only to deceive the gullible:

> ...the revolution attempted to carry out every, or almost every, step of its attack under the appearance of defense. There is no doubt that the refusal to permit the transfer of troops was a serious aggressive act of the revolution; nevertheless this attack was undertaken under the slogan of the defense of Petrograd against a possible attack of the external enemy. There is no doubt that the formation of the revolutionary committee was a still more serious attack against the provisional government; nevertheless it was carried out under the slogan of the defense of the Petrograd Soviets against possible attacks of the counter-revolution.*

Errors of Trotskyism (London, 1925).

There is little doubt that the recent "confrontations" at universities used a similar tactic: after police intervention was provoked, masses of students were mobilized to defend "academic freedom" from police intervention. But the basic purpose of the leaders was power (however childish the fantasy that it could be got by capturing the dean) and revolution. The grievances against police were but pretexts.

Antidemocratic movements—whether they use rightist or leftist symbols—intend to use violence aggressively while pretending defense. This is indeed logical. Those who feel entitled to stay in power without the consent of the majority—which is the nondemocratic intent—surely must be willing to get power by the same violence by which they are prepared to keep it. Antidemocratic groups find it expedient not to advocate violence only as long as they are weak. Therefore, while the advocacy of violence should remain a sufficient ground for illegality, it should not be an indispensable ground. We should be able to outlaw antidemocratic organizations before they grow strong enough to engage in violence. Else we might be too late. We should not be compelled to wait until the antidemocratic organization generates a danger "clear and present" enough to make it hard or impossible to outlaw it effectively.

Democrats themselves are able to renounce political violence only because political freedom is received in exchange. Even if antidemocrats were nonviolent in principle (rather than only when expedient) democrats would not peacefully accept defeat by them. Defeat at the polls is acceptable only as long as the losers have the implicit assurance of the victors that the game will go on. They can try again: there is always another election. But if antidemocrats were to win, the losers would not be allowed to play again. The rules would be rigged so as to keep the new government in power regardless of popular wishes, which democrats would no longer be allowed to affect.

Before considering these practical matters further, it will be shown that democratic principles permit us to define and outlaw subversive activities without confining ourselves to outlawing the practice or advocacy of violence.

However important its nonpolitical effects, as a political system democracy is but the right of citizens to compete freely for a limited governmental power and to award it freely to one of the competing parties. The right is perennial and inalienable. The power of governments in a democratic system is so restricted that they cannot impair the ability of the citizens to oust them by a peaceful vote. Liberties required for this—freedom of speech, association, and voting—are therefore protected constitutionally and safeguarded by checks and balances.

The fathers of our Constitution were successful in protecting us against a government that might keep itself in power by taking away our rights. No attention was paid to the possibility that some citizens might be persuaded to give away their democratic birthright and invite others to do so. Yet large groups abroad have done so. If our right to choose the government freely is *inalienable*, then we are not entitled to give that right away any more than the government is entitled to take it away. We cannot then elect a government that does not recognize the right of the people to oust it peacefully or that denies the necessary civil liberties. Nor, if freedom is to be inalienable, can invitations to alienate it be recognized as a legitimate part of the democratic process.

Here I can imagine someone grumbling that, basing my argument on the word "inalienable," I have made freedom compulsory: citizens are not to vote on it and no organization may tempt them to get rid of freedom. But the alternative—which would permit the use of our political freedom to abolish it, while seeming to pledge more freedom—actually would ensure less.* Laws that do not allow men to deliver themselves voluntarily as slaves guarantee more freedom than laws that allow men to be enticed into slavery. Therefore, once we abol-

---

*Compare John Stuart Mill: "The principle of freedom cannot require that he should be free not to be free. It is not freedom to be allowed to alienate his freedom."

ished involuntary servitude, we also refused to recognize any right to voluntary slavery or to enticement into it.

But there is more: by installing a government which is to be the irremovable and total master of their fate, those voting to become voluntary political slaves would necessarily compel some of their fellows into involuntary servitude. They would not only irreversibly mortgage their own future; they would also deprive of political freedom those who want to keep it. Even if you should feel that your freedom is so total that you have a right to alienate it, with what right could you take away the freedom of others? You may be entitled to suicide, but not homicide. Yet, unless the decision to abolish political liberty is unanimous, the suicide necessarily would become homicide. All the members of the minority would be deprived of their birthright—political liberty, which is but another name for democracy—against their wishes.

Nor is that all. Any vote by which we abdicate our right to future free election also robs our children of their heritage of freedom. To allow democracy to be overthrown by violence is to surrender their freedom. But to allow citizens to vote against democracy is to allow them to sell their children into slavery.

We are the beneficiaries of freedoms won in the past. We possess, but we do not own, this precious heritage. We have a right to use it, but not to give it away or to destroy it. We are trustees, not owners; and we cannot give away what is not ours. As custodians of the democratic heritage, we have no more right to use our possession of democracy to give it up and deprive our children of it than an occupant of the White House has to sell it or give it away.

Our heritage permits us forever to elect and to replace governments as we see fit. Our fiduciary duty requires us to keep this trust intact for our children, to protect it against those who want to rob us of it by violence, as well as against those who want to seduce us into selling it for a mess of pottage. It is not ours to give. Hence, we have no business voting it away; and no one has any business trying to corrupt us into doing so. We ought neither to permit advocacy of the ballot to extinguish democracy nor allow advocacy to resort to violence. For the end, the surrender of power to a group which would not recognize the right of our children to oust it peacefully and legitimately, nor permit them to do so, is vicious in itself regardless of the means used. To advocate violence to overthrow a democratic government is to propose illegal means for an illegal end. To advocate a vote to overthrow democracy is to advocate an illegal end to be achieved by means that lose their legitimate character to the extent to which they are used for that end.

But would it not be unwise to bar invitations to abolish democracy by a vote? Prohibitions, however well justified in principle, might not have the wanted effects or might produce injurious ones. Prudence enjoins to make laws only when desirable effects seem likely to preponderate. What then can we hope to accomplish here, and what evils are likely to attend the interdiction of organized subversive propaganda and the attendant police investigations and actions?

It is earnestly feared that free speech would be destroyed if invitations to destroy free speech—to surrender democracy— were disallowed. But could not a law to preserve democratic freedom be so drafted and interpreted that it does not defeat its purpose? Is it actually impossible to separate freedom of speech, which is to be protected, from organized propaganda against it, which is to be barred?

We discuss and study quite freely many things now for which the law does not allow organized propaganda. We are free to discuss and study all crimes though none can be advocated—at least not to the point of actually conspiring to engage in it. Why should our judiciary be unable, then, to apply a prohibition of propaganda against democracy without invading studies and free discussions of democratic and antidemocratic systems and ideas? Our institutions, such as the universities and even the courts themselves, rest on the conviction that expression of opinion, logical analysis, and fact finding can be separated from organized propaganda. (A conviction which some professors and lawyers have lately tried to undermine—but not, so far, successfully.) If there were no difference between criminology and propaganda for crime, political science and advocacy of political systems, or if judges and teachers could not discern those differences, how could universities, how could any institution, offer courses and conduct discussions dealing with the perversions of the human mind?

The courts have always distinguished literary, scholarly, or conversational discussion, even personal advocacy, from organized propaganda and organized conspiracy to commit illegal acts. Of course, we cannot forbid a man to think as a Nazi, or even to persuade his friends to Nazi views. However, he is not allowed to conspire with others to prepare for or to commit violence. We could as easily forbid organized propaganda to abolish democracy by vote and the organization of groups and parties devoted thereto. The courts have long decided whether a man has alienated from another the affections of a woman—without noticeably impairing free discussion between the sexes, or having a chilling effect on this freedom. Surely the courts can, without impairing freedom, decide whether an organized group, in concert, deliberately alienates the affections of the citizens from democracy, let alone conspires to overthrow it.

The legal prohibition of subversive organization is far from unprecedented in democracies. I have not heard any liberals object to the German law prohibiting the organization of a Nazi party or to the Italian law prohibiting the organization of a Fascist party. Some liberals who at home ceaselessly assured us that such laws are incompatible with democracy promoted them abroad. (Though freedom from consistency was never listed among our constitutional rights they must have won it.) I do not know how effective these laws are. But nobody has contended that they interfere with freedom of discussion in these countries, or that they have impaired democracy there.

Some liberals sincerely fear that if Communist propaganda were prohibited, their own activities might come next. Actually liberalism is as far removed from Communism as one political philosophy can be removed from another. Yet they fear that people might not distinguish. The psychology of that fear has a dreary fascination. A political psychoanalyst might translate the anguished lament of some liberal patient's subconscious as follows:

> Half the fun of being a liberal is going out on dates with Communists, or Panthers, or with the newest leftists. Of course, I wouldn't go all the way. Only debauched people, who went all the way—and came back—see anything obscene or dangerous in my flirtations. People who say I should discriminate just don't realize that I'd have no one left to be unafraid and broadminded with.

Or the patient's subconscious, being notoriously inconsistent, might splutter:

> I never could tell fellow liberals from fellow travelers. If I can't, it proves that no one else can.

No greater disservice could be rendered the liberal cause than to suggest that liberalism is so hazy a matter that it is difficult to distinguish from antidemocratic conspiracies. Liberals who pretend that liberalism is nebulous, for the sake of denying that their minds are, either unwittingly endow the world with their own confusion, or deliberately sacrifice liberalism to their belief in their own infallibility.

To be sure, laws against antidemocratic conspiracies might be abused to punish persons with unpopular ideas who either are not antidemocratic or do not engage in conspiracies. What laws cannot be abused? We have executed innocent men for homicide. Shall we, then, have no laws? Laws to bar subversive conspiracies need not be less clear, nor the court proceedings less careful, than those for homicide cases. The evil to be remedied, the danger to society from the abolition of democracy, seems no less, while the chance of abuse is not intrinsically greater.

It is often thought that the danger from subversion is recondite and action therefore premature. This is an odd idea. If there are only a few people engaged in criminal activities, should we not control them? Should we wait until there are more?

Even if satisfied that the danger is clear, well-meaning people often deny that it is "present." The interpretation of the majority of the Supreme Court in the 1951 prosecution of Communists was that Mr. Justice Holmes' "present" did no more than reiterate his "clear."* The court rejected as absurd the contention that preparation for the overthrow of the government must have been likely to succeed if the danger is to be "present." For obviously the government could then act only when it might well be too late. The court also avoided interpreting "present" to mean "imminent," though I suspect that Holmes might well have had in mind the proximity of the danger. If so, I should agree with Mr. Justice Jackson's concurring opinion in the *Dennis* case: We should abandon the Holmes formula. If you are trying to kill your wife by feeding her poison it does not matter whether it is to be effective in an hour or in a year. How near death you brought her, how fast, might influence the size of the penalty but it is irrelevant to the criminality of the action. What matters is only that your attempt involved a clear danger to her.

Grant that we prohibit, more clearly than hitherto, conspiracies to overthrow democracy—efforts to institute either peacefully or by violence a government that would prevent its own ouster by abolishing the democratic liberties that might be used to oust it peacefully and legally. How can we enforce the prohibition? Wouldn't any attempts to enforce it have a "chilling effect" not only on antidemocratic conspiracies—which is what we want—but also on free discussion or advocacy of nonconformist or radical views which do not go so far as Marcuse's "dictatorship of the elite over the people" or "intolerance against movements from the right and toleration of movements from

*In the *Schenck* case (1919).

the left"* or "the withdrawal of toleration of speech and
assembly from groups and movements . . . which oppose the
extension of public services, social security, medical care,
etc."?** Movements such as those advocated by Prof. Marcuse
certainly should be "chilled." And since his followers, if and
when they take him seriously, will conspire to bring about the
"withdrawal of tolerance" and the "dictatorship of the elite" he
advocates, it is the duty of all law enforcement agencies to
infiltrate them, and to keep informed about them by electronic
and other means—so as to be able to apprehend and bring to
conviction those who actually engage in illegal acts. Democracy
cannot otherwise be defended. We need not wait until the bomb
is thrown or the riot ignited. Law enforcement agencies should
be informed about plans to assemble it, or, to stir up the riot.
And where there is reasonable suspicion such means as wiretapping should be used. They cannot harm the innocent. But
they should help chill, apprehend, and convict the guilty.

The advocacy of revolutionists, then, is not a right deserving
of protection in a democratic system. This means that revolutionists ought to be viewed as criminals, and that governmental
action against them must be measured against the right of
citizens without regard for the damage possible to such illegitimate advocacy. Instead, the rights we must worry about are
the rights of free men: privacy, and the other rights which even
suspects have, and from this a balance struck in the social
situation of our time.

Always the practicalities must be considered. To find out
whether suspicion is justified, information must be gathered
about those suspected. In the end, that information may show
them to be not guilty. Those whose conversations have been
overheard feel, quite understandably, annoyed. Yet it seems the
discomfort and the annoyance of having one's private conversations listened to by strangers—and very few persons would

*Marcuse, op. cit., p. 109.
**Ibid. p. 100.

face this possibility—is a small sacrifice to bear if such surveillance leads to the apprehension and conviction of actual criminals.

To find out whom to apprehend and to indict, law enforcement agencies must collect information about suspected persons, some of whom may indeed by quite innocent. But how are the guilty to be told from the innocent, unless all those suspected of guilt can be investigated? To reiterate, it is embarrassing to know that quite private matters—however innocent—may become known to some FBI agents. But this embarrassment is a low price to pay for the apprehension of criminals. And a necessary price.

5. The Domestic Intelligence Mission
Editors

At Princeton University in October, 1971, more than 50 scholars, lawyers and professional FBI-haters gathered for a conference on the FBI, sponsored by the "Committee for Public Justice." Without doubt, the participants thought themselves to be contributing careful, reasoned analysis to a study of the structure and role of the FBI. But they added nothing.

The fault lay in their hopelessly narrow framework for evaluation of the FBI. Yale law professor Thomas Emerson set the ground rules for discussion—to the hurrahs of most everyone in attendance—with his list of the general charges against the bureau. His thesis: (a) the FBI has assumed the posture of opposing radicals and radical change in society; (b) the radicals are exercising mainly free expression protected by the Bill of Rights; and therefore (c) the FBI ought to be limited to concerns directly related to enforcement of specific laws against criminal violence and "general surveillance" of radical movements ought to be dispensed with. The not-very-surprising conclusion: the FBI's domestic intelligence apparatus must go, in Emerson's view.

This outline obviously does not support an objective discussion of the FBI's proper role in intelligence work. No one at the conference recognized any such difficulty, of course; they were content to taunt in absentia anybody who might suggest that some radicals pose a threat so serious that the government ought to resist them. Most scholars would not admit that such a threat could exist today, and in any case, in their view there could be no interest which would compete with the value of

Free Expression unfettered by a snooping FBI. Throughout the conference no one seriously considered the rights of other (non-radical) citizens; nor was there mention that the public and its government have the inherent power to protect themselves. Without discussion of these problems any conclusions about the FBI and the Bill of Rights were prejudiced from the outset.

The Princeton Conference is illustrative of a crisis in the public's comprehension of internal security situations and the FBI's internal security role. It is certain not many people would agree with Professor Emerson—the general public disagrees with Emerson on whether and to what extent *dissent* ought to be permitted, and on whether and to what extent *protesters* are to be allowed the confrontation tactics to which they are prone. But whichever of these points of view prevails, nothing whatever has been settled as to the proper role of the government internal security forces such as the FBI.

The bureau's internal security function is much misunderstood as a result. This is especially true because here the investigator enters into the delicate area of political dissent, and minds are heavily influenced by whether or not one agrees with the dissenter. The Communists were at one time the central issue. To some these radicals were criminal conspirators; to others they were dissidents whose views were unpopular, but not conspirators. Persons in intellectual circles tended particularly to the latter viewpoint; for they had social and professional contact with some self-professed Communists and found them—lo and behold!—to be people like the rest of us and too nice to be "conspirators." On the other extreme were those who tended to adopt a conspiratorial theory of world history, attributing all the world's problems to a giant conspiracy composed of Communists, socialists, fellow travelers, and, according to some, international bankers and financiers.

The latter theory—which is often laced with anti-Semitism—was recently expounded in *None Dare Call It Conspiracy,* a book sponsored by the John Birch Society. It is roughly the same theory put forth early in the 20th century by Nesta Webster in a series of books that were read in a prison cell by the young Adolf Hitler and which led the Nazi directly to his theories of anti-Semitism. Little wonder then that such thinking has been viewed askance by many.

The question of the FBI's internal security role has not been addressed by the extremists. It simply cannot be understood in terms of Emerson's view that the bureau is opposed to radical change in society, nor in terms of the counter-argument that the FBI is merely enforcing the law (or failing to) against certain conspiracies. Both views are off target. It may be that the FBI has in a sense opposed radical change, and it may also be that the bureau has investigated radical conspiracies; the fact is, the task of protecting the internal security of this nation may have these effects. But they touch only peripherally on the question of propriety and constitutional authority.

The question is: has the FBI's domestic intelligence provided necessary and sufficient protection for the public? This basic consideration, it seems, has been submerged in a quagmire of debate on the surface issues.

In a free society there is a prejudice in favor of tolerating all but the most violent attacks on society. It would be pleasant indeed if we safely implement this standard. Those to whom we have entrusted the safety of the nation, however, cannot afford the luxury of such wishful thinking. Everyday experience shows them that such over-tolerant standards are a mere pipe dream: they don't work.

The framers of the United States Constitution were not so sure of the invulnerability of our form of government. In the Preamble to the Constitution it was stated that the government was to insure domestic tranquility, provide for the common defense, and secure the blessings of liberty to ourselves and our posterity. The federal government was thus plainly given the power to meet the threat of subversion.

The federal government is primarily responsible for this task. Indeed if the several states ever had jurisdiction in the domestic security area, it has been largely eliminated by Supreme Court decisions nullifying state sedition and syndicalism laws, as in the case *Nelson* vs. *Pennsylvania** where the court, for all practical purposes, held that the field of domestic security was an exclusive prerogative of the federal government.

Of course, the FBI is the institution which, by various statutory and executive provisions, has assumed the primary role in this field. In September 1939, the FBI was given primary jurisdiction to investigate violations of several specific statutes covering "political" crimes as well as the broad authority to investigate "subversive activities." The subsequent passage by the Congress of the so-called Smith Act, the Internal Security Act of 1950, the Communist Control Act of 1954 and other legislation covering loyalty and security matters, extended the bureau's primary investigative jurisdiction respecting violations of specific federal statutes, though not necessarily that of intelligence gathering under the more broad "subversive activities" wording of the 1939 presidential directive. It should be noted that this original directive of September, 1939 was later specifically reaffirmed and restated by President Roosevelt and has, likewise, been restated by succeeding presidents. Thus, under the existing statutes and the broad presidential directives granting it authority, it is virtually impossible for the FBI to act *ultra vires* in the internal security field, at least with respect to the scope of its authority, a conclusion that has been agreed to by Senator Sam Ervin (perhaps the most highly regarded constitutional scholar in the Congress).

FBI officials are quick to point out, however, that one can emphasize too much its internal security function, given the fact that only about one-fourth the bureau's manpower resources are devoted to national security matters. This is true, but it is in the area of its national security work that the FBI becomes most embroiled in the epic struggle between freedom and tyranny, and it is understandable that the critics dwell on this dramatic function of the agency.

The FBI has a responsibility in this struggle to all the citizens

*350 U.S. 497 (1956).

of this nation, to "preserve, protect and defend" the Constitution of the United States, the system that derives from it, and the freedoms guaranteed by that system. In recent years, the conflict has centered on new leftist groups which threaten violence and disruption, terrorism, and openly attempt to disrupt the government's authority to govern. The internal security problem has changed in nature, but the nation's need for internal security has not. Like it or not, after all the attempts at detente, America still has foreign enemies, and foreign governments continue to threaten our national security. So long as this is the case, the services of the FBI, or some agency like it, will be needed to ensure our protection.

6. Espionage—An Old Problem Still with Us
Lawrence V. Cott

In the spring of 1960, the United States suffered a black eye as the Soviet Union propaganda machine broadcast the news around the world of shooting down Francis Gary Powers' spy plane over Sverdlovsk. The U.S. State Department, reacting with some offsetting propaganda, produced at the UN a timely report from J. Edgar Hoover. The report read in part:

> At the very time Premier Khrushchev was advancing to the podium to speak [about the Powers U-2 flight] before the United Nations General Assembly . . ., two Soviet espionage agents were cautiously surveying a street corner in Springfield, Massachusetts, in preparation for a clandestine meeting with an American whom they were attempting to subvert. At the very time that Khrushchev was declaring that a means must be found to stop mankind from backsliding into an abyss of war, Vadim A. Kirilyuk, Soviet employee of the United Nations, was attempting to induce this American to furnish information regarding United States cryptographic machines and to secure employment in a vital United States government agency where he could obtain classified information for the Russians. While this meeting was taking place Kirilyuk and the American were under observation by Leonid A. Kovalev, another Soviet employee of the United Nations who was conducting a counterveillance. Unknown to the Russians, however, this meeting was also being observed by special agents of the FBI who obtained photographs of the Russians.

The State Department had complained about this to UN Secretary-General Hammarskjold and the Kirilyuk family had left the U.S. in January, 1960, without any public announcement.

That the FBI was able to provide the State Department with a spy story at that moment in 1960 was no mere coincidence. Instead it revealed that even in the age of "peaceful coexistence," espionage against America continues and is as extensive as ever.

The story is largely untold, not least because untold tales are in the nature of espionage intelligence work. But the tip of the iceberg has shown at times. For instance, in the 1960 report Director Hoover also reported a 1957 incident that included exciting instances of suspense and surveillance around the UN building itself. Hoover was careful to demonstrate that the FBI agents had not violated the sanctity of the UN, while a Soviet KGB man had. The case was that of Vladimir Arsenevich Grusha, first secretary of the USSR delegation to the UN. The report says it best:

> On the night of March 5, 1957, Dhanapalo Samarasekara, a Ceylonese national employed at the UN Secretariat, New York City, was observed by special agents of the Federal Bureau of Investigation (FBI) to enter the Ceylonese Delegation to the UN. At 7 P.M. on that date Samarasekara was observed on the fourth floor of that building opening what appeared to be a file cabinet and examining some papers. He was observed to have left the delegation shortly thereafter carrying an airline-type handbag. He drove to an area where Vladimir Grusha was observed standing on a corner. Approximately one hour later Samarasekara was observed to return to the same area where Grusha was seen getting into Samarasekara's automobile. After driving a short distance, Grusha left the car and Samarasekara returned to the Ceylonese Delegation. He was at that time observed on the fourth floor of the building where he was observed opening the same file cabinet he opened earlier in the evening. He was then observed carefully placing a red book in the cabinet. He left the delegation shortly thereafter. It was subsequently learned that the Ceylonese code book was red in color and that the code room of the Ceylonese Delegation was located on the fourth floor of the Ceylonese Delegation building.

The FBI referred the matter to the Justice Department, which took it up with the State Department, which declared Grusha persona non grata on March 25, just 20 days after the incident. The U.S. Mission to the UN requested the dismissal of Samarasekara from the secretariat, and after a hearing he was dismissed. The Ceylonese, presumably, changed their code book, the locks on their file cabinets, and they probably no longer issued keys to Ceylonese who were not members of the delegation or code clerks.

As details of the case were publicly revealed, it became evident that the FBI had made some kind of penetration of a Soviet apparatus in this country—certainly the KGB must have considered the possibility—and that the FBI was watching Samarasekara's action from afar *before* he even came near Grusha, noting his patrol past Grusha and then the meeting an hour later. That is, the bureau knew that espionage acts would take place that evening, and also knew where they would take place, at two locations, before they actually occurred.

Grusha was just another in a long line of Soviet "legals" who ran afoul of the bureau. The legals come into the U.S. every year, carrying their own passports (however, the Soviet Foreign Office may have cooperated by issuing it in a false, i.e., KGB, name) and go about their cover jobs for a few months or until they think the FBI has examined them and concluded they are harmless. Then they set to work. Those attached to diplomatic missions may have immunity, in which case if they are caught at espionage all the FBI can do is report the facts to the State Department and it, in turn, may ask Moscow for a recall. Other legals, however, come without immunity, because their cover jobs are the menial ones of the translators and chauffeurs, the nursemaids and housewives.

The principal covers for such legals are the Soviet embassy in Washington, the USSR Mission to the UN in New York* the Byelorussian and Ukrainian Missions to the UN (same as the USSR Mission), the United Nations Secretariat, Soviet consulates, Amtorg Trading Corporation (the Soviet purchasing company) TASS, and other minor Soviet operations from the

---

*An entire book, *Red Spies at the U.N.*, by Pierre J. Huss and George Carpozi, Jr., Coward-McCann, 1965, has been written about this subject.

office of Aeroflot to the student exchange program.

From the record we can assume that the FBI has a number of Soviet citizens attached to these locations under discreet round-the-clock surveillance. A 1957 case demonstrates the profits to be gained.

It was during the day of April 5 when bureau agents manning an observation post overlooking the Russian embassy at 1125 16th St. N.W. in Washington took interest in a strolling man who approached the embassy building along the sidewalk in front and acted furtively. The man paused, quickly threw an object over the fence onto the lawn, and hurried on. Whether any Russians inside the building saw what happened is not known, but within minutes the FBI had recovered the object.

It was a letter addressed to the Russians, from Air Force Captain George H. French, bombardier of a B-36, offering to sell, for exactly $27,500, documents and diagrams on atomic weapons and the Strategic Air Command. The letter said to contact the seller at a certain room in a New York hotel the next day.

Two FBI agents, backed up by Air Force investigators, kept the appointment and posed as Russians making arrangements for the purchase. After the bargain had been struck the agents flipped out their credentials and identified themselves. French collapsed on the bed, moaning, "I knew it, I knew it." He was court-martialed and sentenced to a life term at hard labor at Allenwood, Pa., but was released in 1963.

These are espionage cases, and espionage is only one category of the internal security responsibility of the Federal Bureau of Investigation. Other threats to America's internal security are posed by the possibility of foreign-directed sabotage and infiltration of government agencies. But the latter categories are possibilities which have been reduced to nearly insignificant potential—largely due to FBI and other government agency vigilance. Foreign-directed sabotage in the U.S. is unheard of today, and government infiltration by disloyal or potentially disloyal persons—those subject to the influence of hostile foreign interests—has been controlled in large measure by the routine of government employee loyalty programs, in which the FBI has an important role.

The lack of reportable events in these latter two categories should not mislead the observer into thinking the problems are nonexistent. This misconception could lead to a false judgment of the FBI internal security work. The fact is, the very lack of sabotage and infiltration incidents is proof of successful discharge of the FBI's responsibilities in these areas.

Counter-espionage on the other hand, has been a tough assignment for the bureau. There have been notable successes, and there have been cases which, from 20/20 hindsight vision at least, have involved less than fully effective effort by the FBI. The critics, of course, dwell on the latter; but here is where it should be remembered that only the toughest category, the espionage cases, is being considered. Even granting some validity to the critics' remarks, it is only fair to state that in the overall internal security field, the bureau has performed excellently.

How good then is the FBI counter-espionage operation? It should be noted at the outset that the bureau's record, good or bad, has been built even while near extreme caution has been taken to observe civil liberties and good ethics—something not normally the concern of intelligence agencies in other parts of the world. Some critics, including writers represented in this book, advocate a type of intelligence operation which would have the FBI cast such caution to the wind. Admittedly, "dirty" tactics could have netted more spies, but is that in itself sufficient justification? However this question is answered, the fact that the FBI has seldom undertaken this sort of intelligence operation, primarily because of its respect for civil liberties and ethics, must be entered into the equation. This is a severe limitation, and, considering its effect, any judgment as to the FBI counter-espionage record cannot be too harsh. To the contrary, those who criticize the effectiveness of this bureau function must recognize the implications of their position: the only way to improve FBI counter-espionage is to take its caution-padded gloves off.

In this light, the FBI has an enviable record of thwarting foreign espionage while preserving civil liberties. Moreover, with only a portion of the less than 9,000 special agents, the FBI faces a situation in which the United States is the primary target for an array of large and experienced intelligence organizations, from the Soviet Union and its satellites, from Communist China, and from Cuba.

The Soviets, with an apparat of experienced undercover agents, present the main threat. Soviet espionage operations in the United States are conducted primarily by (1) the KGB *(Komitet Gosudarstvennoy Bezopastnosti)* or the Committee of State Security, known more popularly as the Soviet Secret Police, a successor organization to the Cheka, OGPU, GPU, NKVD and MGB-MVD; and (2) by the GRU *(Glavnoye Razvedyvatelnoye Upravlenye),* or Soviet military intelligence. In its organization and activities, GRU is similar to military intelligence departments of other countries with responsibility for espionage involving our armed forces, mobilization plans, and new weapons. KGB is responsible for information regarding pro-Soviet or anti-Soviet trends, agreements, secret treaties, and other "political" intelligence. In practice, the activities of the two agencies have overlapped and jurisdiction has not been sharply defined. For instance, Alger Hiss, in a position to furnish high level political intelligence, nevertheless reported to the GRU. In addition to its other duties, KGB has always had the right to "screen" all other Soviet agencies, including GRU, and to recruit informers from among their personnel. This function, as well as other areas of overlap, has created much rivalry and antagonism between the two agencies.

In addition, KGB and GRU are fed information from and exercise a measure of control over the intelligence services of East Germany, Poland, and Czechoslovakia, and to a lesser degree, the services of Hungary and Bulgaria. (The Rumanian service has probably been denied to them in recent years, and the Mongolian service is little known).

Against these Soviet networks stands the American intelligence establishment. Although it has been the primary responsibility of the FBI since the delimitation agreements of 1939 and 1940 promulgated by President Roosevelt, some of the responsibility for thwarting espionage rests with, for instance, the State Department, whose personnel should be able to detect fraudulent passport applications (to name one contribution), some with the Customs and Immigration and Naturalization services, which should be able to detect fraudulent passports much favored by agents; some with the Federal Communications Commission, which should be able to detect illegal radio transmissions; some with the military intelligence agencies, which should be able to detect and prevent penetration of their ranks and facilities; and some with the Central Intelligence Agency, which should be able to detect the operations set in motion from abroad.

All the agencies are supposed to coordinate their counter-espionage efforts through the FBI and the evidence accumulated indicates that, notwithstanding one or two isolated cases where rivalry or jealousy has clouded issues or confused the joint labor, cooperation has been steady and beneficial for the total counter-intelligence program.

This is the counter-espionage establishment in the U.S. It is at a natural disadvantage in a free country, and in any case espionage is especially difficult to perceive or to thwart. Intelligence agents who recruit spies do so in a sophisticated manner, appealing to feelings of disloyalty, ideological enchantment, loneliness, desire for recognition, lust for money, or sometimes the no-gloves treatment—blackmail based on threats to expose debts, heterosexual or homosexual misconduct, prison records, or threatened vengeance on relatives in Soviet-controlled countries.

The counter-espionage organization has to detect an intelligence operation in which the principals may meet at a *treff* (a

Russian intelligence term dating back to the days of the czars denoting a meeting between agents) only once every six weeks and then only for 15 seconds; or maybe they never meet at all, carrying out their exchanges—information in one direction, money and encouragement in the other—through dead-drops (or *duboki*), those easily overlooked short-time hiding places for small packages.

Who are the spies? They change with the season. In the 1930s and 1940s most Soviet espionage agents in the U.S. spied for ideological reasons—they were Communist Party members, or ex-members dropped from the party at KGB orders, or willing sympathizers. In the 1950s most of the spies recruited were mercenaries, chiefly disaffected military personnel who wanted to "get even" for petulant personal reasons and would do it for money. Today there are still some of those around, but the FBI is now faced with an appalling new task—a virulent anti-American alienation infects tens of thousands of Americans, who are thus espionage potentials, and the KGB and GRU have only to pick the best-situated.

How are the spies detected, identified, and used or apprehended by the FBI? Chiefly, information comes to the bureau via defectors or patriots contacted by the Soviet apparat. The bureau, of course, tries to develop its own information, but this requires penetration of the spy network itself, and this in turn usually requires "defectors in place" (spies who defect and remain in position). In a disciplined and dedicated KGB or GRU, defectors in place are nigh impossible to develop except through blackmail or the like—items not in the FBI bag of tricks.

So the initial information is generally volunteered to the FBI, and here the bureau has wisely looked to its reputation. It has established a public image of rectitude, integrity, and devotion to duty—attributes that encourage the person with a story to tell to go to the FBI. This is one of the reasons that the FBI must retain its public image, and that is why many of the uninformed attacks on the FBI damage not just the bureau but the national security as well.

In addition, the FBI learns about foreign intelligence operations, principally from five sources: (1) Contacted espionage targets: engineers, file clerks, diplomats, servicemen, who are approached by intelligence agents and relay the information to the FBI. Usually then the FBI controls this target, leading the intelligence agent along and feeding him some information while endeavoring to identify the agent's other contacts. (2) The defected foreign intelligence agent: literally scores of KGB and GRU agents, up to the rank of general, have defected to the West, to the CIA overseas or the FBI here, and have given exacting details, uncovering vast networks. (3) Disaffected cooperators, ex-spies—Whittaker Chambers · and Elizabeth Bentley are two who went to the FBI and told what they knew. (4) The methodical and difficult surveillance of probable or known intelligence agents, chiefly Soviet "legals" (e.g., diplomats legally allowed in this country), by whatever means that are found necessary. (5) Other intelligence or counter-intelligence organizations. Many espionage cases have been reported to the bureau as a result of leads obtained by the intelligence or counter-intelligence agencies of friendly foreign powers or from the CIA as a result of its overseas operations.

In category (1) the FBI has turned in an excellent record. American officials and businessmen who have been recruited by Soviet agents (and Soviet efforts remain the FBI's chief problem) have been used against the Soviets for periods up to four years with good results. In most of these cases the FBI waited patiently for the Soviet principal to show himself again to lead trailing G-men to other contacts.

Also, Soviet intelligence defections to the West have had a devastating effect on KGB and GRU operations, and usually throws entire networks into disarray for months, even years, before they are re-established or dismantled. In the 1930s there were important agents who came to our side—General Walter Krivitsky and Alexander Orlov to name two. During the 1940s there were Ismael Ege, and the Soviet code clerk in Canada, Igor Gouzenko, who had the foresight to smuggle out documentary evidence of an intricate network riddling the Canadian government and military and scientific establishments reaching into the United States. KGB and GRU agents have come over in platoon strength—Peter Deriabin, one of the most important ever to defect, Yuri Rastvorov, Nikolai Khoklov and Evgeny Runge, to name just a few. They were, for the most part, overseas operatives, but all shed some light on KGB-GRU operations in the U.S.

The defectors in this country have been few. The first full-time "illegal" (a truly secret agent illegally introduced into the country with a false identity) to defect was Reino Hayhanen, the hard-drinking aide posted to help Col. Rudolph Abel. Another illegal who defected was Kaarlo Tuomi, who had a great deal to tell and who cooperated with the FBI as a double agent for years.

In another instance indicating both the cooperation of friendly foreign counter-intelligence agencies and the testimony of co-conspirators, David Greenglass and Harry Gold, principals in the Rosenberg spy ring, became willing cooperators with the bureau after their arrests, and not only helped to convict their ring-leaders but provided additional leads for follow up.

In category (4), the surveillance of "legal" establishments, the FBI has scored its greatest coups, the result of endless man-days spent by agents over the decades patiently waiting and watching while Soviet and Soviet-bloc diplomatic personnel make their rounds. The watchful agent never knows when the casual bump in the supermarket might be the contact for passage of micro-film or money, he never knows when the innocent family picnic might not be just a country outing but an opportunity to service a dead-drop in the woods.

It was in early 1943 that FBI agents watched the third secretary of the Soviet Embassy in Washington, a man who called himself Vassili Zubilin. His real name was Zarubin, and he was an important intelligence officer. The surveillance paid off when Zubilin was seen contacting Boris Morros, a Hollywood motion picture producer. Morros, who may have once been sympathetic to the Soviets and had relatives in the USSR, was later observed making further connections with Zubilin.

Four years after he was seen being contacted by Zubilin the FBI approached Morros and questioned him. To the agents' surprise he readily agreed he was part of an espionage apparat, had been recruited by Zubilin, and even more surprisingly his sympathies had undergone a change (some of his relatives had died).

After checking on Morros and ascertaining that he was indeed a turned agent, the FBI faded into the background and let Morros continue his music-publishing, his picture-producing, and his spying. The FBI's contacts were almost as brief as the Soviets'—for years Morros was handled by only a few agents working out of the Los Angeles and New York offices of the FBI. On Morros' trips one agent attached himself to the producer as his "male secretary," and Morros became the classic example of the double-agent played relentlessly over the years for maximum benefit to the national security.

One thing to note is that the FBI counterespionage has so often had to deal with an American political establishment which was unwilling to believe that Soviet espionage existed.

A case in point, Jacob Golos, a long-time Soviet agent in the U.S., was convicted in 1940 of failing to register as a foreign agent—this was the old make-do statute used because of difficulty in proving espionage. He received a suspended sentence, and went right back to what he was doing before—accumulating intelligence for the Soviet Union and recruiting spies. The FBI, with only a few thousand agents at that time, simply didn't have the manpower to check him out and make sure he had gone straight. The times were tense and German and Japanese espionage agents were also afoot.

It was Golos, operating with all the resources of the Communist Party and aided by his faithful paramour, Elizabeth Bentley, who laid down a network of sources within the U.S. government—information wells that could be tapped to produce vital data from every sensitive government department save one, the

FBI. Had the climate been different, had the security men, diplomats, and senior bureaucrats who went to the White House not been rebuffed when trying to warn of Soviet attempts at subversion and espionage—the allegations were dismissed as fanciful and alarmist—the FBI would have pursued the matter more vigorously.

Whittaker Chambers tried to warn the nation's leaders in 1939, and was laughed off. The FBI, to whom he only belatedly told the story, and then only part of it, believed him, because his information checked out. But, in this age of trust in the Soviets, the bureau could do little, save following up the leads and informing the proper government officials.

Elizabeth Bentley also defected from the Soviet intelligence apparat in those days, illustrating the usual mode of FBI espionage detection. She, like Chambers, was a courier for the Communists, and thus had seen the key personnel in the set-up. But the results of their disclosures, while involving spectacular charges of disloyalty in high government circles, was less than a counter-espionage coup. The information was too long delayed.

Chambers waited more than a year before he told his story to anyone in government, but he waited *ten years* before he told the whole story and produced the documentary evidence to support his charges.

Miss Bentley, too, delayed telling the whole story. Thus, in both the Chambers and Bentley cases the apparatus was alerted first by the defection and then later by the ensuing investigation, and the paraphernalia that generally gives credence to tales of espionage had long since been disposed of.

Later, when the two testified before the House Committee on Un-American Activities, the full extent of the Ware Group (with which Chambers worked) and the Nathan Gregory Silvermaster and Victor Perlo networks (Bentley's) became apparent.

In those early Communist espionage cases most of the principals escaped punishment, but there were convictions, with FBI help, for the lesser charges of contempt or perjury—Edward Joseph Fitzgerald, William Ludwig Ullman, William Remington and Franklin Victor Reno. Alger Hiss, onetime assistant secretary of state and then president of the Carnegie Endowment for World Peace, was convicted of perjury in 1950 (after two trials) for, among other lies, denying under oath that he knew Chambers.

Others named by Chambers-Bentley escaped punishment but have made clear their current attitudes—Perlo is now the Communist Party's top economist and Frank Coe is Communist China's senior American-in-residence and may still be a *Soviet* intelligence agent.

The Hiss case was a victory the FBI justifiably must share with the Congress. One case in which it gets all the credit is the Jack Soble ring.

From 1947 to 1957 the FBI had a man operating inside a Soviet espionage ring. He was Boris Morros, mentioned earlier. The skillful playing of Morros against the Soviets must stand as a monument to FBI patience, and is a lasting reminder of the great courage of Morros. During that decade Hoover and the few agents who worked the case had the satisfaction of knowing that on one occasion an FBI informant, Morros, was in Moscow, undetected by the Soviets he was betraying, discussing his espionage work with no less than Lavrenti Beria, head of the Secret Police. (The Soviets returned the favor a few years later when their double-agent, Kim Philby, who was head of the counter-intelligence section of Britain's MI-6, discussed espionage shop talk with J. Edgar Hoover. To Hoover's and the FBI's credit it must be added that it was only upon FBI insistence that Britain was pressured into recalling Philby. The FBI edict, reportedly, was a strong one: "Either get rid of Philby or there will be no cooperation between agencies.")

Finally in 1957, as the Russians' confidence in Morros appeared to wane, the bureau moved to destroy the ring that had been built up by Vassili Zubilin, the Soviet Washington embassy official. Arrested and convicted were the leaders, Jack Soble, his wife Myra, and Jacob Albam. Over the years they had collected nuclear and military information, industrial secrets, and they labored ceaselessly to keep tabs on those who were Stalin's special fear, the Trotskyites.

As the Soble ring was broken up some of its outlying members ran for cover. Alfred Stern and his wife, Martha Dodd Stern (daughter of the onetime U.S. ambassador to Germany), fled from Mexico, where they had settled, to Eastern Europe. Jane Foster Zlatovski and her husband George Zlatovski, onetime U.S. Army intelligence personnel, escaped extradition by remaining in France.

By diligently working on every fragment that Soble had unwittingly given Morros the FBI was able to identify another source, Ilya Wolston, a graduate of the U.S. Army intelligence school and later a State Department employee in West Germany. Wolston was Soble's nephew. He was never tried for espionage, but was convicted in 1958 of failing to appear before a grand jury.

Another Soble ring spy was anthropologist Mark Zborowski, who had worked as a language consultant to the army during the war. During that time Zborowski worked at what he was best at—betraying Trotskyites to Stalin. Alexander Orlov says he knew about Zborowski in 1937, when Zborowski was attached to the Trotsky family in Paris, and suspects Zborowski had a hand in the mysterious death of Leon Sedov, Trotsky's son. Zborowski was convicted of perjury (he had denied under oath that he knew Soble) and went off to prison.

Yet another Soble ring figure was not brought to justice for many years. This was his brother, Dr. Robert Soblen, who was finally convicted of espionage in 1962, and then jumped his $100,000 bail and fled to Israel. Deported to the U.S., Soblen stabbed himself on the plane, was hospitalized in England, and there committed suicide by poison, cheating the prison.

Another spy ring in the U.S. had stolen the atomic secrets that gave the U.S.S.R. the hydrogen bomb. This was the Rosenberg group. The Rosenberg espionage ring was unraveled because of an FBI tip about Klaus Fuchs, a tip never fully explained.

Director Hoover insisted that the FBI informed the British that Fuchs, who had been cleared by the British and worked on the joint U.S.-British-Canadian development of the atomic bomb, was a Soviet agent. The British authorities, using well-modulated tones and infinite skill, persuaded Fuchs to talk, and eventually he admitted espionage, ultimately implicating Harry Gold, his courier. Gold led to David Greenglass and Greenglass led to Julius and Ethel Rosenberg.

The FBI could be criticized in the Rosenberg case (several members of the ring escaped behind the Iron Curtain) for the almost slow-motion picture of the arrests: Gold was arrested May 23, 1950; Greenglass June 16; Julius Rosenberg July 17; and Ethel Rosenberg not until August 11. Another principal in the case, Morton Sobell was tracked down to Mexico and arrested there on August 18. He had fled New York on June 21, shortly after Greenglass was arrested.

However, enormous problems faced the bureau. The persons arrested did not cooperate and the agents were probing unexplored territory. Each falsehood had to be run out and then the liar confronted once again. Literally hundreds of agents worked the case and it was a triumph—the Rosenbergs convicted and executed for transmitting atomic secrets in time of war; Sobell imprisoned for 30 years (he served 18); Gold and Greenglass sentenced to long prison terms for their crimes, despite their tardy cooperation. The Rosenbergs were convicted upon the best kind of evidence, testimony of their accomplices, and for Greenglass it meant sending his sister and brother-in-law to their deaths, and himself to prison under a 15-year sentence. He was released from prison in November, 1960, having served ten years. Gold was paroled after serving 16 years of a 30-year sentence.

There were successful parallel prosecutions based upon the testimony of Gold. Alfred Dean Slack, who had stripped Eastman Kodak and other companies of many industrial secrets and also turned over chemical formulae for processing RDX (a powerful explosive), was convicted of conspiring to commit espionage and sent to prison for 15 years. Abraham Brothman and Miriam Moskowitz, other Gold contacts (and Golos' too), and also implicated by Bentley, were convicted of related crimes.

Prosecution of the Fuchs-Rosenberg ring was after the fact—after the most important atomic secrets were provided the U.S.S.R. This is an honest criticism of the FBI mode of intelligence, however, only if, as before stated, the implications are understood. To have busted the case prior to the act of espionage would have required a most thorough penetration of the Soviet apparat, and that would have required a different, and dirty, mode of counter-intelligence. It can be noted too, that had government security risk programs been in adequate operation at the time (they were not) the spies would never have got next to the atomic secrets. This fault was not the burden of the FBI. Honest criticism must note these facts. However, much denunciation of the FBI counter-espionage operation is not that honest.

This is partly due to misconception and misinformation, but some criticism is plainly mendacious or deliberately misleading. An example is the performance of ex-agent William Turner who can produce some of the strangest points on which to score the FBI. For instance, he castigates the FBI cryptanalysts because they couldn't solve the enciphered microfilm found in a hollow nickel turned up by a New York newsboy. This coin was inadvertently placed into circulation by Soviet agent Reino Hayhanen, and the FBI could not break the message until Hayhanen defected and told them the key phrase, which was a line from a well-known Russian folk tale.

In his own private attempt to destroy the FBI's reputation Turner laughs at the FBI agents who could not guess that key phrase. But it was a personal cipher key which no one could have guessed. (An equivalent challenge for Turner—this author's key phrase is part of the first line of a 20th-century American song. Guess away, you have 50 years.)

Turner's game is to show the bureau up as incompetent. The fact is, however, that the FBI is thoroughly competent, though not of course perfect. It is the Communist agents who, for all their experience in espionage, are turned up on occasion as the sad sacks of the espionage field. The mistakes Soviet agents have made, had they made them before the eyes of counter-espionage men, would have ended their undercover careers on the spot. Luckily for them many occurred in everyday America before everyday unsuspecting Americans.

Documentation for real illegals is difficult but not impossible for the Russians to obtain, but in the case of "Mr. and Mrs. Robert Baltch," the two illegals who became known to the FBI, the documents were those of people not only real but living perilously close to the Russian imposters. The real Robert Baltch was born in the U.S. and lived briefly in Lithuania with his parents before all of them returned to the U.S. in 1947, on U.S. passports issued at the embassy in Moscow. Young Baltch entered the Roman Catholic priesthood and at the time the illegal agent, Alexandre Sokolov, was using his identity in New York City, the real Father Baltch was living only 150 miles away in Amsterdam, New York.

Mrs. Baltch, the fictional Soviet illegal, had assumed the documentary identity of a woman born in 1930 in Springfield, Mass., who at that time was living at Norwalk, Conn., an hour's drive from Manhattan. Such were the difficulties the KGB Center had in providing authentic backgrounds for illegals. Yet, it was easy for such errors to go unnoticed. Had one of Father Baltch's parishioners chanced to run into the Robert Baltch who taught at the Berlitz school in Manhattan he would never suspect espionage at work—duplication of names in America is rather commonplace.

But had the phony Robert Baltch, language instructor, applied for a driver's license in New York, and had Father Baltch had one, there was some risk of motor vehicle clerks spotting the duplication, though they may not have suspected espionage. Fraud for the purpose of passing checks, or some similarly mundane illegality or misdemeanor, more probably would have crossed their minds.

Perhaps to escape just such possibilities, the phony Baltches spent little time in New York and moved off to Baltimore, where they were far removed from the persons whose identities they had acquired; this had the advantage of giving them a real background of living elsewhere (New York), and they were also closer to what was their ultimate destination all along —Washington, D.C.

Soviet intelligence is a creature of habit and one day the habit may prove embarrassing. Gordon Lonsdale, or Konon Molody, a KGB illegal, established a cover business operation in London, as a dealer in juke boxes. Evgeny Runge, the high-ranking KGB officer who defected in 1967, had operated under deep cover near Bonn, West Germany, as a salesman of juke boxes. General Walter Krivitsky, who defected in 1938, had worked as an illegal in The Hague, running a small antique shop as a cover. Peter Kroger (Morris Cohen), part of Lonsdale's ring, worked in London as an antiquarian book dealer.

Lonsdale-Molody deserves closer examination. Molody had assumed the documentary identity of a real child, Gordon Lonsdale, born August 27, 1924 at Cobalt, Ontario. The real Lonsdale migrated to Finland and then to Eastern Europe in the 30s and disappeared without a trace. When the phony Lonsdale was arrested in London he protested that he was indeed the young man from Cobalt grown up. But medical records at Cobalt showed the baby Lonsdale had been circumcised immediately after birth, and Col. Molody was not circumcised.

This was not the only time the KGB was tripped up on the matter of circumcision. In 1961 Shinbet agents in Tel Aviv arrested Lt. Col. Israel Beer, who had spent 22 years at the heart of the Zionist movement and was a confidant of Premier David Ben-Gurion. Beer, who posed as a refugee Austrian Jew, was belatedly given a physical and found to be uncircumcised. One can only marvel at Beer's capacity for privacy even while serving in the army, and wonder also about the competence of the KGB.

So espionage can be a comedy of errors. But it is largely a dead serious and difficult business.

FBI Director Hoover once spoke of the enormous task of catching the illegals. "The most difficult to uncover," he said, "are those deep cover spies operating in our country with no ostensible connection with the foreign principal. Once within our borders, these individuals easily blend into our population, and their detection and identification requires time-consuming investigation." All of that, and a great deal of luck.

Much has been written about the Soviet Union's most successful master spy in the United States, the man who became known as Col. Rudolph Ivanovich Abel, but who traveled under the name of Andrew Kayotis, painted in Brooklyn as Emil Goldfus, was arrested as Martin Collins and was known to his subordinate, Reino Hayhanen, as Mark. British historian E. H. Cookridge, citing unnamed sources, thinks the man's real name was Col. Alexander Ivanovich Belov.

Abel was caught as the result of a combination of deficiencies in the KGB, and conversely the efficiency of the FBI. Although he had worked undercover and undetected in the U.S., off and on, for nine years, he had his goofs. The KGB made its first mistake in 1952 when it assigned a KGB lieutenant colonel, Reino Hayhanen, as Abel's aide, documented with a cover identity of a Finn, Eugene Nikolai Maki.

Hayhanen was a heavy drinker and for four years did little as he lived in rural areas around New York City, building up a genuine American residence background to supplement the phony "legend" provided by the KGB. He had several meetings with his superior, whom he knew only as Mark, but relations were strained. Abel must have been appalled at the boozing, scowling understudy, and after prolonged tension between the two, Moscow ordered Hayhanen back for new instructions. He left the U.S. by ship April 24, 1957, landed at Le Havre, and rendezvoused in Paris with another KGB agent.

Hayhanen was in a black mood, and after pondering the possibility of liquidation or a turn at hard labor in the forests and mines, he defected, walking into the American embassy May 6 and gushing out a story of KGB intrigue to startled diplomats. After a security agent was summoned, Hayhanen, by way of providing bona fides, extracted a nickel from his pocket and broke it open—it was hollow.

After preliminary de-briefing in Paris the prize was flown off to the United States five days later, to be questioned for days by FBI agents specializing in Soviet espionage matters.

Moscow must have known Hayhanen was on the loose, but could not guess whether he had succumbed to the pleasures of Paris, simply "going private," or had gone over to the enemy. For its own security the KGB masters had to assume Hayhanen had defected and had to alert its network, including Abel.

If Abel was warned he didn't betray it. Months later, after he was apprehended and as his life was re-constructed, it was determined the colonel had been in Daytona Beach, Florida at the time of Hayhanen's defection, doing some painting (as Goldfus) and nobody knows what else (there are plenty of military bases in the state).

Somewhere Abel must have been tipped off by Moscow: "Vic has not arrived; he has gone over to the enemy; take precautions." Whatever the signal Abel must have known of Hayhanen's disappearance and prudence would have insisted that he take some degree of evasive action to elude pursuit.

In fact, when Abel returned to New York he was wary. He did not immediately return to Brooklyn art studio where he was known as Emil Goldfus, and he didn't revisit the upper Broadway area where he had lived in a variety of hotels in recent months under various names. He checked into the Hotel Latham at 28th Street and Fifth Avenue, near the garment district, registering as Martin Collins, an identity he could document.

For all the stories written about Abel, there has yet to be one calling him a blunderer. Yet, for all his training, for all his suitability for a dangerous illegal mission in the United States, the truth is Abel blundered.

Trusting Vic as little as he had, Mark had blundered not once, not twice, but three times. Three times he had taken Hayhanen to his Brooklyn studio, and while Hayhanen couldn't give the FBI the address of the place, he could and did take them there. A prudent man would not have trusted his private identity, his personal redoubt, to anyone. Hayhanen did not know the name Mark used or where he lived, but he knew where he worked, and then the FBI knew.

Then Abel took some extreme risks, There was something at the studio he had to have, some device—perhaps a cipher pad, a listening schedule, *treff* instructions—so despite the dangers, knowing Hayhanen had gone sour, he went back.

The night of May 23, seven weeks after Hayhanen's disappearance in Paris, Abel took a subway to Brooklyn and went to his studio. For weeks the FBI had kept the building under surveillance. Agents watched the windows of the Goldfus studio through binoculars. At 10:45 on the night of the 23rd the light went on in Emil's studio.

The FBI agents, finally rewarded for their long vigil, watched and waited. The master spy busied himself in the room until nearly midnight, and then turned out the light and left. Agents followed him when he left the building, through the subways, onto a bus and off of it at 27th and Broadway, and then along Fifth Avenue for a block, where the quarry turned the corner and vanished.

It was a crushing disappointment. The FBI did not want to tip him off, had tailed him loosely and lost him. But now tne FBI knew Mark was in town, that he would visit the studio and that he had probably not detected the tail (a remarkable achievement for the FBI, considering the few persons abroad in that part of Manhattan at midnight).

The FBI went back to square one, resuming the watch on the studio. It wasn't until *three weeks later* that this patience paid off again. Mark came again, and so great was Abel's confidence that he went, by subway, and foot, directly to the Latham Hotel. Now the FBI had a residence.

The bureau decided on the direct approach, to try to double Abel. On June 21, 1957, a joint team of FBI agents and Immigration officers pounced on Abel at his room in the Latham. He was charged with illegal entry into the United States, but an FBI agent left no doubt they knew who they had. "Colonel," one said, "we have received information concerning your involvement in espionage."

There followed the strange ritual dance of espionage and counter-espionage, the KGB matching wits with the FBI. Abel was whisked off to an immigration holding camp in Texas, offered freedom and a princely sum for cooperation, in exchange for exposing his network and doubling against his service.

When it became apparent that he would sacrifice his personal freedom, he was indicted for espionage conspiracy, tried, and sentenced to 30 years in prison.

Abel never talked and in 1962 was swapped for U-2 pilot Francis Gary Powers. Hayhanen remained in hiding in the United States until his death in 1961 in a mysterious auto accident in Pennsylvania.

Hayhanen's defection, which had netted Abel, turned over one rock disclosing a low-silhouette American spy. He was army master sergeant Roy Adair Rhodes, who had yielded to a KGB sex trap while working at the American embassy in Moscow, and had given the Soviets information on embassy personnel. Rhodes was court-martialed on espionage conspiracy charges, found guilty, and sentenced to five years in prison and a dishonorable discharge.

The FBI gets a clean bill of health in the Abel case. Abel's operations were superhumanly undetectable until Hayhanen provided the first lead; the FBI then used every fragment of information available, invested enormous patient hours of surveillance of that deserted art studio in Brooklyn, and took every advantage of Abel's blunders and arrogance to nab him.

In her biography, *Abel* (Trident, 1970), Louise Bernikow analyzes her subject to smithereens and finally guesses that for all his nine years as an illegal in the U.S. Abel probably didn't get anything. In what was an otherwise excellent account of the case she finally hypothesizes that Abel spent his time reading *Scientific American* and sending microdotted summaries of it back to the Moscow Center. She conceded he was a spy, but concluded he didn't have any agents and didn't do anything harmful. Her ability to deceive herself into believing her spy really wasn't a "wicked spy" is similar to biographer Sam Waagenaar's *Mata Hari* (Appleton-Century, 1963). Waagenaar had produced the definitive book on the beautiful Dutchwoman, and then chose to distrust the overwhelmingly convincing French intercepts of German messages about their agent H-21 and trusted instead the judgment of her close friends and his own heart that she was not. Let biographers of spies be wary of the proximity fuse.

Abel, at least, was a dedicated agent, cause for pride by his Soviet superiors. Others have not been such prize recruits. The Tuomi case is an accurate indicator of how good the bureau can be when it has a weaker individual in its clutches. In this case the FBI was able to manage and then exploit a major defection, wisely concealed its advantage from the Soviets, and through friends tried to gain an even greater advantage over the Soviets and sow a little fear in the Lubianka. It shows also how the latter scheme was finally aborted by the wagging tongues of two hostile ex-FBI agents.

The Tuomi story is in many ways the Baltch story, and it was the Baltch case that first got the headlines, while Tuomi was barely mentioned. It was in 1963 that the FBI announced the arrest in Washington of the Baltches, two deep cover agents, and the arrest in New York of Ivan and Alexandra Egorov, two Soviet legals. Attorney General Robert Kennedy noted that the four had obtained and dispatched to the USSR "information relating to United States rocket-launching sites, military and naval installations, troop movements, shipping and military waterfront facilities" and much more information that was of a sensitive nature.

On Sept. 29, 1964, the trial of the Baltches got under way in a Brooklyn court and almost immediately ran into a battle between the demands of justice for the people of the United States and the necessity to obscure an American intelligence coup for the greater security of the United States and all its people. The government announced that one of the witnesses against the Baltches would be Kaarlo Rudolph Tuomi, another illegal who had defected.

Several reasons were later given for dismissal of the charges against the Baltches. The arguments in court were (1) that the U.S. did not want to reveal, at defense demand, the home addresses of the 75 FBI agents who had worked on the case, nor Tuomi's address, and (2) that much of the evidence had been obtained by a listening device installed in the Baltches' apartment. Faced with adverse rulings by the trial judge, the government chose dismissal rather than trial.

It is also possible that Tuomi himself was a reason for the government's choice probably because the U. S. did not want him subjected to close cross-examination, especially about the date of his defection. At the time of the announcement government spokesmen were a little fuzzy about when Tuomi began cooperating—whether it had been for weeks, for months or for years.

By 1970 Tuomi discussed his defection in an article in *Reader's Digest* which revealed that Tuomi was turned into a double agent by the FBI almost from the instant he crossed into the United States from Canada as an illegal. Almost his entire time as an illegal operative in the U.S. had been managed by the bureau.

Tuomi was born in Michigan of Finnish parents, went to the Soviet Union as a youth, and was raised a Russian. He fought in the Red Army in World War II and then became a teacher of English at Kirov. Caught up in an indiscretion by the KGB, he was blackmailed into informing on his neighbors and co-workers to the satisfaction of his masters, who noted his proficiency in English. He was touched with the magic wand—tapped for assignment as an illegal agent in the U.S. He was trained for months, and the KGB prepared an elaborate "legend," a phony life's story, for him.

It lacked some important details that can snare a deep cover man. He would not be able to account for not having a Social Security card until he was in his 30s, he could not fake a military record or a draft board exemption, and the Russians worried to the end that the eternal nemesis of the American taxpayer, the Internal Revenue Service, would someday inquire why 1959 was the first year he filed a tax return.

Nevertheless Tuomi, the tyro deep cover man, made a practice run through Europe, then was given money and temporary documents and on Dec. 17, 1958 he walked off a ship in Montreal, and caught a train to Chicago under yet another false identity.

He set out on several weeks of wandering through Michigan and Minnesota, the locales of his real childhood and of his phony legend, familiarizing himself with neighborhoods and towns. He picked up a copy of his baptismal certificate, and visited a cemetery where real relatives were buried.

Then he caught a train to Vancouver to check out his fake Canadian background (a cover for his lack of military service in the U.S.) and returned to the Midwest. At Port Huron, Mich., he remembered later, he was jostled on a train by an unruly drunk, but arrived in New York unscathed, and sent a signal postcard to the Soviet UN Mission announcing his safe arrival. Then, on a schedule worked out in Moscow months before, he began visiting the four dead-drops in the New York area assigned to him. One contained a message complimenting him and welcoming him to the U.S.

Then he set off on a second familiarization trip, and he came to grief in Milwaukee. The story is told in *Reader's Digest*. After three months, Tuomi says, he was picked off the street in Milwaukee one night by four men, one of whom was the drunk from the train at Port Huron.

They were FBI agents. They took him to a hunting lodge, stripped and searched him, and then bargained with him. The KGB hadn't prepared him for this. How had the bureau got on his trail? If they knew about him three months before, how much more did they know? If they were expecting him in the U.S., then how deeply had American intelligence penetrated the KGB?

It was a classic performance of turning the enemy's agent. Tuomi was in an impossible situation, and agreed to double, and for the next four years the KGB illegal in the United States reported to the FBI.

He took an apartment in Queens, and found a job at Tiffany's. Moscow was impressed, just as Moscow was impressed by all the Hollywood luminaries Boris Morros knew.

In February 1961 Tuomi was given a new cipher system and put to work as a spy. He was told to check New York docks and the military installations in the area, encouraged to produce intelligence on seaborne commerce in and out of New York, and so, with FBI help, he left glittery Tiffany's and took a laboring job on the waterfront.

In September, 1961 Tuomi was told to go to Yonkers for a secret meeting. He was met by Aleksei Ivanovich Galkin, one of his instructors in espionage in Moscow, and who was then first secretary of the Byelorussian Mission to the UN. Now a counter-surveillance was mounted by Pyotr Egorovich Maslenikov, first secretary of the USSR's UN Mission. Tuomi and Galkin walked and talked for hours, watched by Maslenikov, all of them watched by FBI agents. One of Galkin's new instructions was to develop information about the U.S. submarine base at New London, Connecticut.

Tuomi worked, picked up his "mail" at the dead-drops and let the bureau read it (and the bureau also watched to see who serviced the dead-drops), checking out missile sites in New York and Vermont, and riding out a panic that gripped Soviet intelligence in mid-1962 (during the Cuban missile deployment) when the KGB finally caught a real live Western spy right in Moscow, Colonel Oleg Penkovsky, who had passed Soviet secrets to the CIA and British MI-6.

Then on July 3, 1963 the FBI arrested the Baltches and the Egorovs and Tuomi's work was done. Former FBI agent William Turner, in his hostile book, *Hoover's FBI* (Sherbourne Press, 1970), provides an account of how the FBI discovered and handled Tuomi.

Turner gives acknowledgement to another ex-agent, Nelson H. "Skip" Gibbons, in a foreword to the book. In the text it becomes apparent that Skip Gibbons was one of Turner's best friends in the bureau, and Skip left the FBI with little love lost, having failed to meet the agency's weight standards (Turner gives several reasons why Gibbons didn't).

The way Turner tells the Tuomi story:

> Nelson H. Gibbons had been a house hero in the FBI. . . .
> he had pulled off an unprecedented feat by single-handedly
> uncovering a Soviet spy. I remember an espionage desk supervisor telling the story at in-service training, holding Gibbons up
> as an exemplar of an alert and determined agent. Assigned to
> a rural area in the Detroit division, Gibbons learned about a
> man who had come to town to obtain a copy of his baptismal
> certificate at the Roman Catholic church. He sensed something
> wrong and began to tail the man. It turned out that he was
> Kaarlo Rudolph Tuomi. . . .

The story sounds reasonable and Turner probably got it firsthand. He does not reveal the source of Gibbons' information, but it seems likely that someone at that church had his suspicions about Tuomi and called the FBI. Someone at that church who had confidence in the FBI, who knew the FBI from its public image, probably phoned in the first tip that indicated a Soviet illegal was afoot.

Had the FBI not had that reputation, Mr. Gibbons, in all likelihood, would not have received the phone call, and would not have become a "house hero in the FBI," and Bill Turner would not have heard that story which he tried to turn around to savage the FBI's reputation.

Whatever the true circumstances of Kaarlo Tuomi's defection—whether he was turned almost immediately after arrival or whether it wasn't until 1962, as E. H. Cookridge has it in *Spy Trade* (Walker, 1972), it caused a serious dislocation in Soviet intelligence and showed the FBI could still play the double-agent game well, years after Boris Morros.

The foregoing are the more thrilling spy stories. However, counter-espionage is usually anything but thrilling. It is a matter of tiresome surveillance.

This surveillance pays off at times. Perhaps one day someone will erect a small obelisk or similar memorial in a parking lot at one of the railroad stations around New York City in remembrance of what the FBI surveillance has there accomplished against Soviet espionage. The KGB and GRU have an ingrained habit of setting up *treffs* between handling agent and spy in suburban railroad station parking lots of the Penn Central and the Long Island Railroad.

It was on a night in the 1960s in the parking lot at the Lynbrook, New York station that Robert Glenn Thompson, one of the Russians' better American spies, knew he had been "made" by the FBI.

Thompson, from Detroit, had enlisted in the air force, and was posted finally to the Office of Special Investigation in Berlin. This was the air force's counter-intelligence office, and Thompson was its file clerk. After years of heavy drinking and an imagined harassment campaign from his CO, Thompson slipped off to East Berlin one night, called up a Russian intelligence agency (the phone number was obtained from his office files), and eventually agreed to be a spy. He ended up bugging the entire office space of OSI, and photographed many of the air force's most sensitive papers. Before taking new orders back to the States he slipped into East Berlin again and was flown off in a Russian jet to a special week-long course on espionage at a Russian base near the Black Sea.

Thompson wound up at Great Falls, Montana, reported his arrival by microdot postcard, and began accepting varied assignments. He checked on people in Minnesota, and in one instance photographed a Polish wedding in Hamtramck, Michigan. One of his Montana contacts in 1958 was clearly a Soviet deep cover illegal—a Great Falls bar waitress who had been one of his instructors at the Black Sea base. Thompson followed Moscow's instructions for years, but was gradually trying to break away, moving his family east, all the way to Long Island. But there the Russians again found him and maintained his cooperation. While he turned down an assignment to go to Canada and locate Igor Gouzenko, he accepted a detail to provide plans for the gas lines in Queens and other areas of New York.

The Russians, he discovered, were paranoid about the FBI, seeing agents everywhere, and their frenzy drove them so much they asked Thompson to get plans of the FBI offices at Mineola and Babylon, N.Y., to set them up for burglary or bugging.

Then one night while meeting his Russian handler at the Lynbrook railroad station Thompson says his eye caught just the barest twinkle of a red light flashing inside a parked panel truck, and he knew immediately that he had been caught by the FBI, photographed by infra-red light.

In a ghostwritten article Thompson can't help but swashbuckle a little, bragging about his keen senses that detected bureau suveillance, but he says he didn't mention it to his Russian superiors to imply that his soul was touched by a patriotic pulse. More likely he was protecting his $300 stipend, and feared the Russians' panic and wrath when they discovered they had been detected.

During all his years of wholesale ransacking of air force secrets for the Russians, Thompson had not been suspected. He was only spotted because the FBI, in its patient and painstaking way, had followed Fedor Kudashkin, an interpreter attached to the USSR delegation to the UN, to that railway station at

Lynbrook. Thompson was convicted of conspiracy to commit espionage in 1965 and after entering a guilty plea he was sentenced to 30 years in prison.

The story of Soviet espionage has no ending. Its latest chapter is in today's newspaper. If not today's, next Thursday's.

Two of the most recent subjects of FBI vigilance, and citizen cooperation, were two Russian civilians, both international civil servants, both translators employed at the UN. One was arrested in the parking lot of a Chinese restaurant on Long Island, the other on a street 3,000 miles away. Both had the same mission: acquisition of military and technical secrets about U.S. defense.

Aleksandr V. Tikhomirov, 37, was arrested Feb. 7, 1970 by FBI agents in Seattle just moments after he had given $300 to an air force sergeant in return for information about anti-aircraft and missile defenses in the Pacific Northwest. After four days in the Seattle jail Tikhomirov was released, the charges dropped, and he was expelled from the country. The airman had cooperated with the FBI all along, having turned to the FBI almost by instinct, knowing it would properly handle the matter. Had the airman lost confidence in the FBI—and the anti-FBI campaign seems designed to shake public confidence—the airman might not have pursued the course he did.

About nine months after Tikhomirov was expelled, UN translator Valery I. Markelov, 32, dropped in on an industrial exhibit in the East and engaged an engineer from Grumman Aircraft in conversation. A friendship flowered and Markelov asked for first one favor, then another. He wanted technical articles translated. He began to ask questions about Grumman's work, then about the new F-14A Tomcat and its weapons systems. Finally he gave the engineer a copying machine (the better'to run off material), then money, then a 35mm camera. Then he asked for specific classified information on the Tomcat, and the engineer, who had reported every contact to the FBI, met Markelov for his last free meal in America at that Chinese restaurant.

There will be more Tikhomirovs and more Markelovs, and there will be more Morroses and Tuomis, and always the KGB and GRU will know there will be the FBI.

If the Soviet intelligence service has been with us since almost immediately after the October Revolution, the flags are now hoisted, indicating that the Chinese Communist intelligence service is only just getting started. The FBI is aware of it, and has taken steps to counter it.

In his 1970 testimony (for the fiscal 1971 budget) before the House Appropriations Subcommittee, Hoover spoke about the Chinese problem. He identified the then principal pro-Peking Communist party in the U.S., the Progressive Labor Party (PLP). "The Chinese Communists," he said, "subsidize the PLP through the purchase of its various publications. PLP leaders have been in periodic contact with Chinese agencies and leaders have on occasion visited the Chinese mainland."

At the same time Hoover noted the waning of PLP, as it became eclipsed by a new pro-Mao Communist party much more fervent and violent, Revolutionary Union (RU).

The FBI kept a close watch on RU, whose members busied themselves with six-hour long political sessions, familiarizing themselves with carbines, shotguns, and pistols (firing twice a month for score), and drawing up lists of political leaders to be dealt with. RU leaders made trips to Communist China and replaced PLP in Peking's favor (PLP has since denounced Mao, for among other things treating with Richard Nixon). Still the organizations serve Red China's espionage as the Communist Party serves the Soviet's.

"During the past year," Hoover told the congressmen, ". . . we have experienced a definite increase in our Chinese investigations due to the stepped-up intelligence activities on the part of the Communist Chinese aimed at procuring highly coveted technical data both overtly and covertly, and the efforts of the Chinese Communists to introduce deep cover intelligence agents into this country."

If Hoover could comment on what was being skulked after,

he obviously knew who was doing the skulking. That he could speak of Chinese deep cover agents indicates that some of the penetration has been detected and countered.

Hoover's 1969 testimony first spoke of the Chinese probes. In one instance a Chinese American businessman tried to send electronic equipment that could be used in aerospace research, missile tracking and radar to the China mainland. He mailed the embargoed equipment, labeled as replacement parts for printing equipment, to a Hong Kong merchant temporarily in Toronto. Canadian authorities, using FBI information, caught the culprit for making a false customs declaration and he served 60 days.

Hoover also worried that 20,000 Chinese immigrants poured into the United States each year, principally from Hong Kong. Most, of course, are genuine refugees from tyranny, but the FBI director was duty bound to observe that "this provides a means to send illegal agents into our nation."

Hoover assessed RU as an intelligence threat: "RU leaders are seeking to work with other militants and to gain influence within the Students for a Democratic Society and other new left and Negro protest movements. There is little doubt that some members of organizations such as these will be entirely receptive to recruitment as intelligence agents for clandestine operations on behalf of Communist China. In this regard, one of the founders of the RU is a longtime Communist named Leibel Bergman who first turned against the Communist Party, U.S.A., and then dropped out of a leadership role in the Progressive Labor Party before turning to the RU."

Since this word from Hoover, Bergman has moved from the RU base camps around San Francisco, Berkeley, and Palo Alto, to northern New Jersey. His move to the metropolitan New York area came at, approximately, the time the People's Republic of China was seated at the United Nations and swept into Manhattan with a large staff.

The other Chinese threat Hoover called to the attention of Congress and the nation was the case of the Hong Kong seamen. There are about 40,000 of them, members of the Hong Kong Seamen's Union, which is Mao-oriented. Many of these seamen have home addresses in Mainland China and their families live there. When they come to the U.S. on merchant ships some of them jump ship. Thousands desert their vessels here every year and Hoover declared that these desertions "constitute a serious security threat."

Espionage buffs compare the Hong Kong seamen threat to the case of the Japanese naval officers in Hawaii. There, in 1939-41, U.S. Naval Intelligence stumbled onto what the Imperial Navy was doing. A Japanese merchant ship would arrive in Honolulu and 40 seamen would go ashore to sightsee and visit a teahouse or pass the time with a geisha and when the ship sailed two or three crewmen, reserve naval officers on intelligence assignments, would be left behind. They would drop out of sight, blend in with the local population, and spend a month or two touring Oahu and the outer islands acquainting themselves on the ground with the military bases, highways, and fortifications. Their places on the outgoing ship would be taken by other officers dropped off months before. This Japanese operation enabled Tokyo to assemble a pool of officers intimately familiar with Hawaii and its defenses, and their casual and unhurried observations contributed no little amount to the Japanese intelligence files on Hawaii.

When the People's Republic of China was admitted to the UN in late 1971 it was viewed by political leaders, newspaper editorialists, and the man in the street as, variously, the end of 20 years of madness, or the sellout of an ally, or the casting off of the last vestiges of decency by an international body. To the FBI of J. Edgar Hoover it was none of these emotion-charged events. It was the opening on American soil of another office of espionage "legals."

The FBI was ready. While the bureau long has had Chinese-speaking special agents it had concentrated in the 50s and 60s on the most obvious espionage threat, the Soviets. However, beginning in the mid-1960s, before the Peking approach was a gleam in Henry Kissinger's eye, the FBI began quietly sending ever-larger numbers of agents to take the full year's deep submersion Chinese language course at the much-praised Defense Language School at Monterey, California. FBI ranks now reflect an increasing number of agents of Chinese extraction.

When the Peking ambassador presented his credentials to U Thant in 1971 the FBI was prepared for the new espionage threat of the 1970s.

Another more recent threat, Cuban espionage efforts directed at the U.S. have continued unabated since Fidel Castro came to power in 1959. Director Hoover reported on them annually, the phraseology usually warning that with hundreds of thousands of refugees coming into the country each year (the air bridge is now stopped) that Cuban intelligence surely was inserting agents into the refugee flow. His annual warning has stated the situation bluntly, in language hard to misunderstand.

The FBI gave a superb demonstration of its ability to protect the Republic in a sabotage case that involved the Cuban Mission to the UN, and clearly demonstrated that the FBI had made deep penetration of Castro's intelligence net in the United States.

The scene was set in the fall of 1962 at the UN building. The engines that moved the plot were gigantic. The Soviet Union and its Cuban ally were carefully laying down a diplomatic diversion in New York while Soviet ships sneaked missiles into Cuba, and the beginnings of the plot took shape as the diplomats converged on New York. The denouement came six weeks later, after the Kennedy-Khrushchev showdown on the missiles, and it came almost as a spiteful afterthought hurled at the United States for having triumphed, however slightly, in forcing the withdrawal of the Russian rockets.

The FBI has never revealed how it came across the trail of the plot, and ten years later we still know only the skeletal structure and some details, but the Cuban case stands as a solid reminder of the FBI's capacity to contain foreign-directed sabotage.

The plot, which some informed persons insist was Soviet-inspired and masterminded from Havana by the Russian ambassador, was intended simply to wage an ugly sabotage terror campaign in the Eastern United States, panicking the population and showing the nation that its security forces were powerless to act against the unknown saboteurs. It was calculated as a gigantic and bloody embarrassment for the FBI.

The Cubans planned to set off bombs throughout New York City in a coordinated attack—explosions in subway stations, in Grand Central Station and at Macy's block-long department store on 34th Street. Explosives would also be detonated in the sprawling Humble Oil Company refinery at Linden, New Jersey, and the fires they would ignite and the secondary explosions that would be set off would be seen and heard by 20 million people and would clearly demonstrate the impotence of the U.S. security forces.

The chief operations officer of this plot was Roberto Lazaro Santiesteban y Casanova, detailed to the Cuban UN Mission as one of the attaches. He did not arrive in New York until Oct. 3, 1962, traveling on the same plane as Cuba's President Osvaldo Dorticos and Foreign Minister Raul Roa. While the officials held the stage at the UN, Santiesteban dropped out of sight for the next six weeks. Two Hearst reporters, Pierre J. Huss and George Carpozi, Jr., in their *Red Spies in the U.N.,* insist that during that period Santiesteban conferred in New York with Soviet military officials attached to various UN functions.

The arrests came the night of November 16, 1962, only a few days after the big missile showdown. Precisely at 10:26 P.M. at four locations around Manhattan FBI agents jumped the saboteurs, all of whom had begun to move toward rendezvous to carry out the bomb plot that night.

On upper Riverside Drive half a dozen agents hailed down Santiesteban just as he was about to enter his car. The Cuban fought ferociously and tried to swallow a piece of paper he was carrying (later discovered to contain an explosives formula).

At 265 West 71st Street agents arrested Jose Gomez Abad.

21, a low-echelon figure at the Cuban UN Mission and his wife, Elsa Montero, 20, the switchboard operator there, just as they locked up their apartment to begin the night's work.

At East 24th Street and Third Avenue agents surrounded a parked car and arrested Marino Antonio Esteban del Carmen Sueirro y Cabrera, 22, a Cuban employee of a costume jewelry firm. With Sueirro, who was the treasurer of a Cuban social club that was a hotbed of Castroite activity, was 26-year-old Ada Maria Dritsas, an American social worker known for her left-wing views but not definitely known as a Castroite.

In a building at 242 West 27th Street five agents entered and took a rickety elevator to the sixth floor and walked into the Model-Craft Costume Jewelry firm, where Sueirro was employed, surprising the proprietor, José Garcia Orellana, 42, who stood before an open safe. Garcia was president of the Casa Cuba Club to which Sueirro belonged, and they were both active in the Castroite Movimiento del 26 de Julio and in the Fair Play for Cuba Committee.

Before Garcia could make a move FBI agents handcuffed him. In the safe agents found hand grenades, TNT detonators, some incendiaries, and drawings, diagrams, and instruction books on sabotaging trains, ships, oil tanks, and buildings. In the same room, in a seemingly cast-aside fluorescent light fixture leaning against one wall, FBI searchers found more grenades and detonators.

All the would-be saboteurs were taken to FBI headquarters for questioning and then to the Federal House of Detention. The next morning the United States government demanded the immediate recall of Gomez Abad and his wife Elsa. They were named as suppliers of the explosives, and one of the boxes at the loft had a shipping label still affixed—155 East 44th Street, then the address of the Cuban UN Mission.

Sueirro and Garcia were held in jail on $100,000 bail and Santiesteban on $250,000. Though Santiesteban claimed diplomatic immunity, the fact was that he did not yet have it. Bureaucratic holdups, it was said, had delayed State Department approval on Señor Santiesteban, so at the time of arrest he was not yet diplomatically immune.

Miss Dritsas, who was seated in the car with Sueirro, was released after questioning and the FBI said she was not aware of the plot and had only been visiting with her friend Sueirro. She worked at a social center only a few blocks from the Cubans' West 27th Street costume jewelry business.

It is recorded that while Santiesteban, the undiplomat, was in the Federal House of Detention he was visited by Attorney General Robert Kennedy. Reportedly they discussed his freedom as part of the exchange for the Bay of Pigs invaders.

On April 22, 1963 (Lenin's birthday, incidentally), five months after their capture, the three Cubans were given permission to return home (the Gomezes had left almost immediately) and the U.S. threw in a fourth for good measure—a Castroite who had killed a young girl during a wild shootout with anti-Castro Cubans in a Manhattan restaurant. Garcia, the naturalized American seized at the safe containing the grenades, was permitted to return to Cuba with his wife and two daughters.

How the FBI got onto the Cuban sabotage plot has never been revealed, but some years later in another case the FBI admitted that for years it had been tapping the phones of the Cuban UN Mission and those of some of its employees. It becomes apparent that the bureau was in on the plot at an early date—by the time of Santiesteban's arrival, surely. That seems the more logical explanation, rather than the chatter about bureaucratic fumbling, for the delay in granting diplomatic status to Santiesteban and it explains, as well, the government's decision not to prosecute and blow the mission.

In late 1970 word leaked to newsmen—and the leakage occurred within the State Department not the Justice Department—of yet another Cuban espionage attempt by a modernday Mata Hari. Jennifer Enid Miles of South Africa was 26, a beauty who in a town where eligible young females outnumber men by five to one had a string of beaux. Some reporters said the bureau lost track counting her boyfriends after tabulating more than a hundred. The story sounds apocryphal—the FBI would not stop counting.

Miss Miles, an employee of the South African embassy, centered her attentions on men working throughout federal Washington. After many months of watchful waiting, and recording the affairs in her apartment, the Justice Department forwarded the FBI's "documented evidence" to the State Department and it became a matter taken up with the UN. Two Cuban intelligence officers, Rogelio Rodriguez Lopez and Orlando Prendes Guiterrez, whose cover jobs were counselor and first secretary, respectively, at the Cuban UN Mission, were declared persona non grata. Miss Miles gave a long statement to the FBI and then voluntarily left for home, to share the same regard from her countrymen that Dhanapalo Samarasekara receives from the Ceylonese.

Miss Miles admitted that she was in the service of Cuban Intelligence. Some of her gentlemen callers recalled later that she never hid her feelings, sometimes openly stating she supported Castro's revolution, giving rise to speculation that one of her missions might have been to see if she could set off any harmonic vibrations. If after revealing her sympathies one of her male friends had conceded that he, too, secretly admired Fidel, then he would be designated as a source to be developed. This is sometimes how important sources, the genuine spies who have access to secret papers, are spotted by espionage talent scouts. Miss Miles, it was later revealed, came by her Cuban sympathies by personal experience—she had spent four months in Cuba. Doubtless some of it was spent in intelligence technique training.

The FBI has had its eye on the Cuban traffic and the site of a swollen Cuban embassy. Mexico is the only Latin country, save Chile, that has a Cuban embassy, and there the FBI has the largest contingent of legal attaches in any U.S. embassy. Mexico City is also home to a large Soviet embassy, and it is obviously the out-of-country headquarters for major intelligence operations directed against the colossus to the north.

In recent years, J. Edgar Hoover warned of the espionage potential of American youths who have traveled to Cuba to have their revolutionary fires stoked. Said Hoover, "Some 1,300 members of the Venceremos Brigade, for example, went to Cuba to cut sugar cane. While there, they were subjected to heavy doses of revolutionary propaganda and constantly reminded that they were the vanguard of the revolution in the United States, The *members of these groups provide the Cuban Intelligence Service with excellent recruitment possibilities.*"

A giant talent pool for the future. Thus, the age-old problem of espionage is still with us, and at least the men who handle the espionage cases at the FBI recognize the enormity of the problem. In one of the stolen Media documents we glimpse the FBI spotting a person who might have been contacted at some time by the Soviets and asked to do a little betrayal. Had he been contacted he probably would have contacted the FBI and reported the attempt and been played off against the Russians again in the endless game of wits. But he might not have. The FBI did not gamble with the nation's security. They wrote it up and filed it. The FBI document was confidential and there was no embarrassment to the individual because of the quiet FBI manner.

It was only after the burglars had made the Media documents public that that individual was embarrassed. The Media burglars, undoubtedly domestic American misfits, proved a valuable ally of the KGB in the raid by compromising an FBI source and an FBI technique until then unknown to the KGB.

The FBI will find another source and develop another technique.

The Ethical Approach to Counter-Espionage / Editors

In his book *I Spy,* published in the USSR, the veteran Soviet agent Kim Philby declared that, during the period of his operations (and those of his sub-agents, Guy Burgess and Donald Maclean) in London, Washington and elsewhere, the FBI was perhaps the least efficient counter-espionage agency of those of any major power. While the Philby statement on this score was largely dismissed as Communist propaganda, as indeed most of his book was, his assertion deserves a closer look.

Although Philby was ideologically committed to Soviet intelligence, his overt training and work experience had been within the British system of intelligence and counter-intelligence, a system that was built along the classic lines of the Europeans who had practiced intelligence for centuries and who still viewed it and its counter-forces as the most obvious of national security necessities. The operational British system had, as one of its parts, a separate unit or service (MI-5) that had the basic counter-intelligence responsibility but, to a degree, worked closely with the intelligence-gathering agency on the premise that one of the most important functions of counter-intelligence is, in fact, the gathering of hard intelligence information about the other side's operations.

It is a system that has been suggested for the United States (and Canada) by some critics of the FBI who have suggested, like Philby, that the bureau's approach to espionage investigations might not be the best.

These critics are not, by any measure, libertarians, but rather are hard-minded pragmatists seeking to increase the efficiency of U.S. domestic counter-intelligence operations by the creation of a separate domestic intelligence agency. The argument is that the FBI is fundamentally a law enforcement body, that its agents are trained primarily as law enforcement officers and that, therefore, the FBI is not equipped to do an intelligence job. Moreover, it is said the bureau tends to view all cases, including espionage cases, in the law enforcement mode. It is fully geared for the collection and preservation of evidence, the seeking out of potential witnesses, and the adherence to procedural "due process" that are all necessary to prepare a case for *prosecution.*

The advocates of a separate service point out, however, that prosecution should not be the primary aim of a counter-intelligence force. Rather, they say, the mission of such a service should be the protection of the nation's security at all costs and through the use of any means needed to perform that mission. They say that such a mission requires a degree of training, temperament, and dedication different from that found in the average FBI agent. They also recognize the fact that it would be difficult to have the average FBI agent—trained as he is to operate within the rule of law, and bound by his organizational discipline as well as his legal background to preserve the rights of defendants as carefully as he seeks to preserve admissible evidence—adapt himself to operating in the counter-intelligence service, complete with all of the secret and dirty (though less flamboyant) attributes of a James Bond including, incidentally, the "license to kill."

The hard fact is that this latter mode is how the classic counter-intelligence service operates at its most efficient level and how it produces the most desirable results within a purely national security context. The mission of any counter-intelligence service is decidedly *not* to put people in jail except as a last resort. The mission is to preserve the security of the nation by denying to an enemy or potential enemy all information deemed by appropriate authorities to be vital to the nation's security, to deprive him of the weapon of his own intelligence system while, in turn, using whatever assets may be available to discover as much of his secret information as possible or, in other words, to get the highest degree of efficiency from one's own intelligence weapon. This means that when a counter-intelligence service discovers an illegal agent of a rival service, it does not take steps to imprison or deport him. The counter-intelligence agents watch him or grill him, learning what they can from the spy and trying to use him if possible, and if not possible, they attempt to thwart him in his mission using the most practical, expedient and secret means.

Those who have criticized the FBI for the relative inflexibility of its rules and regulations or for the severity of its discipline are, for the most part, aware that both the rules and the discipline are designed to attain the highest degree of efficiency *and* to protect the rights of citizens, all within the law enforcement mode. Critics have castigated the bureau's catch-all disciplinary infraction, "embarrassment of the bureau"; but imagine for a moment the scope and degree of FBI embarrassment were a team of agents found to be interrogating a Soviet "illegal," without benefit of warrant or counsel, in an otherwise deserted Wisconsin fishing camp or a remote Virginia hideaway.

We note, parenthetically, that in at least one case, that of the double agent Kaarlo Tuomi, the FBI did, in fact, use the classic grilling technique with an illegal, and by so doing made a valuable double agent. Apparently Tuomi, after having been under FBI surveillance for a period of time, was picked up by agents, taken to a remote location for a period of days after which he not only talked freely to the agents but also agreed to cooperate with them in the classic double agent role. The net result of his cooperation together with other time honored counter-espionage techniques including wiretaps, and even more sophisticated technical gear, resulted in the apprehension of a number of illegal Soviet agents who had assumed false American identities. It would seem obvious that this result was a much more useful one than an effort to collect evidence against, arrest, and try Kaarlo Tuomi who, under those circumstances, may well have revealed nothing to his captors.

In any event, let the critic of the FBI's handling of espionage cases be consistent in his criticism. He cannot, like William Turner, take the bureau to task on the one hand for alleged fast and loose approaches to civil liberties (a charge he fails to document) while at the same time criticizing the bureau for handling counter-espionage activities in a law enforcement mode in which the proper concern for civil liberties restricts the bureau in a way that materially reduces its efficiency in that field.

7. Developing the Internal Security Mission
Andrew Seamans
with the Editors

On March 28, 1933, German Ambassador F. W. von Prittwitz sent a letter to Secretary of State Cordell Hull, requesting an investigation of a threatened assassination of the new Chancellor of the Reich, Adolf Hitler. The threat was contained in a letter, which von Prittwitz enclosed with his petition, and allegedly came from a "Daniel Stern," who wanted the Nazi leader's hide for his atrocities against the German Jews. Stern, if ever he existed, was never found, but the FBI Nazi investigation authorized by President Roosevelt was productive.

Von Prittwitz probably had not realized that an FBI investigation into the mysterious Mr. Stern would quite logically have to include some amount of delving into the activities with which the German Embassy was involved. It did, and the information developed in an extensive but short-term FBI investigation would one day be of great advantage in wrecking German plans in the United States.

More investigation was needed, however. In the following year President Roosevelt, concerned about domestic Fascist plans, held a White House conference with J. Edgar Hoover, Attorney General Homer S. Cummings, Treasury Secretary Henry Morgenthau Jr., Labor Secretary Frances Perkins, and Secret Service head W. H. Moran. The group decided several things: the only legal excuse for investigating the Nazis would have to be based on immigration law; there was no explicit authority for the investigation FDR wanted, and neither were there rules for conducting it; and legally, the President had to order the investigation.

139

There was no fanfare, but from these two episodes came much needed intelligence information on the Nazi threat. As the war approached, the mission assumed much more importance and FBI espionage investigations jumped in number starting in 1938.

Perhaps this limited mission was all that was necessary against the Nazi threat. For the most part, Axis internal subversion in the World War II era was not the work of a sophisticated network of internal organizations. It was chiefly the work of either individuals recruited by the Germans or actual aliens sent in with the express intention of committing sabotage acts. Such cases as U.S. Army deserter Guenther Gustave Rumrich and John Semer Farnsworth were conducted as lone wolf-type schemes with assists from actual German agents. They were not matters involving domestic fifth column groups like the German-American Bundists.

Rumrich was arrested on February 15, 1938, for a sad-sack attempt to pilfer plans for the U.S. East Coast defenses. Following FBI investigation the army deserter was picked up by New York City police detectives and State Department agents. He had actually tried to pass himself off as Secretary Cordell Hull in an attempt to obtain passport forms. Rumrich's efforts won him two years in jail.

Farnsworth on the other hand was not a deserter; he was kicked out of U.S. military service. The Naval Academy graduate was dishonorably discharged in 1927, and six years later started working for a new employer—Imperial Japan. Farnsworth was a paradoxical character, according to Booton Herndon in his biography of the late news commentator Fulton Lewis Jr.* It was Lewis who accidentally came upon the naval outcast and brought him to justice. The Axis spy had wanted $20,000 and a five-day headstart from Lewis in exchange for the exclusive story of how he sold information on ship movements,

*Booton Herndon, *Praised and Damned: The Story of Fulton Lewis Jr.* (New York, 1954), pp. 32-39.

maneuvers, photos, ship specifications, etc. to the Japanese. But Lewis turned over all the data on the heavy drinking ex-serviceman to the FBI. Farnsworth was quickly arrested, convicted and sent to prison, where he eventually died.

The major group of Fascist sympathizers in the United States was the German-American Bund, which reached its high-water mark with a rally in New York's Madison Square Garden. Despite the fact that in the parade 18,000 demonstrated their loyalty to the little paperhanger from Austria (with much arm saluting and gesturing), the Bund was never any real threat to America. It was *not* the vehicle used by the German government for sabotage or subversion. The Germans preferred operatives trained in the Fatherland to any rank amateurs of the Bund.

Interestingly, many professional internal security specialists believe that the danger from the Nazi-sympathizers within the U.S. ended when the Soviets were thrust into the war by Hitler's stupidity in attacking Russia. "Once Hitler attacked the USSR," Harold Ranstad told this writer (he had retired from the FBI in 1955 after 21 years as a special agent), "I thought the internal danger [from the Nazis] was over."

Prior to the invasion of Russia, the official Communist party line had been "peace" with Nazi Germany. That invasion turned the domestic Reds around, and their cry was now "war." The reason the internal security experts thought the internal threat was over after this switch, was that they knew only the Communists at the time had the capability for dangerous espionage and subversion. Had the Soviets remained allies of Hitler, it was possible that the Communist apparatus would have worked for the Nazi cause against America. The Communists understandably feared that successful Nazi underground work would awaken the American government to the need for internal security measures—and they had their own reasons for not wanting that to happen.

To that time, no agency had undertaken a continuing intelligence mission against enemy spies or domestic organizations bent on overthrowing the government, or subverting it. America long had the luxury of blithely ignoring such threats to its constitutional form of government, although the history of much of the rest of the world was fairly written in terms of revolutions and coups. Now, however, the nation was being drawn into the wars promulgated by European ideologues, and now that same ideological impetus was being given organizational impetus by Communists and revolutionary socialists at home. No longer could America be so sure that its constitutional government would not be subverted, and that foreign enemies would not attempt to bring the war to this continent.

President Roosevelt was aware of this, and decided that some agency would have to undertake the internal security mission that had long been common in other nations. The agency he chose was the one most immediately available, the Federal Bureau of Investigation. He issued a directive, made public on September 6, 1939, which read:

> The attorney general has been requested by me to instruct the Federal Bureau of Investigation of the Department of Justice to take charge of investigative work in matters relating to espionage, sabotage, and violations of neutrality regulations.
> This task must be conducted in a comprehensive and effective manner on a national basis, and all information must be carefully sifted out and correlated in order to avoid confusion and irresponsibility.
> To this end I request all police officers, sheriffs, and all other law enforcement officers in the United States promptly to turn over to the nearest representative of the Federal Bureau of Investigation any information obtained by them relating to espionage, counterespionage, sabotage, subversive activities and violations of the neutrality laws.

This decree by Roosevelt, along with directives issued by the chief executives who have followed, are the essence of the FBI's authority in the field of internal security. It resulted in a new intelligence mission on a continuing basis, but it also was the first step in altering the mode of internal intelligence work to a form quite unique in the nations of the world. But before this can be readily understood, the story of FBI efforts to protect democracy before the FDR directive must be told.

The early twentieth century approach to protecting American democracy is in striking contrast with today's legalistic approach. In those years treason was treason, and sedition was sedition. Radicalism was an alien idea, and since most of its advocates were not yet citizens, the authorities put in actual effect the "America—Love It or Leave It" policy which was only sloganized by latter day advocates of patriotism.

Radicals were becoming very active in America after the turn of the century. Some of them were out-and-out anarchists; more of them were socialists, such as the Industrial Workers of the World (IWW—the "Wobblies"); and toward World War 1, the Bolshevik Communists were on the scene. These radicals opposed American participation in World War 1, and the situation became ugly.

The extremists struck on June 2, 1919; nine bombs exploded in eight different American cities. Targets: top government officials and leading industrialists and the system in general. Two men were killed by an explosive device in Washington at the home of newly appointed Attorney General A. Mitchell Palmer. The two were believed to be the would-be assassins.

Just one month earlier, 29 bombs had been mailed to noted personalities, including three cabinet members, a Supreme Court justice, four senators, two House members, a U.S. district judge, two governors, and business bigwigs John D. Rockefeller and J. P. Morgan.*

Actually these attempted bombings were not merely failures in the sense that none of them succeeded in their intended destruction or in scaring off opposition, but they also served a counter-purpose in mounting a public outcry for the scalps of those responsible for planting them. The ultimate result was the now infamous Palmer Red Raids.

Palmer appointed Francis P. Garvan as assistant attorney

*Don Whitehead, *The FBI Story* (New York, 1956), p. 44.

general and former Secret Service Chief William J. Flynn became director of the Bureau of Investigation (BI). The attorney general then set up the General Intelligence Division (GID) led by J. Edgar Hoover, special assistant to the attorney general. The weapon to be used by the Justice Department was a (Love It or Leave It) deportation statute passed on October 16, 1918. The GID's chore was to enable the attorney general to "cope with the marked growth of radicalism and the dissemination of anarchistic propaganda."*

When it came time for the actual arrests and deportations of the radical immigrants, the jurisdiction for the raids was within the scope of operations of the U.S. Department of Labor, not Justice. The Labor Department lacked the funds for the task. So Labor issued the warrants and the BI and Immigration Bureau officers made the raids.

The first raids were conducted in November of 1919, and two months later a 33-city dragnet was spread in an effort to wipe out the mixed bag of anarchists, Reds and other ultra-left agitators. Thus netted were such as Alexander Berkman, who served 14 years in prison for attempting to murder Carnegie Steel Corporation head Henry C. Frick during the bloody 1892 Homestead, Pennsylvania strike, and his sometimes lover, "Red Emma" Goldman.

Berkman, Goldman and 247 of their comrades were ordered deported under the 1918 Alien Exclusion Act and were sent to the newly born Soviet Union aboard the army transport ship *Buford,* which was dubbed the "Red Ark" by newsmen. One story has it that several congressmen even journeyed to New York to witness the departure, and as Red Emma boarded the vessel a lawmaker shouted "Merry Christmas, Emma," to which Goldman replied by thumbing her nose.

This mass exodus of assorted immigrants did not end the violence, however. On September 16, 1920 a horse-drawn carriage was parked across Broad Street from J.P. Morgan and

---

*Editors of *Look* Magazine, *The Story of the FBI,* (New York, 1947).

Company near the corner of Wall Street in New York City. Shortly after the unobtrusive driver climbed from the cart and left, a thunderous explosion rent the air and 330 of the noontime crowd were caught by the blast. Of these, thirty, including an employee working inside the Morgan building, were killed. Authorities found the bomb had contained not merely dynamite, but cast-iron window sash weights, one of which was hurled through a window on the 34th floor of a nearby office building.

Although the murderers were never caught, the incident increased the pressure on Palmer to do something to stop the leftist violence. And Palmer did act. On December 29, 1919, just over a week after the "Red Ark" set sail with its cargo of deportees, the youthful assistant in charge of the GID, John Edgar Hoover, submitted his famous brief (the "Martens Brief") on the status of the Communist Party to Attorney General Palmer. In this classic document, Hoover theorized: "The Communist Party is an organization advocating and teaching the overthrow by force or violence of the government of the United States and members thereof believe in and advocate and teach the overthrow by force or violence of the government of the United States.*

Hoover's legal work reviewed the history of the U.S. branch of the Soviet apparatus in some detail. It also enunciated the identical wording used by the domestic leftists and their Bolshevik counterparts in their International Communist Congress. Among those similarities were such revolutionary statements as the necessity to "destroy the producers" in order to "deprive the bourgeoisie of political power and function as a revolutionary dictatorship of the proletariat." In addition, the Bolsheviks were intent on torpedoing labor unions, such as the American Federation of Labor, which were "united with imperialism."

Chief target for the Hoover document was Ludwig Christian

---

*James D. Bale, *J. Edgar Hoover Speaks concerning Communism* (Washington, 1971) contains the entire text of Hoover's brief, pp. 266-288.

Alexander Kaslovitch Martens, who had come to the United States as an official representative of the new-born Russian Soviet government. It didn't deter Martens one bit that he was a diplomat without portfolio (the U.S. and Soviets had not exchanged ambassadors), as the "diplomat" had other things in mind. Martens reportedly had about $200 million with which to set up an effective Communist operation, but his stay was destined to be of short duration, thanks to the BI.

On the night of January 2, 1920, the Bureau of Investigation ushered in the Roaring Twenties by raids against radicals in 33 cities. Agents and, unfortunately, volunteer patriots rounded up about 2,500 assorted aliens, including Ludwig C. A. K. Martens. The BI men were armed with about 3,000 arrest warrants. And by the time the episode ended 446 aliens had been returned to their lands of origin as undesirables.

This was not the final result of the Palmer Red Raids. There were two other important side effects. First, there was an outburst of protest against the tactics employed by the attorney general; and second, both Communist groups—the Communist Party and the Communist Labor Party—submerged. As Theodore Draper aptly wrote, they "converted themselves into conspiratorial organizations."*

As to the zeal with which the government agents conducted the Palmer Red Raids, charges and countercharges flew back and forth like grapeshot and cannonball at the Battle of Gettysburg. Men who had screamed for Palmer to take action following the bombings which killed so many innocent citizens were now raising their voices in calls for the attorney general's scalp. Congressional committees were convened. Civil libertarians leaped to the fray with their tarnished shields and rusty swords. And the furor raged on, while the subversives continued their planning.

In all fairness to the critics—without going into all of their motives—there had been definite policy mistakes by the Justice

*Theodore Draper, *The Roots of American Communism* (New York, 1957), p. 205.

Department and BI, and there was definite abuse by the legion of volunteers who helped in the raids. These mistakes almost wrecked the fledgling unit which was to become the FBI in a few years.

The Red Raids also stood for many years as a bogeyman for the extreme left. Years later, as former FBI informant Herb Philbrick describes it, Party members were in a panic state as a result of a warning from O. John Rogge that:

> [Rogge's] ex-boss, Attorney General Tom Clark, was preparing to use a New York grand jury investigation on subversive activities as a springboard for the launching of a new series of raids against the Communist Party. Rogge said they would duplicate the notorious Palmer Raids of the 1920s. . . . The top brass scrambled for cover. District leaders fled the Little Building headquarters and ran into hiding out of the city, taking the party's important records with them . . . it was not until several days after that date that the party relaxed its vigilance and sheepishly emerged from the bushes. No one ever explained this raid which did not come off. The party crowed about its security system and took credit for upsetting the government's plans; but I, for one, was never convinced that any such raid was planned in the first place.
>
> The "Palmer Raid" scare brought new tensions into the party. We avoided the telephone. Notices of cell meetings became friendly invitations, such as, "Dear H. I am having a few people in Wednesday evening at eight. Hope to see you then. N." There was no address, and no full names were used.*

Thus about a quarter of a century later, the Reds still had the fear of the Palmer Raids like a Sword of Damocles hanging over their heads.

The Palmer Raids had been the cause of the comrades' flight into the underground in the first place, but they also persuaded a lot of innocent Americans, who had seen the Moscow-controlled Red organizations as something other than what they were, to drop their party affiliation. Party membership estimates

---

*Herbert A. Philbrick, *I Led 3 Lives* (Washington, 1972), p. 236.

plummeted from 60,000 to "a hard core of 10,000."*

It was during these early years that an unusual story was taking place beneath the social stratum—the tale of Agent K-97; Francis A. Morrow, alias Francis Ashworth. Morrow lived in Camden, New Jersey, with his wife and two daughters. He worked at the local shipyards as a shipfitter. Theodore Draper, in his book *The Roots of American Communism,* describes Morrow as "a short, slight man of nondescript appearance. Not quite forty years old [presumably around 1919], he seemed prematurely middle-aged, chiefly because of his graying hair.**

Though not in the image of Ian Fleming's James Bond, K-97's services were of great value to the Bureau of Investigation and the nation. Morrow had been a member of the Socialist Party, and linked up with the emergent Communist Party in 1920. His party name, according to Draper, was Comrade Day. Comrade Day, however, was, in addition to participating in an English-speaking Red group on one evening and attending a study class on another, moonlighting as a dollar-a-day employee of the Department of Justice. His occupation: an agent for the Justice Department dealing with subversive operations by the Reds.

Day *ne* Morrow *ne* K-97 became a section organizer by forming his own cell of five comrades in Camden and was recognized as an up-and-coming party functionary for his efforts. Actually the cell consisted of Day, Mrs. Day, his son-in-law and two friends, all in the service of the Department of Justice.

One of the most valuable services K-97 performed was helping a drunken Communist Party district secretary decode a message via a code key on an application blank for a U.S. postal money order. Quite naturally the secret found its way into the hands of the GID of the Bureau of Investigation. Thereafter the Reds' secret communications were opened to surveillance.

K-97's greatest service to the cause of internal security was

* Whitehead, p. 61.
** Draper, op. cit., p. 366.

yet to come. The bureau wanted inside information on an up-coming Communist Party convention, and K-97 was instructed to get inside the conclave. There was only one way this could be arranged, and this was to be named to the delegation by the Philadelphia-Camden district convention.

Day-Morrow-K-97 could only manage a third-place finish, thus becoming first alternate, which wouldn't have entitled him to attend the underground meeting unless a delegate could not make it for some reason. But K-97's luck held when it was de-cided that the district could send three delegates.

K-97 was unable to inform his Justice superiors of the loca-tion of the top secret meeting due to an intricate, road rally-like method of directions. Delegates were led to the meeting place by following instructions to various checkpoints which con-tained further directions to other points. The secret agent's roundabout trip took him first across the Delaware River to the City of Brotherly Love where at a Workers Party district convention, a CPUSA man aimed them toward Cleveland. In Cleveland, yet another party operative sent the three delegates on to Detroit. From Detroit, the delegates were told to go to Grand Rapids where they were given train tickets for St. Jo-seph, Michigan. But, before leaving Grand Rapids, Morrow fi-nally managed to get off a letter to Washington.

At that time, Jacob Spolansky, a Russian-born former army intelligence agent, was working as a Bureau of Investigation officer in the Chicago office. Spolansky received a terse message from bureau Director William J. Burns. The directive read: "Secret convention of Communist Party now in progress some-where in vicinity of St. Joseph, Michigan. Proceed at once to locate same and keep under discreet surveillance." Spolansky hopped aboard a train and arrived in St. Joe on August 18. He was accompanied by a fellow agent and friend, Special Agent Edward Shanahan.*

---

*Three years later, Shanahan became the first agent to die in the line of duty, shot to death by a professional car thief.

By questioning the local sheriff, writes Spolansky in his book *The Communist Trail in America,* the agents determined that the only place nearby big enough to accommodate a large secret rendezvous was Bridgman, a dozen miles away. So the two men accepted the local lawman's offer of a ride and made their way to Bridgman. In Bridgman they were told by the local postmaster that "a bunch of foreign-looking people...got off the train and went toward the lake."* So the FBI agents headed toward Lake Michigan in a heavy downpour, and met with success by happening upon a drunk wandering through the woods with a flashlight. The drunk was a party member.

Garbed in work clothing purchased in a Bridgman general store, Spolansky and Shanahan spent all of the following day attempting various means of getting a closer peek at the spot believed to be used as the "convention" site—a farm owned by Karl Woolfskill.** On Sunday, the 20th, they walked directly to the farmhouse and asked if they could be put up for a while. But Mrs. Woolfskill, a gaunt, middle-aged woman, told them there was no room due to an 86-member singing society that was taking up all available room, including barns. Spolansky and Shanahan certainly had found their prey.

Later that day, the hunted caught sight of the hunter in the woods on Woolfskill's farm. Spolansky was, in fact, spotted by one of the main targets of the bureau—William Z. Foster, one of the most militant Communist leaders, a man who rarely attempted to conceal his dedication to the Communist Party principles or his zeal in trying to ram these perverted ideals down the throats of Americans.

After sighting the overall-garbed agents, the Communists became suspicious and several of them fled, including, naturally, Foster. The Reds did not run like a pack of lemmings on their suicide trek, however. Instead, they chose to light out in an

---

*Jacob Spolansky, *The Communist Trail in America* (New York, 1951), p. 24.
**Spolansky uses the spelling "Woolfskill," but Draper spells it "Wulfskeel."

orderly high-man-first fashion. First out were the Comintern (Communist International) representatives, then the groups facing arrest on a variety of charges, and last the lower strata operators, including Morrow (K-97).

After checking with the Washington headquarters, Spolansky and Shanahan, who had been joined by four other agents arriving on Sunday and Monday, set the raid for Tuesday, August 22.* On that day, the net closed with the aid of about 20 volunteers from Bridgman. But all of the conventioneers had escaped except for 16 stragglers, some of whom had stayed behind to destroy incriminating documents. Naturally, K-97 was caught up in the dragnet.

When a fellow agent whispered to Spolansky that the Red who had identified himself as "Francis Ashworth" claimed to be K-97, the agent was caught in a dilemma. He didn't know K-97. Spolansky had the man brought to him. Morrow (K-97) identified his Philadelphia Bureau contact and told Spolansky that he had to get loose to retrieve priceless data on the convention grounds, including cables, coded messages, communications from Russia, and a vast amount of incriminating literature, including a valuable list of those who had attended the Bridgman fete. The special agent told Morrow he couldn't let him go, but he did send one of the other agents out to dig up two potato barrels containing the prize catch. Upon checking with William J. Burns, BI director, Spolansky was told to hold onto the "prisoner" and not to let him loose "under any circumstances." It was then Spolansky knew that the man in custody was indeed K-97.

When Morrow was finally released an elaborate scheme was concocted to supply him with a cover story. One of the local deputies was a doctor, and he bandaged Morrow as if he had

---

*Draper claims there were four agents in on the raid (p. 371). According to Spolansky's own account, however, there were six Bureau agents—Shanahan, Maurice Woolf, Louis Loebl, Charles Scully, Frank Fay and himself.

been badly beaten by the captors. Thus K-97 was given his freedom in exchange for a promise not to press "brutality charges" against his assailants.*

Spolansky was determined to track down the escaped Foster, and with an able assist from Chicago Police Department Detective Sergeant Lawrence McDonough, he did. The two men merely went to a known Communist meeting place in the Windy City, walked in and took over the session in progress. They exited with thirteen comrades in tow, including not only Foster but the man who would later become the Red kingpin in the U.S., Earl Browder.

In March of 1923, the captured Reds were brought before a judge, and the key witness was Francis A. Morrow, alias Comrade Day, alias Francis Ashworth, alias K-97. Just as would occur a quarter century later when that "good party member," Herbert A. Philbrick, would step forward and blow his cover as an informant for the FBI, Morrow was free to rejoin society without a stigma.

Morrow's testimony linked Foster and Earl Browder beyond a doubt to the Communist Party and the party, in turn, was indisputably linked with the masters in Moscow.

Draper said the trial showed Morrow was not the only member of the Red network who was feeding data to the bureau. He notes that at the trial of home-grown Communist Charles Ruthenberg, the accused was queried on a report the government had received about a secret party leaders' gathering in New York some seven months after the Michigan raid. "The incident seemed to confirm an insistent rumor in radical circles that the Department of Justice had a secret agent in the Central Executive Committee of the Communist Party," writes Draper.** The group was tried under Michigan's state syndicalist law.

However, penalties never actually burdened party officials. Only Ruthenberg was sentenced (to five years) but he died dur-

*Ibid., p. 372.
**Draper, p. 371.

ing an appeal from the case. The others remained in a legal limbo until all charges were finally dropped in 1933 by then attorney general of Michigan Patrick O'Brien, who had been active in the committee set up to help the defendants. Obviously, the affair was whitewashed.

These early BI efforts to protect the country from undemocratic forces were but occasional exceptions to America's otherwise secure belief that it was safe from the radicalism even then ravaging Europe. True, World War I sabotage had shaken this belief for a time. But neither the nation nor the Bureau of Investigation was prepared.

When Congress declared war on Germany in April of 1917, there were a mere 300 Bureau of Investigation agents on hand,* charged by President Wilson with overseeing the activities of over a million men registered as enemy aliens. And this in addition to the conduct of the other everyday tasks of the bureau.

Even with this handicap, however, within the first 24-hour period following the war declaration, 63 of these aliens were in custody. During the nineteen months of U.S. participation in the Great War, 6,300 were placed under arrest, though most of these were granted paroles.

Despite these arrests, the WWI period saw a toll wrought by saboteurs, including the bombing of Black Tom Island in New York Harbor on July 30, 1916, which shattered windows with shock waves that echoed a hundred miles away. John H. Lufbery, a now-retired resident of Rahway, New Jersey, which lies some 20 miles or so from the blast site, recalls having to eat outside the house at the curb because of the continuing blasts emanating from the island's two million pounds of dynamite. Three men and a child died in the holocaust.

Less than six months later, an explosion rocked Kingsland, New Jersey, home of the Canadian Car and Foundry Company, touching off about 500,000 3-inch shells at that muni-

*Whitehead, p. 23.

tions assembly plant.* The final estimated damage in these two sabotage acts: $50 million.** Yet there was no federal sabotage legislation that could be used against the perpetrators of the acts.

The bureau was not by any means asleep during WWI. In fact in contrast to present methods that attract criticism about the bureau going too much "by the book," the BI staged one particularly noteworthy raid on the neutral Swiss consulate in New York that would drive today's civil libertarians up the wall. Learning of valuable papers stored on the premises, BI agents bored through the walls into a storage room of the consulate to get them. Working hurriedly, they broke seals and tape from the packing cartons, removed the evidence and resealed the packages, leaving no trace of their evening incursion.***

Don Whitehead in his book *The FBI Story* notes that BI Division Superintendent Charles DeWoody reported that the books and papers obtained disclosed code methodology of the Germans, as well as data on securing information on delivery of war materials, and on the German intelligence network's activities in the United States from the outset of the war.****

The outbreak of WWII almost a quarter century later would find the FBI better prepared for countering internal subversion. And one reason for this could well be the chaos during the first war caused by the vigilante-like American Protective League (APL), organized by Chicago ad executive A. M. Briggs with the blessing of A. Bruce Bielaski, who headed the bureau from 1912 to 1919, and Attorney General Thomas W. Gregory.

Founded in March of 1917, the APL was intended as a means of shoring up the nation's security. Its purpose was to assist the undermanned BI. But, as is often the case, what works

*Editors of *Look* Magazine, *The Story of the FBI* (New York, 1947), p. 12 of introduction by J. Edgar Hoover.
**Whitehead, p. 29
***Ibid., p. 31.
****Ibid., p. 31 and 32.

perfectly in theory may fall far short of intent when put into practice. Many APL members abused their limited authority, using their seventy-five cent badges as justification for violating the rights of citizens sometimes guilty, but too often innocent, of subversive activities.

At its apex, the APL boasted a quarter-million members, the bulk of them non-active. Although the activist numbers were few, their effect was often fearsome. There was a spirit of vigilantism which swept the nation during the era of the league. One resultant act was the lynch-murder of Wobbly executive Frank Little by six masked renegades in Butte, Montana.

In contrast with the APL chapter in the bureau's history was FBI Director J. Edgar Hoover's position on requests for the re-institution of a similar group of private citizen-investigators. Hoover told the House Appropriations Subcommittee in hearings on the 1941 Justice Department funding that "self-designated groups . . . some of them super-patriotic in character, some very well-meaning, and again some selfish in that they have a desire to secure personal aggrandizement or financial gain" would not be acceptable volunteers for the bureau's counter-intelligence work.* Twenty years later the director expanded on this in the *FBI Law Enforcement Bulletin,* April 17, 1962. Hoover advised would-be G-men to: "Refrain from making private investigations. Report the information you have to the FBI and leave the checking of data to trained investigators."

At any rate, to the credit of the men in charge of the FBI, the APL was disbanded forever three months after the close of the First World War.

And after that war, the war that would end all wars, Americans again rested easy. The Palmer raids ended; so did the radical violence, by and large; and so did concern about domestic undemocratic forces—including the new and more sophisticated organization, the Communist Party.

*Harry and Bonaro Overstreet, *The FBI in Our Open Society* (New York, 1969), p. 37.

At the time, of course, no government agency had effective jurisdiction in security cases. The FBI had acted previously only because attorney generals had so directed it. A new attorney general, Harlan Fiske Stone, in 1924 ordered intelligence operations ended by limiting bureau investigations strictly to violations of the law. His new BI director, J. Edgar Hoover, determined that investigations of radicals could not be based on federal statutes and terminated any such operations.*

The early raids on the dens of radicalism, however, had driven the Communist Party underground. It was not until the Communist Third International and the new policy of "revolution now" that the domestic party again surfaced. It was then a depression era in the United States and the newly apparent activity of American Communists began to concern some officials once again. One of these, of course, was the man who had studied the Communists before 1920, J. Edgar Hoover. In 1936, Franklin Roosevelt, who had two years earlier directed the bureau to investigate the activities of agents for the foreign Nazi power, broadened the investigation. In discussions with the bureau director, FDR was apparently convinced of the necessity for continuing coverage of both Communist and Fascist activities in the political life of the country.

The bureau investigated the situation, starting in 1936, and supplied an intelligence picture which was to be the basis of President Roosevelt's 1939 order, as well as of new internal security legislation. As practiced to this day, internal security intelligence in this country was the personal brainchild of J. Edgar Hoover.

In this connection it is important to note that other U.S. agencies, namely the Department of State and the army, were available for domestic intelligence assignments. Had Roosevelt not chosen Hoover's agency, American domestic intelligence would probably have developed along considerably different lines under some other agency.

*Alpheno Mason, *Harlan Fiske Stone* (New York, Viking Press, 1956), p. 151.

Hoover's approach was that of a criminal investigative expert. This was evidenced at the outset by the instructions issued by the director to the FBI field offices pursuant to FDR's 1936 request. His instructions were "to obtain from all possible sources information concerning subversive activities being conducted in the United States by Communists, Fascists and representatives or advocates of other organizations or groups advocating overthrow or replacement of the government of the United States by illegal methods."* Hoover was clearly looking for evidence which would support federal legislation making certain modes of revolutionary or subversive activity illegal. This was the legal authority Hoover was searching for by which to counter the totalitarian movements.

Had the State Department, for instance, received the assignment, it probably would have formulated an intelligence mission concerned mainly with foreign agents, and it probably would not have looked for any legalistic crutch to justify action against domestic subversives.

The FBI's view of its assignment was also unmistakeably influenced by Hoover's (and others') conviction that the Communist Party was a puppet of Moscow, and thus not really in the same category as other domestic political groups.

This view certainly was correct as far as the Communist International was concerned. The policy of national party subservience had been firmly established at the 1920 Second World Congress of the Communist International (Comintern). At this congress delegates adopted the notorious 21 points required for admission to full status in the Comintern. Among these were: that all party publications must have Communist editors; if Communists cannot succeed legally "a combination of legal and illegal work is absolutely necessary"; propagandizing in the army must be conducted, even if prohibited by law; each party must foment and agitate in rural areas, within trade unions, workers' councils and other mass organizations; "parties be-

*Whitehead, p. 159.

longing to the Communist International must be built upon the principle of democratic centralism...[that is] organized in the most centralized manner," under "iron discipline" with leaders possessing power and authority; dissenters must be weeded out; "every party that desires to belong to the Communist International must give every possible support to the Soviet Republics in their struggle against all counter-revolutionary forces"; and "all decisions of the Congresses of the Communist International, as well as the decisions of its Executive Committee, are binding on all parties affiliated to the Communist International."*

Subsequently, these guidelines, or more appropriately chains, were strengthened. In 1921 the Comintern Executive Committee decreed that the national congresses must follow the Comintern congresses in order that decisions could be ratified by the national parties. This was tightened even further in 1922 with an edict that all Comintern delegates would arrive in the Kremlin uninstructed by their local congresses. Control was assured over the U.S. party when Moscow sent representatives to supervise U.S. Communist meetings, take part in decision-making and give orders to the local Reds in the name of the Third International.**

While over the years this policy has become more sophisticated, there has been really little to alter the chain of command. This was confirmed for Hoover on September 14, 1936, by the U.S. ambassador to France, William Bullitt, who had served as ambassador to the Soviet Union. Hoover later wrote, "Mr. Bullitt told me that the Communist leaders in Russia make every effort to put spies in all foreign government agencies, and particularly those agencies which are engaged in or charged with the responsibility of knowing about subversive activities. He made this statement in connection with the possibility of Communists entering the employ of the Federal Bureau of Investi-

---

*J. Edgar Hoover, *Masters of Deceit* (New York, 1959), pp. 52-53.
**Ibid.

gation."* (There has never been any evidence showing a successful infiltration of the bureau.)

Of course, domestic Reds are rather touchy about charges that they are Soviet puppets. In 1964, at Rutgers University in New Jersey, high-ranking CPUSA officer Arnold Johnson was asked by a student to name three subjects on which the U.S. party differed from the official Kremlin line. Johnson merely scoffed at the youth's query, calling it a foolish question, and called for the next question, probably with the hope that it would come from one of the friendlier members of the audience. To this day, the CP has no answer to this still-pertinent question.

Obviously something more than "fraternal relations" (the present CPUSA characterization) exists between the American Communist Party and the Kremlin. Thus, Hoover and the FBI could successfully apply the theory as justification for legal sanctions, which became the basis for the bureau intelligence operation.

Before 1940, however, legal sanctions were largely lacking, and while the intelligence was established on a continuing basis by Roosevelt's directive made public in 1939, Hoover's apparent idea of a proper intelligence mission was not yet in effect. Legal action against the Communists was possible in only very limited circumstances.

One such situation came about as a result of Communist efforts to recruit Americans for the Spanish Civil War. In 1936 when the war broke out, the forces of the pro-Communist Abraham Lincoln Brigade sent some 3,000 Americans to aid the Spanish Loyalists. Most of these men never returned. Those who did in many cases became enemies of the Communist philosophy; conversely, some became more firmly committed to that cause.

Many of the recruits were lured into taking part by various subterfuges, including promises of lucrative posts in Spain,

*Whitehead, p. 160.

cash, travel accommodations, even the sexual favors of young female adherents to the party. These actions by the radical organizations were in violation of the statute against recruiting U.S. citizens to fight in foreign conflicts. And in February, 1940 the Department of Justice and the FBI moved in.

The bureau's decision to conduct the raids on the brigade people at pre-dawn was to cause a furor, as seems to happen in any case involving the arrests of the Reds and their fellow travelers. But the feds took careful precautions to short-circuit the expected outcries. Doctors were on hand to examine the suspects—to prevent the charges of brutality. Breakfast and lunch were brought in while the Reds awaited the arrival of a federal judge. Between the meals agents sent out for refreshment for any who requested it. Moreover, anticipating possible charges of sex offenses, a matron was placed in charge of the one female arrestee.

Despite all the precautions, the Red agitators, with the aid of the ever-present newshounds who fawn over practically every criminal or enemy of society as a knee-jerk reaction, found their *cause célèbrè* in the fact that the defendants, excepting the lone woman, were brought into the FBI office in handcuffs. This policy had come into practice after a suspect two years earlier shot an agent to death. The real reaction, however, was against the handcuffing *en masse* to a chain by U.S. marshals, standard procedure in Detroit for large groups of arrestees. Many newspapers published photos of this as if the FBI had done it. The denials received scant publicity.

One of the arrested suspects was Harold Hartley, chairman of the Detroit Chapter of the International Labor Defense (ILD), described as the American section of the International Red Aid, headquartered in Moscow. Several knowledgeable witnesses have attested to the fact that ILD was controlled by the parent Moscow party. Later, on April 27-28, 1946 the organization was merged with the National Federation for Constitutional Liberties to form the Civil Rights Congress, which has also been cited by authorities as a Communist front group.

Harry J. Schweinhaut, head of the Civil Rights Division, Department of Justice, investigated the specified charges of agent misconduct for three weeks. The investigator obtained signed statements from 98 persons, including most of the defendants and their families. None of these statements was obtained by coercion.

The result: the G-men were completely cleared of any use of brutal or illegal arrest procedures or questioning or of denying the prisoners prompt access to counsel. It had been the decision of the U.S. attorney that the arrests be made simultaneously. He had so instructed the agents, because of a tip-off that at least some of the birds were ready to fly the coop in the case of an impending raid. In fact, there were already several members of the International Brigade in self-imposed exile in Mexico and four of the 16 indicted did in fact disappear before the FBI move. Additionally, the choice of the predawn hour for the round-up was to assure that all of the defendants would be at home. Only one defendant said any attempt was made to compel him to make a statement. The one aspect of the raids that might have left cause for doubt was in the seizure of certain evidence, and here too it was found that the agents were merely carrying out the U.S. attorney's orders.

The volatile critics of the FBI must have been pleased when the charges against the members of the Abraham Lincoln Brigade were dropped. But if it was the pleasure of having bested the FBI, the pleasure was short-lived at best, for Attorney General Jackson quickly set this idea to rest. Jackson fully supported the bureau, pointing out that the indictments were being dismissed for reasons completely removed from the FBI agents' conduct.

The bureau action in the Spanish Loyalist case was based on a statute peculiarly applicable to a specific activity of the Communists. A wider ranging authority came in the enactment of an amendment to the Hatch Act, the amendment becoming law on July 19, 1940. The Hatch Act, as amended, made it illegal for a federal government worker to belong to any political party or organization which preached the violent overthrow of our constitutional government—a reasonable prerequisite for remaining a member of any society where the citizens maintain the right to vote. Penalty for violation of the act was not imprisonment but rather simply dismissal, the theory being: why should the taxpayers finance those who would destroy their legally constituted government?

However, not all federal employees were investigated. The Hatch Act was not a blank check for witch-hunting. The only employees to be checked out were those who, for some reason or other, were subjects of complaints.

It is interesting to note that one of the favorite themes of bureau critics is that the bureau *could* misuse its power in some way or other. It is only on very rare occasions that one of the vocalizers cites a case in point, and even then their charges have never been proven true in the bureau's history.

At any rate, in reviewing the six years from the amendment of the Hatch Act to 1946, Hoover stated: "In some cases the bureau established that the employee was a member of the Communist Party and in some instances the employee admitted such membership. However, because the bureau was unable to establish membership in the Communist Party at the time the case was being considered by the employing agency, no administrative action was taken against the employee."* This was in all probability to protect those who in their youthful idealism had joined "cause" groups that turned out to be Red fronts.

This writer asked former "Communist" Herb Philbrick, who was feeding back data to the FBI all the while he was in the party, what precautions were taken to protect these innocent dupes.

"I've actually been called into cases to testify when there were some people innocently involved," said the noted expert on the

*Whitehead, p. 280.

Communist apparatus. "Many times I've been called in and put under oath in cases involving government security, jobs with government and immigration and naturalization. They would say to me, 'Here's the name of a person being investigated, and the record shows the fellow was once a member of the Cambridge Youth Council* or whatever, cited as a subversive organization by the attorney general. What about this guy? And I've often been able to testify that the fellow was an innocent dupe who didn't have any idea what was going on or that the group was Communist or Communist-controlled. In other words we've been able to clear the innocent through testimony."

Asked if this clearing testimony was at the request of the bureau, Philbrick said: "Yes. In fact each time that I'm called the bureau contacts me and says there's something coming up."

Philbrick's own case is an excellent example of a man getting involved in a Communist front group by accident. As a young salesman in Boston, Philbrick was sucked into the "peace" movement of his day—1940—only to later find it was not the kind of peace a 25-year-old American would want for his nation or his descendants. It was the kind of peaceful society that one may find behind an Iron or Bamboo Curtain; a peace where poets mouth hollow praise for the regime if they wish to continue their "free" expression; or where Jews are free to live their lives providing they shut themselves off from the religion of their forebears.

"Well, I found out this organization was infiltrated," said Philbrick, "and I decided to quit the thing. Then I figured the bureau ought to know about it. So I went to them, and they suggested I go back in to stay and see what else we could find out."

However, Philbrick's experience and expertise in the Com-

---

*The Cambridge Youth Council was the branch of the "peace" movement which Philbrick joined, only to find it was firmly in the grasp of the Soviets' domestic puppets. See *I Led 3 Lives*.

munist Party affairs was not shared by many government officials in the World War II era. For that reason, the Hatch Act provision was not effectively employed and Communist infiltration into government became an increasing problem. The FBI could do little, since its investigations of employees depended on requests from within the government agencies. This fault was repaired, but only after infiltration had become a scandal, by President Truman's and President Eisenhower's government employee loyalty programs.

Infiltration of Communists into government, moreover, was not FBI Director Hoover's first concern before then. Instead, he was aiming a knockout blow at the radical organizations themselves.

Director Hoover's theory of action, developed in the course of the 1936-1939 FBI investigation, was quite evident in the enactment of the Smith Act in 1940. This act outlawed conspiracies to overthrow the government by force, precisely the legal sanction Hoover viewed as a basis for proceeding against domestic subversives. It would, however, take nearly a decade before the FBI was ready to make its case.

In the meantime, the act was tested against a Communist splinter group, the Trotskyite Socialist Workers Party. FBI investigation resulted in a 1941 case against 18 members of the Socialist Workers Party (SWP), who had infiltrated a labor union. This FBI investigation was actually made easy by an internal feud in the labor union, as one-time SWP recruits became willing witnesses for the Department of Justice. The SWP defendants were convicted of unlawful conspiracy, and the convictions were upheld on appeal. The Supreme Court refused to review the convictions on three occasions.

It was not such easy going against the Communist Party, however. Information usable as evidence in a case against that party's higher echelon members was not sufficiently available. Then as now, the FBI was not infiltrating its own special agents into the party, and was therefore dependent on voluntary defectors or other informants like Herbert Philbrick. On the other hand, no few of these were available, particularly after the internal party strife in the 1930s and after the Communists were revealed as martinets in the Hitler-Stalin pact.

Former FBI Assistant Director Stanley Tracy tells of how the FBI utilized its informants. Tracy is in an excellent position to know of the inner workings of the bureau, having spent more than two decades as an inspector and as assistant director.

To FBI officials, the value of the informant cannot easily be measured. Tracy cited the example of Mary Stalcup Markward, a beautician who joined the Washington, D.C. section of the Communist Party at the request of the FBI in 1943. Mrs. Markward remained in the party until forced to end her informant-infiltrator career due to physical impairment caused by multiple sclerosis. During her term of membership the courageous native Virginian rose in rank within the party, eventually becoming membership director—a role which permitted her to leak the names of every single member in the D.C.-Maryland unit to the FBI. This, Tracy pointed out, led to a suspension of the use of membership cards by the Reds.

Mrs. Markward informed the FBI as to the various divisions of the party and the devious methods it used to protect its own from being uncovered, such as dropping from the party rolls those who might, if uncovered, lose their value—a procedure which might well have worked were it not for informant Markward. This "dropping" of members from the official rolls belies the view of those critics who stress the "wasted" time spent by agents looking into people who dropped out of the party. Fortunately, the bureau is run by pragmatic men who realize that the Communist Party is anxious to throw them off the trail by varied methods, such as the use of sleepers, followers who remain totally inactive for a time only to re-emerge when the heat is believed to be off.

In addition to the information Mrs. Markward gathered on the membership of the local party and its D.C. organization, the beautician also supplied a good deal of data on the use of various front clubs in different categories by the party. She named building trades clubs, students' clubs, civil rights clubs, and government workers' clubs—eighteen groups at one point which had been infiltrated and used by the Communists. Some, under the guise of being patriotic organizations, used such respectable names as the Thomas Jefferson Club or the Abraham Lincoln Club—names not exactly designed to produce images of Communist totalitarian front groups.

Stan Tracy said the FBI does not act merely on the strength of the data supplied by a single informant, except as a means to ascertain where further investigation is warranted. Instead, it compares data from different informants to see if they coincide or conflict.

Herb Philbrick, for example, said he had the impression on several occasions that there were other informants operating in areas where he was working. "Occasionally I'd run into something, and the bureau would say 'Back off! Stay away!' And this meant somebody else was already there," said Philbrick. The former undercoverman said he never knew if this meant another FBI plant was involved or, perhaps, an operation of another governmental agency, but he was aware that it was being covered.

As the Philbrick and Markward cases show, the FBI was in fact penetrating the CPUSA with informants during World War II, but the knockout blow was not ready. The government had higher internal security priorities at the time—Axis espionage and sabotage.

The internal security work of the FBI during WWII is probably the bureau's best chapter in the record of its efforts to protect democracy. The threat was obvious, and all concerned were aware that the Axis enemy would attempt sabotage and espionage. The FBI spared no effort, and greatly increased its manpower, at first primarily to assist in beefing up the security of our industrial plants.

The FBI had prepared a categorized list of Japanese aliens who might work for the enemy. Within three days of the declaration of war, the FBI had quietly taken into custody 3,846 enemy aliens. This was in contrast to the scandalous mass round up of some 120,000 mostly Americanized Japanese, ordered by Treasury Secretary Morgenthau.

Enemy sabotage and espionage were repeatedly thwarted by the FBI during the war. Kurt Ludwig, Hitler's prize spy, was trailed by FBI agents and caught. The bureau developed double agents, and it extended its operation to South America where intrigue matched any of the best spy thriller novels, with the FBI generally getting the best of the enemy agents. And German saboteurs failed entirely. One group was chanced upon on Long Island while landing from a U-boat. They thought they had talked their way out of the situation but became terrified as they mulled over their mission in a New York City hotel, and thereupon turned themselves in to the FBI. A quick investigation netted all eight of the enemy agents.

An episode told by a law enforcement officer active during the war illustrates the fact that many of the FBI internal security investigations were not quite so earthshaking as the celebrated cases above. Rep. John Hunt (R.-N.J.) prior to being elected to Congress in 1966 spent much of his adult life in police work, and is a graduate of the New Jersey State Police Academy, Harvard School of Police Science, U.S. Army Intelligence School, and the FBI National Academy. He was an officer in the New Jersey State Police's Criminal Investigation Division during the war and he knows first-hand what it was like to work with the FBI then. Prior to his enlistment in the U.S. Army, the congressman worked with federal agents on cases of suspected subversion, and he rates the bureau high, both in cooperation with local law officials and in protecting the innocent.

"They would come to us," said the Garden State lawmaker, "and ask us if we would make the investigation of a suspected subversive for them, either *in toto* or in cooperation with them, depending on how busy they were."

Sometimes these cases were amusing. Hunt recalled one instance in particular. "The agents did a fine job on him," said the congressman. "What actually happened was this man got into a Camden bar and started shooting his mouth off. Somebody called the local police when he began to shout, 'Hitler was right.' We went in with the FBI men and investigated. It just so happened I knew the fellow. In fact his son-in-law was a member of the police department there. He wasn't anti-American, he had offered to serve in the American Army immediately. He'd go fight for the Americans, but he wasn't going to fight for anybody else. But he was anti-Semitic. He didn't make any bones about it."

Hunt said the cantankerous old man, who spoke broken English, had served in the Austrian cavalry in World War I, then had come to the United States and raised his family. "When he was sober he was just the opposite. So we couldn't figure him out. Drinking made him a bigot," said Hunt. "When he was sober he was a patriot. Here was a guy with a split personality, but a nice fellow, raised a good family—law-abiding and whatnot. Got mad as hell because they came in and took him out of the bar room. He was really scorched. All he kept talking about was he paid for a drink and they wouldn't give it to him."

Critics of the bureau, during World War II, have gone on record accusing it of taking a more lenient posture regarding the Fascist left than against Communist left. In July of 1943, *The Nation,* which has made its anti-FBI fervor into a near-crusade, published a two-part article by an anonymous government worker, whose authenticity was vouched for by the leftist Washington editor for the magazine, I. F. Stone. In the attack by the civil servant, dubbed XXX by the portside publication, the FBI's investigators were accused of emphasizing possible Red affiliations of government workers rather than seeking out Nazi sympathizers. XXX said agents asked more questions about sympathy with labor unions, Jews and Negroes than with the Nazi-led Axis powers.

But mere opposition to the Hitler regime was of course not enough to ensure loyalty to the traditional free system of this Republic. And too many Americans believed that the Soviet Union was friendly merely because of the war alliance. The FBI knew the Communists in America posed a menace. It is common knowledge that the domestic Reds adopted a sort of instant patriotism—but only after Hitler broke the mutual non-aggression pact in June of 1941. But even this was only the surface image, the expedient "line." It is to the credit of the FBI that the battle against the visible enemy in Europe and its home-grown minions didn't deter the surveillance of our other foes who had become, of necessity, loyalists for the duration.

Nor was this duplicity of the Reds lost on their followers. In the wake of their whirling dervish act the party lost some 20,000 supporters, according to Whitehead. It didn't last, however, as by 1944 the party had recouped these losses with new recruits or returnees and membership reached an estimated highwater mark of 80,000. The bureau maintained an estimate of nearly a million Red front activists, some knowing, some unknowing. Meanwhile the party boasted that for every actual member there were ten willing followers. On the other hand, it was during this period that the party was being penetrated by people like Herbert Philbrick.

For nine years, Philbrick led his three lives — citizen, Communist, and informant. The cover wouldn't end until April 6, 1949, when it was revealed in a packed courtroom in New York City. There Judge Harold R. Medina, U.S. District Court for the Southern District of New York, would for the first time publicly hear the odyssey of the FBI informant. It was there that eleven Communist Party officials learned, as others have so often, that one of their "comrades" was not as dedicated to their doctrines as they had been led to believe. All eleven were found guilty and sentenced to the maximum five-year jail terms.

This, finally, was Hoover's and the Justice Department's knockout blow, based on the Smith Act's outlawing of conspiracies to overthrow the government. With the testimony of informants like Philbrick the case for conspiracy was proven, and upheld by the Supreme Court.

The successful prosecution sent the party into an apparent spin. "As a result, the party to a large extent went underground in the first large-scale underground operation since the early 1920s," wrote J. Edgar Hoover in his classic *Masters of Deceit*. "Party offices were closed, top party leaders went into hiding, records were destroyed. Courier systems were instituted and clubs broken up into small units, if not completely disbanded. For about four years, from mid-1951 to mid-1955, the party in protecting itself spent energy, time, and money that otherwise would have gone into agitation and propaganda."

Thus, Hoover's legal attack seems to have at least staggered the Communist Party. But the party was weak-kneed for other reasons too. Other things were not going well for their cause in the postwar period extending into the 1950s. For one, Communist infiltration and espionage rings had been exposed. Alger and Donald Hiss, both respected high government officials, were revealed as part of a Communist cell and Soviet espionage ring. The revelation exploded in an incredulous Washington when Whittaker Chambers, a Communist defector, testified before the House Committee on Un-American Activities in August, 1948. Others—Harry Dexter White, N. Gregory Silvermaster and Victor Perlo, for example—were similarly exposed by Chambers and another defector, Elizabeth Bentley.

Far from accepting the Communists as liberators of the American workers, the public had somehow gotten it in their heads that Communists were their enemies. The Fuchs-Rosenberg case did not help matters for the Reds. Fuchs and Julius and Ethel Rosenberg were ideological Communists and party members who, with David Greenglass and Harry Gold, had stolen and transmitted to the Soviets America's vital atomic secrets. Their convictions once again demonstrated Soviet Communist treachery in America.

The American mood in the period was precisely what the Communists feared most—the public was aware of Communist designs and did not want to tolerate Communists or others likely to be under Soviet influence in sensitive positions, governmental or private. This was later referred to as the "McCarthy era hysteria," deriving from the campaign of Senator Joseph

McCarthy to root out security risks (and Reds) from government agencies. It was indeed an "hysterical" period to those who insisted on tolerating Communists in government.

While this was happening, the FBI and the Justice Department were pursuing their legal war against the CPUSA. Seventeen second-string party members were subjected to a nine-month trial after the FBI meticulously prepared the proof that they were a part of a conspiracy to smash the U.S. government. Thirteen of the defendants were convicted when the jury returned on January 21, 1953.

In 1950, the McCarran Act was passed, creating the Subversive Acitivities Control Board. The act provided that organizations such as the Communist Party and its members had to register as agents of a foreign power. The FBI promptly prepared the case and in October of the same year the SACB was petitioned to compel the CPUSA to register. A long legal struggle was begun, ending only after the federal courts made prosecution under the act ineffective almost 15 years later.

All these things had the domestic Communists on the defensive for the first time in their history, although the organization was too intransigent to throw in the towel. The party was no longer "legit." Its membership nosedived to a hard core of no more than 20,000 by most estimates. Once-held dreams of leading the American proletariat in an uprising were put aside, and the party was not much of an influence on anything.

Nevertheless, toward 1960, the Communist Party began to re-emerge, at first cautiously but then more openly as their lawyers began pulling the teeth out of the Justice Department-FBI legal offensive—with the Warren Court's blithe cooperation. Then too, the New Dealers, who by the late 1950s represented orthodoxy itself, devoted great effort to hold back the wave of anti-Communism which had swept the land. It finally became safe once again for Communists to come out of hiding.

Still, the party had lost its leadership of the radicals and their movements. It remained for others to rekindle the revolutionary flame left smoldering by the CPUSA. The impetus of the Marxist ideology still advanced even though the organized party faltered, and the influence of the ideology, coupled with the lack of will of the Americans who should have combatted it, accomplished what the Communist organization could not. But that is a story for other chapters.

8. Internal Security Today
Editors

The voluble detractors of the FBI cannot understand why the FBI ought ever to have opened cases on many of the non-Communist radical groups. Among these detractors is another of the very few disaffected ex-agents, Robert Wall, who recently dropped out of the FBI, and more recently dropped out of the American mainstream, becoming first a leftist and then an emigrant. In his defecting process he bounced into the open arms of very radical Frank Donner, an old "Smith Act lawyer" and one of the organizers of the October, 1971 Princeton Conference on the FBI. At the conference, Wall "testified" to his outrageous ("naive," he said) conduct in the course of his security investigations with the bureau. His remarks were released in the *New York Review of Books* of January 27, 1972.

Wall places quotation marks around "security" when he refers to his former "security" work. This quite emphasizes his one and only offering: that, in his mind, FBI intelligence operations have little to do with internal security. The FBI, according to Wall, picks on "politically deviant" groups, which are in the opinion of the FBI a threat to the nation, but which to Robert Wall are nothing more than peace groups, and part of a political movement with which he cannot find fault. This characterization, to Robert Wall, is all that matters. If the target "peace" groups meet his approval, he can find "no rational criterion" for the FBI investigations.

Thus, the disaffected agent describes present-day FBI internal security work as no more than a strong arm mission against dissident leftists.

The bureau without a doubt has more comprehensive jurisdiction standards than Wall will admit, and one suspects that rather than being a serious critic he has succumbed to the class war mentality of his new-found new left friends. If so, one cannot entirely trust Robert Wall's eyesight and hearing, nor his recollections about the FBI. Events acquire untrue and sinister twists for such people, whose alienation from American society is so severe that their preconceived vision of truth dictates their mind's perception. Consider as an illustration of this phenomenon the female leader of the Philadelphia Resistance who complained to an ABC-TV commentator that one day, out of the blue, the FBI knocked on her door and trashed her apartment. She was sure in her mind that just that sort of brutal harassment occurred before her very eyes, but she neglected entirely facts needed for an objective view of the incident. For example, the fact is that the special agents requested entry to the premises with a search warrant. And it is fact that the agents conducted a legal search of the apartment after legally breaking through a door which the occupants would not open. But she perceived the event as pure harassment. The FBI was, to her mind, intimidating the Philadelphia Resistance, and search warrants, forced entries pursuant to such warrants, and subsequent (lawful) searches are matters her mind "lost" in quest of her vision of persecution.

Similarly, Robert Wall's version of FBI intelligence has been twisted in retrospect, according to his new-found leftist perception. He did not see any proper internal security purpose to the bureau's new left intelligence, because he did not see anything illegitimate in the target groups. He looked back on his work with the bureau and with this new perception, could view the effort as being only silly or sinister. But a serious student of the FBI cannot rely on Robert Wall's five senses for the facts.

A case in point is his revelations in the *New York Review* about the FBI investigations into the Institute for Policy Studies. He cites the institute investigation as an example of how there are "hardly any limits on the bureau's activities in compiling information, particularly information about the new left," implying that the IPS was no more than a legitimate think tank constituted of "former government officials, lawyers, journalists, radicals and others ..." who do no more than research, write, and talk. Wall credits himself for opening the FBI case on the institute, but wrote that after determining it was only a think tank, he closed the investigation.

But another agent reopened the case. In Wall's words:

> About a year later another agent newly assigned to the squad came to see me with the closed file of the institute and asked whether I thought the case ought to be reopened. This agent, like so many others, had strong right-wing views and could not believe that the institute was merely sponsoring seminars and doing the other work I had described. It seemed necessary to him to think that a grand new left conspiracy existed. In spite of my opposition, he had the case reopened and began a full-scale investigation of the institute. He began monitoring the checking account of the institute to determine where its money was going. He asked for telephone company records and compiled a list of the institute's long distance telephone calls. He attempted to place informants in the institute as student interns and gathered every available paper published by it. Individual investigations were then opened on the people who worked for or received money from the institute.
>
> When I left the bureau in April, 1970, the case on the institute was still being investigated with gusto, and a huge collection of papers and reports on it had accumulated. So far as I have been able to determine, the FBI has found no evidence whatever of any illegal activity by the IPS, but the institute continues to be investigated.

To Wall, the Institute for Policy Studies should never have concerned the FBI, and most certainly the bureau should never have monitored the organization as extensively as it did. If that position were to be accepted, however, one must have a standard substantially different from that which gives the FBI official jurisdiction to keep tabs on organizations like the institute. The IPS is, true enough, a think tank, and to be sure there is no evidence that the institute plans in the near future to lead a legion of new leftists into expanded, shooting, guerrilla warfare against established government. In that sense, the IPS is not in league with the more violent elements of the new left. But Wall ignored some things by implying that the organization has no deeper connection with illegal and illegitimate efforts of the new left than as an enclave of quiet leftist sympathizers prone to sitting in overstuffed chairs, tobacco pipes in hand, intellectualizing over the historical significance of it all.

In fact, IPS could be well characterized as a collector of armchair guerrillas, men whose revolutionist temperaments do not quite outweigh their emotional need for respectability within the society which torments them. This also happens to be about what the more militant new leftists think of IPS "research fellows." *Progressive Labor,* an organ of Progressive Labor Party (PLP), in August, 1971 labeled the institute "...a 'left'-liberal, pseudo-radical outfit supported by money from big foundations..." whose main purpose is to convince radicals to operate within the system. IPS is truly revisionist, in the PLP view, and the opinion is not too far from the truth.

If the IPS, with its Ford Foundation grants and its trustees drawn from high officialdom* has a measure of respectability, it has nevertheless sampled activity at the skirts of violent revolution. It thus serves as a sophisticated link between the respectable pseudo-radicals and the not-so-respectable new left with its disruption and violence. As such, IPS ought to qualify for some degree of FBI investigation, for to argue otherwise is only to say that police investigation cannot cover those who travel to and fro in the misty world between legitimate intellectualizing and overt revolutionary activity, the latter being more obviously the proper subject of an intelligence assignment.

The fact is, IPS goes to the brink just about everywhere its "senior resident fellow," Arthur I. Waskow, travels. Waskow,

---

*At various times IPS trustees have included: Richard J. Barnet, formerly with the State Department; Arthur Larson, undersecretary of labor under Eisenhower; Thurmond Arnold, former federal judge; Philip M. Stern, once deputy assistant secretary of state; and Marcus Raskin, aide to McGeorge Bundy in the Kennedy administration.

formerly an assistant to ultraliberal Congressman Robert Kastenmeier (D. Wis.) and once a staff member of the Peace Research Institute, joined the IPS staff in 1963. Since then he has helped plan several of the major disruptive new left-government confrontations of the past decade. These confrontations conform to a Waskow theory of street politics, as published in *Saturday Review* in 1965, that revolutionists will gain increasing acceptance as they force "tyranny" (i.e., the government) to stop the radical activities. It is not the intention here to overstate the importance of Arthur Waskow, nor of the IPS, to the militant radical movement; but Waskow *is* one of the strategists for the revolutionists' confrontation tactics, and he and the IPS must therefore share the blame for the resultant violations of public order.

While serving with IPS, Waskow developed close contact with the leadership of the then upcoming new left, including SDS, the New Mobilization Committee to End the War in Vietnam (New Mobe), and the National Conference for a New Politics, organized in Chicago in 1967 with his help. In league with such groups, he is credited with helping to plan the violent confrontation between demonstrators and Chicago police at the 1968 Democratic Convention.* But he had a neat distinction to offer the street demonstrators after the Chicago convention. He said the lesson of Chicago was "guerrilla politics—not guerrilla war." His strategy was to recruit new street demonstrators with a "political course of action, not new street tactics." The distinction may have assuaged the fears of his more moderate peers, but if they thought it meant he would encourage radicals to work within the system, subsequent history must have been a disappointment.

Instead of politics in the accepted sense, Arthur Waskow, with new left leaders Rennie Davis and Tom Hayden, Michael Lerner (a former SDS activist), and Sidney M. Peck (a former Wisconsin Communist Party official), developed a plan to "lib-

Barron's, February 13, 1969, page 9.

erate" the nation's capital. The plan was presented by Waskow and Lerner at a June 1970 "Regional Action Conference" held in Milwaukee. The strategy involved Waskow's guerrilla politics, which turned out to include such tactics as blocking the bridges and highways to the Pentagon and the CIA headquarters in an effort to stop certain functions of the government. This was the initial organization of the May, 1971 "Mayday" demonstration in Washington, D.C., which was quelled by the district police and the Justice Department only after mass arrests of about 12,000 demonstrators.

Perhaps it cannot be said that the foregoing is typical of the IPS involvement in the violent adventures of the new left movement. The fact remains, however, that the institute traffics in the same revolutionary substance which intoxicates all the less respectable revolutionists. For this reason, particularly important in an age of volatile movements bent on the nation's destruction, the FBI would be shirking its responsibilities if it ignored the institute.

On the other hand it would have been wrong for the Federal Bureau of Investigation to overreact. The IPS involvement with "the revolution" has not, according to any available evidence, been such as to merit, for instance, an attempt by the government to undermine or destroy the institute itself. But such has not been the nature of the FBI intelligence assignment of this case, Robert Wall's protestations notwithstanding.

In point of fact, the FBI investigation of the Institute for Policy Studies was and is a classic example of a low key intelligence operation gathering data on the non-Communist left. Even the stories told by Wall fit this mold, and he greatly exaggerated by implying otherwise. Quite probably special agents (as alleged by Wall) did monitor IPS checking accounts and telephone records, did once or twice seek to infiltrate informants, and did open investigations of IPS's staff and associates. Most certainly the bureau collected and continues to collect every IPS document and publication available. Yet these are not the techniques which could properly be characterized as investigating "with gusto" as Robert Wall said. It is a case of occasional low-level surveillance and intelligence reporting, and is in no wise preventive or restrictive of IPS activities. The IPS assuredly does not act "chilled."

Such considerations, of course, are not within the new leftist thinking of Robert Wall, who, well after leaving the bureau, all of a sudden determined that the FBI was trying to suppress a "broad-based national political movement," and therefore "acted as a national political police." For Wall, and other critics like him, it is enough that the movement, euphemistically labeled the "anti-war movement," was a political movement; police action against the movement was then *ipso facto* political police repression. But such criticism is not born of a reasoned analysis.

Granted that in one sense the "anti-war" movement was political, this does not establish that the FBI response was political. Nor does the assumption of impropriety necessarily follow even if the bureau response could properly be characterized as political. Yet it is precisely the propriety or impropriety of the FBI's investigation of the new left which is at issue, and the question must be answered on a more adequate basis than the *dégagé* use of the term "political" and the accompanying sinister assumptions in which Robert Wall deals.

The FBI unquestionably has ample criminal laws upon which to justify broad investigations into this "political" movement. The criminal violence so often a part of the movement's "politics" is itself an adequate basis for police action, both to obtain intelligence about forthcoming criminal violations, and to prevent them. But on this point, Robert Wall attempts to cover his trail a bit, saying that during his surveillance of radical groups he never once found any evidence "that would lead to a conviction for criminal violence."

What does this assertion prove? Nothing much. It does not demonstrate that the bureau's justification for his investigative work was a sham, for several reasons: a) the FBI may have reasonable grounds to believe that a target radical group is or will be involved in criminal violence; b) Wall himself may not have been able to uncover any criminal violence in which a target group planned to or actually did participate; and c) prevention of criminal violence is not the only proper objective of FBI penetration and investigation into radical groups. Leaving the last point till later, it is obvious that, after the highly visible violent twist which the anti-war legion took in the late 60s, law enforcement agencies had to concern themselves in some form with the movement. Robert Wall has to confess that he never noticed a thing, however; otherwise he could not characterize as a sham the law enforcement purpose of FBI radical investigations. Wall had to view the FBI efforts as a sham because he believed at the time of his confessions that the FBI was a national political police. His conclusion colors his proof.

By hiding criminal revolutionary violence behind a smokescreen of "politics," the bureau's enemies attempt to portray it as politically oppressive. By this argument they deftly ignore all the usual and proper law enforcement objectives of the FBI new left operations. Wall, for example, revealed what he thought was a more active FBI intelligence mission within the new left. He told of how the agents delighted in messing up movement rallies and of sowing dissension in the ranks of the new left. It has recently been revealed that the bureau had attempted such measures, but Wall's confessions were exaggerated.

He wrote for instance, that:

> A frequent tactic was to leak stories to the press and television shortly before any mass march or rally. This was easy enough to do. Agents in our offices would write often fanciful press releases warning that violence was expected on the day of the rally, or that the organizers of the march were in contact with Hanoi, or that some known Communists were active in organizing the march. Our superiors in the Internal Security Division at FBI headquarters would then pass on the information to conservative newspapers, which published it immediately. The purpose of such stories was not only to influence the general public but to scare away those whose commitment was weak and

thereby reduce the number of persons who might otherwise attend.

This revelation was a clue to a new policy at the bureau, a change that meant the FBI in 1968 began unwrapping the legal rationale which had sheathed its internal security operations for more than 30 years. And it was not the target of those years of criminal justice proceedings, the Communist Party U.S.A., but a new revolutionary phenomenon, the new left, which impelled the development.

Responding to what seemed at the time to be a dangerous wave of anarchy, violence, and revolution in the ostensible form of an anti-war and anti-establishment movement, the FBI in May, 1968, began affirmative counteraction against various segments of the movement. This was the basis of Counterintelligence Programs (Cointelpros) Internal Security—Racial Matters.* The apparent aim was to neutralize the threat. The means employed were to be disruptive counteractivity and exposure of the duplicity and deviousness of the organizations and their leaders.

Wall wrote about another FBI active intelligence operation seemingly from personal knowledge. He said:

> In one case we addressed a letter to the leaders of the National Mobilization Committee (NMC) which said that the blacks of Washington, D.C., would not support the upcoming rally of the NMC unless a $20,000 "security bond" was paid to a black organization in Washington. At the same time we instructed some informants we had placed in the black organization to suggest the idea of a security bond informally to leaders of the organization. The letter we composed was approved by the bureau's counterintelligence desk [sic] and was signed with the forged signature of a leader of the black group. Later, through informants in the NMC, we learned that the letter had caused a great deal of confusion and had a significant effect on the planning for the march.**

*Memo from Director, FBI to SAC, Albany, May 12, 1968, (released to public, December 6, 1973).
**Washington Post/Potomac, March 5, 1972, page 36.

The New Mobe rally to which Wall referred could only be the November 15, 1969 "March on Washington," which was sponsored by NMC and participated in by extreme factions of the SDS, the American Friends Service Committee, and a number of other more moderate antiwar activists. The March on Washington occurred near the peak of an increasingly disruptive and violent nationwide anti-war—i.e., revolutionary—movement. The Washington demonstration was intended as a forced "moratorium" on the war, and aimed at disrupting the capital city. The New Mobe demanded "no business as usual," seeking a general strike of sorts. Here was a clear threat to federal government operations, and the Nixon administration decided that the march would not be handled simply as another demonstration. The potential disruption was too massive, and the Justice Department did not mean to permit it. Instead, Justice decided to confront the situation head on, trying to disrupt the demonstration itself.

A cointelpro-type operation was implemented. The FBI attempted, by using fake letters, to split off the Washington black peoples' organizations from the radical New Mobe leaders. But contrary to Wall's contention, rather than being a common FBI practice, it marks the first known example of a departure in FBI methods against the left.

Additionally, the FBI engineered public disclosure of the pro-Communist and far-left connections of the confrontation organizers. This was done by getting the information (which, incidentally, had been previously exposed by writers and public admissions of those involved) to a party in the administration who could be expected to pass it along to reliable columnists. This the individual did, passing the information to columnist Roland Evans, who with Robert Novak, in their November 12, 1969, column blew the cover off the Communist and Trotskyite organizers of the confrontation.

The decision actively to counter the Washington demonstrations was the sort of affirmative mode of response to a revolutionary threat which is classic counterintelligence. It was a qualitative change, resting on the assumption that the government was entitled to use extra-legal resources to interfere in the revolutionary affairs of the left.

Yet, because they did so in this case by no means demonstrates that similar active measures are frequently applied against radicals. There is only one other Washington confrontation that was treated similarly, and that was the May, 1971 "Mayday" demonstrations in that city, an affair which even more justifiably called for affirmative and preventive action by the government. These two instances are in fact exceptions, and fairly drastic departures at that, from past FBI practice in its new left intelligence.

Robert Wall intends to portray a Federal Bureau of Investigation which was involved in a political-ideological war against the American left. His picture is false. The FBI has not contended with any part of the radical movement in that fashion. The fact is, the FBI has conducted its security intelligence mainly along the lines of a law enforcement operation.

Yet, the initiation of the Cointelpro-New Left program, on May 12, 1968, clearly marked a new FBI emphasis on the non-Communist new left. How did this change occur?

To be sure, it was resisted by J. Edgar Hoover. There was a policy dispute at the highest levels. Assistant to the Director William C. Sullivan, who was in charge of all investigations, was the primary advocate of the new emphasis, and was certainly responsible for Cointelpro. He was removed from the bureau in October 1971, as the result of a dispute which it now appears was intermeshed with the ending of Cointelpro as a continuous program. The intelligence operation was being implemented outside the FBI by the White House, and probably was the cause of a dispute between Hoover and the White House.

Sullivan, understandably, has not revealed quite what his policy differences were with the late director. Oddly, at the time of his removal from the bureau, the media had the story turned around.

As a *Washington Post** story goes, the former assistant to the director was an advocate of a new approach in domestic intelligence, which theory is probably accurate to this point. Conflict arose, according to this report, in that J. Edgar Hoover was not happy with Sullivan's concept of internal security investigations, which is probably not quite accurate. But the *Washington Post* speculated further that in the early 1960s Sullivan argued to change the FBI's intelligence emphasis from the Communist Party to the Ku Klux Klan and the like, which is ridiculous, even though he did reason that such right-extremists deserved more FBI attention.

What was inarticulately reported by the *Washington Post* was that Sullivan had a more sophisticated concept of domestic leftists than did Hoover. Sullivan is quite knowlegeable on the subject, of course. However, the *Post* and others add a bit to the former bureau official's viewpoint, an interpretation consistent not with Sullivan's situation but rather with the anti-witch-hunt syndrome of the *Washington Post* writers and others. Those afflicted with this syndrome think Hoover saw a Communist under every bed (to employ a hackneyed phrase), an attitude in seeming contrast to the fact that Sullivan advocated de-emphasizing Communist intelligence in favor of something else, and favored greater concentration on crime (he advocated other bureau changes as well).

The *Post* misread the situation entirely. William Sullivan did seek intelligence emphasis different from J. Edgar Hoover's emphasis on the Communist menace. Granting this, it can in no wise be said, first, that Sullivan pooh-poohed the internal security threat from the extremists of the left, and second, that he incurred his boss' wrath for the change in emphasis he sought.

Actually, Bill Sullivan advocated a more sophisticated operation against the left, de-emphasizing the capital "C" Communist Party dominance of the movement. Far from being removed

---

*Washington Post, October 3, 1971.

for that advocacy, he *prevailed* and the FBI in fact adopted his approach in large part, in Cointelpro.

The unbelievers scoff at a straw man when they deride the FBI's and Hoover's concern for the "Red menace." Themselves still living in the "McCarthy era," these critics insist that the FBI today is still chasing down non-existent Reds in the radical movement, implying that the object is to taint legitimate dissent with the Communist label. That was never done unfairly by the FBI or its director, but the critics miss the further point that the "Red menace," Communist subversion and the like, is no longer the primary justification for bureau action against the left that it once was. For years, no high official of the FBI, including its late director, has viewed the present radical movement as a Communist problem. The bureau's official position is that under the laws and executive directives given the agency, the FBI internal security objectives are the Communist Party and related organizations, and "totalitarian organizations." The Communist movement is a prominent objective; yet totalitarian groups are listed independently, and other subversives are targets on two separate bases: (1) threatening the violent or forceful overthrow of the government; and (2) conspiring against the rights of other citizens.

J. Edgar Hoover's testimony presented to the House Subcommittee on Appropriations on March 17, 1971 illustrates the FBI view. Introducing the subject of internal security, Hoover said:

> The FBI experienced a sharp increase in investigative work in the internal security area during the past year. New left and black extremists stepped up their violent and terroristic tactics. Old-line Communists revived efforts to influence the American people and Communist countries intensified their intelligence operations targeted against the United States.

He then detailed activities of the "revolutionary left," namely the Students for a Democratic Society, Weatherman, Venceremos Brigade, People's Coalition for Peace and Justice, National Peace Action Coalition, Resistance in the Army, the Communist

Party USA—the party being named as one among many—Progressive Labor Party, Black Panther Party, Student National Coordinating Committee, Nation of Islam, and other general listings labeled as "Other Terrorist Groups," and "Local Black Extremist Groups," including also "Klan-type Organizations" and "Other Hate-type Groups." Communist background is not mentioned other than for the PLP, where Hoover notes the *sentimental* connection of that party to the Chinese Communists, and for the Black Panthers, where Hoover mentioned their own brand of Marxism. With such scant mention, this presentation was hardly an attempt to blame organization Communists for all revolutionary activity in the nation; rather, it was an accurate portrayal of the nature of various radical groups, with emphasis on their terroristic action and their sympathies with foreign and Communist movements.

Hoover's statement in 1971 was markedly different in emphasis from testimony he had given on the internal security subject in earlier years. The point is, the emphasis in 1971 was essentially the emphasis William Sullivan advocated. In fact, Sullivan was responsible for preparing this part of the statement, according to ex-FBI personnel who note that he would have been expected to do so as assistant to the director in charge of all investigations—intelligence and criminal. That being the case, it appears that, at least by 1971, Sullivan's sophisticated view of leftist organizational dynamics was officially recognized in the bureau; and if his view of the problem and threat was accepted, then he must have also changed to a degree the FBI's investigative emphasis—but not, of course, in a way the *Washington Post* would have accepted.*

It would appear, then, that criticism of the FBI's enchantment with the "Red menace" is in error, or at least is itself outdated. The FBI has recognized the existence of the so-called "new left," it has correctly analyzed the radicals' independence

*One of Sullivan's ideas was that more FBI manpower be put on Soviet-bloc espionage in this country, which was done as well.

of foreign discipline, and it has determined quite accurately the revolutionist and terrorist nature of the movement.

The changed emphasis became necessary as the radical threat changed. As a Communist menace, the left was the domestic adjunct of a foreign danger, international Communism. Communists and their followers did the bidding of a potential enemy power, and on that basis it was within the legitimate police power of the United States government to investigate the movement continuously for internal security purposes. This was the primary rationale. Now, when the revolutionists seem to seek this nation's destruction without direct assistance or at least without waiting for orders from abroad, the rationale would be inadequate. This is implicitly recognized in the bureau's present emphasis on the violence and violations of democratic processes promulgated by the new left. The primary basis for responding to these threats is that the government and the people are entitled to reasonable measures of protection from domestic totalitarian forces, illegal acts of intimidation, and, of course, terrorism. More than a new emphasis, this is a qualitative change, dictated by the same in the radical movement.

The question now is whether the new emphasis has resulted in more appropriate and sophisticated investigations of the new internal security threat. First, let us explore the FBI techniques when the Communist Party is the primary target.

FBI Communist Intelligence

The CPUSA remains an FBI target, of course. The bureau does not even have the authority to decide that it should *not* be. The FBI cannot on its own volition terminate its investigative jurisdiction, a point which it seems must repeatedly be brought to the attention of some of the bureau's detractors. It can be noted that various of the laws and executive orders provide the FBI ample and obligatory authority for broad and continuing investigations into the CPUSA and related organizations. Courts have limited the scope somewhat, but none have gone so far as to determine that the Communists are not properly the target of general investigation.

It remains to be determined whether Cointelpros meant any significant change in FBI intelligence practice. However, the programs underscored a qualitative change in the bureau's domestic counterintelligence *modus operandi.* From a unique criminal investigative operation, the bureau moved toward the more commonly understood counterintelligence operation, which is counteraction. Cointelpro envisioned no criminal prosecutions of the intelligence targets, but instead involved extralegal action designed to deny the target groups their revolutionary aims. This was quite different in principle from the internal security domestic intelligence which J. Edgar Hoover had developed in the 1936-1939 period, which was incorporated by implication into the 1940 Smith Act. The act supported the 1950s prosecution on criminal charges of the higher echelon Communists and the party itself, but it was killed by the Supreme Court in the 1960s. For thirty years the legal basis of the FBI's domestic internal security intelligence had been the notion that Communists and subversives acted in violation of specific laws and could therefore be prosecuted in the courts. In 1968, the FBI recognized a broader principle of government power and duty, and began conducting counterintelligence operations independent of the prosecutorial notion.

It was a step which had to be taken, but which J. Edgar Hoover and the FBI had long resisted in their domestic intelligence. To understand this, we need to assess the situation of the FBI's internal security domestic intelligence at a time just preceeding the 1968 development, when the FBI conduct of the mission remained in the criminal justice style.

This was the style of operation against the Communist Party U.S.A. It can be noted that various laws and executive orders provide the FBI with ample authority for broad and continuing investigations into the CPUSA and related organizations. The courts had by the early 1960s severely limited the sanctions against the party and its members—removing any hope of effective prosecution. But none had gone so far as to determine that the Communists were not properly the target of general investigation.

The purpose of the bureau's investigations of Communists had been twofold, both aspects requiring a continuing or open-end surveillance. First, it was intended to support prosecution for criminal offenses—violation of the Smith Act or the SACB order to register, or involvement in some other criminal conspiracy. Secondly, it was intended to guard the security of government operations against infiltration by a group which was demonstrably the domestic arm of a foreign power.

But even regarding the latter function, the nature of the bureau investigations was basically of the criminal investigative sort. The FBI did not treat American Communists as foreign agents or spies; FBI agents did not go deeply undercover within the Communist movement for disruptive operations. Rather the FBI respected the procedural rights of domestic Communists as for all citizens, and proceeded against them generally in the manner of a law enforcement agency acting only to secure obedience to the laws. It was not a full scale counterintelligence operation that, in intelligence parlance, would have involved tactical, strategic, and disruptive activities of undercover agents.

Originally, the Communist investigations had been designed to support prosecutions which would cripple the CPUSA. Instead, as we have seen, this mission was instead itself crippled by the Supreme Court. Additionally, by the middle 1950s, the operation of government security—removal of security risks by government loyalty boards and like agencies—had become a routine matter, supported by the information in the bureau's Communist files, but not otherwise heavily involving the FBI. What then, could remain as the operating purpose of the CPUSA investigations?

The answer is that the FBI's remaining practical purpose was simply penetration for the sake of penetration. The bureau had continued to penetrate (via informants) the Communist Party, not in order to disrupt or dissolve the party, nor always to uncover illegality, but for the sake of penetration itself.

Bureau investigation of the Communist Party involves everything from reviewing public statements of the party officials to developing informants in the party's high councils; but the purpose is simply to determine what the party is doing, who is involved, and what other "innocent" groups are drawn into the Red net.

Communist intelligence, it should be noted, often involves FBI contact with non-Communists and non-Communist organizations. In these cases it is the Communists who remain the target, not the others. Other cases involve non-Communists in their own right, but here the FBI objectives are changed somewhat. In the bureau the demarcation is between the "old left" and "new left," as explained in detail in the section on non-Communist domestic intelligence.

For example, the American Friends Service Committee, a Quaker political group is non-Communist, and usually does not act so as to merit investigation, but it has been subject to continuing FBI intelligence of a sort. The reason is that the Communists attempt to use the organization, and the FBI is responsible for watching such efforts.

Continuing intelligence against the Communists involves in practice a large amount of file maintenance. Open files are kept up to date on the whereabouts and activities of known Communists. An open file means that, unless intelligence data pertinent to a case comes to an agent's notice in between time, the file is reviewed periodically (or the case re-opened) every 90, 180, 270, or 360 days, depending on the priority category of the file. Informants are checked or short-term physical surveillance is undertaken in order to determine whether the Communist or ex-Communist remains active, is again active, or otherwise. The agent then recommends a priority status for the case and closes it again. He will also either certify that the subject should be continued in the active files or report that the case should be dropped entirely. It is a routine; it fills the files; but it is the most important practical aspect of any valuable intelligence assignment.

Inside informants, of course, are the most important element in the FBI Communist Party intelligence. However, the number of informants in the party is not necessarily the most accurate measure of the degree of penetration. It is the quality of information that results, as one informant in a key position may have access to more of the party's secrets and membership information than a hundred more casually connected informants. An estimate of the degree of FBI penetration is impossible, and the figure will change from year to year.

In fact, no reliable information has ever been made public as to even the number of informants within Communist organizations. In 1962, former agent Jack Levine took a sensationalized stab at a figure, saying that the FBI had in 1961 nearly 1,500 informants within the party.* The CPUSA then had fewer than 10,000 formal members. In this critical statement Levine, who had been a special agent for less than one year, intended ridicule of the bureau. But he succeeded only in demonstrating his actual lack of intimacy with bureau work, which intimacy he was selling to *The Nation* Magazine as his credentials for criticizing the FBI. The 1,500 figure he cited was fantasy.

Levine had no way of knowing how many Communist informants the FBI had. No mere special agent is privy to that information and only a few high ranking bureau officials could make such an assessment. A writer intending sincere criticism of the bureau would have had to admit this fact. Instead, Jack Levine found headlines with the sensational figure, cited as if it were a known fact among agents.

Whatever the number of informants the FBI does have, the bureau appears satisfied with its success in obtaining them, at

*_The Nation_, October, 1962.

least in the lower echelons of the Communist Party. It is probably true, as Jack Levine reported,* that the FBI director in
1960 ordered a slowdown in recruitment of Communist informants, except for any which could be obtained at high policy-
making levels. This order illustrates FBI recognition of the
point made earlier: the number of informants is not what matters; it is the intelligence material they can develop which is
the continuing need in the bureau's view.

The Communist investigations are the responsibility of the
Domestic Intelligence Division of the FBI. This would imply
that the usual sort of intelligence work takes place. But again,
in practice the bureau conducts the assignment more on a law
enforcement model, which severely limits an intelligence function in the commonly understood meaning of that function.
As an example in contrast, the foreign security work of the
Central Intelligence Agency and the military includes intelligence operations more active in nature than penetration and
information gathering, although the latter is the primary effort. Sometimes in CIA or military foreign intelligence work
agents undermine enemy forces, support counter-forces, and
initiate counter-agitation. This is a full intelligence operation—
in intelligence jargon, one which includes *tactical, strategic,* and
disruptive activities of undercover agents. Coercion and blackmail are accepted tools of the profession. This is in contradistinction to the FBI Communist intelligence which has no similar mode of operation.

To be sure, the bureau has at times utilized its Communist
insiders—its informants—to play tricks on the party.** The special agents to whom the informants report are at times quite
happy to encourage their contacts to mess up whatever they
can (without risking the party's suspicion). In the real world,

---

*op. cit.

**In Jack Levine's *Nation* article, he reports that one Communist Party infor-
mant, who was responsible for the party's own security, framed loyal party
members as FBI agents. Levine is again reporting only agent scuttlebutt, but
the story is not unlikely.

this is not an unexpected occurrence. FBI agents are, after all, the ideological enemies of the Communists. Yet, more often the FBI informants are discouraged from such affairs, since the bureau considers them informants, not counter-agents, and wants information, not clandestine adventures. However, one point stands out: bureau policy has never allowed FBI special agents themselves to go into deep cover missions.

Objective observers would have to agree, moreover, that such indiscretions as did occur were of a different mode than the "active intelligence" operation sometimes practiced in foreign intelligence work. Informants in the party are invariably volunteers, often well-meaning radicals who have been approached by Red recruiters.* Higher echelon informants are nearly always defectors,** and arrive at the FBI doorstep in small droves after Communist International squabbles and unpopular Soviet misadventures, such as the Soviet invasion of Hungary and the Mideast conflict. These are the FBI's informants. The bureau has not blackmailed, threatened exposure, or otherwise intimidated them into becoming informants. They come to the FBI, and that is evidence of a more passive intelligence operation than might be employed.

In fact, some FBI special agents have been frustrated at this restraint, which they view as lack of aggressiveness in the intelligence field. They lament the fact that the bureau does not often develop "defectors in place," intelligence parlance for informants recruited while active in the target organization. A gentle operation does not succeed at this, since Communist activists are generally ideologically motivated and cannot be appealed to on gentle terms. To obtain defectors in place, the agents would have to get nasty. They will not, primarily because the bureau under J. Edgar Hoover would not permit an active, full-scale intelligence operation. The point is, this is the

*Herbert Philbrick and Boris Morros are prominent examples of these.
**Whitaker Chambers and Elizabeth Bentley were valuable defectors who contacted the FBI.

conduct more of a law enforcement agency than of an intelligence agency.

It is also the conduct of a police unit which as a matter of policy has a high respect for the procedural rights of its targets, even sworn enemies of the nation, and even if the bureau thinks them undeserving. If domestic intelligence were conducted actively in the sense foreign intelligence is, domestic Communists would be subject to direct and immediate sanctions, without regard for the procedural niceties which are involved by proceeding against them through the criminal justice system. No other country deals with a substantial domestic revolutionary element as a law enforcement problem, and it is a mark either of the FBI's respect for the American system of political rights or of its caution that the Communist investigations are conducted on the law enforcement model.

Still, given the authority, the Federal Bureau of Investigation would surely undertake a more active intelligence mission against the Communists, for the present intelligence experience is largely a frustrating one. It is frustrating not because the FBI has been unable adequately to penetrate the Communist Party—it has accomplished that—but because the bureau is constrained not to deal the party the death blow which a more complete intelligence operation might permit.

Attempts to prosecute the CP have ultimately failed over the years. In the 1950s, the Justice Department and the FBI did prosecute the top leadership of the Communist Party in an attempt to dissolve the party. As a prosecutorial effort it again conformed to the law enforcement mode of operation, and ultimately served mainly to demonstrate that the approach would not work. Between 1949 and 1961 FBI investigations resulted in the conviction of 109 top Communists,* 104 of whom were tried under the Smith Act provision against teaching or advocating the overthrow of the government. A 1957 Supreme Court decision** let most of the convicted Communists off the

*1962 Report of the Attorney General.
**Yates vs. United States 354 U.S. 298 (1957).

hook, and only 29 ever served any time in prison. Today, Supreme Court rulings effectively preclude prosecution of Communists, although they may occasionally be prosecuted under general criminal and criminal conspiracy statutes.

It is arguable whether the prosecutions and convictions of Communists would have been effective even had the Supreme Court cooperated. True, the CPUSA apparently feared the legal proceedings, and after the *Dennis* case, in which 11 national Communist Party officials were convicted (convictions which were upheld in the Supreme Court case *Dennis* vs. *United States* 341 U.S. 494 [1951]), the party hierarchy went into hiding and the party members went underground. The CP membership rolls also stagnated in the period, but that is more likely the result of the anti-Communist climate in America at the time than of the Justice Department's legal effort. Whatever effect the prosecutions did have, the fact remains that they did not foil the CPUSA, which continued functioning as before. This is true despite the fact that the prosecutions were permitted by court decisions at least for a period of five years.*

The results of Communist prosecutions necessarily would have been spotty and long delayed by defense attorney maneuvers, even if the Supreme Court had upheld the convictions. In the meantime, the party had ample time to organize around the legal proceedings, selecting a second string leadership and avoiding further prosecution by submerging. In no way could the prosecutions have decimated the party, and the cost of the FBI intelligence apparatus was the surfacing of too many informants. The bureau risked blowing its whole operation every time a defense attorney demanded that a judge authorize a peek at the FBI files.

Because of such problems, coupled with changing political situations, FBI investigations of Communists since 1957 have not resulted in prosecutions of party members under the

---

*Although most of the convicted Communists remained free for years as their cases were appealed.

Smith Act. The government continued to proceed on a different path, still with prosecution in mind, seeking to force the party and its members to register with the Subversive Activities Control Board.* After a decade of legal maneuvers, a hint of success appeared when the Supreme Court in 1961 upheld the validity of the order to register.** But even this hope was dashed when a lower federal court later ruled that the party or its members could not be punished for failing to comply with this same SACB order. Not giving up, the Justice Department produced two FBI informants in the party who were willing to register, and retried the case, winning another conviction of the party for refusal to register. However, when the Court of Appeals reversed the second conviction, the Department of Justice hung up its gloves.

More than 15 years of legal battling against the CPUSA thus ended in dismal failure. Cointelpro was a change, but designed not to bust the party. Rather, it meant to separate the CPUSA from the new left.

It should be noted that we have been referring here to the FBI penetration of the Communist Party, and not the counterespionage work of the bureau, where the FBI mission is decidedly less delicate toward its targets, and the results less frustrating. Nowadays CPUSA intelligence involves only peripheral contact with espionage operations. This is so, incidentally, at least in part due to the FBI penetration of the party.

A Soviet espionage apparatus exists, but is dependent on the CPUSA only for recruitment of occasional spies. The American Communist Party does not control the espionage work, nor does it contribute significant numbers of spies, for the simple reason that they cannot be trusted to perform secret spy missions. One reason they cannot be trusted may be that the Soviet GRU knows American Communists to be generally inept; but another is that an espionage apparatus dependent on CPUSA

---

*Pursuant to the Internal Security Act of 1950 and the Communist Control Act of 1954.

**Communist Party vs. SACB 367 U.S. (1961).

members would surely be uncovered by the FBI—as a result of the heavy penetration of the party. This may be an indirect result of FBI Communist intelligence (doing little to dispel its other frustrations), but it is an important one.

The FBI penetration has had another indirect but important impact on the American Communist Party's potential to harm the nation—it has greatly reduced the Communist capability to affect American government policy. Again, this may be inadequate considering the results the FBI, if empowered, could accomplish with more direct action against the party, but it is a major historial accomplishment.

The American Communist Party has in the past attempted to affect American policy by means more immediate than appeals to public opinion and fomenting revolution. The party would like to do both, of course, but a Communist underground has more immediate and obtainable goals in mind, aims that fit short-term Soviet foreign policy. The Soviets expect their American underground to impede, perhaps seriously, perhaps even entirely, American government efforts which oppose Soviet and Communist designs in the world.

The means to that end employed by the Communist underground are not well understood, particularly by those most closely affected. For one, Communists have at times infiltrated government agencies where they can influence or directly formulate American policy in favor of Soviet strategies. Few people want to think that an American would perform such a function for a foreign government (they do not even want to think America is in a conflict), but it was done by such as Alger Hiss, Harry Dexter White and others who came to light in the post-World War II days and early 1950s. Today we hear scant mention of any who have infiltrated the government as Communists, reflecting several things: (a) the mania of present orthodoxy against so-called McCarthyism; (b) the utter willingness of non-Communists in the government voluntarily (if unknowingly) to serve Soviet strategy; and (c) on the positive side, increased awareness of the problem by responsible government agencies including the FBI. This is one area where the country has adequate laws safeguarding internal security.*

The American government control of infiltration has been largely successful. This would not have been possible without FBI penetration of the party, which dovetails with the security laws and government employee loyalty programs. For these programs, the FBI information on Communists which is routinely entered in the FBI files is routinely made available to other requesting government agencies in name checks by the Civil Service. It is a simple procedure which reduces in government jobs the number of foreign agents and those under their influence. The FBI itself conducts more thorough security investigations of persons being considered for employment in designated sensitive positions. By law, security risks are not entitled to serve in such positions, although it is not the FBI which decides the merits of each case.

The FBI's participation in government employee security programs has been a success in keeping Communists out of the government since 1950. In another area, however, success has been denied. The Communist Party has long aimed to infiltrate and dominate other organizations in this country. Penetration of the party has not impeded that effort in the last decade. Functioning primarily as a law enforcement agency, the FBI had been able to do little about this problem, for the laws which could deal with it are lacking or unenforceable.

Identification of Communists and uncovering their infiltration into legitimate groups has long been an object of FBI penetration, but the information obtained is of small effect when no direct action is taken. Before Cointelpro-Communist Party-U.S.A. that had been the case, and Communists enthusiastically worked the situation to advantage.

The FBI policy on this matter had been that public exposure of Communists is the key to countering party control of non-

---

*President Eisenhower's Executive Order 10450 promulgated an effective program to reduce the number of "security risks" in government employment.

Communist movements, but that the FBI would not make the information available on its own. Director Hoover was most concerned about the problem and strongly urged others to tackle it. Testifying before the House Committee on Un-American Activities, on March 26, 1947, Hoover explained this, saying:

> The aims and responsibilities of the House Committee on Un-American Activities and the Federal Bureau of Investigation are the same—the protection of the internal security of this nation. The methods whereby this goal may be accomplished differ, however ...
> ...The Communists have been, still are, and always will be a menace to freedom, to democratic ideals, to the worship of God and to America's way of life.
> I feel that *once public opinion is thoroughly aroused as it is today, the fight against Communism is well on its way.* Victory will be assured once Communists are identified and exposed, because the public will take the first step of quarantining them so they can do no harm. Communism, in reality, is not a political party. It is a way of life—an evil and malignant way of life. It reveals a condition akin to disease that spreads like an epidemic and like an epidemic a quarantine is necessary to keep it from infecting the nation.

It may be that for the Communist Party, or more broadly, the old left, this uniquely soft intelligence operation in the mode of law enforcement is adequate and proper. There is insufficient evidence that the party, whatever it may have once been, today entertains any serious thought of coming to power in America. That being the case, the threat represented by the CPUSA and the old left is primarily that of an agent of the Soviet Union, which seeks by illegal means to influence American policy in favor of the goals of Soviet policy. Penetration of the party, along with the FBI's intelligence functions, control the extent of that threat, even though a more thorough counterintelligence effort would likely end the threat altogether.

Since 1968, the FBI apparently initiated a Cointelpro-Communist Party-U.S.A.* Like the other Cointelpro actions, this meant that the bureau intended to disrupt certain activities of the CPUSA. Presumably, this FBI program was developed on the basis of some intelligence information which indicated the need for affirmative counteraction against the Communists. In any case, it amounted to a departure from previous and long held FBI intelligence principles.

There is no evidence, however, that regarding the old left Communists, the bureau changed in any significant degree its actual practices and means of investigation. Cointelpro-Communist Party-U.S.A. may have been a new principle of operation, but it does not appear to have been the full scale (tactical, strategic, disruptive) counterintelligence *modus operandi.* FBI agents, for example, have not gone deeply undercover within the party. There have been no significant defectors from the party ranks, nor have any persons been exposed publicly as Communists. There are simply no outward signs of the counterorganizational and ideological war against the CPUSA that a full counterintelligence operation would have produced.

Moreover, there is no evidence that Cointelpro-Communist Party-U.S.A. involved the sort of underhanded methods most counterintelligence operations involve. If a new principle of domestic intelligence, it still did not mean that the FBI would resort to blackmail, kidnapping, intimidation, or other coercion of its intelligence targets.

The Cointelpros, it is clear, were not aimed at the sort of problem usually presented by the old left and Communists. Instead, the new *modus operandi* was developed in response to a new threat, a movement generally referred to as the new left. Cointelpro-Communist Party-U.S.A. was a program designed to counter the party program as it regarded this movement. The FBI—we do not know precisely how or with what success—attempted to separate the party from the new left and otherwise reduce its influence in that movement.

*This was one of the programs ended in March, 1971, according to a memorandum (Airtel) from the Director, FBI to SAC, Albany; March 28, 1971.

The FBI response to the new left movement is a story in itself.

Non-Communist Domestic Intelligence

Irresponsible critics of the FBI lose their cool particularly regarding the domestic intelligence missions. These are "Investigation of Opinions" in Max Lowenthal's opinion,* "intimidating presence in force against legitimate protest," according to the disaffected ex-agent William Turner,** or the work of "political police" in the words of a chorus of other FBI-haters like Isadore F. Stone and Fred Cook.

More responsible critics worry about the *potential* for intimidation inherent in the FBI's files, its presence on campus, and its coverage of leftist meetings and demonstrations. Yet, it is always the potential that worries them, since they have precious few hard facts with which to mount a case against the FBI. Still they wonder (rhetorically of course, since they always seem to know) whether FBI intelligence coverage of radical groups is repression.

All the left-liberal critics, responsible and otherwise, haul out the tired "McCarthyism" charges against the bureau.*** The Reds are "ghosts" which J. Edgar Hoover and his bureau have always used to taint legitimate dissent by calling it Communist or Communist-infiltrated, according to these critics.

Such an analysis may assuage the consciences of the left-inclined who would otherwise be implicated by their ideological and organizational proximity to the Communists, but it is long out of date as a serious criticism of the FBI. The critics them-

---

*Lowenthal, *The Federal Bureau of Investigation* (Harcourt Brace, N.Y. 1950).
**Turner, *Hoover's FBI* (Sherbourne Press, Los Angeles, 1970,), p. 212.
***The most recent example in the literature is Turner's book, ibid. In fact, the McCarthyism analysis is the framework of his comment on the FBI's domestic intelligence.

selves talk of ghosts, it appears. As discussed earlier in this chapter, FBI domestic intelligence emphasis has changed. No longer is the Communist menace pre-eminent on their list of security threats. The FBI mission is much broader than suspected Communist fronts. Bureau domestic intelligence is more interested in the so-called new left.

No doubt before too long the leftist critics will charge that the new left menace is an FBI ghost as well. We can hardly wait. In the meantime, a fair appraisal of the Federal Bureau of Investigation's efforts concerning the non-Communist left is in order.

It should be noted first that, just as the bureau emphasis in domestic intelligence changed in the late '60s, so did the bureaucratic structure of the Domestic Intelligence Division of the FBI. There had long been an Espionage Section and a Communist Section of the division. All radical groups under investigation had been the responsibility of the Communist Section. As the new left evolved into the revolt of the 1960s, it was soon clear that the Communists were not in control. Consequently, the Domestic Intelligence Division organized a new left section. The Communists were in effect demoted to "Old Line Communists"* and remained the responsibility of the Communist section.

A new left section means in practice that the Washington FBI headquarters has specialists in the field who administer and coordinate the cases opened by special agents in the field offices. It does not necessarily mean that each field or resident FBI office will have a squad of agents who work on nothing but non-Communist domestic intelligence cases. The New York, Chicago, District of Columbia, and other large field offices have special new left squads, but the smaller offices do not. The determination whether the office has such a squad rests simply on the number of new left matters available for investigation in the region covered by each field office. Thus the new section

---

*See J. Edgar Hoover's characterization of them in the 1972 Federal Bureau of Investigation appropriation document.

of the Domestic Intelligence Division does not at this time amount to a major reorganization within the bureau. An internal FBI memo from the special agent in charge of the Philadelphia office* illustrates how the new bureaucratic structure affects the investigations. It reads:

> During the recent inspection this office was instructed to separate security matter supervision to create a "New Left" and an "Old Left" desk.
>
> Squad No. 3 was designated to be the "Old Left" desk. While retaining espionage and foreign intelligence matters, it will handle the investigations of all organizations and individuals who fall in the "Old Left" category. Generally, "Old Left" means the Communist Party and the various splinter and Trotskyite groups which have been in existence for many years. The youth groups and satellites of the Communist Party and these splinter groups are also to be handled in the "Old Left" category and on Squad No. 3.
>
> Squad No. 4 was designated to handle "New Left" matters which includes both organizations and individuals. This is a relatively broad term [meaning] newly formed organizations with leftist or anarchistic connotations. Among other things, desk No. 4 will be responsible for such matters as SDS, STAG, underground newspapers, commune investigations, the Resistance.
>
> It is not contemplated that such organizations as the Women's International League for Peace and Freedom, SANE, AFSC, etc., which have long been in existence and are now attempting to polarize themselves toward revolting youth will be considered within the investigative purview of "New Left." To include such organizations would defeat the purpose of setting up a flexible activist group designed to deal with violent and terroristic minded young anarchists.
>
> A New Left Events Calendar will be maintained by Squad No. 4 secretary. When from reviewing underground newspapers, calls from outsiders, complaints or informants we know of a demonstration gathering, educational, or similar event planned by a New Left group, it should be given to SA Davenport who will coordinate this calendar. He will log it with No. 4 secretary. This will enable us to answer all kinds of queries

*This memo is apparently part of the stolen Media papers. The source of information is Brandeis Professor John Elliff, who has seen them.

about the date we know a particular event is scheduled. It will correlate the knowledge of all.

According to the Philadelphia SAC, the intent of the new left section is to introduce some flexibility in handling the violence-prone non-Communist radicals. Additionally, the preclusion of an organization such as the American Friends Service Committee (AFSC), indicates that the FBI concern with them continues to be one of Communist infiltration and other similar internal security problems, and accordingly the old Communist squad (renamed the old left squad) continues coverage of these cases.

The organizing of Cointelpro-New Left would seem to indicate in itself that the bureau has recognized that different objectives and/or methods are necessary in an intelligence assignment against some of the non-Communist radicals. The following critique, illustrated by examples, tends to the conclusion that the FBI in concert with President Nixon's Justice Department has quietly changed the tack in this area of domestic intelligence. The critique also suggests that more qualitative change is required before the non-Communist intelligence operation will have evolved into the sophisticated type of operation necessary to any successful governmental response to the left-radical movement which may re-emerge as a true security threat.

Naturally, no outside observer can quite predict the correct FBI reaction to specific organizations, people, and events. The bureau is dependent in large part on the specific intelligence information available. For this reason, it is not intended here to advise the bureau that, for instance, it should change the nature of its intelligence concerning the Black Panthers. Only the FBI has information accurate enough to suggest whether or not this ought be done. Yet, the guesses and estimates fitted into this critique will, it is hoped, articulate the type of considerations that should be reviewed in evolving the FBI's domestic intelligence work.

There are only a few known examples which illustrate the development of Cointelpro-type of FBI counterintelligence against the new left. They could represent the tip of an iceberg. It is more reasonable to conclude, however, that the Cointelpros never became extensive operations.

Cointelpro-New Left was obviously concerned with demonstration situations. The FBI practiced some mild interference with the organizers of the disruption, but it would be very unlikely that the bureau acted in this manner in any large number of occurrences. Since Cointelpro operations were under Washington headquarters' tight control, the bureau could not have managed to administer more than a few.

Nothing has come to light on what Cointelpro-New Left accomplished between demonstrations. If the FBI wanted really to smash the movement, the first thing would have been to organize and maintain a left-front of its own, devising to confuse the movement from within and scatter its adherents. If that were done, it is still the best-kept secret of the times. Seldom would such a government front escape the awareness of the leadership of the real movement. It wasn't done, we must conclude.

Informant penetration? Of course, the FBI energetically recruited new left informants, and most of its Cointelpro-New Left operations must have depended heavily on them. The FBI otherwise would have had to send a fair number of its own agents into deep undercover assignments. Again there is no evidence that this happened, and given the bureau's long-standing policy against deep covers, it is safe to assume that Cointelpro-New Left did not change that policy.

Yet, only disciplined FBI agents going deeply undercover could have accomplished much in the way of sophisticated counterintelligence without risking exposure. Cointelpro-New Left did not send agents undercover for these assignments, and it is clear from this fact that Cointelpro-New Left was no more than a shy experiment with disruptive counterintelligence.

Cointelpro was ended, except for special situations, by Director Hoover in March, 1971.*

The "new left" is, of course, a press invention, and a sloppy one at that, as it is used to lump together and sometimes legitimize, a vast menagerie of radical groups. The FBI has open cases on a large number of the groups, whatever their label, and has had investigative contact with many more. Nationally, FBI investigations cover at least the following: Students for a Democratic Society (SDS); the Weatherman (former SDS faction); Youth International Party (Yippies); White Panther Party; Venceremos Brigade (a "travel service" to Communist Cuba); People's Coalition for Peace and Justice (formerly the National Coalition against War, Racism and Repression, and evolved out of the New Mobilization Committee to End the War [New Mobe]); National Peace Action Coalition (NPAC) and its parents, the Socialist Workers Party (SWP) and the Young Socialist Alliances (YSA); Resistance in the Army, an organization within the military sponsored by the NPAC; Progressive Labor Party (PLP); and the Black Panther Party and related organizations. These are the presently prominent organizations commonly referred to as the new left, although the FBI considers the Trotskyite-Communist SWP and YSA and the formerly Maoist-Communist PLP as Communist splinter groups.** Besides the nationally prominent organizations, the bureau has cases, most of them open, on hundreds of radical groups more locally oriented. For example, the Philadelphia Resistance, various radical Catholic groups, local radical "communes," underground newspapers and similar organizations are subject to FBI scrutiny across the nation.

Other non-Communist radical organizations, usually nonvi-

---

*Memorandum, Director, FBI, op. cit.
**Meaning in practice that they merit coverage of the old left section of the Domestic Intelligence Division, with the clear objective of that intelligence category. The PLP, however, is new leftist in its terroristic approach, and to the extent YSA becomes involved in potentially violent confrontations, it would also be a case for new left intelligence.

olent even if militant, are investigated by the FBI or have contact with FBI investigations in the course of FBI intelligence
regarding other matters. This includes such organizations as
SANE, the American Friends Service Committee, the Institute
for Policy Studies, the Southern Christian Leadership Conference, and the Nation of Islam, an openly racist black power
group. These examples illustrate a variety of investigative matters engaged in by the bureau relating to a variety of radical
groups not of the new left sort. The FBI posture toward these
groups, however, is often quite different, and decidedly more
limited in methods and scope, than the open-ended casework
against the violent and terroristic new left. Nevertheless, the
Federal Bureau of Investigation has cause for more than occasional contact with a large number of left-radical groups. Hardly an organized radical group has escaped the FBI span of investigation.

This, of course, drives the liberal and new left critics respectively up their ivory towers and to their barricades. William
Turner is the most fun to watch denouncing the broad scope
of FBI intelligence. His one-time compatriots in the bureau evidenced "near-pathological hatred of leftists," Turner laments.*
No doubt the intelligence agents love their work, but it is nonsense to imply, as Turner does, that the bureau has chased
after radicals because the agents (and the late Mr. Hoover) personally disliked the radicals. Bureau responsibilities necessitate
various investigations into many organizations, whether the
agents like it or not.

Turner is willfully blind to any threat from the left—that is
the reason he is anguished over the mental attitudes of the special agents, and that is the reason he is bemused at "Hoover's
ghost," the Communist menace.** His illustrations are rather
bad examples as a result. He laughs at bureau investigations into

---

*He is, however, frightened of the *Power on the Right,* the title of his rather
McCarthyite book on right-wing organizations.
**Turner, op cit., p. 198.

the W.E.B. DuBois Club,* never quite admitting the established fact that the clubs were organized by the Communist Party and dominated by it from their inception. Would Turner have the bureau cover such an organization in its intelligence work? He would not. The Communist Party itself didn't think much of the clubs, he writes. Obviously, they could not be much of a threat to anything.

The party never conceded it, but in point of fact, the DuBois clubs were the main youth arm of the Communist Party until they were disbanded during 1969 and 1970 with a new Communist youth front quickly taking their place. The replacement group was the Young Workers Liberation League, openly organized by the CP in February, 1970 in order to take better advantage of the new left style of action. To say that the FBI should not have concerned itself with the DuBois clubs is to say it should not have bothered with the CP, and of course Turner would say just that. But the American public, as represented in the executive, the Congress, and courts, has long disagreed, and they set the jurisdictional scope of the FBI.

Investigative coverage of the new left groups continues the FBI's gentlemanly approach to law enforcement. One thing stands out in the FBI's entire left-intelligence performance: *special agents do not work deeply undercover in the radical movement.* Bureau agents recruit informants within the movement, but they do not themselves infiltrate the ranks. This is the elemental factor which makes it impossible for the bureau to become involved in a full-scale left-intelligence mission: an effort to disrupt and destroy the revolutionary left as an effective threat to the U.S. Informants cannot be relied on for such ideological warfare. More often they tend to *agent provocateur* efforts in maintenance of their cover, and this is quite the opposite of a proper counter-insurgency operation. Only professional FBI undercover men could promulgate a war on the left, and the FBI has so far refused to employ the technique.

*Turner, op cit. p. 20.

With J. Edgar Hoover gone, it is possible or even probable that FBI agents *will* quietly go undercover. Hoover would not permit it. He had his reasons, and understandably shied away from "dirty" cop business like this. Bureau sources have told the editors, however, that agents were sent undercover in several instances, without Hoover's authority. These were short-term missions, and do not detract from the general conclusion that the FBI did not employ undercover techniques. But they are an indication of a need felt within bureau ranks, and a director less conscious of potential bad publicity will surely move in that direction.

Nearly every other police agency which deals with radical criminality does infiltrate policemen into targeted radical groups.

Another difficulty with the present FBI procedure is that informants are often prone to trouble, and are suspect to juries in the prosecution of those spied on. Boyd Douglas, a convict-informant in the recent Berrigan brothers case, was not believed by the jury; nor did the informants in the Chicago 7 trial prove to be weighty witnesses. These tendencies are apparent to FBI officials and indicate again the likelihood of a new policy permitting agents to go undercover within the left.

Obviously, FBI undercover operations and other covert efforts of this type would have political effects on the so-called peace movement. This does not by itself make the operation improper. The propriety or impropriety is determined by two considerations: (a) whether the federal government has the legal power to suppress the radical left with affirmative police action; and (b) whether the actual police actions undertaken, some being admittedly underhanded, ought to be prohibited or restrained on various ethical and political grounds.

Philosophizing on these points is left to other papers in this book. But the position here may be stated very briefly that a) the federal government has the inherent power to defend itself fully against undemocratic ideologies and activities, and b) since the target groups themselves employ underhanded and illegal methods, it is sometimes necessary to do the same in defense (but as little as possible).

Drawbacks of the usual FBI role in the anti-war demonstrations of the late 60s and early 70s are illustrated by records and testimony in the federal trial in Chicago of Bobby Seale, Rennie Davis, Abbie Hoffman, Tom Hayden, et al., commonly referred to as the "Chicago 7" after Seale's trial was separated. These conspirators caused severe disruption at the 1968 Chicago Democratic Convention. Yet, under guerrilla lawyers William Kunstler (pinch hitting for Charles Garry) and Leonard Weinglass (serving as Kunstler's second string), the controversy about the trial itself soon eclipsed the furor over the demonstrations and the police response. The drama of the Chicago 7 courtroom disruption thus unfortunately obscured the historical and philosophical significance of the Chicago convention demonstrations. Score one for the new left.

The organization and execution of both the demonstrations and the government response contained all of the elements of a confrontation between classic revolutionary force and government authority in the American law enforcement tradition. But the government did not respond as if the challenge were of the revolutionary sort. Here was a massive threat to order in one of America's great cities, but much more, a threat to the democratic process of the nation. And it was a bold threat; sensing power in the leftward thrust of Senator Eugene McCarthy's campaign, the withdrawal of President Lyndon Johnson, and the mass of revolutionary-minded and malleable youth headed for Chicago's streets, the leaders of the demonstrations held what they thought was a powerful fist in the face of Mayor Richard Daley and the Democratic Party. Daley and his party, of course, did not give in to the threat, but the fact remains that the street troops made a serious assault on one of the country's two major political parties and thus to the democratic process. It was the fist of revolution that was raised; yet government authority viewed the ensuing fracas and bloodshed as a law enforcement problem.

The police reaction was not even based upon the legal frame-work which is supposed to protect America's internal security. Chicago's city police acted only to preserve order, in their minds at least. That was their main responsibility, and the performance of Chicago's finest is not the subject of this book. The U.S. Justice Department and the Federal Bureau of Investigation are, however, charged with protecting internal security. An objective observer would have to adjudge their response to the Chicago disturbances a failure.

The salient policy decision which was *not* made by the Justice Department-FBI in the face of impending disorder in Chicago, is exactly the policy decision which *was* made in the previously discussed Washington, D.C. demonstrations, and at Miami. This was the decision to have the FBI and the police take positive steps to quell the demonstration before and during its occurrence. In Washington in 1971 and in Miami in 1972, the FBI actively disrupted the revolutionist effort. In Chicago, it was not done.

Basically, Justice and the FBI considered the Chicago demonstrations to be Chicago's problem except to the extent federal jurisdiction was conferred by the anti-riot and conspiracy laws. This does not mean that the bureau ignored the affair. FBI intelligence within the anti-war movement was at the time quite extensive, and it appears that bureau field offices across the country were particularly interested in information about the radicals' plans for Chicago. Still, the demonstrations themselves were the province of Chicago police.

It is apparent from exhibits introduced in the conspiracy trial that the FBI had developed much intelligence information relating to the organizations which became involved in the convention disruption. However, testimony of several FBI informants and agents at the trial showed that the bureau had a more immediate concern than background intelligence for the Democratic convention demonstration. The testimony makes it clear that the FBI was preparing a conspiracy case against

David Dellinger, Rennie Davis, Abbie Hoffman, Tom Hayden and others.

The star among the FBI's witnesses at the Chicago trial was Louis Salzberg,* a sometime freelance photographer from New York City. He came to the FBI's notice after publication of one of his photographs, in which a hammer and sickle flag was contrasted with a small American flag, both displayed at a street meeting in Harlem. Whatever his politics, Salzberg considered some of the anti-war organizers dangerous, and in early 1967 was a willing recruit as an FBI informant. His recruiter, an agent in one of the New York offices known to Salzberg only as Phil, was a smooth operator who appealed to Salzberg's patriotism in securing him initially for the relatively harmless assignment of supplying photographs to the FBI. From this humble beginning, the recruit became increasingly involved with left-wing groups in New York City. He obtained official positions with the Vietnam Vets for Peace and the Fifth Avenue Vietnam Peace Parade Committee, and he joined the "Crazies." Ultimately, he cultivated close relations with none other than David Dellinger and Abbie Hoffman, and was by that time a prize informant for the New York FBI.

For a time Salzberg was spending many hours in leftist activities at no drain on the bureau's budget. With a family to support, his extensive activities as an informant would have had to be terminated unless he began to receive compensation for his time. Only then did the FBI begin paying him—about $10,000 over a two-year period. This sum underscores the importance the bureau attached to his information and to his infiltration into the targeted radical groups. Before paying an informant such a sum, the agent-contact must request authorization from his superiors in the field office and obtain approval from Washington headquarters.

*Dwayne Oklepek, a Buffalo, New York state university student was a primary inside informant who testified. He had infiltrated Mobe as a summer assignment for Chicago columnist Jack Mabley, and later reported to the FBI. He was not an FBI recruit, however.

Still, the FBI obtained Salzberg's efforts cheaply. Salzberg took the risks, and they were not all that slight. As an FBI informant in April, 1967 he became embroiled in difficulties with the New York police, being arrested along with others in connection with a demonstration at a speech by Vice President Hubert Humphrey. The bureau's handling of his arrest is curious. Salzberg had to obtain legal defense from a leftist lawyer's commune, and later swore at the Chicago conspiracy trial that the FBI never consulted with him in his trouble nor offered assistance. By not involving the bureau in his defense, Salzberg kept his cover, and appeared willing to take his chances. As it turned out, of course, he surfaced at the Chicago trial before his own trial date, and was off the hook.

In any case, Louis Salzberg was in a position in 1968 to provide the FBI information about what Hoffman, Dellinger, and others were planning for the August Democratic convention. He did this at the FBI's specific request, and later went to Chicago along with the antiwar horde, also for the FBI. It is interesting to note that the FBI emphasized to him that he was to report what the movement leaders said about Chicago. In one instance, Special Agent Robert Mills asked Salzberg to attend a New York meeting at which Tom Hayden was the speaker, and specifically directed him to report what Hayden said about demonstrations in Chicago. This he did, to the exclusion of other intelligence information. Culminating his effort, Salzberg later testified at the trial about Hayden's speech, much to the dismay of Hoffman and Dellinger.

Other informants for the FBI were requested to report damaging utterances made by the Chicago defendants prior to the demonstrations. The FBI interest obviously went beyond intelligence purposes—a conspiracy case was being prepared.

Frank Sweeney, a New York advertising executive, was in 1968 a casual informant for the FBI. He had volunteered his services to his neighbor, an FBI agent, and had been attending radical meetings for six years as assigned by the bureau. In July, 1968, the FBI requested he attend a public meeting of the Fifth Avenue Peace Parade Committee at which Tom Hayden was a speaker. His report to FBI agents covered Hayden's remarks on the upcoming Chicago demonstrations. He later testified to Hayden's "inflammatory" speech at the Chicago trial.

In the same period, New York FBI agents themselves were discreetly watching radical rallies and meetings with an eye to gathering evidence for conspiracy charges. In July 1968 a radical group sponsored a demonstration near New York City's Waldorf Astoria. The New York FBI field office had procured leaflets which advertised the rally and Special Agent Robert Casper and several other agents decided to attend. Standing discreetly on the sidelines, the FBI men each took particular care to note for later report what one rally speaker, Jerry Rubin, had to say about Chicago. Casper later testified at the conspiracy trial that the bureau's purpose at the rally was more general, but it is clear that Rubin was of primary interest.

While the New York FBI had agents and informants gathering evidence of the Chicago conspiracy, other field offices were doing the same as the opportunities arose. A San Diego television reporter, Stephen Gilman, had volunteered to become an FBI informant in March, 1968. He apparently had the capability of obtaining information and photographs concerning the SDS chapter and other leftist groups around San Diego and San Diego State College; for the bureau quickly accepted his offer and soon insisted on compensating his expenses and time at about $200 a month.

As an informant Gilman attended a meeting of SDS and other groups at the San Diego college in July, 1968. David Dellinger was the featured speaker, and the informant wrote down his exact words in a particularly damaging quote, a quote referring to disrupting the government and then: "I am going to Chicago to the Democratic Convention where there may be problems. I'll see you in Chicago." This exact quote Gilman reported to his FBI contact and later testified to in the Chicago trial of Dellinger. Background intelligence would not have required exact quotes. A conspiracy case would, and it is apparent that Gilman was helping the FBI prepare such a case in this instance.

Thus, the interest shown by the New York and San Diego FBI illustrates that the FBI was investigating a federal case against the Chicago 7 prior to the convention. Similarly, FBI agent activity during the demonstrations seemed directed mainly to eventual prosecution in contradistinction to any efforts to suppress the revolutionary action in Chicago's streets, a function which was left to the Chicago police. Agents and informants, such as Salzberg and Oklepek, of course, were in the Chicago crowds. But these men made no attempt to confuse or quiet the demonstrators. They did keep the Chicago police informed of the confrontation plans of the demonstrators, but mainly they were reporting back more evidence of the Chicago 7's leadership at the scene—again for the federal riot and conspiracy charges.

The rest of the 1968 Chicago story broke violently into the homes of millions of startled Americans via television and other media. The city of Chicago and the convention were disrupted and upstaged by violent confrontations between demonstrators and Chicago police. The federal government and the FBI had made no effort to head it off or suppress it. Instead, they prosecuted the perpetrators, the Chicago 7 and Bobby Seale, this after the fact in the usual custom of the criminal justice system.

Still, the prosecutorial objective of the FBI pre-convention investigation was a new chapter in FBI new-left intelligence. It marked the first major attempt by the Justice Department and the FBI, newly armed with federal laws against rioting and conspiracy, to confront head-on the self proclaimed revolutionaries in the new left.

An assessment of this effort nevertheless reduces to a conclusion that its successes and failures were mixed. The prosecution of Davis, Dellinger, Hoffman, Hayden et al. did result in convictions of several defendants on the charge of crossing state lines for the purpose of inciting a riot (convictions since reversed), but resulted in acquittal on the conspiracy charges, just as similar conspiracy cases have since shown themselves unprovable in court. In the meantime, the Chicago 7 used the trial as a *cause célèbre;* and since that time remained free to continue their movement activities. Indeed, several of them organized (less successfully) similar confrontations at the 1972 Miami Republican and Democratic conventions.

Most importantly, the government's prosecutorial response did not adequately meet the situation in Chicago at the time. True, the demonstrators were unable to storm the convention itself, nor did they have unqualified success in fomenting a massive revolution in the nation—both objects of the Chicago 7's dreams. Nevertheless, every objective the demonstration leaders could have *reasonably* hoped for was achieved. Chicago was theirs for a week. Subsequent prosecution of the conspirators was no response to this threat, and the legal proceedings hardly gave pause to the left as it continued and increased disruptive demonstrations in ensuing years.

It is reasonable to believe that it was partly in recognition of this fact that the Justice Department and the FBI under President Nixon developed a qualitatively different response to some subsequent leftist upheavals. The distinction between, for instance, the November 15, 1969 "March on Washington" and the August, 1968, struggle in Chicago's streets was the decision by Justice to influence the course of the latter demonstration, hopefully to reduce its disruptive and revolutionary potential. Jurisdictional problems, of course, were laid aside in the Washington, D.C. confrontation, that city clearly being the Justice Department's more direct concern. In Chicago, the department and the FBI were constrained to deal mainly within the confines of federal law, which did not suffice to avert the threat at the convention site. Even with these differences, the decision actively to oppose the Washington demonstrations evidenced a new and positive response to a revolutionary threat. It was a qualitative change, still not approaching a full-scale intelligence operation, but at least resting on the assumption that the government was entitled to use firmer techniques to interfere in the revolutionary affairs of the left.

From such mild interference, the Justice Department with Washington, D.C. Police Chief Jerry Wilson, graduated to a much more sophisticated police response in the May, 1971 "Mayday" capital city struggle. Operating with the benefit of FBI intelligence, the Justice Department and Chief Wilson knew they faced serious disruption from thousands of youth who would stop traffic, block entrance to government buildings, and willingly face arrest. Rennie Davis and John Froines, two of the organizers, promised that so many would face arrest that the law enforcement facilities would be inadequate and the disruption would not be stopped. Exactly that could have resulted, except for the counter-strategy of the government authorities. Chief Wilson did not wait for Davis and Froines. Employing trickery, the Washington police routed thousands of demonstrators from a Sunday night "rock-fest," thus successfully dispersing most of the youth before they could be organized for the confrontations the next day. The next day and throughout the week, thousands of demonstrators were arrested and detained, most of them *before* they could illegally jam traffic in the district. By these methods, the capital disruption was minimized.

For once, the police with the Justice Department's and FBI's active assistance had out-foxed the revolutionary movement leaders. Police forces had taken steps humanely but firmly— there is no more accurate word—to "repress" the demonstration. It worked. Very few injuries resulted. The radical movement was left with only unappealing legal issues to complain about, and its rather tarnished pride.

In Miami, at the 1972 conventions, Dellinger, Seale and others were right back at it. The situation this time was different at the Justice Department and FBI, however; no rerun of the Chicago riots was going to be permitted. The few leftist troopers who showed up in Miami (no more than 1,500) for the GOP convention were utterly disorganized, discouraged, and outnumbered. Only one significant demonstration was launched and this occurred too late for the purposes of the "confrontation engineers." The FBI, the Secret Service, and the local police would like to think they were at least partly responsible for the organizational mess Dellinger found at Miami Beach's Flamingo Park. It was the combined policy of these agencies to keep the demonstrators disorganized, and agents and informants worked undercover at the park to assure this.

Perhaps the left was in disarray by its own efforts. But there were individuals known to the editors of this book who stood on the stage at Flamingo Park and purposely sought to divide and confuse the demonstrators. In any case, the Zippies, the Vietnam Veterans against the War, the Panthers and the Yippies would not agree on a common strategy, and they went their own ways until the last day.

The authorities' response to Mayday and the Miami convention was thus a considerably more sophisticated model for police action in disruption situations which actually constitute a threat to government operations. Investigations of illegality or potential illegality, police attempts to keep the demonstrators within the law, and arrests and charges for prosecutive purposes—the trappings of traditional law enforcement objectives —all took second ranking to the main police objective, the suppression of a threat to governmental and democratic functions (charges against the demonstrators were dropped). Prosecutions after the fact would not have suppressed the threats in May, 1971, or August, 1972. The examples demonstrate that only the extra-legal suppression of certain revolutionary causes is an adequate response to legitimate internal security threats.

This is not to say that all police departments ought to treat all demonstrations in such a manner, or have a free hand to do so. To the contrary, most demonstrations threaten public order but *do not* involve an imminent threat to internal security. Where internal security is not primarily at stake, order-keeping and prosecutive objectives ought to remain the police purpose.

Only in the face of a grave internal security threat should federal and local authorities throw off the law enforcement cloak and beat the revolutionaries at their own street games. One hopes that, when new battle lines are drawn, the FBI will have again the authorization to engage in at least limited counter-revolutionary activities. Should this authority be granted, one can be sure the FBI will, with its customary thoroughness and efficiency, do much to protect the nation from the violent ideologies of the left.

9. Intelligence—A Part of Law Enforcement

Frank G. Carrington
with the Editors

Crime and Revolution/Editors*

"Tonight at 7:00 P.M. we blew up the New York City police headquarters" began the note, labeled "Communique No. 2" and sent on June 9, 1970 purportedly from the "Weatherman Underground." Several hours before, a police station in New York was in fact rocked by a bomb explosion.**

On a dark evening in January, 1972, two young police officers, one of whom happened to be black, were walking their beat as usual in a lower Manhattan section. Gunshots cracked. Both officers fell dead, murdered in an ambush from some unseen corner. Next day, the United Press International office

*The editors are indebted to a paper drafted by Justus van der Kroef, Chairman, Political Science Department at Bridgeport University, for a basic draft of part of this chapter.
**Harold Jacobs, ed., *Weatherman* (Ramparts Press, 1970).

received a letter from the "George Jackson Squad" of the "Black Liberation Army" claiming responsibility for the ambush of the "two pigs."*

On August 16, 1970, Robert Fassnacht, a University of Wisconsin graduate student, decided to work late on some experiments in a lab situated in the university's Sterling Hall, a building which housed also a mathematics research center connected with the U.S. Army. Late into the night, Fassnacht was still working when a small cadre of fanatic leftists parked a light panel truck next to the building. A short time later the truck exploded with a thunderous burst, blasting apart laboratories, classrooms, and portions of the army research center, and snuffing out the life of Robert Fassnacht.

Charged with this bombing-murder were four young radicals,** one of whom was a writer for the *Daily Cardinal,* the student newspaper, and was quite well known among activists on campus.

Certainly, such acts of violence are not "privileged" deeds even if they are, in a certain morbid sense, politically motivated. The perpetrators, the bombers, arsonists, and murderers, are as criminal—if not more so—as any who victimize their fellow men. And as criminals, they ought to experience the full penalties of the criminal justice system. Every available means of crime detection, every available method of assuring their arrest, and every available means of legal prosecution ought to be used against them.

Police intelligence, including in certain instances the informant and surveillance operations of the FBI, is the most important means of detecting these crimes. Of course if they are not detected they cannot be prevented, so advance intelligence is critical. The Fathers Berrigan case is an illustration.

Whatever their protestations of innocence and whatever was not proven to the satisfaction of a jury, it is clear that Fathers

---

Washington Post, January 30, 1972.
**At this writing, only one, Karlton Armstrong, has been apprehended.

Philip and Daniel Berrigan and others had formulated a quixotic plan for terrorizing the government in Washington, D.C. Heating ducts and tunnels could be blasted, according to their discussion, and they could even kidnap high government officials. Now, whether or not these mad dreams materialized to the extent of a conspiracy provable to a jury, they existed in letters and notes traveling by courier between one of the Berrigans already in prison and others of the radical clan. Unfortunately for them, the courier, a cellmate of the fanatic father, happened to pass the information along to the FBI. This was one crime of terror which would never occur. Bureau agents would have been ready if and when the Berrigans' little army headed to the front.

Yet, there are some who would effectively deny the nation this means of protecting itself from future spasms of terroristic crime. They would either limit, dismantle, or altogether forbid police intelligence systems as those systems affect radical groups (the Berrigans, the Black Panthers, etc.) because, they say, the intelligence effort "chills" unfettered expression of dissent. Granting that it would, must we for that reason alone discontinue the practice of surveillance and infiltration when related radical activities are criminal?

Put another way, the question is a challenge: what do those who would limit police intelligence operations in the political area propose to do about the crimes of violence perpetrated by revolutionists and politically motivated psychopaths? No answer is forthcoming from their corner. In their quest for absolute protection for the rights of radical activists, they neglect wholly the interest the public has in protection from bombings, arson, and murder.

The editors have in this book urged a broader concept of the domestic intelligence function of the FBI, one that extends beyond purely law enforcement objectives. Reasonable persons, we admit, could question whether or not this should be done. Not so with the law enforcement intelligence objective. At a minimum, FBI intelligence work related to crime detection must command the support of every fair-minded person. However one views the proper breadth of FBI intelligence coverage of radical groups, one cannot reasonably question that to the extent it is related to the detection of terroristic crime, FBI infiltration and surveillance of revolutionary organizations is well within traditional limitations on police powers. No amount of concern for free dissent can outweigh the need for protection against terroristic crime.

Although we think it ought to be a secondary objective, the editors do not mean to deemphasize the importance of the crime detection aspect of the FBI intelligence operation. Indeed, where totalitarian political movements involve themselves in terroristic actions, the concern for protecting democracy and the concern for protecting against crime merge.

For this reason we treat this aspect of the FBI intelligence operation as one of its contributions to law enforcement. In fact, it is one of its most important law enforcement functions. This is because much of the terrorist action is either organized or encouraged by national organizations. Local madmen assassinate police and plant bombs, but national organizations back them up with materials, manuals, escape networks, and defense lawyers. And national organizations support traveling organizers who deal in the revolutionary substance of the terrorist acts. Only a national police intelligence network, then, can begin to cope with the underlying national basis for terroristic crime. This is a job for the FBI.

It should be noted that in the area of terroristic crime, as in most other criminal matters, the FBI has a limited role; state and local police are responsible in the first instance for protecting the public from criminals, including radical terrorists. Local police departments do not depend on the FBI for the necessary intelligence. Any large police department infiltrates undercover police officers into as many radical groups as it can find. Within certain organizations, the FBI develops informants of its own, of course, and information is traded between the various agencies. But the larger intelligence force is not the FBI's; it is, rather, the aggregate of the local police intelligence networks. Still the FBI is an important part of this "early warning" system. One hesitates to label it as a central collecting and coordinating function, for the communications among the various police agencies involved does not necessarily channel through the bureau. But the FBI function is akin to this. It is the bureau which, in pursuing information related to its jurisdiction, develops and provides to all law enforcement agencies the broader intelligence picture on terrorist groups. Many of the bits and pieces of this information come from local police, but it is the FBI which fits them into the pattern of national radical movements. This sophistication is necessary to detect and control criminal terrorism.

The editors turn to Frank G. Carrington, a lawyer and former police official, and presently the executive director of Americans for Effective Law Enforcement, for a view of the FBI intelligence role in the area of terroristic crime.

The Need for Intelligence Activities in Dealing with Terroristic Crime / Frank G. Carrington

If the extent of domestic subversion consisted of a few deranged individuals such as the pathetic American Nazis who posture about harmlessly, then a massive intelligence program involving surveillance, infiltration, the use of informants, and other similar investigative techniques would be pointless. Unfortunately, this is not the case. Certain disaffected persons, fueled by actual or imagined grievances against American society and bolstered by an attitude, in some quarters, of almost insane permissiveness toward their activities, have made a calculated decision to promote and practice terrorism—riot actions, ambush assassinations, and other revolutionary terrorism. The danger from this is clear, present, real, and substantial.

In view of the recent climate of domestic terror in the

United States, the nearly unanimously expressed view at the Princeton Conference on the FBI, that the bureau was engaging in *too much* investigation of political dissidents, borders on the lunatic. The Princeton conferees were agreed that there should be a sharp curtailment on such intelligence gathering activities as infiltration and surveillance of radical groups, the keeping of intelligence files, and the practice of electronic surveillance.* The FBI's elite critics at the Princeton Conference divided, roughly, into two camps on the intelligence-gathering issue. The first group, whose champion was Professor Vern Countryman of Harvard Law School, took the position that there should be no political surveillance whatever by the FBI; the second "moderate" group grudgingly admitted the need for FBI intelligence work in cases of actual criminal conduct (e.g., bombings, arsons, attacks on law enforcement officers) but would restrict surveillance activities to those cases in which an actual crime had been committed or was imminent.

Both schools of thought deserve some comment. The "Countryman Theory" is frightening. It can be best summed up by a colloquy which took place between Professor Countryman and this writer at the Princeton Conference. After I pointed out to him that a recent racially motivated bombing of school buses in Pontiac, Michigan—perpetrated by the Ku Klux Klan —had been solved in a matter of days by the FBI through the use of precisely those techniques of infiltration and surveillance which he so roundly condemns, the following dialogue then took place:

> Countryman: "Well, my judgment would be that if the only way to detect that bombing is to have the FBI infiltrating political organizations, I would rather the bombings go undetected."
>
> Carrington: "No matter whether somebody was killed?"
>
> Countryman: "Yes. Yes, there are worse things than having

---

*This view is, incidentally, just the opposite of the opinion of the majority of Americans as evidenced by public opinion polls.

people killed. When you've got the entire population intimidated, that may be worse. We put some limits on law enforcement in the interests of preserving a free and open society or
at least we try to, and every time we do that—things like the
privilege against self-incrimination, things like the 4th Amendment—every time we do that, that involves a judgment that
even though some crimes and some crimes involving the loss
of life will go undetected, it is better in the long run to have
a society where there is some protection from police surveillance."

Carrington: "I'm not really sure that the family of Robert
Fassnacht who was blown up at Wisconsin or the families of
the kids that were killed in the Birmingham church bombing
would agree with that."

Countryman: "I'm sure that the families of the victims would
not agree in any of the instances that I've mentioned, but I
don't believe that most of us would say that for that reason we
should repeal the 4th and 5th Amendments."

No one else present saw fit to question these heartless pro-
nouncements. It is disturbing to hear from a member of the
law faculty of Harvard University a view subordinating the
value of human life to his abstractionist views of constitutional
absolutism. It is more disturbing that his views provoked no
rebuke from the other supposedly thoughtful conferees.

No one had even remotely suggested that the Fourth and Fifth
Amendments be repealed. The question was whether or not it
was useful in our society to have an organization—specifically
the FBI which gathers intelligence via the use of infiltration
of extremist groups with a view toward preventing or, failing
that, solving murders committed by terrorist bombers. Professor Countryman said it was not.

The "moderates" do not go quite so far as Professor Countryman. However, they argued that surveillance of political dissidents should be limited to those cases in which a specific
crime had actually been committed, or in which such a crime
was imminent. This is fantasy. Intelligence gathering against
potential criminal acts is, by definition, a preventive function,

and it is too obvious to bear extended argument that in order to ferret out the lawless elements of a violent so-called political movement, intelligence must be gathered in depth from the whole of that movement. The more limited the search, the more limited the results in prevention of crime.

For instance, when a crowd gathers to protest one thing or another, the result may be anything from a peaceful demonstration to a full-scale riot. The police cannot know in advance which alternative the gathering may choose. But the police have a sworn duty (a) to prevent property destruction and violence, and (b) to calm down or disperse a crowd which becomes riotous. It follows that they have a concomitant duty to gather advance intelligence, to watch the gathering, and if necessary, to arrest those who incite the crowd to riot and disperse the other demonstrators. The police cannot work in the dark. Good intelligence may well make the difference between an orderly legal protest and an ugly riotous mob scene.

The question of keeping files on dissident subjects is similar. Eyes rolled with horror at Princeton at the idea that the FBI and other agencies were keeping "dossiers" on people whose only desire was to exercise their constitutional rights of freedom of speech, etc. But we know that terroristic crimes are plotted in secret and usually at some length. If say, an R.O.T.C. building were dynamited, the crime would usually be very difficult to solve if the authorities had to start from scratch after the bombing. On the other hand, if the authorities have gathered prior information that A is a dedicated exponent of removing the R.O.T.C. from campus, by violence if necessary; that B, who meets with A, has a knowledge of explosives; and that their associate C has been seen casing the R.O.T.C. facility, then the authorities may be able to prevent a crime, or at least apprehend the criminals. *This* is a purpose of intelligence files and without them the revolutionary criminal would be relatively free to practice his terrorism with impunity.

But, say the pseudo-libertarians who would curtail intelligence gathering in the "political" area, the actual threat of bombing, mob action, and assassination is not sufficiently great to justify the "repressive climate" which police intelligence gathering creates. This is nonsense, and it brings us to the point of this chapter: revolutionary terroristic crime is indeed a grave threat to life, property, and, in the final analysis, to the existence of freedom in this country.

The Climate of Violence

No nation has ever been totally free from the activities of the politically motivated criminal, but in recent years revolutionary violence in the United States has risen to an unprecedented level. Bombings and acts of arson, mob violence, assassinations, and the murders of figures of authority—particularly law enforcement officers—have become relatively common occurrences. These are the types of crimes in which preventive intelligence is most needed. If we are faced with "political" crimes then those involved at all levels in the "political" groups from which such crimes emanate must become the object of preventive scrutiny by law enforcement agencies.

Bombings and arson are the most spectacular of revolutionary criminal activities. Neither the lunatic fringes of the right or the left has a monoply on them. A fine man, a Negro named Vernon Dohmer, was burned to death in his home in Georgia by racial bigots; and few will ever forget the horror of the church bombing in Birmingham, Alabama which killed four little Negro girls attending Sunday school. In the recent past, a wave of bombings by left-wing extremists erupted all over the country.

During the year July, 1970 to June, 1971, according to the Bomb Data Center of the International Association of Chiefs of Police, 1,858 bombing incidents took place in the United States—863 with explosives and 995 with incendiary devices. 17 lives were lost and 178 persons injured. 537 of the incidents were "politically" motivated and the targets included governmental buildings, police and judicial facilities, military installations and commercial and manufacturing properties (including 34 bombings of the Bank of America in California)—in short, just such targets as represent the "establishment," the "enemy," to the revolutionary terrorist.*

This wave of terroristic crime has by no means ceased. According to the FBI, in the period January through September 1972 there were 1,486 bombing incidents in the United States in which 21 persons died and 133 were injured. If anything, the number is increasing.

Assaults against law enforcement officers and government officials are another hallmark of the terrorist. According to the 1971 Uniform Crime Report of the FBI, during the period 1967-1971, that period in which revolutionary and terroristic crime reached a growth peak in this country, 45 law enforcement officers were murdered in cowardly ambush attacks. They were gunned down for no other reason that that *they were law enforcement officers.* Such attacks are intolerable. They strike at the very foundations of society. Such crimes have common elements in motive, planning, and execution. If infiltration and surveillance by the police of some of the groups which the Princeton conferees euphemistically call "political" could have prevented just one of these ambush attacks, the preventive intelligence effort would have been entirely justified.

Assassination is a favorite method of the terrorist. Oswald, Sirhan, and Bremer were all politically motivated. Such killers or would-be killers evidence a climate of violence in the United States. It is obvious that police agencies should have full authority to thwart it. It is equally obvious that if preventive intelligence—in this instance especially the effective use of intelli-

---

*"Bombing in the United States; July 1970, June 1971," by Jane P. Morton and Gary Persinger, a publication of the National Bomb Data Center, Research Section, International Association of Chiefs of Police, 11 Fistfield Road, Gaithensburg, Maryland 20760.

gence files—could have stayed the hand of the assassins, the course of history would have been changed considerably.

Riots have become a part of the American mythology. Detroit, Watts, Washington, D.C., and scores of other cities have been rocked by mob violence with enormous loss of life, personal injury and property damage. On this nation's college campuses in the school year 1969-1970, according to Committee on Internal Security of the House of Representatives:

> A total of 1,785 demonstrations were recorded by the close of the school year, FBI Director Hoover announced. Sit-ins and building seizures numbered 313; ROTC installations were attacked in 281 instances; 73 protests involved military recruiting on campus; and 101 actions opposed government research or corporate recruiting. In addition campuses were plagued by 246 instances of arson or attempted arson and 14 bombings. *As a result of disruptions, 8 individuals died, 462 were injured and damages exceeded $9,500,000.00*, the FBI chief reported.*

While concededly some of these riots flared up from a given incident, other riots were *started*, particularly in the campus situation where such fringe-left groups as the SDS were active. There is no necessity here to recount the entire history of mob violence in this country in recent years. As everybody knows, a great deal of violence *has* occurred—often at the hands of those groups which the civil libertarians would insulate from police surveillance because they are "political." The need for intelligence gathering techniques in this area grows in direct proportion to the threat of violence and that threat is obviously present.

One aspect of the Princeton Conference was intriguing. While there was no absolute unanimity on the subject, there was a consensus that intelligence techniques which the conferees felt to be "off limits" when applied to "political" groups

---

Anatomy of a Revolutionary Movement: "Students for a Democratic Society." Union Calendar No. 750, 91st Cong. 2nd Session, House Report No. 91-1565. P. 150. (Italics added.)

were quite permissible where focused against organized crime.
There is simply no question that organized crime is a threat
to this country, the more so because of the secrecy that conceals
its operations. But political violence is also a threat. Crime is
crime. Those who take the position that all legal investigative
techniques should be utilized against organized crime should
take the same view about political terrorism. In fact, if deliber-
ate revolutionary terrorism is not "organized crime," what is
it?

We live in a climate of violence. Some of this violence is random: a robbery of a liquor store, a killing over a card game.
But other violence is planned and nurtured by revolutionary
"political" criminals. Bombings, ambushes of police officers,
many riots and assassinations do not just happen. They are
carefully planned. Far and away the best way to deal with them
is to prevent them with prior knowledge developed through
intelligence techniques. No individual or group which presents
even the potential for such violence should be immune from such
lawful investigative techniques as are available to law enforcement authorities.

The FBI has some intelligence techniques available to it. The
courts of this country, including the Supreme Court of the
United States, have consistently refused to interfere with legitimate intelligence gathering techniques. If we lived in serene
and peaceful times, it might be possible to agree with the
Princeton conferees that police powers be somewhat curtailed.
But we do not. So long as lunatics of either fringe, right or
left, choose to express their discontent in violence, the FBI and
its counterparts at the state and local level have a clear duty
to protect innocent citizens. Intelligence gathering is a major
part of this protection and, despite the views of the elitists at
Princeton, this law enforcement power must be utilized to the
fullest extent possible.

10. The Uses of Police Power

Editors

At 4:00 A.M. on August 10, 1965, Dale B. Menard was lying on a park bench in a Los Angeles park. He was unshaven, and his dark clothes gave him an unkempt appearance. Two police officers approached him.

The officers had earlier received a complaint of a prowler in the area. Menard fit the description. They arrested him.

The suspect was taken to the precinct station, booked, and fingerprinted as in the regular procedure. Subsequent investigation revealed that no burglary or other crime had been committed in the area of the arrest, so Menard was released.

However, as was the usual procedure, Menard's fingerprints and a notation of his arrest were forwarded to the Federal Bureau of Investigation. These were processed and placed in the bureau's fingerprint identification files along with a record which read:

Date arrested or received: 8/10/65
Charge or offense: 459 PC Burglary
Disposition or sentence: 8/12/65
Unable to connect with any felony or misdemeanor—in accordance with 849b(1)—not deemed an arrest but detention only.
Occupation: student

Mr. Menard was very unhappy about the arrest, but he was even angrier at the fact his fingerprints and "arrest record" were now on file at the FBI. He wrote letters to the Los Angeles Police Department and to the bureau, demanding that the file be destroyed. The bureau responded that it had not the authority to do any such thing.

Feeling wronged, Menard took his case to Washington, D.C., where he filed suit in Federal District Court. He asked that the courts compel the FBI to expunge his fingerprint file. While the courts would not do that, exactly, a Washington, D.C. district judge did ultimately enjoin the bureau from disseminating the information contained in the file to private employers or non-law enforcement agencies outside the federal government. This order was issued in June, 1971.

In the following year, another legal proceeding was held in another court. In this latter case, two soldiers, an informant, and a government employee were witnesses against a man who had spoken unkindly of the government, and moreover had done so to a newsman, who thereupon published his statement. The testimony of these witnesses, and the introduction in court of the anti-government news report was enough proof. For his actions the man was found guilty as charged, and was sentenced to two years in prison, five additional years in a corrective labor camp, and five more years in "domestic exile." On top of this, he had to pay part of the expense of the legal proceedings against him. It cost him 100 rubles.

The latter case, of course, did not occur in the United States. It was a proceeding in Moscow City Court. The defendant, Vladimir K. Bukovsky, who had already spent a good part of his life in confinement for mandatory "psychiatric treatment," had illegally "slandered" the Soviet government.* The contrast between this Soviet case and the U.S. district court case is obvious. It is a contrast between a system which spares no effort to smash an independent individual who spoke against the Soviet government, and the American criminal justice system which goes to extreme lengths to curtail its own operations where they may adversely affect an individual. In the U.S. case, a court ponders the damage an individual's reputation might suffer even if his arrest was fair and legal, as a result of possible dissemination of arrest information. In the Soviet case, a court ponders only the matter of establishing the trial record necessary to order a dissident to the work camps.

It is no exaggeration to judge as a police state that system which sends Bukovsky to the salt mines. Only the most biased sort of mind, however, could lump in the same category that system which enjoins its own Federal Bureau of Investigation from disseminating too widely some not very incriminating data on Mr. Menard. The distinctions are clear.

Yet, there are those who denounce the FBI information processes as practices of a police state. One such partisan critic is Frank Donner, who heads a project aimed at legally disarming this system. Donner appeared at the October, 1971 Princeton Conference on the FBI to present a paper on FBI informants, "the keystone of the [FBI's] political intelligence system," as he put it. Presumably, Donner is aware of the systematic abuse of police powers in the Soviet Union; nevertheless he hotly contended that:

> It is precisely this free-floating political intelligence function, based on the unchecked power of selection of surveillance ends and means, that identify [sic] the FBI as a secret political police unit—and which clothes the director with such unique *repressive* powers. (Emphasis added.)

---

*See *Chicago Tribune* story compiled from report of Alexi Tumerman, March 1, 1972, p. 22.

Did Donner simply overstate his case? No. Upon questioning, he refused to alter his view that the FBI is a secret political police and its "informer" operation proves it. To Frank Donner, then, the FBI is no different from the KGB which Bukovsky feared.

Clearly, Donner is among the prejudiced critics referred to earlier. But one is not content to leave the matter at that, for the information gathering and filing processes of the FBI, while certainly not of the police-state sort, must nevertheless be measured against the libertarian standards embodied in American law, and against the ethical standards upon which American society is based. To these measures must be added a judgment of the worth of the system—an assessment of the need for FBI intelligence and files.

Bureau information gathering consists of field intelligence and file maintenance. Field intelligence can be either FBI investigation or data retrieval from other federal, state or local agencies (e.g., the fingerprint-arrest records). FBI investigation, as treated here, involves: (a) surveillance, which requires judgment on the use of wiretaps and other electronic listening devices; (b) informants; (c) the treatment of suspects and others by FBI agents; and (d) controls on the potential abuses in these areas. (These subjects are discussed specifically in later chapters.)

Since the intelligence power of the federal government is clearly established, the only problem is the potential abuse of that power. In matters of both criminality and national security, the federal government must of necessity have FBI field investigations, and these cannot be properly performed without the second aspect of information gathering: file maintenance. The power of government to compile and keep files is corollary to its intelligence function. It follows that if the FBI filing system becomes problematical, it is due to the *abuse* of the system, not the system itself.

Many of the bureau's detractors, in particular those who charge "police state," do not want to accept the obvious. Instead, they attack FBI intelligence as if it were somehow illegal or mean in itself. They try to deny that the bureau has an intelligence function in the internal security field as well as in other criminal violations. It is the FBI's intelligence function which drives the Frank Donners to their rash statements. Because FBI internal security investigations vary from the practices commonly accepted—even by the Donners—for criminal investigations, this variance is used as proof of impropriety. But the difference between the bureau's two types of investigations is minor, and would hardly support a charge of police state tactics. The FBI conducts the security intelligence assignment in the very same mode as its criminal investigations, although the two differ considerably in their purpose.

Criminal investigation is aimed at bringing to justice a specific criminal (or criminals) for a specific crime. This type of investigation has a beginning and an end, each easily definable: it starts with the commission of the illegal act, and ends with the judicial process. But security investigations are frequently nebulous. Rather than a definite, short-range goal of apprehending a suspect, the aim of any security investigation is the neutralization of a subversive threat, an espionage threat or other threat to the constitutional form of government. This is a continuing intelligence mission, and it seldom has a definite prosecution or other sanction as its end object. FBI investigations in the security field have, over time, pinpointed foreign influence among domestic revolutionary organizations and provided intelligence data of continuing value to other government agencies on the objectives and activities of these groups. This intelligence coverage has also provided assistance to local authorities in such matters as police killings, fire-bombings, and, recently, air piracy. Almost by definition, this involves gathering much peripheral information which does not have specific, immediate application.

FBI investigations of internal security matters should not, in a word, be criticized for failing to produce immediate arrests, prosecutions, and convictions of criminals; such is not its purpose. But some critics will not recognize the distinction, e.g., Yale professor Thomas Emerson, who absolutely would not permit FBI investigations of radicals except to apprehend bombers and arsonists. Surely, the federal government's legitimate information gathering powers are broader than that. Intelligence information is necessary to protect constitutional government as well as to enforce criminal law. It cannot be said, then, that the FBI's security intelligence function has been abused in this regard.

Just as the FBI's intellectual enemies swing wildly at the very idea of intelligence investigations, so do they attack the bureau's files. These, by their very existence threaten the basic rights of millions of American citizens, according to some "civil liberties" advocates. "At the very least," says Aryeh Neier, a national official of the American Civil Liberties Union, "millions of people have been injured by the data kept by the FBI."*

Neier refers to the identification operations of the FBI, which fill the fingerprint and arrest files. He is worried more about the dissemination of derogatory information from those files—a process admittedly susceptible to unintentional but real abuse, as found by the district judge in the Menard case. While these records exist at the expense of the mental serenity of ACLU officials, it is not arrest records but rather a mass of other files in the bureau that cause them the greatest distress.

The investigation files derived from internal security investigations are characterized as "dossiers" by those who would do away with them. The term "dossier" is used because of its dramatic, sinister connotations—it conjures up visions of secret files which contain, in addition to personal data, all those things which some vicious establishment prosecutor will some day use against the file subjects.

The fact of the matter is, the FBI investigative files are indeed secret, and should be (except in litigation), to protect civil liberties. But they are in no wise files compiled of adverse data

*Aryeh Neier at October, 1971 Princeton Conference on the FBI.

for use against persons the FBI wishes to target for trouble. They are investigative files and no more.

These files, by their very nature, can be no more, since they are simply the results of agent investigations—they contain *reports*. Every case, every physical surveillance, every interview of an informant, every interview of a suspect or associate of an investigative target, and every bit of information pertinent to a case is the subject of an agent report. Copies of these reports are sent to Washington headquarters. There, agents, clerks, or secretaries do nothing more than review and file the reports in the proper case files. No one processes them further, no one compiles the data into summary reports on the individual subject of a file; and no one compiles lists of subversives, criminals, or any such thing. The files are thus reports from the field on investigations performed, reports which are merely maintained in a central location of case files. This is not what could properly be termed a system of "dossier files."

Allan Belmont, an assistant to the director in charge of FBI investigations, explained FBI procedures in testimony in 1964 before the President's Commission on the Assassination of President Kennedy (Warren Commission). The testimony reads:

> Mr. Belmont. A case is opened by the FBI upon the receipt of information indicating a matter within the jurisdiction of the FBI. We restrict our investigations to those matters which are within our jurisdiction.
>
> The office of origin is the office where the major part of the work is to be done. Thus it should be the controlling office of the investigation.
>
> Normally, if an individual is under investigation, it will be the office where he resides. There will be in many cases investigation to be conducted by other offices. Those offices that have investigations in that case are considered auxiliary offices, and will cover the investigation sent to it, sent to them, by the office of origin or by another auxiliary office, if a lead develops within that area that requires attention elsewhere.
>
> I may say that the office of origin can be changed and is changed if during the investigation it becomes apparent that

the focus of the investigation has shifted to another area.

It is logical, therefore, that that office which bears the brunt of the investigation should be in possession of all the material pertinent to the investigation and should be charged with the supervision and running of the investigation and the direction of it.

In the event the office of origin is changed at any given time, the previous office of origin will forward to the new office of origin all material pertaining to the case so that it will have a complete file and the necessary knowledge to run the case.

Mr. Stern. Can you tell us a bit more about how information is maintained and how it flows through the system from headquarters to office of origin, to the auxiliary office or in the other directions that are possible?

Mr. Belmont. Since the information is maintained in a standard and uniform filing system in both our field offices and our headquarters so that there is complete uniformity in the handling of information, our main filing system is at headquarters. Consequently, we need here all pertinent information in any case. Consequently, the reports and information developed during a case are sent to our headquarters for filing.

It is pertinent to observe that we conduct close to two million name checks a year for other agencies and departments of the federal government. Consequently, we must have here all pertinent information so that a name check will reflect the information in possession of the bureau.

When a report is prepared in our field office—an investigation—and there are leads or investigation to be performed in another office, copies of this report are designated for that office, together with the lead or the investigation to be covered. Upon receipt of that the office gathers the background information from the report and proceeds with the investigation.*

Belmont's testimony gives no hint of FBI headquarters taking an active part in compiling the files. The information is fed in from the field. Much of it is raw data, none of it is evaluated except as to the reliability of the information, and the only concern of headquarters is whether the reports indicate FBI procedures and policy has been followed in the investigations.

*Hearings of the Commission, May 6, 1964.

This is illustrated by the following testimony of Allan Belmont at the same hearings:

> Mr. McCloy. Well, we had testimony here yesterday that in a preassassination investigation of Oswald that they learned he was a defector, they had interviews with him, and then they marked the case closed.
>
> At one stage it was reopened and then it was closed again because, as I gather it, there was no indication other than his defection that would lead to their, to the agents', feeling that this man was capable of violence or that he was a dangerous character in any sense.
>
> I gather that whether or not he was thought to be a dangerous character or whether he was capable of violence would be settled by the man in the field office, in the office that had charge, the man who was in charge of the office that was dealing with that case locally, is that right?
>
> Mr. Belmont. That is a judgment that he would render, but that judgment would be passed on by our headquarters staff.
>
> Mr. McCloy. Passed on by Washington?
>
> Mr. Belmont. Yes, indeed. In this instance by the Domestic Intelligence Division.
>
> Mr. McCloy. In this case then the decision to close that case, I am talking always about the preassassination business, was approved or tacitly approved by the Washington staff.
>
> Mr. Belmont. Not tacitly approved. Approved.
>
> Mr. McCloy. Approved. Well, you mark the paper approved or you just accept it, accept the file with a notation "return for closing."
>
> Mr. Belmont. When the closing report comes to our headquarters, it is reviewed by our supervisory staff, and if we do not agree with the action then the field office is notified to continue the investigation. That is a decision of substance.
>
> Mr. McCloy. Well, I can understand that but I gather when the report comes in you simply let the report lie unless you feel from your examination of it that it justified further action. You don't notify the field office, do you, that the closing of the case is approved?

Mr. Belmont. No, Mr. McCloy. With the volume of work that we have that would be an unnecessary move.

Mr. McCloy. I can understand that.

Mr. Belmont. It is, however, thoroughly understood through our service, through the system that we follow, that if that report comes in and it is reviewed and it is filed here, if there is disagreement as to the handling of the closing of the case or any other matter pertaining to the investigation, the [official FBI opinion] will then go out with instructions to the field.

This gives a good picture of the function of the files in FBI investigations. Files are, after all, fundamental to law enforcement and internal security investigations, as they are to the administration of any organization or business. In this perspective, the "dossier" criticism is ill-considered. Certainly, as long as the investigative functions of the bureau are legitimate, the corollary function of investigative files cannot be denied. But a question remains: is this power exercised correctly in everyday FBI practice? Or is it abused? This is not so easily answered, and we shall explore the subject in some detail. Some general considerations are in order.

In Mr. Menard's lawsuit, the issues were broader than one would surmise at first glance. Menard's fingerprint file and arrest record might be considered unfortunate or unfair, since he had not committed an offense; nevertheless the file could not damage him except by its disclosure. The judge apparently recognized this point, and enjoined the broad dissemination of the arrest information. The judge could have done better by restricting the information to FBI use only. Had Menard's arrest record been strictly maintained according to FBI policy—that is, as information filed *in confidence* for use in FBI investigations—the possible damage to Menard would have been minimized. In any event, it is obvious that the effect of the court ruling in Menard's suit was to endorse the value of confidential FBI records as a *protection for the individual.* This protection should hold as true for FBI investigative reports as for the fingerprint-arrest system. However, it seems the very people who

bemoan the damage to Mr. Menard can see only sinister implications in the secrecy of FBI operations and reports. Secrecy,
of course, is always suspect in American government. Yet one
cannot come down on one side of the issue when lack of confidentiality in the arrest files is challenged, and on the other side
when the FBI refuses to submit its files to public scrutiny. The
critics do come down on both sides, by unfairly imputing to
FBI officials a desire to "hide" their investigations.

Public scrutiny of FBI records is precisely what was demanded by the contributors to the Princeton Conference on the FBI
—including Aryeh Neier, the same man who at the same conference worried so ponderously over the damage done by disclosure of arrest information. An "overseer board" with *"access
to all bureau records and activities"* and an ombudsman also with
"access to bureau materials" were proposed by those meeting in
Princeton. Yet the conferees agreed that Neier was absolutely
correct about the need for sealing the fingerprint arrest files.

There is a conflict in principles involved here, and it is certainly not resolved by charging wrongdoing against the bureau
on both counts. As early as 1792, the founders of the United
States had occasion to confront the question of public disclosure of sensitive and potentially damaging information. At that
time, in the midst of the Aaron Burr conspiracy case, Thomas
Jefferson and Alexander Hamilton agreed that it was the executive's responsibility "to communicate such papers as the public
good would permit, and . . . to refuse those, the disclosure of
which would injure the public."*

The tradition has continued, and the FBI, an executive
agency, weighs seriously its responsibility to the public interest.
J. Edgar Hoover in 1956 wrote an article for the *Syracuse Law
Review* in which he recognized the rhetorical difficulties of the
bureau's position, and to a remarkable degree anticipated
today's attacks against the bureau. Speaking of intelligence and

---

*The Writings of Thomas Jefferson, p. 303-304, Washington, D.C. 1903, Thomas
Jefferson Memorial Association.

law enforcement agencies, Hoover said:

> The people are fully entitled to a general accounting of the operations and accomplishments of these (intelligence and law enforcement) agencies, but to open their files to public scrutiny would be the grossest violation of the trust which resides in these agencies—a violation which unquestionably would jeopardize the lives, welfare and reputation of many fine citizens and might lead to the absolute destruction of our form of government.*

The FBI agent follows two rules in his investigative reports: good English and neutral reporting of all information which he obtains. The second standard, it must be agreed, is not only vital to any investigation, but an extra protection for the individual. Consider what disasters might result if the reports were both slanted and open to public scrutiny.

The incorporation of all intelligence information in reports is an assurance that the information is available to all the agents working the case, and it is a key to headquarters' control of its field investigations. The reports often contain sensitive information in that: (a) individuals contacted in the course of investigations expect protection of their own privacy; (b) unproven data in the reports could unfairly damage other persons; and (c) the bureau's informants risk much by disclosure of their positions. All these considerations require that FBI reports be maintained in confidence. The choices are only two, in reality: either the reports are kept in confidence, or the reports will no longer record all the agent's information. Although the latter case would tragically change the nature of the FBI, it is exactly what would happen, should the prying eyes of a public overseer body or ombudsman search the FBI's investigative files.

To illustrate the need for confidential reporting, imagine what would happen if Special Agent A reported a meeting of himself, another agent and an Informant B who swears that

Syracuse Law Review (Vol. 8, No. 1, 1956.)

Professor C is a Maoist and has raised several hundred dollars among his academic colleagues for forwarding to a leader of a migrant labor union which the national ("Maoist") Progressive Labor Party favors. Now, Agent A must record this information, as he receives it, since the FBI has the duty of gathering intelligence information on the PLP. However, C is probably acting legally, B's information that he is a Maoist may not be trustworthy, the migrant labor leader may be no party to the PLP's designs, and C's colleagues may be entirely innocent of knowingly participating in a revolutionist's scheme. What a different picture would result if it became public that the bureau had a report in its files which "indicated" that Professor C was a Maoist, and that he and his fellow academicians supported PLP and a union leader with PLP connections. This may not be the case at all; yet, Agent A's report could be read to this effect. The harm from disclosure of such a report is obvious.

Imagine also what would happen to Informant B, who likely is a part of the same academic community, if the report were made public. The history of similar events (e.g., what happened at various Eastern colleges in the wake of disclosure via the "Media papers" of FBI informants in the academic world) is that for the informant, disclosure would damage his livelihood. "Academic freedom," as practiced, has not included tolerance for the patriotic Mr. B.

The FBI thus protects its sources. This is true even in reports which circulate to other agencies. Bureau memoranda based on informant reports in these cases use a code for the source. A separate paper which does not leave the bureau, names the informant or other source.

The important thing to bear in mind is that FBI investigative files are working files rather than evaluative memoranda. Unverified and incomplete data are reported; conclusions, except in functional matters, are left for others. Professor C, for example, is reported to be a Maoist by Informant B. Agent A may make a functional evaluation adequate to recommend or advise against opening a case file on C; he may have other in-formation that confirms or contradicts B's contention. Whatev-er the situation, the reports comprise an incomplete picture of Professor C and it is obvious that C has had no chance to deny the reports. His mention in an FBI file is thus fraught with possible unfair damage to his reputation. It will not, however, cause actual damage, nor even give cause for second thoughts on his part, unless the file becomes public.

All these characteristics of FBI investigative files have been recognized as vital to the type of investigative agency desirable in a free society. J. Edgar Hoover resisted proposals which would have required either disclosure or FBI evaluation of its investigative reports. In 1950 it was proposed as an amend-ment to the legislation establishing the National Science Foun-dation that the FBI certify the loyalty of scholarship grantees. Hoover advised against making the FBI responsible for judg-ing the loyalty of anyone, and persuaded the Congress to main-tain the FBI only as a fact-finding agency.

In those years, FBI files and investigations were involved in controversy. Again and again, bureau officials had to explain that the FBI was "a service agency. It does not make policy; it does not evaluate; it secures facts upon which determinations can be made by those officials of the United States government who have the responsibility for taking whatever action is indi-cated."

This is quoted from a November 17, 1953 statement by J. Edgar Hoover before a hearing of the Senate Committee on the Judiciary, which was delving into the Truman administra-tion's appointment of the late Harry Dexter White (who had been revealed as a key figure in a Soviet espionage ring) to the International Monetary Fund.

In the same year, Attorney General Herbert Brownell re-vised Attorney General Tom Clark's previous Departmental Order 3229 to prohibit disclosure of FBI records except upon the attorney general's authorization. The confidential nature of FBI work was thus being formalized.

About the same time, the publication of FBI papers, as required by Federal Judge Albert Reeves in the trial of Judith Coplon (for passing information to Russian agent Valentin Gubitchev), was a godsend for those who wished to portray the bureau as a bunch of giggling tattle-tales. Reported in these papers, for instance, is the statement of an informant that associates of Miss Coplon ran about their house nude.* What lawful interest, the critics asked, could the FBI possibly have in such information?

Plainly, this information taken by itself was trivial and embarrassing. It was, however, information related by an informant, and the rather free nature of his neighbor's activities was one reason his suspicions were aroused sufficiently to contact the FBI.** Should the agent have deleted the statement from the report? It may have proved worthless; but it may have borne on the credibility of the informant, or on the services Miss Coplon may have performed for the Soviets. No, the report—as part of a working file—would have been inaccurate without the remark concerning nudity.

J. Edgar Hoover, in his November 17, 1953 Senate testimony, had a basic answer for the critics who laugh at such "superfluous" information. He remarked: "Since we are not an agency for decision as to action, we are legally, morally, and in good conscience obligated to relay all information and facts we secure to the responsible officials and agencies of government."

In any case, the best protection for individuals who are directly or peripherally involved in FBI investigations is to maintain the bureau's files in confidence. Secrecy, in this matter, is a desirable government practice.

As discussed earlier, the bureau record in this regard has been excellent, as far as its investigative files are concerned. Even though much information exists in the files which some unscrupulous official could use for his own aims, it simply has

---

*Alan Barth, *Harper's Magazine,* March 1954.
**Remarks of Barry Goldwater, reprinted in *U.S. News and World Report,* April 16, 1954.

not been done. And the confidentiality of the files has the force of law.

The exception has been the criminal identifications records, which are disseminated outside the FBI's effective control. By law, most federal banks are permitted this information for "official use." But what further use for it than credit records do the banks have? Some thought should be given the use and potential abuse of these records. The FBI is not the place to look for a scapegoat. The bureau acts as no more than a collection and dissemination service for fingerprint records. If it is to do more, Congress will have to give it the power.

The subject of bureau files is not fully discussed without mention of the Security Index which has crept into the nightmares of the bureau's intellectual enemies. The index, true enough, existed, and probably continues to exist in modified form. At one time, it was a contigency list of those radicals (mostly Communists) whom the FBI would detain in the event of actual hostilities with a Communist power—quite like the list of Axis aliens and sympathizers which enabled a quiet, selective round-up of potential enemy agents at the beginning of American entry into World War II.

The index was compiled upon the recommendations of special agents who were responsible for evaluating the individual as to his inclination to help the enemy in time of war. Here is an "evaluation" on the part of the FBI, but again, it is a functional judgement: the decision actually to detain those on the list would be up to the President. FBI agents have been assigned the task of knowing the whereabouts of those on the list, in case the President should issue such orders.

A Security Index of the same sort today would be unmanageable for the simple reason that it would have too many names. The old list never numbered more than several thousand.

Whatever the nature of the list, can the power to prepare such a contigency list be denied? The power of the President to detain enemy adherents has the requisite precedents. The intelligence function which determines beforehand who is an enemy agent is a necessary corollary to that power.

So why the recurrent fuss over the Security Index? Because it is the single file system of the FBI which has a parallel in the dossier files of the police states. People on the Security Index list have been marked in one sense, as the unfortunate Bukovsky was marked in the Soviet Union. The parallel goes no further, however. One who is listed on a contigency basis as a probable enemy agent in time of war, is in a far different situation from one who is marked, like Bukovsky as a present enemy of the state and subject to state harassment or worse at any time. The former situation is compatible with a democracy with the most minimal capability of defending itself; the latter occurs only in an all-powerful police state.

11. Wiretaps in Perspective

Daniel Joy
with the Editors

One of the first administrative orders issued in 1924 by the just-appointed director of the FBI, J. Edgar Hoover, forbade all wiretapping. The 1928 edition of the FBI's *Manual of Rules and Regulations* directed that:

> Wiretapping, entrapment, or the use of any other improper, illegal, or unethical tactics in procuring information in connection with investigative activity will not be tolerated by the bureau.

This policy continued through 1931, but Attorney General William D. Mitchell, who was then assuming his position, reversed Hoover's wiretap ban. In a memorandum prepared in January, 1931, the FBI regulation regarding wiretapping was changed to read:

> Telephone or telegraph wires shall not be tapped unless prior authorization of the director of the bureau has been secured.

Hoover, in turn, announced that he would not authorize the electronic surveillance unless approved in advance and in writing by the assistant attorney general in charge of the case. The amended regulation continued in force until March 15, 1940 when Attorney General Robert H. Jackson announced *on the advice* of J. Edgar Hoover that the Department of Justice was re-instituting the wiretap policy as it appeared in the 1928 *Manual.* Although it would no doubt bring cries of disbelief from certain of today's critics, Hoover made his point to Jackson in a March, 1939 memorandum, following widespread charges of indiscriminate wiretapping.

> While I concede that the telephone tap is from time to time of limited value in the criminal investigative field, I frankly and sincerely believe that if a statute [to legalize wiretapping] of this kind were enacted the abuses arising therefrom would far outweigh the value which might accrue to law enforcement as a whole.

As a result, Attorney General Jackson announced that the practice of wiretapping would be stopped until and "unless Congress sees fit to modify the existing statutes."

Could this same Federal Bureau of Investigation subsequently threaten the privacy of American citizens with extensive use of bugs and wiretaps? This has been precisely the fear of some, but they have spoken only in generalities.

If this fear were placed in the perspective of what and how electronic surveillance can be employed *according to the law,* then the question would be reduced to answerable proportions. Then the question would be one of fact—has the FBI conformed to the law in its use of these techniques? It could still be argued that the law is too permissive in this regard, but anyone unwilling to address the facts of the issue presents no more than nameless anxieties. Of course this concern is not new, nor is it a recent development that the critics have refused to address the facts. In the late 1940s and early 1950s, critics, many taking aim at the Federal Bureau of Investigation, charged that wiretapping and electronic eavesdropping were being used far too extensively. The matter became such that FBI Director Hoover, when announcing on January 13, 1950, that the bureau was operating fewer than 170 telephone taps (and these were limited to national security cases) said, "This fact contradicts the hysterical utterances of those who would have us believe that wiretapping by the FBI is unrestricted and is utilized on a wholesale basis." President Nixon also said it was "hysteria" 21 years later in reference to charges that telephone tapping was extensive.

The controversy continues. In the *Washington Post* of February 27, 1972, Roger Wilkins suggested that technological advances in investigative work amounted to a "silent creeping. . . revolution" which all but threatened to destroy the private person's right to privacy. But such statements do not tell us anything. What are the facts? Is the private citizen, traditionally secure in his privacy, realistically and objectively threatened by the use of technological information gathering devices?

Although one might get a different picture from those who currently contend that the privacy of the individual is not secure, the matter of wiretapping has a significant history. Records indicate that the New York police, in 1895, less than two decades after the telephone was invented, used wiretapping to detect criminal conspiracies and to investigate committed crimes. Interestingly, in 1916, the *New York Times,* commenting on a New York State legislative investigation, editorialized: "The *Times* feels too few wires have been tapped, not too many, and that the exposé has hurt the cause of justice."

It was an issue in those days too. As early as 1905, the California legislature prohibited the interruption of telephone conversations. Other states, almost half of them, took the same or similar actions. Technological advances in eavesdropping were even then suspect.

Federal law, perhaps reflecting the authority of states in matters of criminal law and individual practices, was for all practical purposes silent on the question until 1928 when the United States Supreme Court ruled in the case of the *United States* vs.

Olmstead, * a federal prosecution against bootleggers. The prosecution, arising in the state of Oregon—a state which had prohibited wiretaps without court order—was based on information secured by wiretap. In holding admissible the evidence, the Supreme Court ruled that the activity was not unconstitutional because there was no unlawful entry or seizure of tangible things.

However, in 1934 the Congress adopted the Federal Communications Act, which included a prohibition against intercepting and divulging any wire communication. Interestingly, one of the elements of the crime was in divulging information from an electronic eavesdrop. Thus, this language effectively proscribed a wiretap product as admissible evidence, but it was susceptible to interpretation whether electronic interception was permissible in the case the contents were not divulged.

As noted, the modern FBI did not employ the technique until 1931, and then at the insistence of its superiors. After that, Hoover prevailed on a new attorney general to rescind the policy.

This order rescinding authority was Attorney General Jackson's order in 1940, but the reinstituted regulation was short-lived. On May 21, 1940, President Franklin D. Roosevelt, in a confidential memorandum (printed in full in the June 19, 1967, issue of the *New York Times*), issued a directive to the Justice Department as a result of the growing challenge to law enforcement inherent in the internal security stress in the days leading up to World War II. The Presidential Order read:

> It is too late to do anything about it after sabotage, assassinations, and "fifth column" activities are completed.
>
> You are, therefore, authorized and directed in such cases as you may approve, after the investigation of the need in each case, to authorize the necessary investigating agents that they are at liberty to secure information by listening devices direct to the conversation or other communications of persons suspected of subversive activities.

---

*277 U.S. 438 (1928).

In elaborating his views on the extent of use of wiretaps, President Roosevelt limited the use to two items of investigation: first, in those cases where sabotage or espionage are suspected, and second, in the domestic crime of kidnapping, which included extortion.

The regulated practice continued until modified by President Truman, who, on July 17, 1946, directed Attorney General Tom Clark to use, when appropriate, wiretaps in cases involving domestic security cases or "where human life is in jeopardy."* Then, an additional modification came in an order issued by President Lyndon Johnson which eliminated all wiretapping and other electronic surveillance except in cases affecting the national security and in which the attorney general had approved the action. But in another turnabout, Attorney General John Mitchell and President Nixon quickly rescinded this order when they took office.

Through all the modifications, the procedures for establishing electronic surveillance remained tightly drawn. At a minimum, the director, who in turn got the consent of an assistant attorney general, had to authorize the surveillance in writing. Thus, for the last quarter century, when wiretaps were in use FBI policy has permitted the installation of wiretaps, even in national security cases, *only* with advance written authority of the attorney general.

This authorization procedure was legally sufficient for years, based on the Supreme court ruling in the 1928 Olmstead case. But in 1967 the court decided that in non-security cases, warrants had to be obtained, and in 1972, the court required the same for domestic national security cases.

Responding to the change in course required by the 1967 court ruling, Congress passed the Safe Streets Act of 1968, substantially altering federal law regarding wiretapping and electronic surveillance. Making the distinction between private and

---

*This memo was also printed in the June 19, 1967 issue of the *New York Times*.

public (i.e., law enforcement) use of these tools, Title III of the 1968 act replaced the blanket prohibition instituted in the Federal Communications Act of 1934. Making use of the legal reasoning and constitutional law suggested in the 1967 Supreme Court case, this section authorized court-approved wiretaps and electronic surveillances, except that the attorney general was authorized to instruct federal authorities to undertake wiretaps and the like when the national security is involved. As a safeguard, the Congress also required court officials, in conjunction with law enforcement officials, to report annually to the Administrative Court of the United States the number of taps and surveillances authorized under the procedures detailed in the Safe Streets Act.

The latter provision was probably a sop to those who feared widespread use of the devices. Yet the extent of tapping and other electronic surveillances continues to be an issue of some magnitude. The reports, filed pursuant to the act, still have not eliminated or even diminished the nagging fears.

It should be noted parenthetically that if these reports cannot be believed, the lie would be of a magnitude unbelievable in itself. In his testimony before the House Appropriations Committee on March 2, 1972, Director Hoover pointed out the FBI's selectivity in the use of even this court sanctioned surveillance method. He stated: "As an example of this selectivity the FBI obtained 150 court orders for installing electronic devices during calendar year 1970 and 258 court orders in 1971." Though a single court order may authorize more than a single wiretap or microphone surveillance, these figures hardly seem to substantiate the fear of widespread surveillance.

It certainly is not a large number of taps in comparison to the breadth and scope of organized crime activities throughout the United States. For example, an adequate electronic surveillance of organized gambling activities would require a massive operation, since a great deal of the gambler's routine business is conducted by telephone. The series of raids on bookmakers' "wire rooms" and on numbers "banks" have shown that the telephone is a primary tool in the gamblers' operations. Nearly every adult male in a large U.S. city has had the experience of walking into a tiny corner "cigar stand" in which several men were employed and four to six telephones were immediately visible. Multiply this one location by a couple of dozen and the reader can begin to comprehend the massive scope of even a small local segment of organized crime activity.

But the hysterical do not want to believe the reports. In a major analytical essay, published by the American Civil Liberties Union, Herman Schwartz, a professor of law at the State University of New York at Buffalo, contended that electronic eavesdropping is considerably more widespread than the FBI, Hoover, or the government would have one believe. Yet in several different points in the essay Schwartz indicated that he just "didn't know" how extensive wiretapping was. He doesn't know otherwise but *for sure* he will not believe the government reports.

Similarly, a major series of reports in the *Washington Post* in February, 1971 catalogued a number of charges, most of which challenge the integrity of the Hoover testimony on the use of electronic surveillance. But their evidence is sparse indeed.

Post reporter Ronald Kessler quoted former Attorney General Ramsey Clark, along with several of those famous "well-informed (albeit unnamed) sources," to the effect that the FBI regularly "thinned out" its operating taps in order that Hoover might "honestly" testify as to the number of taps and surveillances. Although the reporter attempted to present this charge in a flat, "matter-of-fact" tone, it was actually an article filled with disconnected innuendo. Kessler cited a number of alleged, but unsubstantiated, charges by former agents (William Turner and Walter Sheridan) to suggest that Hoover authorized extensive bugging. Kessler quoted a "well-qualified" (again unnamed) source who contended that the FBI maintains, via a lease from the Chesapeake & Potomac Telephone Company of Washington, D.C., 450 lines for purposes of tapping in on phone conversations. Not elaborating on the source's qualifications (which is a serious failing with so many of the charge-makers), Kessler reported that his man knew of the situation (how is not reported). Beyond the unnamed spokesman's testimony, the only other evidence presented was a statement from a telephone company spokesman who denied the allegation and stated that the lines were "special test circuits" having nothing to do with wiretapping. Kessler quotes another (unnamed) former FBI "soundman" (read: wiretapper) who said that he had seen one of the "tech rooms" maintained by the bureau in a downtown Washington building formerly housing the Post Office. The tech room is used for monitoring lines which the bureau has tapped into. If they are relevant at all, these items are supposed to prove the case that the FBI is extensively and illicitly tapping phones and otherwise eavesdropping on the citizens in general.

The single, authoritative testimony came from Ramsey Clark, who as attorney general refused to authorize FBI wiretaps except in national security matters. Clark said, "Mr. Hoover, according to information given to me while I was at Justice, will pull taps off before he testifies, and he couches his language [sic]. Of course, you have to thin them [the taps] out anyway . . . I don't think the Hoover testimony ever purported to give the full extent of FBI wiretapping." It is interesting to note that Clark provides only hearsay testimony without any indication that he had firsthand knowledge of such a practice. In addition, he tries faint praise in implicating Hoover in an immoral deception of the Congress. Second-hand information from an "authoritative" source is still second-hand information. In court it wouldn't be admitted as evidence at all.

When Clark says that "Mr. Hoover will pull taps off before he testifies," he tacitly admits that the figures furnished by the FBI director to the House Appropriations Committee are, in fact, correct at the time of the testimony. Mr. Clark concedes, as well, "Of course, you have to thin them out, anyway," suggesting that the procedure is not unusual, only that the timing is designed to place the best possible light on the testimony, a tactic not entirely unique to the FBI insofar as government is concerned. One may presume that the number of wiretaps operated by the FBI varies from day to day or month to month, and that the number given by the director in his Appropriations Committee testimony doubtless represents a low point. However, a review of ten years of Hoover testimony reveals that the *average* number of reported wiretaps in "national security" cases is about 50 so that even if at the high point the figure were ten times that reported, the number would be around 500, hardly a wholesale or widespread use of the wiretap.

We are compelled to guess at the high figure, assuming Mr. Clark's assertion to be true; but interestingly, Mr. Clark himself could have made that unnecessary had he chosen to do so, or had he believed that his argument might have been bolstered by so doing. As attorney general, if he were at all aware of his office procedures, he did not have to guess at the number of wiretaps in effect at any one time nor did he have to rely on hearsay. Each and every wiretap in operation in a case involving the national security is placed only after prior written authority is received from the attorney general who may thus maintain an exact count, assuming he is sufficiently concerned to do so. Even if he is a shoddy administrator and has not maintained adequate records, he may at any time determine the number from his subordinate, the director of the FBI. That Mr. Clark chose to rely on innuendo in a situation in which precise knowledge had been available to him would, thus, seem to indicate that the real high-side figure was never high enough to outrage Mr. Clark's libertarian sensibilities at the time.

While evidence was lacking, the matter would not rest. Four months later, the FBI, through the testimony of Director Hoover and Associate Director Clyde Tolson before a House Appropriations Subcommittee, denied the Clark and Kessler allegations (*Washington Post,* June 9, 1971). To clarify the matter, it was reported that Attorney General Mitchell had approved fewer than fifty taps and surveillances via microphonic devices in national security cases that were then operating. This was reported in a Ken Clawson article appearing in the July 9, 1971, *Washington Post.* Clawson quoted Justice Department sources from interviews on the previous day. Kessler's reports were thus authoritatively denied by both Hoover and Justice.

Only if there were proof of a wholesale cover-up of taps and other eavesdropping would there be grounds justifiably to conclude that there is or was extensive federal bugging. The critics have never explained why the bureau or the Justice Department would attempt to fabricate a number (like 53). Even if the number were ten times that, it would seem that our fears for the integrity of an individual's phone circuit would still be minimal. What does seem likely, or at least very possible, is what former Attorney General John Mitchell suggested. He said in early 1971 that the idea of extensive bugging was becoming a national paranoia, that even congressmen have the feeling that *someone* (the FBI or CIA, no doubt) is tapping into their conversations. What is any more difficult than to challenge a *feeling,* a subjective determination?

This feeling is fueled at times by irresponsible charges. In 1966 the question arose regarding the FBI's use of electronic interceptions without the requisite authorizations. Senator Robert F. Kennedy of New York made the charge indirectly by claiming that certain taps had been made of telephones in the investigation of a Las Vegas gambling case during the years 1962-63, but that he, as attorney general, had approved no electronic surveillance except in cases involving the national security. The implication was, of course, that someone, probably Hoover, had authorized the taps on his own, without authority to do so.

Notwithstanding the assertion by Senator Kennedy that he had not authorized any electronic surveillances except in national security cases, Director Hoover produced, at the demand of Congressman H. R. Gross, an authorization signed by Robert Kennedy as attorney general, dated August 17, 1961. Concerning the controversy, the *Washington Post* of June 27, 1966 reported that a former official of the Justice Department said, "Hoover would never engage in any of that wiretapping [Las Vegas and Washington, 1962 and 1963] and bugging without authority from the attorney general." More specifically related to the actual charge, the *Post* story by reporter Richard Harwood continued:

> Another Justice Department figure with knowledge of FBI eavesdropping told the reporter, "Anyone who claims that Hoover had no authority for what he did . . . is just not telling the truth.
> "And anyone who says Bill Rogers, Bobby Kennedy, and Nick Katzenbach [all former attorneys general] didn't know what [Hoover] was doing, doesn't know the facts."

In every other case in which specific charges of unauthorized wiretapping have been leveled against the FBI, the bureau has been able to present specific refutation of the charges in the form of letters of authorization signed by the attorney general. It has answered the broad, non-specific charges with categorical denials—what else can it do?—coupled with annual disclosures to the House Appropriations Committee of the number of wiretaps in operation. It is difficult to imagine what further steps the FBI could take in order to achieve the maximum possible credibility in this area.

In sum, factual material on the question has been regularly presented to the public; the FBI's accounting is in turn supervised by the Justice Department and the President as a part of the normal operations of the executive branch. A preponderance of the available evidence confirms that wiretaps and bugs have been used by the FBI only in a very limited fashion.

Without question there is imperfection, and even equivocation in some instances, in the institutions of man, including the FBI. The question is whether we should say "especially the

FBI," as someone like Ramsey Clark would contend we should. But when the fabric of faith and truthfulness is so broken that a man cannot normally believe what others, government officials or not, tell him, then a crisis of significant proportions looms. This is not in any way intended to chill the investigative zeal of those seeking to dig out intolerable and unconscionable situations. But when unsupported charges become repeated so often that the recognition factor of the charge vests it with a patina of truth, truth itself is on the threshold of breakdown.

Former special agent, FBI critic and Princeton Conference participant William Turner, cloaking himself with the mantle of the inside authoritative source, again provides an example of the particle of fact, highly seasoned to induce a belief of widespread abuse. Turner devotes an entire chapter of his book, *Hoover's FBI,* to the subject of electronic surveillance (and is honest enough with the reader to express his view, based on purely philosophical grounds, that all electronic surveillance should be discontinued). He cites some specific instances, in cases involving organized crime activities and national security matters, in which wiretaps or microphone surveillances were used. As to *misuse* of the wiretap, however, he relies solely on his own editorial comments and some from the *St. Louis Post-Dispatch* and the *San Francisco Chronicle.* The newspapers' opinions understandably reflect the same view as that held by Turner, namely that there should be no electronic surveillance whatever. Turner's use of innuendo, on the other hand, may better be judged by what Turner leaves out of his recitation.

The opening sentences of his chapter on wiretapping, beginning at page 315, sets the tone: "Not long ago, at a San Francisco cocktail party, I had the strange sensation of hearing a voice from the past that I couldn't quite place. I studied the face—it was totally unfamiliar. Then it dawned on me: the voice was one I had heard many times while monitoring wiretaps years before. It belonged to Robert Treuhaft, a well-known civil liberties lawyer and husband of famed author, Jessica Mitford.

The tap on the Treuhafts was one of more than a dozen the FBI had installed in the San Francisco-Oakland area in the early 1950s." So it is that the reader is asked to regard Mr. Treuhaft as a "well-known civil liberties lawyer," husband of a prominent author and a person one would meet at a San Francisco cocktail party. The scenario thus suggested by innuendo is: FBI harassment of an especially virtuous citizen. The facts tell a different story. One Bessie Honig, herself a former member of the Communist Party, testified in 1957 that she "also worked with other party members, including Decca Treuhaft [Jessica Mitford] in party headquarters".* In its issue of December 19, 1946, the *Peoples World,* West Coast newspaper of the CPUSA, shed more light on Mrs. Treuhaft when it reported, "The Twin Peaks Club [of the Communist Party] whose $1,500 quota is the largest of any neighborhood branch, has had only 15 members active in the [fundraising] drive. And yet, due to the fine work of individual members like Decca Treuhaft, county financial director of the Communist Party . . . " And again, in June, 1957 Dr. Jack M. Patten testified before a hearing of the House Committee on Un-American Activities that he had been a member of the professional section of the Communist Party on the West Coast and, as such, had known both Robert Treuhaft and his wife, Decca Treuhaft (whose real name he thought to be Jessica) as members of the Communist Party.**

Turner may not believe these are sufficient reasons to justify the installation of a wiretap. It is clear, however, that Turner deliberately denied his readers an opportunity to make an honest judgment of their own. And describing the Treuhaft tap as "one of more than a dozen," Turner seems to make a poor case for his charge of indiscriminate FBI tapping.

*Report and Order of the Subversive Activities Control Board in the case of *Attorney General* vs. *California Labor School,* May 21, 1957.
**Report, *Hearings Held in San Francisco, Calif.,* Part I, Committee on Un-American Activities, U.S. House of Representatives, p. 1109-1171 June 18-21, 1957.

Turner adds another bit of innuendo when, on page 318, he states, "Although the annual announcement of the number of wiretaps in operation helped to reassure the public that the FBI was not promiscuous in its practices, it only hinted at the actual scope of electronic eavesdropping. In the first place there existed in the field what we called 'suicide taps'—those not authorized by Washington that would have killed the career of any agent caught installing them." Turner then hints, darkly, "But—you cannot train and equip people for electronic intrusion and expect them to hold themselves in check." (Why not?)

We must assume that Turner has knowledge of wiretapping because he was an FBI "sound man," an agent specially trained in the technique of installing and using wiretaps and microphones. This is not a course of training received by every agent in the FBI. It is a highly specialized field in which only a few agents are trained. This means, as we consider the "suicide tap," that not one, but two agents are involved and are risking their careers—the agent to whom the particular case is assigned and the specialist who, by reason of his training, must install the tap. Turner is quite correct when he describes this kind of tap in terms of "suicide." Its discovery by the bureau would result in severe disciplinary action and possible discovery by an outsider would, undoubtedly, result in dismissal. Under these circumstances, the necessity of a two-agent involvement in such a scheme reduces its possibility almost to zero at the outset— while suicide is not uncommon, double suicide is.

Turner further fails to tell us how the agents involved in such a matter would account for the use of the equipment or, even more difficult, how they would account for the time used to monitor the clandestine tap. Finally, assuming all these obstacles could be overcome and all of the bureau's careful inspection processes circumvented, Turner fails to suggest how the agent in the field will report the information he has thus illicitly obtained since all information in an FBI agent's report must be attributed to some source. If the naive reader of

Turner's book jumps to the conclusion that the agent will simply report the source as "confidential," he is mistaken for, while the bureau protects the identity of confidential sources from outside dissemination, an agent may not conceal the identity of sources from the proper bureau authorities.

Obviously, none of these restraints constitute absolute barriers to the installation and use of an unauthorized wiretap and the law of averages would suggest that some have probably been successfully installed. The restraints, imposed by the administrative rigidity about which Turner complains elsewhere in his book, do argue against his hint that the device of the "suicide" tap is one used casually by lazy agents seeking an easy shortcut on a tough assignment. They argue, further, that the concern of the FBI in the matter of the unauthorized wiretap is no less than the concern of the libertarian and constitutes the strongest safeguard against abuse of whatever authority the FBI may have to install wiretaps.

The wiretap and more sophisticated electronic surveillance paraphernalia have their proper place in the free society, but only when their use is reasonable, limited, and court-approved. It is ostrich-like to contend that, because these devices can be misused, they ought not be used at all. If we were to accept this notion as a fundamental principle, man would be unable to do much of anything. The challenge to the free society is so to construct the restrictions on electronic surveillance that its use will be limited to that which is both just and necessary. The United States has put its faith into the judicially supervised warrant procedure. In attempting to control, rather than to eliminate, the use of the wiretap, the Congress attached its warrant practice to the use of taps. Those who would employ the tap or make use of some other electronic surveillance are required to prove the reasonableness, usually to a judge, of both the need and the probable utility of their request. These conditions seem eminently reasonable to reasonable men.

12. Thoughts on the Use of Informants

Mary S. Meade
with the Editors

Introduction/Editors

Frank Donner is a lawyer. He is one of the most persistent critics of the FBI's use of confidential informants, at least in the field of internal security matters—a field sweepingly described by Donner as "political." Like many other FBI critics, Donner has had little complaint about the use of the informant in criminal cases. When the informant works among radicals, however, he spares nothing in his criticism, which is based essentially upon his own political leanings.

At the Princeton Conference on the FBI, Donner delivered a lengthy polemic on FBI "informers" used in the "political" sphere. This contained no surprises given his premise that all alleged threats against the nation's security from within the United States are "myths." However, even within the limitation imposed by his own predisposition, Donner's presentation contains many sweeping distortions and untruths.

For example, Donner characterizes *anyone* who furnishes information to the FBI (or the police) as an "informer" regardless of motive. A large portion of his paper does deal with motives, to the effect that all "informers" hurt their fellow man and no motive is justifiable in his eyes. And of course all those who furnish information in security cases are "political informers," a class even more reprehensible in view of the sanctity in which Frank Donner holds the political criminal. So it is that in Donner's eyes, arson, bombing, kidnapping or even murder, committed in furtherance of "political" ends, somehow are of a different or higher quality than the same crimes committed for other motives (e.g., profit, to mention one Donner finds unacceptable).

Having denounced the motivation of all informants, Donner then attacks their credibility, charging that the information they furnish is unevaluated and suspect because of their highly subjective view of the matter reported on. The matter of credibility, of course, is one of continuing concern for any investigator who uses informants. His best assurance in that regard is usually another informant who is in a position to report entirely independently on the same subject matter. Yet Donner also takes great pains to criticize alleged proliferation or duplication of informant coverage, mocking the few reported incidents of informants furnishing information about other informants. The fact is, this very duplication provides one of the few real safeguards available to the investigator to ensure a high level of credibility on the part of informants. One of the cardinal rules in handling informants requires that one informant shall under no circumstances know the identity of another. This accomplishes several purposes simultaneously. For example, if there were three informants working within a single organization, the surest test of the reliability of their coverage comes from a comparison of their reporting. If their coverage is accurate, they will almost surely report on one another, enabling the investigator to evaluate all of them and to be sure they are maintaining their "cover." The investigator will then be able to judge whether they are getting out of line, or if any are transgressing that fine line between participant and provocateur.

But Donner sees an informant under every bed. He sees them in massive numbers in every organization and group that advocates even the mildest "dissent," and complains that their presence constitutes a massive "chilling effect" on "progressive change." In the same breath he describes FBI officials who have expressed concern regarding an internal threat to our constitutional system as "paranoid." Perhaps that word would apply better to people frightened of "informers" who don't exist.

To be sure, not every informant is a paragon of virtue, enacting his role with purity of purpose and nobility of motive. For example, the *typical* security informants in the past (and there have been exceptions) have been persons who have first been members of extremist or revolutionary groups and who have, for one reason or another, defected. Their reasons for defecting have varied but, again, the usual defection has resulted from gradual disillusionment with the purposes or methods of the group itself. The breaks are often complicated by emotional readjustments, not the least among which have been feelings of guilt about the act of informing on those who have been the friends and co-workers of the informant. Some have re-defected (and have furnished much of the grist from which the critics draw their material). Others, having been persuaded to accept the most extreme views at one end of the political spectrum, as easily become extremists at the other end. Some have or develop a "spy complex," thinking of themselves as "secret agents" and fantasizing their roles, particularly if they "go public." Some, as the critics are hasty to suggest, furnish information they believe their contacts want to hear. Some become too active and, indeed, become provocateurs. All these are the hazards encountered daily by the investigator who works with informants and no one, even the wildest critic, is more aware of the potential problems than he. Any intelligence operation that either totally believes or totally disbelieves its sources of information is doomed to failure.

Those like Donner who wish to stigmatize the informant have on their side the normal human desire of one person not to cause any sort of harm to another. Donner would like to extend whatever "guilt" this might carry with it to *anyone* who cooperates with the law enforcement official. His attitude is a simple extension of the law of the underworld, the antithesis of the society that accepts the rule of law, democratically arrived at.

The term *confidential informant,* when used by the FBI, is a generic one. The confidential informant is an individual who, by reason of his or her special position relative to an organization or other individuals, can furnish "inside" information that could not be obtained, except with great difficulty, from any other source. It is a relationship that usually lasts for a long period of time, and thus is maintained on a highly confidential basis in order to preserve the source as viable, and also to ensure his safety. He may be, and frequently is, compensated for the information.

There are some things that a confidential informant is *not.* He is not an employee or an agent of the FBI, and so acts independently of the bureau, completely free of any of the discipline or organizational loyalty that may govern the conduct of an employee. He is not the supplier of a one-shot piece of information no matter how useful it might be. Any citizen may furnish information to the FBI on a confidential basis and that confidentiality will be respected, but he will not be regarded or designated as an informant unless the relationship is to be continued. Likewise, the person who is simply in a position to furnish certain confidential information to the FBI such as a bank cashier, a credit bureau manager, or a university registrar, is not regarded as an "informant," though their identities may be protected because of the sensitive nature of their relationships.

Every law enforcement agency uses informants. Some, not including the FBI, use their own employees in "undercover" roles, fulfilling essentially the same functions. But, whether it be in the realm of narcotics, organized crime, street crime, or internal security matters, inside information is absolutely essential to the daily performance of the investigator's job.

The law enforcement officer, FBI or otherwise, literally uses the informant as an investigative tool as he would use a records system, laboratory, or any other tools at his disposal. He does not have to recruit an informant as a paragon of virtue; indeed, the more useful the informant proves to be, the less likely it will be that he fits the virtuous mold. The investigator need not be concerned with motive, even if it is crassly materialistic or vengefully evil. He need be concerned only with the end product—the information furnished by the informant, its accuracy, and its usefulness in the investigative area in which the agency is concerned. A policeman's gun is a tool, though it is regarded by some as being evil *per se.* But in the care of a trained, cautious, and stable officer a gun is used only in defense of life and thus becomes a positive force, in its own way, in the social order. In evil or careless or unstable hands, the gun clearly becomes an instrument of evil. The same may be said of any tool used by the lawman—including the informant. The tests to be applied must consider not only the tool but the character and nature of the man or organization that uses the tool. This judgment should be remote from the emotional matters of motivation or character raised by Donner and others. It should be based on all available facts. It must account the results—how the informant's information is used by responsible authorities. The article which follows will discuss the FBI's use of informants in this perspective.

It is usually the case that the use of an informant is viewed subjectively in relationship to the viewer's feeling about the group or individual upon whom the informant is being asked to inform. This being the case, the FBI's use of informants in its various areas of criminal jurisdiction has almost never been publicly criticized. The same cannot be said for bureau informants in the security field. Here the criticism has been loud and frequent and, almost always, based on the political leanings of the critic.

The reader should consider, as he reads, many of the practical drawbacks connected with the use of informants, remembering however that their use cannot and should not be entirely abandoned. In overcoming some of the objections, we should consider the relative advantages that might be achieved by the FBI's use of undercover agents—FBI employees, responsible to FBI administrative and disciplinary control—who assume "underground" roles in either criminal or security cases. This would not change or even alleviate the objections of the critics, who object for their own highly parochial reasons to all FBI security investigations. Such a procedure, however, would increase the level of credibility regarding security information in the minds of the more objective majority and could certainly raise the level of credibility of such agents called as witnesses in criminal cases.

The Ethics of Being a "Stool Pigeon" / *Mary S. Meade*

Every major police force and investigative agency utilizes, at least occasionally, either undercover agents or informers, as they are notoriously known. Most, indeed, use both. In some police agencies, greater emphasis is placed on regularly paid employees who operate undercover, and, in their line of duty, incur the grave risks of consorting with radicals, conspirators, and criminals, while reporting in secret to their police superiors about the actions and plans of the organizations into which they have infiltrated.

Other police or law enforcement agencies rely more heavily upon the confidential informant—the person who is already a part of the criminal, radical, or conspiratorial group and who furnishes information on a sporadic or regular basis in exchange for money, mitigation of charges, or expiation of conscience. In the past, the FBI has largely used informants in lieu of undercover agents. The confidential informant may not only face a good deal of inherent danger in his position but also has drawn upon himself the apparent loathing of today's journalists, politicians, academicians, and others, regardless of his motives for informing. Indeed the word "informer" is today invested with the overlay and debris of far too many wasted emotions and prejudices. As a result, the informer, no matter who he may be, has been equated with what Marx, Lenin, and their latter-day followers derisively call the "stool pigeon."

But as Robert Louis Stevenson once wrote: "It is not the hangman but the criminal who brings dishonor on the house." It is the criminal, not the informer, who is the enemy of a free society. Those who heap abuse on the informer and not the wrongdoer in effect abet the crime.

The police, especially detectives and their counterparts everywhere, always need information. They must check clues. They must tediously confirm or refute strange little bits of information or news received from witnesses. They must track down people and talk to them for the express purpose of getting information. Myriads of pieces of news or information are useless or trivial or commonplace, and certainly *most* of it is not evil or even incriminating. Isn't a witness to some event justified, if not obligated, in telling the police the truth?

The answer must be yes, if we are to keep any semblance of law and order in our society. It is the duty of a witness to cooperate with the police in the detection of crime and criminals. Only when the information of the witness turns out to be misinformation, only when he has lied or perjured himself in bearing witness, only then must he be regarded as criminal, and certainly then his actions must be despised. It therefore becomes the very serious obligation of the police force or investigative agency to verify information it is given. And not merely to verify it in the same haphazard manner in which Jack Anderson verified his "information" on Senator Eagleton, but to play the role of the devil's advocate seriously in each individual case. It is in this way that the informant plays a constructive role in society's ever constant search for truth and justice, by assisting the various law enforcement agencies in their work against various types of criminal behavior.

The FBI is no exception, and as was reported to me by former Special Agent Ray Carew, the bureau relies heavily on the information obtained from persons who furnish confidential information on a regular basis, or "informants" as they are referred to by the agents. In Carew's words, "This is especially true in the hijacking area where I worked in New York. But it is important to keep in mind that informants are *not* employees of the bureau, and this is made clear to *them,* along with other points, from a checklist of items that the agent is supposed to tell the informant. There are two types of informants, security and criminal." Agent Carew worked only with criminal informants—CIs—as they are referred to in the bureau. Before an individual becomes a CI, he is designated as a PCI, or potential criminal informant. After a PCI furnishes information in two or more cases resulting in an arrest or recovery of goods, there is a request made to designate him as a CI. In other words, the reliability of the informer as well as his truthfulness must be established *before* he is accepted by any of the bureau's agents.

But what determines whether an informant is good or evil? Whether his information should be accepted or rejected? Certainly to be thorough and fair one must consider the nature of what he says and does, his purpose or motivation, and of course the circumstances. If what he says is a lie, his actions are wrong. If his motive or purpose is sinister or vengeful, his conduct in informing is open to question, yet the information he furnishes may be reliable and useful. The circumstances of his act are perhaps most important. For example, if his motives are evil, but his information truthful and helpful toward the capture of criminals, then his *purpose* must be censured, but his *actions* must be permitted. The combinations are limitless, and that is why *each* informant must be examined individually, and the value of *each* piece of information tested.

Ex-agent Carew reminds us that informants are often criminals or conspirators themselves. Surely there are cases when the individual has genuinely reformed, and has been overcome with a sense of righteousness. But perhaps more frequently it is a means of escaping or mitigating punishment for himself. And certainly there will always be those who can be persuaded by the ever popular dollar. But regardless of their motives, these men and women can and do help in the search for justice, and it is most unfortunate that the press and news media today have transferred the common loathing for informants and their actions, as is revealed often luridly in the Sunday supplements, to the FBI, and to other law enforcement agencies that utilize informants. As *Newsweek* put it in a recent article, "The risks of dependence on this kind of intelligence—particularly intelligence for cash—are manifest. The informer's stock in trade is that information, not its veracity but to what degree it satisfies the agent. There is the additional danger of the informant becoming the actor and even the provocateur. Yet the dependence continues."*

Questioned about this, Mr. Carew pointed out that first an informant must prove himself as a potential informant, and *only* when this has been done can he be designated as a regular informant. He said, "Each...informant has a different reason for doing what he is doing...Some CIs become very friendly with the agents, and give information for that reason. In the criminal field the type of person who is a CI is not your normal citizen, and about 99 out of 100 times has a criminal record. But I don't know of any instance where a CI has ever deliberately provoked an incident. *All* information is checked out and investigated. You *cannot* convict a person just on information obtained from a CI."

Ex-agent Carew referred to the same *Newsweek* article which had cited one source as saying that all agents are now required to carry at least twelve informants: "Six criminal, three national security, three racial."** He noted, "They are all wet on that

---

Newsweek, "Hoover's FBI: Time for a Change?" (May 10, 1971), p. 30A.
**Ibid.

point...When I was in the bureau, there was no quota for twelve informants...The bureau wanted you to have at least two CI's *if* you worked on criminal cases. You come by CIs through the various cases you investigate and the thousands of people you talk to during your work...I personally believe that the informant program is well worth the money spent because of the time and money saved by not having to use more agents on an investigation...One CI alone was responsible for information that led to the arrest, indictment, and conviction of over forty members of a hijacking ring in New York. So you can see some of them are very valuable."

Perhaps it should here be stressed that the informant works for or with a particular special agent or agents, not for the bureau. He must be approached only by the agent to whom he is responsible although FBI regulations require that all informants be contacted by *two* agents, first for the protection of the primary agent and, secondly, to ensure the continuity of contact with the informant. A special agent is aware of the identity of only his own informants and usually only a very limited number of agents in a field office are in a position to ascertain the identity of any other of the informants handled by the office. At the bureau level in Washington, only a few agents assigned to coordinate informant coverage and activities in the field would be in a position to know the acutual number of confidential informants handled throughout the bureau, much less their true identities.

Some confidential informants are paid according to the quality of the information furnished by them and, then, only on a "C.O.D." basis. Others are paid on a regular basis since they supply the bureau with a continuing flow of information. Others require no payment, and in fact give their information out of a simple desire to promote law enforcement. Any citizen may furnish the FBI with information on a confidential basis but would not be regarded as an "informant" simply by virtue of that fact.

Surely it would seem obvious that information about crimes

or criminals, or anticipated crimes or potential criminals should indeed be welcomed, even when it comes from "informers" in the pejorative sense. However this apparently is not always the case. In April of 1971, a group calling itself the Citizens Commission to Investigate the FBI publicly revealed the names of seven persons allegedly acting as informants for the bureau. The so-called informants were not ex-convicts, but rather ranged from a college switchboard operator to bank employees and the dean of student affairs at a predominantly Negro college.* Needless to say, the disclosure of their names foiled any further chances of their obtaining more information, and, to be sure, brought down on these people the loathing of many a *New York Times* reader although the news of their "informing" became known through the release of a series of documents stolen from an FBI resident agency—the reprehensibility of which act is consistently ignored. Copies of some of the stolen documents were given to the *New York Times* by a Cambridge, New Jersey organization called Resist, which supported and helped fund community-based groups which opposed the war in Vietnam.** In making the documents public the Citizens Commission explained: "We regret that this action was necessary, but these are troubled times, and the struggle for freedom and justice in this society can never succeed if people continue to betray their brothers and sisters."*** The commission therefore felt that it was *their* responsibility to "inform" on these informants, or, to use their own words, "to betray their brothers and sisters."

Many outspoken liberals have taken up the "commission's" cry, and continually deplore the informant as somehow more reprehensible than the very criminals about whom he informs. In fact, once the news of these alleged informants had been

---

*Bill Kovach, "A Citizens Commission Writes to Seven Persons Who It Says Served as Informers for the FBI," *The New York Times* (April 13, 1971), p. 23.

**Ibid.

***Ibid.

publicized, Dr. Robert D. Cross, president of Swarthmore College was quick to warn these "accused" of their possible dismissal because of their dealings with the bureau. He labeled such connections as "beyond the limits of reasonable cooperation."* And he announced the appointment of a committee charged with "alleviating in every way possible harm unjustly done to the reputation of those given notoriety."** But in fact who was really responsible for this "notoriety"—the informant who relayed confidential information, or the thieves who stole the documents and made them public? Strangely, Swarthmore's president advocates no censure of *their* illegal actions or the publication of materials intended by the FBI to be confidential —primarily for the protection of those named, it should be added. And apparently the Swarthmore incident is encouraging other college presidents to act in a similar fashion.

The president of nearby Haverford College also issued a memo to his college community, reminding them that "we will not be involved in any undercover searching into the thoughts or teachings of a professor, student, or staff member. Anyone on campus who is asked, in his role as a member of the college community, for information to be provided on a covert basis on another member of the community should immediately report that request to the president. Any failure to do so will be considered a violation of college policy."*** The intention of this memo is stunning. What it comes down to is a college *policy* which prohibits cooperation with a law enforcement agency "for information to be provided on a covert basis." The informant, regardless of his motives, be they pure and altruistic, or corrupt and cunning, has been banned unless, of course, he is informing on a law enforcement agency.

On October 15, 1970, President Nixon signed into law the Organized Crime Control Act of 1970 which, in addition to

*Gayle Tunnell, "Swarthmore Informers Warned of Dismissals," *The Washington Post* (April 10, 1971).
**Ibid.
***Ibid.

establishing significant provisions to extend the fight against organized crime, increased the FBI's investigative responsibility in yet another field. This act charges the bureau with the investigation of bombings or attempted bombing of any property of the federal government, or that of any institutions or organizations receiving federal financial assistance. In view of this extension of the bureau's jurisdiction, President Nixon proposed and provisions were made for the hiring and training of 1,000 additional FBI agents. There is no mention whatever in this public law (91-452) of any college or university campuses, either generally or specifically, though most receive some federal funding. Nonetheless soon after its passage, "choruses of perennial alarmists cried out that the FBI planned to saturate college and university campuses with more than 1,000 FBI agents to monitor student activities."* The fact is, most of the manpower added by the appointment of more agents is being used in the many new investigations of organized crime.

But the alarmists rather than the facts were being heard, so finally the late director himself was forced to clear the air: "A thousand FBI agents are not being stationed on the nation's campuses. In fact, none are. This is not to say that *if a bombing occurs* on a college or university campus in violation of Public Law # 91-452, FBI agents will not proceed to the site of the bombing and conduct an investigation. They have no choice in the matter. They are required by law to investigate such acts."**

Perhaps it was the same type of misinformation which led to the spread of the incredible rumor that the FBI used and encouraged the use of Boy Scouts as informants. Here again the anonymous Citizens Committee to Investigate the FBI was responsible for the publication of the information used to support this charge. A document said to be included among those stolen from one of the bureau's offices was made public by the

*Human Events, "FBI Agents Are Not Stationed on Our Nation's Campuses" (July 3, 1971), p. 11
**Ibid.

National Action-Research on the Military-Industrial Complex (NARMIC), a program of the American Friends Service Committee. The document alleged that 20,000 Boy Scouts in Rochester had been recruited as "extra eyes and ears" of the FBI. According to a *N.Y. Times* story, "The committee said the... copies of the documents were received by NARMIC recently from the anonymous Citizens Committee to Investigate the FBI, the group that perpetrated the theft of some 800 documents in nearby Media, Pennsylvania."* The press and news media were quick to jump at the "scandal," and in fact in the space of a week's time the *New York Times* had devoted three major articles to the "Role of Rochester [N. Y.] Scouts as 'Informers.' "** Said the *Times,* "Reports of the alleged FBI document inspired visions of Cub patrols spying on 'suspicious' persons, eavesdropping on conversations, and keeping a wary eye on strangers instead of following the more scoutly pursuits of tying knots and studying Indian lore."***

Yet somehow I did not find myself stealing furtive glances at our own foster child—a "notorious" Boy Scout. In fact the entire absurdity of the situation was only enhanced by the staid and serious treatment it was given by the press. It was certainly given a great deal of coverage, and Gene Cruse, the local scout executive in Rochester found it necessary to clear up the matter. He described a pamphlet which may or may not have been misconstrued by the alarmists. In the pamphlet, the scouts were indeed "enlisted" by the FBI, as well as by the Fire Department, the Coast Guard, the local and state police, the sheriff's office, the Poison Control Center, and Civil Defense. The scouts had been asked to "report such things as faulty traffic signs, blown-out street lights, fires, youngsters playing with matches, trees blown down, flooded viaducts, suspicious strangers in neigh-

New York Times, "FBI Said To Urge Use of Boy Scouts as Informers" (May 15, 1971)
**Homer Bigart, "Role of Rochester Scouts as Informers is Belittled," *The New York Times* (May 19, 1971)
***Ibid.

bors' homes, and suspicious strangers loitering about schools. Asked if the scouts were required to 'snoop,' he said: 'Hell, no, they would report to police only as participating citizens.'"* "We're pawns in somebody's effort to smear the FBI," said another scout official.**

Indeed there are many who would like to "smear" the bureau, and one of their most favored tactics is to discredit the informant and disparage the infiltrator and, by so doing, discredit the information they supply. This was made abundantly clear to me recently, when I had the misfortune of attending a "debate" at the College of William and Mary. The topic was "Oppression in America," or so we were led to believe, and the participants were William Kunstler, attorney for the Chicago 7, and Phillip Abbott Luce, a former member of the Progressive Labor Party.

In a most dramatic entrance, Mr. Kunstler greeted his opponent by calling him an informer and a Judas Iscariot with whom he refused to shake hands. Such informers as Mr. Luce, the attorney proclaimed, "are a danger to a free society,"*** and must therefore be "ostracized by everyone who believes in a free society."**** "There is no room for someone who reports on our conversations," Kunstler said. "Otherwise children spy on their parents, and the Gestapo is everywhere... This is oppression as much as wiretapping." Mr. Luce, author of *The New Left,* repeatedly denied that he is or ever was an informant, and it is clear from a reading of Luce's books and his testimony before congressional committees that he did not furnish information to any law enforcement agency until after having had a complete change of heart and conscience, he left the Progressive Labor Party. Luce tried without success to

*Ibid.
**Robert Sherrill, "Boy Scouts: When Not Helping That Little Old Lady . . ." *New York Times* (May 23, 1971)
***Bill McLaughlin, "Kunstler-Luce Debate Almost Turns into a Fight," *The Daily Press.* Newport News, Va. (April 6, 1972)
*****The Times-Herald,* Wm. & Mary Debate Almost Turns into a Fight" (April 6, 1972) Newport News, Va.

direct Mr. Kunstler's train of thought to the issue at hand. But the attorney was not to be swayed from his objective, and he succeeded in putting his opponent on the defensive and turning the "debate" into a subjective condemnation of informants. He even remarked that "at least Judas hanged himself."*

But a good deal more was ignored here than just the topic of the debate. With a minimum amount of ingenuity Kunstler finessed his audience and opponent into agreeing that, yes, all informants are evil, and, yes, wiretapping is the oppressor's tool. This was accomplished in the space of ten minutes and by means of a simple and apparently unjust accusation. But the point here is this: what if Mr. Luce really had been an informant? What if he really did help indict Fr. Philip Berrigan and six others?** Surely there would have been no comdemnation whatsoever if an informant had been able to prevent the assassinations of John Kennedy, or Martin Luther King. Should we not be just as anxious to prevent criminals from blowing up underground heating tunnels in Washington, D.C.? Or from any other conspiracy or crime that is preventable? It is difficult to find a reason why any citizen, regardless of his motives, should be condemned for having helped to prevent a crime or injustice.

In 1955, the informant who was responsible for the arrest of the notorious Russian spy, Martynov, was praised and esteemed as a responsible citizen. He was a colonel soon to be retired from the United States Army. The Soviet spy made a proposition to him to sell information to the Communists, and the colonel appeared to agree. A meeting with the spy was arranged in New York, and an FBI agent was substituted as the contact. Shortly thereafter the bureau was able to close in, and Martynov, who claimed diplomatic immunity, was declared

---

*Ron Gup, "Kunstler, Luce Debate Oppression in America," The *Flat Hat, The College of William and Mary* (April 7, 1972), vol. 61, # 26, p. 1.

**Boyd Douglas, a jail cellmate of Philip Berrigan, became an FBI informant and star witness at the Berrigan trial on charges of conspiracy to blow up heating tunnels in Washington, D. C.

persona non grata, and was compelled to leave the country. It is true that this colonel was a voluntary, rather than a paid informant, and needless to say it would be ideal if all informants would give their information out of the noblest of motives. But the human condition prevails. We all have our motivations and the world is no Utopia.

It is highly doubtful that ex-convict Boyd Douglas informed on the "Harrisburg 7" out of the same patriotic convictions which moved the retired army colonel. Douglas was a paid informant who probably sought to mitigate his prison sentence, and because of this he managed to lead a "double life" as a federal prisoner and as a trusted member of the anti-war movement. It is certainly apparent that the character of Boyd Douglas is not flawless; he has become an object of loathing by some. But this must not be allowed to cloud the facts. In smuggling letters from Father Philip Berrigan and Sister Elizabeth McAllister to the FBI, Douglas was able to provide the bureau with the most important evidence of their conspiracy charges. In two particular letters exchanged by the nun and the priest in late August of 1970, "they discuss the possibility of a plan 'to kidnap—in our terminology make a citizen's arrest of—someone like Henry Kissinger.' Another of the more than 20 long personal letters . . . [discusses] . . . a 'subterranean project in the district,' which Douglas says is the plan to blow up the tunnels in Washington."* Another news story said, "It now appears that one of the letters Douglas turned over to the FBI may have given away the hiding place of the Reverend Daniel J. Berrigan, Philip's brother who lived underground for $4^1/_2$ months after being sentenced to prison for destroying draft files."** It must therefore be stressed that whether or not Boyd Douglas is an admirable fellow, it is clear, or should be clear, that because he was an informant he was able to supply

*Betsey Medsger, "FBI Informer's Assurance Is Wearing Thin," *The Washington Post* (April 13, 1972)
**Trudy Rubin, "Portrait of an FBI Informer," *The Christian Science Monitor* (March 3, 1972).

the FBI with information which may well have prevented extremely serious crimes from occurring. We must therefore take care not to put the informant on trial for his motives when we should put the criminal on trial for his actions.

Recently the American Medical Association emphasized its belief that citizens, especially professional persons such as physicians, should cooperate with police efforts in the capture of criminals. *The Journal of the American Medical Association* accordingly advertised a "wanted poster" of a young woman indicted for conspiracy to transport illegal explosives across state lines. The young woman was "known to be afflicted with a severe skin condition known as acne vulgaris which could necessitate treatment by a dermatologist."* Another poster appeared in a subsequent issue of the *Journal* asking AMA members to be aware of a former nurse's aid charged with defaulting on a bond and issuing uncovered checks. She was pictured, and described as suicidal. A group of doctors, not wanting to become involved or to be placed in the position of informing, organized opposition to the posters. But the Judicial Council of the AMA reviewed the matter and reaffirmed the "idea that such notices should be published as a public service."**

This type of cooperation on the part of the American Medical Association is the type which the late FBI director believed so important to the success of the bureau. Mr. Hoover always hoped that that cooperation would be voluntary. He once said, "If we knock on a citizen's door, he does not have to talk to us or give our special agents information. This is a decision he must make. We can solve cases only if citizens furnish information."*** It is certainly true that informants, voluntary or paid, save the bureau (and therefore the taxpayers) countless

*Jane E. Brody, "Plea to Doctors by FBI Decried," *The New York Times* (April 23, 1972).
**Ibid.
***Jack Nelson, "FBI Used Cash from Mississippi Jews: $36,500 Paid to Ambush Klan." *The Washington Post* (February 13, 1970).

amounts of money. The recruiting and training of a special agent is a long and expensive venture and the men and women so recruited and trained meet the highest standards of character, judgment and professionalism in law enforcement.

Rigid discipline and education continue throughout an individual's employment as a member of the bureau, thus constantly adding to the education of an agent. Today the 8,600 agents are responsible for the investigation of more than 185 types of criminal and security cases. If there were time and money to train twice as many agents, the bureau still would not be able to solve as many crimes or gather as much intelligence as it does now with the aid of informants. This stands to reason. The informant usually is in the right place at the right time. He is often a witness to a crime that has been committed, or to a conspiracy that has been plotted. Such is typical of the informants who voluntarily give their information to the bureau, or who approach them requesting a "reward." In all cases the information must be thoroughly checked out, and it should here be stressed again that the FBI will not rely solely on information obtained from a criminal informant.

Most informants are specifically recruited by the individual FBI agents. The bureau is well aware that there are certain groups, particularly in the areas of organized crime and subversion, that would have been virtually impenetrable without the aid of these informants. Those who are specifically recruited by the agents are often paid for their work, or at least they are paid for their expenses. But some informants are called upon to penetrate certain lawless and/or subversive groups, posing as members of such groups. In doing so, they incur serious hazards and often risk their own lives. And even if they are doing their work for the worst possible reasons, they nonetheless provide a service to the bureau, a service which has in turn provided information to assist in indicting many a criminal.

Particularly in the field of security investigations, we must not overlook the importance of the disenchanted informant or "defector" as the case may be, who has been vitally important to our national security during the hot and cold wars. Theirs is perhaps the most difficult information to divulge, for in bearing witness to the facts they are also renouncing their one-time friends and associates.

I recall an episode in my father's life concerning his client Bella Dodd, the once important Communist Party official in New York State. She began to have doubts about the Communist Party after being a faithful functionary for many years. Two events in particular were to disillusion her, a disillusionment begun in 1939 with the short-lived rapprochement between Hitler and Stalin, and culminated in 1945 with the callous and savage manner in which Earl Browder's former devotees and henchmen turned on him, on orders from Moscow. Earl Browder had been the head of the CPUSA for years, and Bella Dodd genuinely regarded him as a friend; as did, according to appearances, other party bigwigs.

Shaken and humiliated by these two shattering events, Bella Dodd's loyalty to Marxist principles began to wane, and for strength and consolation she turned to her new friend, Judge Louis Pagnucco of the Family Court of the City of New York. Indeed this man's prudence and congeniality were to have a great effect on her future. After many conversations with the Judge, Bella Dodd knew she would have to abandon her former beliefs and face the reprisals of her comrades. Judge Pagnucco introduced her to his friend, my father, Godfrey Schmidt, asking him to meet with her and advise her in all legal matters. And so for some six months my father and Bella Dodd discussed Communist doctrines and practice. Finally there came a time when Bella knew she must tell her story to the FBI, but for months she remained reluctant to become, in her words, a "stool pigeon." In the end she realized that she had to tell the truth, and she gave the FBI everything she knew. Bella Dodd's information was given in the sincere conviction that she was serving the cause of true human freedom. And she was.

No matter how repugnant the informant or his motives may be in the eyes of the law enforcement officer, the information furnished by him is subject to independent verification; if it is found to be accurate, the informant gains credibility. The character and motives of an informant are considered no less by investigators in judging credibility, but in the final analysis, so long as the information furnished by him is found to be factual, his character and motives become irrelevancies. The accusing cry of "stool pigeon" will not change cold, hard facts, though, of course, it may render them less believable in the minds of some.

In 1970, a Jewish community in Meridian, Mississippi was to realize this fact, and indeed paid $36,500.00 to two Ku Klux Klan informants. A series of nightrider attacks in Mississippi were directed against Negro homes and churches, as well as against the Jewish community. In the fall of 1967 a synagogue and a rabbi's house were bombed, and Jewish leaders began to raise funds to solve the crimes. "On May 27, 1968, a bomb shattered a synagogue at Meridian . . . Finally the FBI and the Meridian police decided to use the reward money to pay the informants (directly) . . . rather than for information leading to the arrest and convictions of the terrorists . . . The reign of terror ended after a shootout. There has been hardly any violence in Mississippi since. And the White Knights of the Ku Klux Klan has virtually disbanded."* Here is a case where the community, as well as the investigative agency, realized the usefulness of the informant's information, and through cooperation with the police brought these otherwise evasive "nightriders" to justice. Some distinction should be made between the "defector" who has made a total break from his former associations and decides to "tell all" to the FBI or another agency, and the "informant," who may, for reason of conscience or cash, decide upon the same break but retains his associations

---

*Jack Nelson, "FBI Used Cash from Mississippi Jews: $36,500 Paid to Ambush Klan," *The Washington Post* (February 13, 1970).

under pretext of continued loyalty and, while so involved, furnishes a continuing flow of information. In the generic sense, the former is not usually classed as an "informant" by the FBI while the latter is. In the same generic sense, the "informant" is certainly not an "undercover FBI agent" or "operative."

Recently a major crackdown against organized crime crushed "four multimillion dollar gambling operations in the New England area." On September 13, 1972, 89 persons were arrested "after a federal grand jury indicted [them] on illegal gambling charges."* It was estimated that the gambling operations netted several million dollars a year in illegal betting. It was established that "the bulk of the information resulting in the indictments was gathered by electronic surveillance devices used by FBI agents with court authorization."** In addition, in this particular case an informant was instrumental in the successful trial. He was Vincent C. Teresa, or "Big Vinnie" as he is known in the crime world. Big Vinnie, a former "gambler, loan shark and swindler . . . became a government witness, and revealed the Mob's secrets to the Justice Department."*** In fact he became the government's key witness, and with his help the police were able to put forth a "major assault on organized illegal gambling operations based in the Metropolitan Boston area."****

One must never lose sight of the basic objective of justice, which we seek in fighting every crime. Naturally that objective would be lost if we were to fight crimes and criminals with illegal and evil weapons. But if, in our fight to preserve law and order, we can encourage one "Big Vinnie" to tell the truth to help preserve the rights of a community of free men, we have accomplished a moral good. Big Vinnie may have aided the police for the selfish reason of mitigating his own punishment

*Herald Traveler and Boston Record American, "FBI Crackdown Nets 89" (September 14, 1972).
**Ibid.
***Ibid.
****Ibid.

(as did Joseph Valachi, who gave information to the FBI on *La Cosa Nostra* from his jail cell), or enriching his own purse; but in encouraging him we will at least have established truth as our goal, and as our means to obtaining true justice. Moreover, we will have encouraged a citizen's active participation in the political life of the society, even though that citizen may be a former criminal. What better type of reform program can there be than one of active participation in the life of the community?

The concept of the informant really is closely related to the idea of freedom. The informant, whatever his reasons, does serve the cause of justice in his community, and thus fulfills an important citizen's responsibility. Aristotle, Thomas Aquinas, Immanuel Kant, and Jacques Maritain, among many, affirmed the responsibilities which freedom imposed on citizenship. Maritain commented, "The famous saying of Aristotle that man is a political animal does not mean only that man is naturally made to live in society; it also means that man naturally asks to lead a political life and to participate actively in the life of the political community. It is upon this postulate of human nature that political liberties and political rights rest. . ."*

*Jacques Maritain, *The Rights of Man and Natural Law*, trans. D. C. Anson (New York, 1951), p. 84.

13. The Gentleman's Force

Charles Rice
with the Editors

Americans seem willing to understand and tolerate a "Dirty Harry" or "Popeye Doyle" on the local police force. Since criminal elements respect no ethical limitations, it seems only just that the police reply in kind. Movie cop-heroes sometimes treat their criminal suspects in a way movie audiences think fair, even if brutal; and in the theater at least, the tough cops get their jobs done. But offscreen, being "ugly" is not necessarily the quality of an effective law enforcement officer.

There is one law enforcement agency which stands as the model of the opposite character. The FBI is this model, and there is no force quite like its special agents. They sleep at home (or alone when in the field), remain sober in public, treat people with courtesy and respect, and they also perform their investigations as gentlemen.

The FBI is truly the gentleman's police agency. Yes, agents

bust down doors, shoot it out with crooks, and deal with unsavory informants. However, no one has heard "police brutality" complaints against the FBI; no one can recall an instance where the bureau agents have manhandled a suspect; and no victim of FBI guns has been wounded in the back while fleeing and not immediately endangering life. These things are not done by special agents, and any who would believe otherwise must invent the "facts" to support his position.

There is nothing inherent in a federal investigative agency which would incline it toward the sort of gentlemanly law enforcement practiced by the FBI. This character was bred into the bureau, and it was one man, J. Edgar Hoover, who did it. Under a different director, the agency could have been quite different in this respect; for its assignments are concerned with as rough a lot of criminals as are the targets of any other police agency.

Director Hoover would not, nevertheless, permit his bureau to become involved in the dirtier business of law enforcement, no matter whether this policy gave the criminals and subversives a decided advantage. His belief was that if the FBI agents were well-trained and dedicated professionals, then they need not employ foul methods. His opinion on law enforcement ethics was often stated. In a 1952 article, Hoover addressed the problem of what officers do outside the reach of immediate supervision. He wrote:

> It is in this area that law enforcement ethics must rise to prevent abuses, such as third-degree techniques, unlawful arrests, unreasonable detentions, illegal searches and seizures. These practices are anathema to civil liberties, destroying the very heart of the American democratic system. They represent law enforcement at its worst.*

Up-to-date scientific methods of crime detection would do the job, in Hoover's view. Technical knowhow on the part of

*37 *Iowa Law Review* 175, 178.

law enforcement would take the edge off the attack against society by criminals. Thus, no need existed for FBI use of illegal interrogations, searches and seizures, and unreasonable detentions.

But illegal methods are not the only taboo in the bureau. (In this regard, the FBI differs little from other modern police forces; the fact is, Popeye Doyle notwithstanding, modern police avoid illegal procedures.) In the bureau, however, ungentlemanly as well as illegal methods are out of bounds.

The distinction is apparent in the FBI's reliance on informants for intelligence operations, both within the criminal and totalitarian-radical syndicates. Under Hoover, the bureau did not have agents in deep cover, making it the only large law enforcement force which does not employ the technique. Undercover assignments can be unsavory, and to date, the bureau has insulated itself from this risk by using non-bureau personnel—informants—for the undercover intelligence assignments.

This is not to imply that the FBI men are cowering individuals who shirk the risky tasks. The bureau has thought it more important in the long run that its agents be known as gentlemen. The FBI properly demands that its personnel be thoroughly reputable in order to be accepted without question anywhere by the public. Law enforcement must be respectable, Hoover often cautioned, because it cannot long perform its functions without public good will. Thus, the FBI is a gentleman's force as a matter of policy.

Everything about the FBI seems to be an embodiment of this philosophy. Its recruitment, training and regulatory policies stress the morality and performance of duty expected of gentlemen (and, now, ladies). Recruitment is aimed at college graduates, mainly lawyers and accountants; training instills in the recruits the respect for individual rights and the techniques of professional, cool-headed law enforcement; and high morals and ethics are enforced in the field. The success of the philosophy is a matter of record, as far as concerns the image of the FBI. One striking indicator is the high esteem in which thousands of former agents are held by private employers.

The philosophy has its controversial ramifications—of late, the most hotly debated is the bureau's penchant for disciplining agents who "cause embarrassment to the bureau." Some critics, somewhat inconsistently with their broader views, contend that discipline for this reason is unfair. But the agents understand the policy; the FBI, their employer, demands that the agents represent the bureau well, and if they cause damage to their employer's image, they expect to be disciplined. They understand that the gentleman's force is expected to maintain its appearances.

Imagery is important in the FBI's contacts with the public as well. In all its investigations, the FBI treats with politeness those it touches. For example, FBI agents interviewing a person, perhaps a friend or relative, who may have information about a fleeing felon, do not employ tactics which would force information out. Third-degree methods, which are illegal, are one way a practical cop can get his information. Threats of other action are also effective, particularly if the person being questioned has something to hide (e.g., prostitutes and addicts who are invaluable police informants for this very reason). But the FBI discourages such tactics. The usual procedure by interviewing agents is to identify themselves, advise the subject that they are looking for the felon, suggest that perhaps it would be best for the suspect if he were to face justice, and straightforwardly request the cooperation of the one being questioned. No tricks and no threats; the agents just ask.

Surprisingly, this approach works quite well for the FBI, not in any small part due to its respected image. Friends and relatives more often than not believe the FBI agents who promise to protect as best they can the life of the person they are seeking. Local police too often have a different image, and do not get the same degree of cooperation.

FBI agents are instructed to treat those they interview in a non-accusatory fashion, and never to suggest antipathy for the suspect. In the same way, agents steer clear of referring to the suspect in accusatory terms. This approach softens the brittle feeling toward law enforcement held quite naturally by one who is asked to give information, and it creates a gentlemanly image among those who have had personal contact with the FBI. The FBI's respect for individual rights is underscored by this approach.

What it means is that the FBI not only stays within the limits of the law in its techniques, but that it goes an extra mile in order to ensure that it does not harm the public. Its caution has perhaps been the most substantial protection against abuse of its power.

This is well illustrated by the FBI's method of interrogating subjects. Most everyone knows, now, that persons can "take the Fifth Amendment" to avoid testifying against themselves in court. It is also widely known that confessions out of court cannot be used against a person in court, unless the confession was "properly" secured.

The latter rule is the subject of the most famous and controversial Supreme Court case in point, *Miranda* vs. *Arizona** where the court decreed specific procedures that police must follow in their interrogation of suspects. Miranda and others had been questioned by the police without being advised of their right to have a lawyer present and their right to remain silent. The resulting confessions were excluded from evidence by the Supreme Court. The court stated the rule:

> *He must be warned prior to any questioning that he has the right to remain silent, that anything he says can be used against him in a court of law, that he has the right to the presence of an attorney, and that if he cannot afford an attorney one will be appointed for him prior to any questioning if he so desires.* Opportunity to exercise these rights must be afforded to him throughout the interrogation. After such warnings have been given, and such opportunity afforded him, the individual may knowingly and intelligently waive these rights and agree to answer questions or make a statement. But unless and until such warnings and waiv-

*384 U.S. 436 (1966).

er are demonstrated by the prosecution at trial, no evidence obtained as a result of interrogation can be used against him. (Emphasis supplied.)

This was not always the rule. The Supreme Court long ago interpreted the Fifth Amendment to exclude from evidence any involuntary confessions or admission made by the accused. Such involuntary statements must be excluded in considering the defendant's guilt or innocence because involuntary statements are inherently untrustworthy and because their admission would violate the Fifth Amendment concept of fair play. Third-degree methods of extracting confessions were thus ruled out. But the list of the suspect's rights as decreed in *Miranda* were new in the law as of that 1966 ruling.

The FBI, however, had not waited for the Supreme Court. It took pains to assure that all the technicalities of its warning procedures were above reproach. The FBI was not about to risk the admissibility in court of confessions it obtained.

In fact, the Supreme Court in *Miranda* reviewed the FBI's interrogation procedures and set them out as a model for state authorities. From a letter to the court which was printed in the decision, the bureau's cautious regard for legal technicalities is made plain. Asked what warning was given individuals "interviewed" by agents, the FBI replied:

> The standard warning long given by special agents of the FBI to both suspects and persons under arrest is that the person has a right to say nothing and a right to counsel, and that any statement he does make may be used against him in court.
>
> After passage of the Criminal Justice Act of 1964, which provides free counsel for federal defendants unable to pay, we added to our instructions to special agents the requirement that any person who is under arrest for an offense under FBI jurisdiction, or whose arrest is contemplated following the interview, must also be advised of his right to free counsel if he is unable to pay, and the fact that such counsel will be assigned by the judge. At the same time, we broadened the right to counsel warning to read counsel of his own choice, or anyone else with whom he might wish to speak.

The FBI warns a suspect at the outset of an interview, and an arrestee as soon as practicable; in all cases the warning precedes an interview for the purpose of obtaining a confession or admission of guilt.

Asked what practice it has in the event that the individual requests an attorney or has an attorney appear, the bureau stated:

> When the person who has been warned of his right to counsel decides that he wishes to consult with counsel before making a statement, the interview is terminated at that point. It may be continued, however, as to all matters *other* than the person's own guilt or innocence. If he is indecisive in his request for counsel, there may be some question on whether he did or did not waive counsel. Situations of this kind must necessarily be left to the judgment of the interviewing agent.
>
> A person being interviewed and desiring to consult counsel by telephone must be permitted to do so. When counsel appears in person, he is permitted to confer with his client in private.

If the individual requests an attorney and cannot afford one, the FBI policy was stated as follows:

> If any person being interviewed after warning of counsel decides that he wishes to consult with counsel before proceeding further the interview is terminated, as shown above. FBI agents do not pass judgment on the ability of the person to pay for counsel. They do, however, advise those who have been arrested for an offense under FBI jurisdiction, or whose arrest is contemplated following the interview, of a right to free counsel if they are unable to pay, and the availability of such counsel from the judge.

Not indicated in the letter quoted by the court is the fact that the interviewing agent usually has at his fingertips a form or two for the suspect's or arrestee's signature. One form declares that the signator has received the warnings, another form declares that he has willingly waived his right to remain silent and have counsel. Most often, the FBI obtains signatures on the waiver forms.

There is a very good reason for this: unlike state and local police authorities, the FBI seldom depends on confessions for proof of guilt. This is so because the FBI rarely arrests a suspect unless it has "the goods" on him already. Quite often the bureau deals with "fugitives from justice," whose confessions are the worry of someone else's jurisdiction. In crimes which come under the FBI's original jurisdiction, the FBI will seldom arrest a suspect until after it has obtained, or believe it will get proof of guilt, but it may keep him under surveillance. When he is interviewed, he usually knows the FBI has what it needs to support a prosecution. In these circumstances, the suspect is prone to give it up and cooperate, and if he doesn't the prosecution has good evidence anyway.

Not many police agencies have the luxury of operating in this fashion. Most must depend a good deal on confessions. The Supreme Court in *Miranda,* by comparing the FBI experience to law enforcement in general, was comparing apples to oranges, and stirred up quite a controversy as a consequence.

The fact remains that the FBI long had been super-cautious in the technical procedures of interrogation. This is an illustration of its long-established policy to operate in a gentlemanly way.

14. By the Book
Donald Albanito
with the Editors

Rigid Rules—Why the Complaints?/Editors

A former head of the Criminal Division of the Justice Department once told Tom Wicker, the media outlet for Robert Kennedy's legal crusaders at Justice, that the FBI bureaucracy had produced a legion of "paper work agents."* According to Wicker, the official said:

> "They go right by the book. They can't innovate, they can't think for themselves, they have to check every move with Washington. Orderly procedure has become more important in the FBI than solving a crime."

Wicker considers this a serious indictment of the Federal Bureau of Investigation and its director at the time, J. Edgar Hoover. FBI procedures are rigid, it is said. Worse, the mass

*New York Times Magazine, December 28, 1969, p. 7.

of "detailed paper work" centralizes control of agents' work and lends itself for use against agents whom headquarters wants to discipline for less than official reasons. Headquarters exercised summary powers over the lives of special agents; quick disciplinary transfers and reprimands and censures are meted out without mercy. Most infamous to Wicker was the iron-clad rule in the bureau that agents and officials report only to the bureau, and any matters which go outside the bureau go through the director.

These are curious complaints, considering that they come from a source one assumes would be concerned about police agencies operating in highly sensitive areas. If the bureaucratic system of the FBI were changed to meet Wicker's objections, would either the function of the agency or its performance as regards civil liberties be improved? That is a question seemingly ignored by the *New York Times* columnist.

Other critics attack on a more personal basis. This is an approach taken by former agent William Turner in a chapter titled "The Cult of Personality" in his FBI book. The personality, of course, was J. Edgar Hoover, and as a dismissed agent himself, Turner's dislike for Hoover's form of discipline is acute, indeed. It shows. He truly hated Hoover.

Nothing is right about the FBI procedures and rules, if Turner's characterizations of a special agent's life can be believed, and he cannot fathom an agency which demands loyalty to itself and its chief. He finds something unsavory in an organization which is so distrustful as to expect rule violations to be reported by fellow agents, which has routine and not so routine inspections, which sometimes wipe out whole field offices. He is absolutely beside himself thinking about letters of censure which cause a "tendency . . . toward caution" among agents.

Generally, Turner cannot be caught lying about facts, although much of his knowledge is based on agent scuttlebutt It is what he leaves out that reveals his stories to be so one-sided, the product of an anti-bureau bias rather than that of concerned research. Never does he state the case for discipline in the FBI, and never does he relate the rules to that need, except as to chuckle about how experienced agents thwart them.

Certainly the FBI does things by the book. This fact stands out to any objective observer. Any agent in this situation will find a certain amount of "Mickey Mouse"—procedures and paper work that seem to be routine for the sake of routine. Agents could also be expected to view as unfair some of the disciplinary actions (or promotions) when firm control is exercised by headquarters. Sometimes agents have not been treated fairly, and some FBI officials have been notoriously short with their underlings. To maintain, however, that such matters taken by themselves prove oppressive, or destructive of FBI performance, is to neglect entirely the merits of an organization which operates by the book.

Americans cherish fairness. As citizens we ought to be most concerned about the impact of the FBI on the life of the nation, and we should not be taken in by those who, like Turner, hurl embittered attacks at the bureau in the form of stories about unfairness to its agents. Instead, the bureaucracy should be analyzed from the viewpoint: what has been the impact, desirable or undesirable, of the FBI as it came to be administered under J. Edgar Hoover?

That is the overall question. The corollary issues are matters of performance and degree: (1) Did Hoover's intention of holding tight control materialize in fact and continue as the bureau grew? (2) Have FBI procedure and discipline accomplished the intended purposes, or have they served to thwart or drive out good agents? (3) Has the performance of the bureau been rendered more desirable in fact by application of its rules or has the FBI fear of embarrassment overtaken the system of internal accountability? (4) Has the control remained reasonably related to better performance, or has rigidity hampered performance? These are the questions discussed by Professor Donald Albanito below.

One question was not considered by Dr. Albanito. That is

whether FBI rigidity has resulted in "stultification of viewpoint," the words Tom Wicker uses to describe the bureaucratic result of the director's tight control. As this story goes, Hoover's over-firm grip on the bureau produced a legion of yes men under him. The implication is that Hoover thwarted the efficient performance of bureau duties. The average citizen would regard such criticism as nit-picking or worse. The bureau has not lacked for creativity or efficiency.

The charge is nonetheless made by many of the bureau's detractors, and it reveals a bias. Can the critics deny that agents have energetically chased kidnappers, car thieves, bank robbers, and, of course, subversives? Certainly not. In speaking to other issues, they commonly bemoan the *over-activity* of agents in these areas. What they really mean to say, then, is that agents who would otherwise energetically participate in the crusades dreamed up by the Tom Wickers are stultified by the bureau. FBI rigidity is not the object of their criticism—it is the bureau's policy and viewpoint, which to the detractors are not as enlightened as their own views. In a word: the FBI isn't "liberal" enough for them.

Whatever the merits of Wicker's enlightenment, it has no bearing on FBI agents as they perform their duties. FBI policy is not established by outside critics, but by the director and his superiors in the executive branch, in accordance with the acts of Congress.

How well this process works is another question. It wouldn't work well if the men who populated the agency were no more than yes men. Actually, agents aren't called on to be yes men unless it comes to carrying out the policy decided upon by headquarters.

It would appear that the critics misinterpret the situation within the FBI if they really think bureau personnel are without the opportunity to speak up. True, differences tend not to be aired publicly, and if they are, the person responsible may be dealt with harshly. Moreover, there is a common viewpoint in the FBI to a degree that would surely alarm the critics. But none of this is the result of any stultification of viewpoint. Differences do exist in the bureau, and are even encouraged when constructive. The agent who fails to offer advice to headquarters when he had such to offer is likely to be reprimanded.

It is not true that agents are uncommonly fearful of reprimands for mistakes made. A former assistant to Hoover tells of one agent who had so many reprimands his file would have bested even William Turner's. Yet he was promoted time and again, because headquarters recognized the initiative of the agent. He was always in tough spots, and he was aggressive. Sometimes he got in trouble, hence the reprimands. But he never got caught making the same mistake twice, and he was promoted even while on probation.

Neither is it true that Hoover surrounded himself with pleasant natured men who contributed no policy initiative. At headquarters, the assistants would meet at executive conferences on Wednesdays to discuss administration and to formulate policy. Hoover seldom was in attendance, but would receive recommendations from the conferences. These were arrived at after discussion and votes which, although it may amaze the critics, were often divided. Those in charge of the respective divisions were responsible in the first instance for policy initiatives in their fields. Upon submission of the recommendations, Hoover would sometimes accept them, sometimes take one side or the other, and occasionally require further consideration. The decision was his, but he would not apply recriminations upon those who had not agreed—indeed he demanded honest discussion. He would not, however, tolerate deviation from the policy once set.

Further, the special agents in charge of the field offices, who were directly responsible to the director, would be regularly called to Washington for policy discussion. Hoover expected them to make the decisions in the field, and thus considered them important to policy input.

This is hardly the operation of an agency that has been robbed of vitality by either a personality cult or a frozen bureaucratic routine. The questions remain however, as to whether the administration of the FBI is adequate to the needs and limitations of an investigatory agency operating nationally. We turn to a management expert for an answer to this question.

The Administration of the Bureau / Donald Albanito

An organization such as the FBI provides a highly specialized service and operates in a highly sensitive area, with civil rights and national policy implications. Consequently, it attains both its highest degree of effectiveness and its greatest regard for its limitations when it is tightly knit, and tightly controlled. But it has a job to do, and for that reason it should he highly mobile and hard-hitting.

These ends are served well by an FBI organization which stands out as a well-controlled and coordinated machine which is highly responsive to commands from the top. In fact, the bureaucracy of the FBI is a classic example of Max Weber's* theory of organization in that specialization, a hierarchy of authority, a system of rules and impersonality are its foundation.

In many ways the late J. Edgar Hoover was the FBI, and in many more the bureau was a reflection of the man who "founded" it, and for nearly 48 years ruled it (internally) with absolute authority. The practicing goals and methods of the bureau always were a reflection of Hoover's personality. Unfortunately such issues as Hoover's autocracy, eccentricity, and age had been the major focus in recent years in most literature about the FBI. While these may have been interesting and may shed a great deal of light on how and why the bureau grew to its present proportions, taken alone, they did not provide sufficient material upon which to make a value judgment of the bureau's accomplishments and effectiveness. To do so re-

*Max Weber, *The Theory of Social and Economic Organization,* Oxford University Press, 1947.

quires a look at both the historical development of the bureau and the FBI as it operates in the world of today.

To many, the FBI stands as the symbol of American determination to preserve and protect the democratic form of government established here almost two centuries ago. A few are convinced that it has wiped out organized crime in the United States and that only J. Edgar Hoover stood between them and communism (especially in the years after 1945). At the other end of the scale, there are a few who have labeled it "the product of a given society, dependent on its myths and failings."* These opinions purport to be evaluation of FBI performance and impact, but in their bias they generally ignore objective appraisal of the bureaucracy which underlies the FBI's action or inaction. Without an assessment of this aspect it is but undisciplined speculation and arbitrary vilification, hardly the substance of constructive analysis.

Moreover, to evaluate the performance of the FBI, one major question must be resolved at the very beginning—that of efficiency. The question is not in the abstract; efficiency must be related to the purpose of the organization in society. What is essential is to understand that the FBI was created within this democracy for a specific purpose; hence its achievements toward its purpose should be the only measure of the organization's efficiency. As Peter Blau notes: "Bureaucratic and democratic sometimes can be distinguished on the basis of the dominant organizing principle: efficiency or freedom of dissent. Each of these principles is suited for one purpose and not the other. When people set themselves the task of determining the social objectives that represent the interests of most of them, the crucial problem is to provide an opportunity for all conflicting viewpoints to be heard. In contrast, when the task is the achievement of given social objectives, the essential problem to be solved is to discover the efficient, rather than the popular

*Sanche De Gramont, *The Secret War*, New York, Putnam, 1962.

means for doing so. Democratic values require not only that social goals be determined by majority decision, but also that they be implemented through the most effective methods available, that is, by establishing organizations that are bureaucratically rather than democratically governed."*

This concept is usually neglected by those who criticize FBI efficiency. Normally, such criticism presumes that the bureau should conform to the critics' own view of social needs, and when performance is lacking in furtherance of these causes, inefficiency or lack of aggressiveness is blamed. Such arguments miss the point. FBI performance must be judged on the basis of its legitimate objectives, which are the business of the society, not on the decisions of bureau officials. Their task is primarily to promote bureaucratic efficiency toward those objectives.**

The FBI was born in the days of President Theodore Roosevelt. Then Attorney General Charles T. Bonaparte advised Congress of talk of an investigative wing to the Department of Justice. He said: "The attention of the Congress should be, I think, called to the anomaly that the Department of Justice has no executive force, and, more particularly, no permanent detective force under its immediate control . . . it seems obvious that the department on which not only the President, but the courts of the United States must call first to secure the enforcement of the laws, ought to have the means of such enforcement subject to its own call; a Department of Justice with no force of permanent police in any form under its control is assuredly not fully equipped for its work."*** The Congress ignored his plea, and the Department of Justice adopted the practice of "borrowing" agents from the Treasury Department's Secret Service to carry out its investigations. These makeshift measures continued until Congress amended the Sundry Civil Appropriation Act. This amendment forbade the Department of

* Peter M. Blau, *Bureaucracy in Modern Society* (New York, 1956,) p. 107. 1956,) p. 107
**See *Ibid.* pp. 61-66
***Whitehead, *op. cit.*, p. 19

Justice and all other executive departments to use Secret Service agents in their investigations of law violations. After the restrictive amendment was approved, President Roosevelt directed Bonaparte to create an investigative service within the Department of Justice subject to no other department or bureau, which would report to no one except the attorney general. On July 26, 1908 Bonaparte issued orders for the creation of an investigative agency within his department—the beginning of the FBI. Finally, on March 4, 1909, the new Attorney General George W. Wickersham conferred on the department's investigative service a secure place and the dignity of the title—Bureau of Investigation.

While having only a few agents and limited crime fighting jurisdiction, the bureau was itself beset with problems. Essentially it lacked character and discipline. At the outbreak of World War I, it was totally unprepared and unequipped to deal with espionage and sabotage. To add to its problems of inexperience, there were charges of corruption which pervaded Washington and touched the bureau.

Wartime security problems were added to the bureau's duties as they arose. But because it was unprepared, and possibly corrupt, from the "Palmer Raids" until Hoover's appointment in 1924, the bureau's reputation was that of a somewhat shady "snoop group," wielded and controlled by politics and a private clique of shysters who had become acknowledged and accepted in Washington. By the time of the Harding administration, the bureau had turned into a politically controlled group of private investigators whose characters were so much in question that one—Gaston B. Means—was suspended because of much adverse public opinion.

Finally, in 1924 in the aftermath of all the bad publicity and exposure of the corruption throughout the Harding administration as a whole and the Bureau of Investigation in particular, President Coolidge demanded Attorney General Daugherty's resignation and appointed Harlan Fiske Stone in his place. Chief Burns' resignation and the appointment of John Edgar Hoover as acting director of the Bureau of Investigation came a few days later, marking the beginning of a decisive change in the operations and public image of the Bureau of Investigation.

In later years Hoover was decried as being interested only in becoming the hero of America or the symbol of truth and justice in the United States. In the late 1920s, however, the Bureau of Investigation was badly in need of a reputation-cleaning, and Hoover's efforts as its director to present a clean, strong, ethical, straight picture of all agents—and especially of himself—were important and effective ways of erasing from the minds of the public the unsavory images created during the Daugherty-Burns-Means era. For his own part Hoover's personal image was one of straightforwardness which stood in bold relief against Burns' unsavory image. In his effort to clean political influence out of the bureau, Hoover instituted strict criteria of education, character, experience, and age for would-be agents.*

No longer would the bureau be a dumping ground where a recommendation letter from a congressman could bring a sure appointment. Hoover hammered repeatedly at the theme: "This bureau is to operate solely upon the basis of efficiency. Influence, political or otherwise, will not be tolerated, and any agent or employee of this bureau resorting to same will be disciplined."** Thus the severe discipline came early in Hoover's reign, and he never let up—a cause for repeated criticism by former agents who felt they had been victimized by it. It was apparent even at its inception, however, that the standards of discipline were intentionally high in order to sustain the good reputation of the bureau that Hoover was then fighting so hard to establish. He never apologized for it and continued to demand the strictest discipline from every bureau employee in regard to public and private behavior and appearance. It may

---

*"Sleuth School." *Time,* XXVI (August 5, 1935), p. 11.
**Whitehead, *op. cit.,* p. 69.

be added that those who entered the bureau did so with a full awareness of the bureau's disciplinary policies.

In addition, Hoover made several changes in bureau organization which since that time have remained bureau policy:

1. All investigative activity of the FBI would be limited to certain violations over which the bureau and the Department of Justice have jurisdiction;

2. Reorganization and regular inspection of all field offices would be initiated;

3. Organization of a nationwide identification file would begin through the consolidation of the Bertillon Measurements of the National Bureau of Criminal Investigation and fingerprint records of the Leavenworth Penitentiary Bureau.*

In addition to the centralization of identification information, there were other organizational changes during the early years. In October, 1926, the Fugitive Division had been created to investigate and apprehend fleeing criminals and in 1930 Congress authorized the FBI to collect and compile uniform crime statistics for the entire nation, containing material volunteered by police and other law enforcement officials. Such statistics have been published quarterly for the past forty years as the *Uniform Crime Report Bulletin.* On September 1, 1932, the FBI Laboratory was established in one room with a single microscope, an early move to use scientific knowledge in crime fighting, and in 1935 Hoover initiated the Crime School, later to become the National Academy, for members of local police forces who come to Washington for courses in psychiatry, ballistics, abnormal psychology, communications, photography, fingerprinting, and practicum in firearms. The purpose of the Crime School was to prepare local officials more adequately to handle law enforcement in their own municipalities, to cooperate with the federal government in catching criminals wanted

---

*Look editors, *op. cit.,* pp. 13-14.

in other areas, and to allow the FBI to concentrate only on federal violations.*

Ten years later, looking back to the early days of his director-ship, Hoover made the following statement summarizing his philosophy regarding the bureau's responsibilities and methods of operation:

> In 1924 I had a very definite opinion of what I hoped the FBI could be, as well as of the caliber of men we needed. The FBI is the investigative branch of the Department of Justice. It has the duty to gather facts which fully establish the guilt of the guilty and the innocence of the innocent. The FBI does not make policy; it is a service agency designed to carry out the responsibilities imposed upon it by legislative and executive directive.
>
> To fulfill this responsibility its work must be prepared impar-tially and judicially. That is why we have vigorously resisted any move which would cause the FBI to evaluate the facts it gathers. Likewise, we do not make recommendations or initiate prosecu-tions. That is the function of other authorities. What the facts prove is not for our determination—it never has been and never will be so long as I am privileged to serve as its director. The opinions I had in 1924 have not changed.**

In June, 1939, President Roosevelt handed the bureau a re-sponsibility which would result in tremendous expansion of personnel, organization, influence, and budget during the war years. The presidential directive placed full responsibility for all espionage, counterespionage, and sabotage matters in the hands of the FBI and the army and navy intelligence services. By agreement, the FBI would be responsible for civilian sus-pects and the army and navy for their own personnel. On Sep-tember 6, 1939, Roosevelt published requests for all law enforce-ment agencies to report information pertaining to espionage, counterespionage, sabotage, subversive activities, and violations of neutrality directly to the FBI.*** This substantial enlargement of the FBI's jurisdiction assigned the bureau the task of intelli-

*"Picked Police Trained by U. S.," *Literary Digest,* August 10, 1935, p. 18.
**J. Edgar Hoover, "What Makes an FBI Agent," *Coronet,* XXVIII (June, 1955), p. 111.
***Look editors, *op. cit.,* p. 21.

gence gathering on a continuing basis rather than on a short-term basis as had been the practice until then.

By the end of the war, the structure of the bureau was amazingly altered and expanded in comparison to its scope during the 1930s. By 1947, the bureau headquarters in Washington was composed of seven divisions each with its own head, called an assistant director, and its own specific areas of responsibility:

> Identification Division, which housed and maintained the fingerprint files;
> Training and Inspection Division, which educated agents within FBI ranks and inspected the workings of headquarters and field offices for efficiency;
> Administration Division;
> Communications and Records Division, which compiled and maintained the bureau's statistics and handled telegrams and long-distance telephone calls;
> Security Division, which handled cases of .espionage, counterespionage, Selective Service violations, and other similar investigations;
> General Investigative Division, under which most investigative responsibilities fell; and
> Laboratory Division, which provided scientific aids in criminal investigations.

The responsibilities of the bureau had expanded to such a degree that in 1949 there were over 120 statutes under its jurisdiction grouped in these four categories: federal job applications, internal security, general criminal investigations, and frauds against the government. In the early fifties, the job of investigating routine federal job applicants was shifted to the Civil Service by Congress.

In summing up the bureau's job responsibilities in 1950 Hoover said:

> The FBI by congressional enactments and presidential directives is responsible for investigating violations of specifically assigned federal laws; the collection of evidence in cases in which the United States is or may be a party in interest; and performing other duties imposed by law.*

*"Hoover Answers Ten Questions on the FBI," *The New York Times Magazine Supplement* (April 16, 1950), p. 9.

In the heat of the McCarthy loyalty investigations, the bureau felt obligated to repeat its assertion that FBI policy was to secure facts, not to interpret them, to apprehend violators of federal laws within its jurisdiction only, and to service other law enforcement agencies.*

Today its responsibilities fall into the same categories as they have historically, one of the most recent additions being President Nixon's request in 1970 of Congress for authorization of federal intervention in cases of campus arson or bombing.**

In recent years the FBI structure has proven quickly adaptable to new and changing situations, new law enforcement techniques and legal tools, and new jurisdictions. From an organization that busted gangland crime waves in its early years, it evolved into a force which now threatens the very existence of sophisticated crime syndicates. From an intelligence agency which dealt with bold but amateurish Nazi spies, and then Communists and subversives, it changed course to handle the domestic radicals who thought the old leftists too moderate. When the civil rights cause finally resulted in FBI jurisdiction, it took that sensitive task in stride too.

These changes were not without struggle and antagonism, of course. These are the subjects of other chapters. Here, it is important to note the changes did' occur, and the FBI structure, instead of resisting, quickly adapted.

Yet, since 1947 the basic structure of the bureau headquarters has remained the same: a number of divisions headed by assistant directors, all responsible to Hoover and his immediate aides—the assistants to the director. By 1971 there were, however, eleven divisions, the newest being the Legal Counsel Division. The other three additions were the result of splitting the Training and Inspection Division, and the Records and Communications Division into four separate divisions instead

*J. Edgar Hoover, Foreword in *The FBI Story* by Don Whitehead, New York: Random House, 1956, p. 111.
**Marjorie Hunter, "President Seeks U.S. Intervention in Campus Terror," *New York Times* (September 23, 1970), p. 1.

of two, and of creating the Special Investigative Division in addition to the General Investigative Division. (L. Patrick Gray dropped the Criminal Records Division, but Director Kelley has reformed it as the External Affairs Division.)

The most recent major development in the bureau is the completion of the computerized National Crime Information Center, which is a connecting network of computers with over 100 police headquarters and 56 field offices around the country.* Stored in the computer are descriptions, *modi operandi,* and records of criminals which are made readily available nationwide. The index does not contain complete detailed information regarding the crimes, but rather it serves as an index to documented files maintained by local agencies on cases involving stolen securities, stolen automobiles, certain categories of stolen property, all federal fugitives, and fugitives wanted for the commission of serious state crimes.**

Throughout, the objectivity and foresight of Hoover was borne out by the fact that the basic policies formulated at an early stage still prevail. These policies were: (a) The bureau would be a fact-finding organization, and its activities will be limited strictly to investigations of violations of federal laws. (b) Investigations would be made at and under the direction of the attorney general. (c) The personnel of the bureau would be reduced as far " . . . as is consistent with the proper performance of its duties." (d) The incompetents and the unreliables would be discharged as quickly as possible. (e) All the "dollar-a-year" men, "honorary" agents, and others not regularly employed would be cut from the rolls. (f) No new appointments would be made without the attorney general's approval, and preference would be given to men of good character and ability who had some legal training.

Once instituted, the basic character of the FBI bureaucracy

*J. Edgar Hoover, *FBI Annual Report* 1970 (Washington, D. C.; The U. S. Department of Justice, October 19, 1970), p. 31.
**J. Edgar Hoover, *FBI Annual Report,* 1969 (Washington, D.C.; The U. S. Department of Justice, October 29, 1969), p. 33.

stuck. However, the process of reorganization itself was painfully slow. Hoover persevered and sought out the support of Stone whenever it was required. This task was doubly difficult since on one hand it was essential to eliminate the slack and enforce strict rules of conduct, and on the other it was equally necessary firmly to convince political leaders that their influence over the bureau's appointments was finally at an end. Hoover believed that men of technical backgrounds were essential for scientific investigation as detailed corroborated evidence was the sole criteria of proving innocence or guilt in the judicial system of the United States. To elevate the bureau to majestic heights of integrity and efficiency was Hoover's objective. With this in mind, he introduced strict policies for training, performance, and personal conduct. Duties and procedures were elaborated in great detail, and routine was systematized and standardized so as to achieve the highest efficiency from all offices. Together with this systematization, Hoover increased the scope of authority of the special agents in charge (SACs) of the field offices over the special agents assigned them. Thus, a chain of command was established within the bureau for the first time whereby responsibility was bestowed commensurate with authority.

Although each of the FBI's divisions exercises supervisory authority over those field office functions within their scope, the SAC is responsible solely to the director for the overall functioning of the field office. To ensure the strict pursuance of these rules and regulations Hoover established a special field inspection system which visited offices and evaluated agents' efficiency, character, and industry. Together with these external evaluations, the SACs are considered responsible for their agents' performance and their own. (Incidentally, their position has, rather than shielding them from reprimand, made them many times more vulnerable. Many SACs have been demoted.) Administrative routine was also systematized, and office practices involved excruciating adherence to detail—an adherence to detail which is the essence of the FBI's success over the years.

In the FBI's reorganization, Hoover had invaluable aid from those people whom Don Whitehead, in his book *The FBI Story,* called "The Anonymous Nine," a term used to describe a management team composed of the associate director, two assistants to the director and the (then) six assistant directors. It should be added that the anonymity attributed to this group tends to reflect FBI lines of responsibility. All communications originating at the seat of government go over the signature of the director and all communications from field offices are over the signature of the SAC. Investigative reports on the other hand, bear the name of special agent to whom the case is assigned.

The structure of the FBI organization since its creation has been a functional one due to the nature of the various specialized tasks involved and the wide range of its investigative jurisdiction. Traditionally organization is viewed as a vehicle for accomplishing goals and objectives. Classic organization theory is based on four main principles—the division of labor, the scalar and functional processes, structure, and span of control. The division of labor is by universal acclaim the cornerstone among the four elements.* From it the other elements sprout out as branches, e.g., the "scalar" and "functional" growth requires specialization and departmentalization of functions. Organization "structure" is dependent on the direction which specialization takes. Finally "span of control" problems result from the number of specialized functions under the jurisdiction of one individual. The "scalar" and "functional" processes deal with vertical and horizontal growth of the organization respectively.** The "structure" is consequently a relationship of functions in an organization arranged to accomplish the objective

---

*Usually this topic is treated under the heading of Departmentation; see, for example, Harold Koontz and Cyril O. O'Donnell, *Principles of Management* (New York: McGraw-Hill Book Company, 1959) Chapter 7.
**These are discussed at length in Ralph Currier Davis' *The Fundamentals of Top Management* (New York: Harper and Brothers, 1951) Chapter 7.

of the organization efficiently. The "span of control" concept relates to the number of persons, themselves carrying managerial and supervisory responsibilities, for whom the senior manager retains his over-embracing responsibility of direction and planning, coordination, motivation, and control.*

Although modern organization theory is not a unified body of thought, it does provide a "system" or integrated overview of an organization. A similar, integrated approach will be adopted here in studying the organizational structure of the FBI: the demands the organization makes on the individual, the personality structure he brings to the organization, the informal organization that exists within the FBI, if any, and the "physical setting" in which the job he performs will be evaluated.

The objectives of an organization determine its structure. Since the objectives of the FBI are primarily investigative and involve the various phases of an investigation—identification, criminal records, laboratory, etc., it follows that the FBI has to be a functional bureaucracy. The only changes through its history have been those of horizontal addition of various divisions deemed necessary in meeting the demands made on the FBI.

The managerial organization of the FBI is made up of one director, two assistants to the director, one associate director, one assistant director, deputy associate director, and eleven assistant directors. These assistant directors each head a division. Four of these divisions—Identification, Training, Administrative, Records and Communications—form the administration of the FBI. They are the responsibility of one of the assistants to the director. Four other divisions—Domestic Intelligence, General Investigative, Laboratory, and Special Investigative—are the responsibility of the other assistant to the director. The remaining three divisions—Inspection, the new External Affairs,

*E. F. L. Brech, *Organization* (London: Longmans, Green and Company, 1957) p. 78.

and the recently formed Office of Legal Counsel—are under the responsibility of the deputy associate director.

Over the eleven divisions, each with its own assistant director, the director rules supreme. Since Hoover was appointed director, even though the bureau mushroomed, he never shared that responsibility with anyone else. Second-in-command is an associate director. Immediately below him are two assistants to the director and a deputy associate director. For over twenty five years, the same few names were present among these top echelon positions. Among these were Clyde Tolson, D. Milton Ladd, Alan H. Belmont, and Lou B. Nichols, who have all retired now from the bureau. There have been a number of changes, however, in the posts of assistant to the director in more recent years.

Ladd retired from his position in 1954 after 33 years of service to the bureau, and three years later Nichols resigned after 24 years.* On the retirement of Belmont in 1965, Cartha DeLoach was elevated to assistant to the director only to retire in 1970. He was replaced by William Sullivan who was forcibly "retired" over an alleged policy dispute with Hoover in 1971.** The director's position itself has been a statutory one under the attorney general's jurisdiction, subject to appointment by the President. In the 1960s, however, the law was changed to provide that future FBI directors will be appointed by the President with the advice and consent of the Senate.

It was often charged as a sign of Hoover's acuity as a politician that he conveniently recalled to public mind the attorney general's responsibility for the bureau's policies during crises such as the wiretapping issue, while in actuality he maintained

---

*Luther Huston, "FBI's No. 3 Man Back in Civil Life," *New York Times* (November 2, 1957), p. 11
**"FBI Aide Resigns in Policy Dispute," *New York Times* (October 3, 1971), p. 29.

sovereignty over the bureau regardless of his nominal subordination to the attorney general. This might also have been as fairly interpreted as a scrupulous observance of both the legal and formal relationships between the FBI and office of the attorney general while, at the same time, retaining for the FBI the greatest latitude of independence from the attorney general as a political appointee of the President. It has been claimed that, for the most part, recent attorneys general have seen to it that they do not cross the director or "know too much about what he was doing."* A different point of view might find this attitude to be the most efficient delegation of authority, but in either event, the choice was that of the attorney general whether exercised by reason of trust in the bureau's performance or of the attorney general's own nonfeasance.

In any case, the FBI continuously strives to meet its increasing responsibilities with the greatest possible efficiency and economy of operation. The implementation of sound organizational concepts and administrative procedures and their constant refinement have been the hallmark of the FBI, as supervised and coordinated by the FBI headquarters in Washington, D.C.

Though policy, activities, administration, and training for the FBI all center in Washington, bureau organization also includes offices both in the United States and abroad. Seventeen foreign liaison offices work with the Washington headquarters to facilitate the exchange of information with foreign law enforcement agencies on matters relating to international crime or subversive activities.

It should also be mentioned that the special agents in charge, who each head one of the bureau's 59 field offices, are in a leadership capacity with the FBI. Foremost, their responsibility is the investigative work of the bureau, performed by agents in these field offices and the over 400 resident agencies, each of which functions as an extension of a field office. SACs are

*"A Dirty Business," *The Nation*, CCIII, 22 (December 26, 1966), p. 690.

responsible directly to the director, and in Hoover's reign this was not mere theoretical structure. Hoover expected each SAC to know what was happening in his field office, and he wanted this information to be at the director's disposal without any breaks in the communication line. Hoover would personally issue orders to the SACs and would personally consult with them on policy.

The importance of this direct command structure cannot be overemphasized. The director's direct command established not only centralized control in Washington, but his personal control of the entire bureaucracy. It ensured that the chief was truly in command, and avoided any possibility of policy breaches which could otherwise occur if the chain of command extended first through levels at headquarters.

It is this characteristic which kept the FBI as a tightly knit unit even as it became a sizable bureaucracy. Everybody worked for the man, as they say in the bureau, even though personnel were spread out far from the director's office. The implications of this are apparent: agents and their superiors must be dedicated to their work because (taking nothing away from their high motivations) they are not insulated by an ambiguous structure from the director; and policies, including such important ones as regard for professional police techniques and regard for civil liberties, are sure to be effected.

It is this agent dedication, assured by the command structure, which is largely responsible for making the rest of the bureau structure perform efficiently and aggressively. There is an uncommon degree of cooperation within the FBI—one part of the organization simply never scuttles an operation of another part. Investigations originating in one field office often require agent time in other field offices, and the work is undertaken in the second office as its own job.

Agent dedication also permits each agent latitude in judgment exercised in the course of his investigations. For all the verbiage about the FBI's administrative and management rigidity, there are in fact broad areas of delegated management responsibility and discretion at the bureau's working level. The system of chain of command is a chain of responsibility for the bureau's day-to-day work; this chain begins at the level of the average special agent who is responsible for the management and working of all cases assigned to him. Within the parameter supplied by the FBI's Rules and Regulations, the agents' management responsibility permits the widest latitude of innovation and imagination. This may be best illustrated by a routine case described by a former special agent who was involved in the case while in the New York office.

The agent and his partner were working the "late shift" on New York's minor criminal squad, so assigned on a rotating basis so that two agents would be available in the office to handle matters that might come up after working hours. One evening the office received a telephone tip that a deserter-fugitive was going to visit his girl friend in his old Brooklyn neighborhood. Although the case was assigned to another agent who had performed no investigation on it, the late shift agents immediately went to the Brooklyn neighborhood, learning there, after checking with the office, that the agent to whom the case was assigned was on annual leave. The two agents contacted everyone in the immediate neighborhood who might see the fugitive, including such obvious contacts as his family and girl friend, but also bartenders, bowling alley proprietors, theater cashiers, and the beat patrolman. After several hours, satisfied that the fugitive was not then in the area and, further, that they would be called if he appeared, they returned to the office.

Shortly after their return, they received a telephone call from none other than the fugitive who said he had heard that they were looking for him and that he would be arrested if he appeared in the neighborhood. Refusing to meet with the agents either in the office or elsewhere, the fugitive declared that he was not, in fact, a deserter but that he had returned to his duty station, Ft. Gordon, Georgia, had been given a suspended sentence and transferred to Ft. Dix, New Jersey, from which post he was calling. The agents hoped to persuade the fugitive to meet them, to turn him over to the military authorities and let them investigate his story but he steadfastly refused to meet with them and vehemently insisted that his story was true. The agents were able to persuade him only to give them the number of the phone from which he was calling and a promise to call back in about an hour.

After checking with the minor criminal supervisor, the agents called the Newark office of the FBI, spoke with a night clerk and after identifying themselves, requested the name and phone number of the resident agent in New Brunswick, New Jersey, near Ft. Dix. The clerk furnished the information by a return phone call which permitted him to confirm the identity of the New York agents. They then called the resident agent in New Brunswick, related the alleged deserter's story and asked him to check on it immediately.

The latter agent promptly called the Ft. Dix authorities and discovered that the fugitive's story was true, that he was listed as "present for duty" at Ft. Dix and, further, that he had called New York from a phone at the Ft. Dix Post Exchange.

Having learned this the New York agents were able to assure the "fugitive" that he would not be arrested if he came to New York City, and in addition, promised him they would return to the Brooklyn neighborhood, retrace their steps and "take the heat off," a task they did perform immediately despite the fact that it consumed about three hours of voluntary overtime.

The resident agent in New Brunswick later confirmed his investigation findings by memorandum for the New York office and the case was closed administratively without an investigative report ever having been written.

The case is, in many ways, typical of how the average agent does his day's work, always conscious of chain of command procedures but in no way unduly restricted by them. Checking only with the lowest level of immediate supervisory authority, they contacted another field office and then dealt directly with their New Brunswick counterpart. No paperwork was required other than the brief memo needed to close the case and the necessary job was done quickly, cheaply, and with maximum efficiency.

At the field office level, the agent is directly responsible, in handling his cases, to the field supervisor who handles the particular classification of the case at hand. The supervisor is responsible, in turn to the special agent in charge who exercises direct supervisory responsibility only on major cases. The field supervisor also has effective responsibility to the bureau supervisors at the Washington desks in charge of the pertinent case classifications. These Washington desks are the link between the headquarters divisions and the field offices, being basically a communication link. There is normally some routine and regular communication between these agents at the supervisory level at which chain of command is bypassed for the sake of efficiency or to retain an "off the record" process of free and open discussion of mutually shared work problems. It is a method predicated on cooperation, which in turn is predicated on agent dedication. Actual internal operating procedures are admittedly not strictly "by the book" but are certainly not discouraged by the bureau, for they serve the very useful purpose of performing the job at hand with the highest degree of efficiency and aggressiveness.

The fact that agents exercise effective discretion in practical matters, however, has not resulted in disunified policy and effort within the bureau. Though the FBI has never been a policy formulating agency as far as its duties are concerned, it does have definite policies for its own internal functions. The soundness of its administrative procedures is borne out by the characteristics of its policies, which are clearly related to the objectives of the FBI and designed for their achievement. The policies are clear, consistent, and have a distinct stamp of functionalism aimed at enhancing efficiency.

The setting of objectives within the FBI was done a long time ago; yet, the soundness of the basic policies outlined by Hoover in 1924 would seem to be underscored by the very fact that they are still in use. In any organization where performance and results vitally affect its continuance, there exists a very strong need for definite objectives and procedures to effectuate them for long periods. This is vital for any organization, and as Peter Drucker says, "Each manager, from the 'big boss' down to the chief clerk, needs clearly spelled out objectives. These objectives should lay out the performance the man's own managerial unit is supposed to produce. They should lay out what contribution he and his unit are expected to make...in other words, emphasis should be on teamwork and team results."*

Traditionally Americans have not been regarded as a disciplined people. In reality, they accept discipline when there is strong leadership to point out the need for it and the goals attainable by such discipline. This is the reason for the acceptance of discipline by the FBI personnel. Investigative work of the FBI is done by special agents, but a wide variety of non-investigative personnel, specialists in various fields, are also employed. All employees are carefully selected and undergo thorough background investigations before employment to assure their suitability.

During his tenure, the Hoover standard of suitability was "excellence." Agents knew this when they "signed on." Additionally each field office is responsible for the proper investigation of matters within its territory. Each is headed by a special agent in charge, who is personally responsible to the director for work done within his geographic area. Sometimes the pressure of headquarters for strict discipline is heavy, and no one is excepted. In the words of one former special agent, "You're expected to call down anyone who is goofing off. If you don't you're reprimanded yourself."** This standard of discipline can be more easily understood when viewed in light of the possibility that at some point an agent's very life may depend on the

*Peter F. Drucker. *The Practice of Management.* (New York: Harper and Brothers, 1951) p. 126.
**James Phelan, "Hoover of the FBI,"*Saturday Evening Post,* Sept. 25, 1965, p. 28.

alertness and efficiency of another agent with whom he may be working. Just as the director keeps close tabs on the activities of each SAC and each office, so the SAC maintains a rigid round-the-clock system of checks and controls over his agents and their activities. Moreover, the SACs and Assistant SACs (ASACs) are called on the carpet as often as anyone, and they get "busted" regularly. Ex-SACs and ASACs remain with the FBI in field offices across the country—as special agents. Yet they all accept the discipline, unless they are a William Turner type.

The rules require dedication. For example, an agent may never be out of touch with his field office or a designated local check-in agency, without reporting in by phone, if he is otherwise out of town for more than two hours.* It is this type of close control rather than the difficulty of assignments which prompts comments such as the following from ex-agents: "The FBI is a wonderful place to work because after that no job ever seems hard."**

In this age of unionized government employees and "employee rights," acceptance of such work requirements is truly remarkable, and the FBI personnel *are* truly remarkable. This is at least partly the result of one of the most impressive features of the FBI: its personnel policies in recruiting, training, and employee benefits.

The process of being appointed a special agent begins with the completion of a ten-page application form at headquarters or at a field office.*** The applicant qualifies physically if he is 23 but not 36 years of age, at least 5'7", has very good hearing, corrected eyesight of 20/20, is a United States citizen willing to serve anywhere in the world, and has the necessary education and experience to qualify for the bureau's Law, Accounting, Science, Language or Modified

*Michael Drury, "The Private Life of a G-Man," *Good Housekeeping,* CXXXI (July, 1950), p. 59.
**Knebel, *op. cit.,* p. 80.
***FBI documents regarding applications.

(professional or special experience) Programs. The next step is a trip at his own expense to the nearest field office for a personal interview by an SAC or assistant SAC of the field office. This interview includes a briefing on the tedium of everyday work as an agent as well as the requirements and danger of the job, the long absences from home, and the confidential nature of the work. He is also told that he may expect promotions only on the basis of merit. If the applicant is still interested, he is required to explain his own desire to join the bureau and then to take an appropriate examination. This test covers his knowledge in his particular area and determines his analytical and investigative aptitude and ability. He will also be required to participate in a mock-up of an investigation interview or in a hypothetical application of a statute to a true-life situation. It is not easy; only one of five applicants interested in an FBI position satisfactorily completes the procedure to this point.

The next step is a thorough physical examination and an FBI-conducted investigation of the applicant's personal life including his career, associations, reputation in the community, family background, and moral standing. If he is accepted, the applicant must proceed to Washington at his own expense to begin training at the FBI Academy.

The rugged application and appointment process was originated by Hoover in the 1920s to erase the Burns-Means type of agent from the bureau's image. Hoover was looking for men who were rugged individualists yet who had the ability to engage in teamwork. The men had to be firmly and conscientiously dedicated to the truth to the point that they could be capable of complete impartiality in investigations.*

Of course, many bright young people, who likely would be excellent agents, are repelled by the rigors of FBI discipline and the do-it-by-the-book procedures. In one sense, this is a loss to the bureau. That does not settle the question, however.

*Hoover, "What Makes," p. 111.

The bureau is looking at the total picture: bright but undisciplined men may be innovative; but the need of the FBI and the country is for an investigative agency which is a disciplined unit; and the latter consideration must control since the bureau is not everybody's "problem solver" but is rather an agency dedicated to performance of functions set by its superiors.

A moral code exists in the FBI too. Hoover imposed strict rules of personal conduct, but he himself lived by them—thus expecting no more of his employees than he did of himself. Rules and regulations exist for each and every aspect of an agent's life—whether on or off duty. However meddlesome this may seem it cannot be denied that by emphasizing extreme discipline, Hoover gradually developed the FBI into a prestigious organization. Under Hoover's direction the FBI became known as an organization that is efficient and incorruptible. He regarded his agents as representatives of the bureau, and as such they have been expected to conduct themselves with the honor and dignity befitting the service of which they are a part. These rigid standards also apply to clerks and other bureau employees. All employees are always expected to give "just a little more" and are compensated for this effort by the job security, benefits, personal satisfaction, and a sense of accomplishment.

Discipline is important but patience, perseverance, and a penchant for detail are other prime requirements. Accuracy and thoroughness are the essence of all FBI activity. As Associate Director Clyde Tolson once said, "Precision is the cardinal virtue of an investigating agency. Many a criminal has been convicted and many an innocent person absolved because somebody took pains to be accurate about an 'unimportant' little fact."

Once in the field, the special agent finds himself involved in little glory-filled work, but rather in a tightly knit, well-disciplined organization which often demands total devotion of his time, effort, and energy,* and a substantial capacity for detail

*Wicker, op. cit., p. 6.

and routine. Whatever activities he may plan out for a workday, he may well be required to interrupt in order to take care of unexpected developments and to stay on the "new trail" until he is relieved or the investigation is completed.* For that reason he is expected to carry enough money at all times to be able immediately to board a train or plane for any destination.**

Does this rigor drive good agents out? Some agents have left because of it, to be sure. Ex-agent William Turner complained in 1970 that his field office assignment in Seattle, Washington was limited to "relatively minor waterfront thefts, chasing military deserters, looking for fugitives, and developing informants."*** It is a practical fact of FBI life, however, that most of the work is relatively routine and, further, that the major cases that do occur are normally assigned to agents who have more experience and who display a greater aptitude for their work than William Turner. This is not to say that the "routine" cases complained of by Turner are without satisfaction, occasional excitement, or, occasionally, significant results. Neither Turner nor anyone else can predict when the "minor waterfront theft" may lead to a major hijacking ring, when the deserter/fugitive may turn out to be a dangerous felon, or when the routinely developed informant may prove to be the key to breaking a major case.

Control, of course, requires paper work in any large organization. In the bureau, there is indeed a large volume of required reports covering all agents' activities. Whether this means that bureaucratic rules and attitudes have pervaded everything in the FBI structure, from standards of dress to loyalty to the director and the bureau (as charged by one former official of the Justice Department****), depends mainly on

*"What It's Like To Be an FBI Agent," *Changing Times*, IX (July, 1955), p. 23.
**Drury, *op. cit.*, p. 59
***Turner, *op. cit.*, p. 14
****Wicker, *op. cit.*, p. 7.

whether it assists or hinders speedy and efficient performance. Secondly, it should be tested on the basis of whether the routines continue to relate to the bureau needs or rather perpetuate themselves for routine's sake.

On the first count, it can only be said that the paper work and routines have not hampered FBI performance, because the bureau has an excellent record of doing its job thoroughly and quickly. The second measure, however, does not earn the FBI quite as high a grade. An example is the FBI headquarters unwritten voluntary overtime rule, which at one point served a purpose—it was a measure of an agent's willingness to work. However, as the bureau began employing it routinely under civil service regulations, it no longer served that purpose. Nearly all agents were expected to do average or above average overtime, a mathematical impossibility. Yet, the standard continued to be enforced until Pat Gray succeeded J. Edgar Hoover.

Similarly, the time in office rule seemed to have outworn its usefulness before it was rescinded by Acting Director Pat Gray. This standard was probably meant to encourage agents to do the paper work promptly and correctly. But it was too rigidly applied, resulting in agents complying with the standard at the expense of their necessary out-of-office work.

However, ex-agents will not cite more than a few such examples. There remains a rigid set of regulations, but as stated previously, the practice is a very workable set of routines, by and large. Bureau officials know that "the book" can go only so far toward establishing good work effort, the rest is left to good judgment. No, the critics are wrong, overly bureaucratic attitides do not pervade the FBI structure. Instead, the structure assures tight and pervasive control, a very desirable feature.

One iron-clad rule is that the agent does not "shoot from the hip." He must plan his case and his schedule rigorously. His reports reflect this. The agent is trained to request a stenographer from the supervisor of the stenographic pool, advising her when he expects to begin dictation and its approximate length. Once dictated, typed, and reviewed, the agent's report is checked, criticized, and reviewed by a supervisor, who initials it and transmits it to the Washington headquarters. It is also initialed by the reporting agent prior to transmittal. By these means authority of the special agent in charge at the field office is greatly increased and the chain of command is strengthened.

Before Hoover, however, the FBI had insubstantial rules and regulations, and the SAC had practically no authority over the special agents. By giving the SACs greater authority over their special agents and making the SACs responsible for the actions of their field agents, Hoover ensured the efficient operation of the field offices. The field inspection system further enhanced administrative efficiency. By demanding absolute discipline and acceptance of anonymity from its personnel, the FBI has obviously become the most prestigious of all federal agencies.

A few critics refuse to consider the management rationales behind the strict policies of the bureau. Instead, they view only the possible hardships. For example, in 1924 Hoover made promotion based on merit a cardinal principle of the bureau's policy, and a special agent supposedly assumed that his advancement would be promulgated on performance and not on seniority or tenure.* By and large, this policy has not been violated, but the critics are certain that favoritism existed. In recent years a few complaining ex-agents have been vocal about the policies of promotion within the bureau which they feel are unfair and unethical. In 1962 both William Turner and Jack Levine complained that the only real requirement for advancement was compatibility with Hoover.** Levine cited "authoritarian, over-demanding perfectionist policies" in a bureau dominated by fear and a Hoover personality cult.*** Nine years later, ex-agent Jack Shaw (who had more reason for disenchantment) put it more explicitly:

It is certainly no military secret, though I am sure, [sic] not

*Whitehead, *op. cit.,* p. 68.
**Turner, *op. cit.,* pp. III-XVI.
***"Questions for the FBI," *New York Times* (October 23, 1962), p. 36.

very well published either, that adulation of the director in some form or other provides the main catalyst in the process of administrative advancement.*

Obviously, any man proud of his long effort with an agency would appreciate the adulation of his employees, and bureaucratic politics being what it is, no doubt some in the FBI sought promotion by playing up to the director. And one would not expect Hoover or his assistants to have often promoted personnel who evidenced a degree of contempt for the boss. These facts prove nothing, however, and the critics entirely misrepresent the situation.

Hoover was not that sort of man. He demanded personal loyalty, to be sure. He also was very impressed with performance. In that sense he had favorites. Stories abound of the director's involvement in promotions. Hoover would at times chance onto an underling and would be impressed. Upon that, an agent's fortunes within the bureau would skyrocket. Other times, good information about an agent would come to Hoover through normal channels, and the boss would have another favorite. The agent who looked good in high publicity investigations could expect a quick promotion. Others who, even if lucky just to be at the right place at the right time but who nevertheless got results (an arrest of a long sought fugitive, for example), could expect at least a merit raise and a letter of commendation. The other side of the coin is that such favorites had to continue high performance, in the director's opinion, or they lost favor, and promotions came more slowly.

Sure, Hoover had favorites. The question is, so what? The fact is that the director was extremely concerned about moving the kind of men he wanted into important positions, and that was his main consideration. Can he be blamed for using his own personal experience and information in that quest? A merit promotion system would be meaningless if personal judgment of those who do the promoting were excluded. With-

*New York Times, Jan. 23, 1971, p. 27.

out it, there could only be the impersonal data comparisons among prospects—a process subject to worse faults, certainly, than the possible apple-polishing involved in Hoover's approach.

The whole structure of the FBI is directed to controlling its far-flung operations. The most apparent control function within the FBI is performed mainly by the Inspection Division. The essence of management control is any action that adjusts operations to predetermined standards. Consequently, much external control is based on feedback of information about activities in the field. This is provided by the Inspection Division's program of field inspection. These inspections are active and continuous. Their actions are at times corrective and restore operations to exacting standards. By reporting directly to the deputy associate director and the associate director, the Inspection Division maintains the incredibly high level of performance standards of the FBI. By retaining independence from all other divisions, the Inspection Division provides factual information so that correct remedial action can quickly be taken. It reports on all activities of the FBI and evaluates all personnel.

The FBI is not merely a robot of efficiency. It is a very human organization made up of very human people. The fact that it is a most prominent government agency should not cloud its early turmoils. One reason for the FBI's present image of incorruptibility and integrity is the quality of direction it received from J. Edgar Hoover. Mr. Hoover's strict discipline and continuing pursuit of perfection elevated the FBI to its present position. The loyalty and dedication that Hoover demanded in the name of and for the FBI contributed to it in full measure and resulted in high motivation and morale of the bureau's personnel. Because of the intense dedication and devotion to duty that exists throughout the FBI, the esprit de corps is phenomenal and J. Edgar Hoover must have looked back with pride at the organization he so carefully molded. Succeeding directors will doubtless have differences in emphasis but it seems likely that all will try to retain for the bureau the same high levels of loyalty.

While dedication, discipline, and control from the top are the FBI's main ingredients in its recipe for an efficient, aggressive organization, other features of the bureaucratic structure also follow rules of good organization. The already mentioned fact that the entire FBI is quite responsive to commands from the top is a feature assisted by the minimal levels of authority existent. Use of modern communications equipment also facilitates the organization's responsiveness.

However, command from the top has not meant that authority has not been delegated as far down the line as possible. One of the first things Hoover did after his appointment was to strengthen the authority of the special agents in charge. He also made special agents responsible for the handling and management of cases assigned to them and, for their performance, to the SAC. For the first time, adequate authority was vested in individuals as far down as the field offices. The SAC was responsible for reports to Washington instead of the agents dealing directly with the bureau. Further, the SACs started to exercise close supervision over the work of all employees assigned to them. This practice has continued and as a result of the foresight of J. Edgar Hoover, a clear-cut line of authority within the FBI exists today.

Moreover, this responsibility and authority of the supervisors is in writing, the subject of an elaborate system of rules and regulations established by the FBI. This system prevents overlapping of authority or gaps in responsibility, and the lines of authority running from the top to the bottom of the organization are clear.

From another angle, in the bureau, each person knows to whom he reports and who reports to him. This "unity of command" principle is required by the rules and regulations of the FBI and is rigidly adhered to. In fact, a departure from this procedure by FBI personnel is looked upon as a violation of the principles of conduct.

Here it should be emphasized that the responsibility of higher authority for the acts of its subordinates is absolute. Accountability of higher authority is a distinguishable feature of the FBI.

Another rule, insofar as is practiced, is that the work of every person in an organization should be confined as far as possible to the performance of a single leading function. The requirements of the FBI are so diverse that this condition is a prerequisite for its functioning. This principle of specialization concerning the "horizontal" rather than "vertical" delegation of authority is evident in such areas as the FBI Laboratory, special investigation, and administration. It extends as well to the sections of these divisions, each having its specialty and each working with supervisors and squads of similar specialists in the field.

A "span of control" concept is apparent in the FBI—another good sign. Due to the highly centralized nature of the FBI, the "span of control" is very small. For example, at the SAC level this extends to the number of special agents assigned. The numbers become progressively smaller as the higher levels of the heirarchy are reached. The line functions have been separated from staff functions, helping to assure that adequate emphasis is placed on important staff activities. The FBI's investigations are carried out by special agents only, and all other personnel perform auxiliary functions—services, advice, and control. As the FBI is highly functionalized, the separation of line and staff functions has come naturally and is distinct. The Identification, Administration, Training, and the Records and Communications Divisions perform staff functions while the Investigative Divisions of the bureau perform the line functions. Since the Laboratory Division plays such a crucial role in investigations, it is also included as a line division. External Affairs, Inspection, and the Office of Legal Counsel provide staff services to the bureau. Due to their importance they are the responsibility of the associate director.

Nearly everything points to good organization in the bureau, but, again, one thing stands out; it is highly centralized and adapted for tight control. This is desirable, considering its responsibilities and the nature of its services. It is well too that this very efficient bureaucracy effectively employs its personnel and utilizes systematized and standardized administrative procedures. The chain of command through the organization and the discreet hierarchical levels of the FBI make it extremely responsive to directives from headquarters. The type of organization in the FBI is similar to the "star" type of organization described by Dr. H. J. Leavitt in his book, *Managerial Psychology.* Accordingly, this type of organization is most efficient in carrying out administrative routine since the response is fast, understanding of the organization is very clear, the number of communications required to complete a task are minimal, and the "top boss" has 100 percent leadership responsibility. The FBI's requirement that individual goals be made subservient to the goals and objectives of the bureau imposes an anonymity on its employees that must be accepted by them. Consequently, team effort and team achievement rather than individual brilliance is the password, although individual bravery and meritorious service are amply rewarded by the bureau. All these things, responsiveness, impersonality, anonymity, and absolute devotion to the bureau from its personnel, are essential to the achievement of FBI objectives and the fulfillment of its responsibilities.

Yet, there can always be improvement. The bureau is not lax on that count either. In analyzing the performance of the FBI and the evolution of its organizational structure, it is evident that this organization is continuously striving for perfection, the hallmark of a dynamic organization. It is also obvious that the FBI is controlled by equally dynamic leadership.

But the FBI must always remain responsible to democratic authority. Under Hoover this need was served well. The FBI has grown over the years solely because it has been given more responsibility either by legislative action or by presidential direction. Rep. John J. Rooney, chairman of the House Appropriations Subcommittee on State Justice, Commerce and Judiciary, has confirmed that the bureau's budget increases were the result "of additional duties given to it gratuitously—and not sought by the FBI—by the Congress itself." So it is our FBI, and perhaps the critics of the FBI should devote their efforts to assigning federal jurisdiction to other federal agencies and stop using the FBI as a catchall. As John Doar of the Civil Rights Division of the Department of Justice said, "perhaps in retrospect there were ways to have made the bureau do better. But in evaluating the FBI's performance . . . let us be sure we do not transfer our impatience with America itself onto the FBI simply because of its visibility, or our prejudices, or because we feel more comfortable criticizing a bureaucracy than criticizing ourselves."

15. Expanding the War on Crime
John Snyder
with the Editors

Jack Wilner, a feature writer for the *Chicago Daily News,* was grappling with the tentacles of a mysterious, powerful octopus which was then squeezing Chicago and vicinity in an ever-tightening grip. The year was 1964, and the octopus was the Chicago Mob. Wilner was fearlessly exposing this monster as best he could in a series of articles running in the *News.*

One day in early 1964, however, Wilner had some information that he thought would be more useful to the FBI than to his newspaper series. He called the Chicago FBI field office, explained what he had to Special Agent Paul Frankfurt, and arranged for a meeting a short time later.

At the meeting Wilner introduced to Frankfurt and another agent, one Charles Smith. Smith was a confidant of certain lower echelon Chicago mob figures. Wilner thought Smith might be a valuable informant for the FBI.

The two special agents listened at length to Charles Smith's story. They listened attentively to his sad tale of financial ruin, but it was not their business. Smith apparently had been a south suburban Chicago land developer active in supermarket developments. In the course of that business, he had devised a combination atomic shelter-supermarket system which he wanted the nation's defense establishment to adopt. In the fall of 1961, Smith said, he had presented his plan to a top aide of Adam Yarmolinsky at the Pentagon. The "defense experts" in that corner of the Pentagon had no interest in civil defense structures, and Smith's problems began. As if the Pentagon's negative attitude on his project were not bad enough, a car accident disabled him for a time, and the banks foreclosed his most recent supermarket project.

Now the FBI agents' interest perked up, for they guessed the remainder of the story, or part of it. Charles Smith, in deep financial trouble, went (unknowingly, he said) to the type of people who would refinance his development when the banks would not. Smith went to Harry Brown, a "mortgage broker," who, for a fee, would help those facing ruin. Brown had ties with the Mob.

Soon, Smith found himself tied up with Chicago's crime syndicate. This was not new to the FBI agents. It happens to many an innocent person. But the informant at this meeting was not the usual innocent. He impressed the agents as something of a super-patriot, but they knew he sincerely wanted to do something about the crooks he was then dealing with. The FBI was interested.

The story became more involved. The "mortgage broker," Harry Brown, was unable to come through with financing for Charles Smith, and now Brown owed him money. Something was unusual about this operation, Smith soon found out. In the course of his frequent trips to Brown's office on Jackson Street in the Loop, the informant soon realized the nature of the men operating from those quarters. Once, Brown told

Smith he had been "held up" in his office; and at other times Smith witnessed what he figured to be fixes and bribes being negotiated at Brown's office. The troubled supermarket developer quickly realized that the office was a front for organized crime.

He began hanging around more frequently at the office, Smith told the bureau interviewers, and he would run errands for Brown and others. He had thus infiltrated into the Chicago mob. Was the FBI interested in an informant? Charles Smith wanted nothing more than to help the FBI crack the influence of the mob in Chicago.

Special Agent Frankfurt was not convinced of the reliability of the volunteer's information, nor did it appear that Smith would be close enough to top figures in the rackets to be helpful in any big cases. Still, he could tip off the agents on some operations, and perhaps serve as a cross check against information secured by the FBI by other means. Besides, the FBI agents would not turn down a volunteer informant at the time. Yes, Charles Smith would work with the FBI after the meeting.

So Smith continued to observe Harry Brown's operation, which in early 1964 was moved to Meadow Brook Country Club. But now the informant was secretly meeting several times weekly with FBI agents, telling them what he observed, what errands he ran, and showing them whatever papers he could copy.

The country club was not as serene as most. Harry Brown was in trouble with some fellow racketeers, and his problems threatened not only himself, but the FBI infiltration, and for that matter, the life of Charles Smith.

Brown's troubles came to a climax one night as a terrified Smith stood by at the country club office. An angry Mafioso threatened Brown and then telephoned wherever it is such gangsters call for a "hit man," and left the morose Brown in the care of Smith at the club. The informant, wanting no part of a double murder in which he figured to be the second victim, left Brown to his own resources and began a hasty retreat, but not without jotting down the license plate numbers of the mobsters' automobiles parked at the country club.

Across the street, Smith telephoned the home of his agent-contact, getting him out of bed. The informant explained the trouble and enlisted the FBI's help in making good his escape. Heavily armed FBI men arrived quickly in automobiles and watched from a discreet distance as Smith entered his own car and drove off. He was not followed by any of the hoodlums and the agents left the area of the club as quietly as they had arrived.

The FBI agents meant to protect the life of their informant, but the bureau had no idea of raiding the country club that night. Nor was anything else done about the shady dealings at the club.

One week later, Smith determined that Harry Brown was still alive, although a bit sore from repeated beatings. Shortly after this episode, the gangland operation in the club moved out, and soon thereafter the FBI told Charles Smith that his services as an informant were no longer needed.

It is not known precisely why the FBI was no longer interested in Smith. Perhaps he had lost his potential for infiltrating the operations of Chicago's organized crime when Harry Brown got in trouble.

However, Charles Smith's experience parallels closely a national trend, and something more is indicated than that the FBI had lost interest in one informant. Smith may not have been the most valuable insider, but he was an insider, and was willing to continue as such. Moreover, the bureau had paid him no more than $300 over a period of six months.

Considering these facts, it is not likely the agents working the case would have dropped Smith unless the FBI was not going to open any cases on the basis of his information. If so, Chicago's mob could have breathed easier.

In point of fact, organized crime lords across the nation were breathing easier in 1964. A U.S. Justice Department campaign against them was ending, and the FBI was, in effect, called off their trails. A new president, and an attorney general with his wings clipped, were factors in a situation that allowed the mob to resume business as usual. FBI Special Agent Frankfurt, and for that matter FBI headquarters, could do nothing.

In the three preceding years, Attorney General Robert Kennedy had mounted a law enforcement campaign against organized crime. Las Vegas was one target; Jimmy Hoffa and union corruption another; and other racketeers soon realized that their criminal operations were being watched (and listened to via wiretaps) by the FBI.

In 1961, at Robert Kennedy's insistence, Congress gave Justice and the FBI some needed legal tools for the campaign. On September 13, 1961, several laws were enacted concerning interstate gambling and interstate transport in aid of racketeering, thus giving the FBI for the first time investigative jurisdiction directly over some of organized crime's important operations. The impact of these laws is apparent from the fact that in 1963, the FBI arrested 144 underworld figures, mostly on interstate gambling law charges,* while in 1960 the FBI could point only to the arrest of Frank Palermo, the "underworld king of boxing."

The attorney general also sought congressional authorization for court-approved wiretaps, and sought to strengthen the hands of federal prosecutors. The latter are compelled by federal law to submit evidence to grand juries, which must return indictments before a person may be tried for crime. Difficulty arose, since adequate evidence in organized crime cases often depended on testimony from organized crime figures themselves, and they would simply "take the Fifth Amendment" in response to the prosecutor's questions. Kennedy wanted authorization to grant immunity from prosecution to such witnesses, in effect compelling them to testify. At the time, however, Congress refused to grant this authorization for wiretaps or immunity.

Nevertheless, the campaign against organized crime made

*FBI Report, 1963.

headway, and the attorney general, who had once before bared his teeth at the mobsters when he was counsel to the Kefauver Rackets Committee in 1957, would not quit until the crime lords were on the ropes. But in 1964, the situation in Washington had changed.

A new president was in command, and Lyndon Johnson had no intention of continuing Kennedy's campaign against organized crime. The new laws would be enforced, of course, but the coordinated and persistent investigative and prosecutive effort, so necessary to success against the underworld, would not be continued.

If this trend wasn't clear in 1964, it became apparent to all who would see when the President appointed Ramsey Clark to the Justice Department. Nicholas Katzenbach was attorney general then, but Clark was the White House contact. It was the President and Clark who combined to end immediately the FBI wiretaps and electronic eavesdropping which Kennedy had authorized. This was formalized when Ramsey Clark was later promoted to attorney general, and the Justice Department quickly issued a memorandum barring federal eavesdropping and wiretapping except in national security cases.*

All the while Johnson and Clark were piously speaking against wiretaps as invasions of privacy, but the privacy of organized crime was the foremost beneficiary of their position. Without electronic eavesdropping and wiretaps, any assault on the rackets was ineffectual.

Some men in the Johnson Administration had plenty to fear from too energetic investigations of organized crime. Besides the fact that administration power was precariously perched on corrupt city machines likely to be investigated, links to the rackets had reached boldly into the White House itself, through LBJ's tenure as the Vice President. And no matter what he

---

*Clark Mollenhoff, *Strike Force,* Prentice Hall (Englewood Cliff, N. J., 1972), p. 105.

could do as President, some of his political associates and cronies were bound to come crashing down about him.

Bobby Baker, for one, was falling. Baker, who had been Johnson's "right hand man," was under indictment for theft, income tax evasion, and conspiracy to defraud the government pursuant to his having misappropriated political contributions of $100,000. Baker's and President Johnson's friend Fred Black was also in trouble.

The Baker and Black cases hit very close to home, and it was Bobby Kennedy's and the FBI's crusade against organized crime which had uncovered the underworld dealings of the two. As attorney general, Kennedy had become suspicious of Baker and Black, particularly because of their association with the Las Vegas mob and gambling figures Ed Levinson and Ben Siegelbaum. The latter two were partners with Baker and Black in the Serv-U Vending Company.

Under Kennedy's direction, FBI and Treasury agents investigated Las Vegas "skimming," or taking money off the top of casino gambling receipts. Bugs and wiretaps were employed by the FBI in this investigation,* so the attorney general was not merely guessing at what was going on. He was certain that Baker and Black were dealing with underworld figures. Kennedy therefore authorized an FBI bug in Fred Black's hotel suite in Washington, D.C.,** where the two fast dealers operated.

All this was in process when an assassin's bullet catapulted Lyndon Johnson into the presidency. Justice Department prosecutions against Baker and Black would now face roadblocks. Thurgood Marshall and Abe Fortas, both cronies of the President and both connected with Baker and Black, now sat on the Supreme Court. The field prosecutors' superiors at the Justice Department in Washington made decisions which de-

---

*Mollenhoff, p. 105.
**Mollenhoff, p. 104.

stroyed the case against Fred Black and nearly did so in the Baker prosecution.

Despite these problems Bobby Baker was convicted and his influence was finally curtailed, although he remained hopeful of getting off on appeal. His Las Vegas friends fared better. The electronic surveillance of the Freemont Hotel, of which Ed Levinson was president, formed the basis for a federal grand jury indictment of Levinson and others in May, 1967. But the Fremont Hotel had friends.

Grant Sawyer, then governor of Nevada, blasted the FBI surveillance. U.S. Senator Howard Cannon complained to President Johnson, who, knowing the contents of the surveillance tapes, knew he had more than a few Nevada politicians to protect. Ramsey Clark's Justice Department, however, had the matter well in hand.

Assistant Attorney General Mitchell Rogovin had a deal to offer. In return for Ed Levinson's ending a civil suit which would have delved deep into the FBI's surveillance tapes, he and another defendant, Joseph Rosenberg, would be dealt with softly. Levinson and Rosenberg pleaded no contest to the skimming charges, the Justice Department moved to dismiss the remaining charges. The years of investigation ended with a paltry $5,000 fine leveled against Levinson and a $3,000 fine against Rosenberg.

The handling of the case in Las Vegas made it obvious that organized crime across the country could now operate with impunity. FBI and Internal Revenue Service investigations would go for naught without tenacious effort at the Justice Department. But instead of that, Bobby Kennedy's crusade was spiked, the electronic surveillance necessary to the effort was stopped, and the investigations which had promised results were effectively snuffed out.

Congress did not agree with President Johnson's and Attorney General Clark's pious complaints about wiretaps. Over their objections, the Omnibus Crime Control Act was passed on June 14, 1968, with a provision authorizing electronic surveillance under federal court orders. But the President announced that the Justice Department ban on wiretapping in most circumstances would remain in effect.

It was not until a new administration took power in Washington that the legal tools provided by Congress in 1961 and 1968 were again put into effective use. A new attorney general, John Mitchell, recognized the value of electronic surveillance to investigations of organized crime. He quickly reversed Ramsey Clark's policy and in February 1969, just after President Nixon took office, Mitchell authorized the first electronic surveillance of organized crime since Kennedy's crusade. At the same time, "Strike Force" teams were activated for investigations. The Strike Forces originated in the previous Justice Department, when the public pressure had mounted against Ramsey Clark's retreat from the war on crime; but until the Nixon administration, Strike Forces were active only in New York and Michigan.

Organized crime lost its influence in Washington in the election of 1968. John Mitchell was intent upon employing the FBI in the Strike Forces to get the results he knew the bureau could get.

Mitchell realized some other things about the underworld. He knew that organized crime was misnamed. It was organized, to be sure, and it was crime; but it was *politics* which had long protected rackets and racketeers. In Chicago or San Francisco, in New Jersey or Miami, or wherever crime bosses operated with impunity, they had tainted the political machines which ran the cities and some states. Attorneys general and presidents, prosecutors and governors, judges and mayors, often owed much to the mob. The name for this is "politics," not "organized crime." *Corrupt* politics.

In the same sense, the law enforcement posture toward organized crime was determined by politics. It was, after all, the politicians who made the decisions. Law enforcement agencies like the FBI had no authority to decide that Las Vegas casino owners would be handled softly, or that the wiretaps authorized by Congress would not be employed. Thus it was not until 1969 and John Mitchell that the federal government mounted a sustained drive against the Mafia and other elements of crime syndicates. Only then did the FBI become adequately involved in a Strike Force campaign against the rackets. Previously, the bureau had had its Charles Smiths, its occasional wiretaps, its occasional "strike force" type of investigation campaign against a crime syndicate, but with little to show for its efforts. The results depended on prosecutions, and the FBI was not in that business on its own. Attorney General Mitchell realized that the FBI was capable of assaulting the Mafia fortresses, and that the bureau had not been properly used by the real decision makers, the politicians.

This situation was quickly repaired by the Nixon administration Justice Department. William Lynch, who had been with Justice since 1961 and was experienced in organized crime investigations and court cases, was named chief of the Organized Crime and Racketeering Section in May, 1969. With Lynch, the Justice Department assembled some of its best lawyers in Strike Forces across the nation. The teams went right to work.

Results began to show just as quickly. With FBI agents carrying much of the investigative work load, court-authorized electronic surveillance, primarily relating to gambling, narcotics and extortion-credit operations, began recording the evidence which would by 1971 have nearly every top gangster in every major city either under indictment or already convicted.

In the three-year period following the first tap in February, 1969, 478 court orders (by all agencies) were obtained for electronic surveillance in federal investigations of organized crime.* These investigations had the underworld on the run, really for the first time. Chicago's Mafia boss, Salvatore (Momo) Giancana, had to find sanctuary in Mexico, after serving one term for contempt. Back home the FBI and the Chicago Strike Force were picking his organization apart. Sam Battaglia, who Giancana had left in charge, was jailed, and the Strike Force was proceeding after the other top dogs, Jack Cerone, "Mil-

*See records of administrative office of the courts.

waukee Phil" Alderisio, Paul Ricca, William Daddano and Sam DeStefano, among others.

Meyer Lansky had to retreat to Israel (which subsequently deported him), leaving behind his Miami and Las Vegas holdings and leaving the national syndicate without one of its most productive schemers. The New Jersey organization lost its leader, Sam ("the Plumber") De Cavalcante, to a jail cell. Joseph Colombo, boss of New York's Joseph Profaci Mafia "family," was arrested by FBI agents along with 30 members of his gang and subsequently indicted on federal gambling charges;* and mobs in Kansas City and New Orleans were losing their people in raids and arrests.

The "untouchable" underworld bosses were finally experiencing the long arm of the law, which reached into their protected fortresses via electronic surveillance.

These crime bosses had long depended on the lesser hoodlums to take the risk of arrest and prison. But the lesser hoods were being picked up in gambling raids. A boost for these raids by Strike Force-FBI teams came in 1970, with the enactment on October 15 of the Organized Crime Control Act. This broadened direct jurisdiction of the FBI and the Strike Forces in organized crime matters. By the Spring of 1971, Clark Mollenhoff reports, over 400 search and arrest warrants in major interstate gambling raids were issued pursuant to this act.**

In 1971, FBI gambling raids netted: 56 persons in a seven state-District of Columbia operation which amounted to a $60 million take per year; more than 50 persons in a Maryland gambling raid; 79 persons in raids on five mob-controlled gambling rings in the New York City area; more than 150 persons involved in a ring extending from Tampa and Las Vegas to Chicago and Michigan; and 30 persons in raids of Philadelphia area gambling operations.*** Additionally, the bureau could

*Colombo was later incapacitated by a bullet wound from an attempted assassination.
**Mollenhoff, p. 231.
***FBI Release, January 6, 1972.

point to the help its 1971 investigations gave to Strike Force, Treasury Department, and local agencies, in more than 500 additional raids which involved the arrests of some 3,500 underworld figures.*

It can only be guessed whether the back of organized crime has been broken; but it is certain that its gambling operations have been badly hurt. Similar efforts by the FBI and energetic leadership by Strike Forces, when directed to other mob operations such as loan sharking, could result in future successes against this criminal monster.

In the meantime, the recent record, one would think, would quiet the critics like Fred Cook, William Turner and Hank Messick, who have contended that the FBI has shied from an effort against organized crime. But no, they continue.

Hank Messick in his latest book, *John Edgar Hoover*** (subtitled: "A Critical Examination of the Director and of the Continuing Alliance between Crime, Business, and Politics"), parrots the line which Cook and Turner established, it being their position that the bureau and Hoover refused to recognize the existence of organized crime in order to confuse the public with a "mythical" danger, communism. Messick goes them still one better, implying—but only by innuendo—that Hoover was in league with the underworld.

These critics must gloss over a critical fact, however. They ask us to presume that the FBI long had it within its power to destroy organized crime. This is plainly in error. It was not until the legal jurisdiction and tools were provided the FBI that it had any capability for a sustained drive against rackets and gambling operations. The fact that when these were granted— in 1961, 1968 and 1970—the FBI participated fully in a massive and successful drive against the underworld, would seem to prove the point.

Another fact ignored by these critics is that it was not the

*Ibid.
**(New York, 1972).

FBI that refused to recognize the need for such a drive. It was the bureau's political superiors. This was the case with Ramsey Clark and President Johnson in the 1960s, and it was the fact in earlier administrations owing their lives to corrupt city machines. This is illustrated by the Pendergrast mob affair in 1947. Politics, in this case brazen politics, frustrated an FBI investigation of vote fraud in the Pendergrast machine-ruled city, Kansas City, Missouri.

Kansas City Star reporters had uncovered evidence of massive vote fraud in the 1946 elections. The Truman administration, having to appear concerned, ordered an FBI investigation. But this was only a public relations gimmick. The bureau agents were restricted to interviewing only the *Star* reporters and election officials.*

Nevertheless, the FBI compiled a 355-page report which was forwarded to the proper authorities. But the U.S. attorney in Kansas City and federal judges could find nothing which merited further investigation by a federal grand jury, and the FBI investigation went for naught. No further bureau investigation was authorized.

Then a state grand jury investigated and returned indictments against 71 persons. Embarrassed, Attorney General Tom Clark defended his office, saying the FBI had "conducted a full investigation." The investigation, of course, had been regarded only as a preliminary effort by the bureau. It was clear that administration officials intended a whitewash of the affair, and the FBI could not open the case, or follow through on its investigation, without orders from the attorney general.

The FBI simply could do little about organized crime until the federal government was committted to the cause. This did not happen until 1961, and after an interlude during the Johnson administration, again in 1969, and it was then the FBI began writing its record of success against organized crime.

It now appears that this record will be only one chapter in

---

*Mollenhoff, p. 56.

a series of success stories. One may hope that the concentrated effort and cooperation involved in the Strike Force work will finally send the political machine-rackets alliance reeling into a deserved oblivion.

It has been similar concentrated efforts which have succeeded for the FBI in past campaigns against crime. It has been this, in fact, along with police agency professionalism, which has been the bureau's stock in trade since reorganized by J. Edgar Hoover. Thoroughness, persistence, and correct action have been common threads through the history of FBI crime fighting, and these have been made possible only because of the bureau's capacity for concentrated and professional effort.

However, concentration of effort has not meant that the FBI has participated in the scheming for centralizing government control in Washington, D.C. The bureau and J. Edgar Hoover steadfastly resisted that trend, and insisted that the FBI should not become a national police force, or a federal investigative agency of more general jurisdiction. Hoover also resisted efforts to combine all federal investigative work in his agency, arguing against FBI responsibility for drug control, for instance, and never coopting the efforts of parallel agencies such as the Secret Service or the Treasury Department which also have certain criminal jurisdictions. The FBI has always observed its legal limitations.

These three themes—concentration of effort, professionalism in investigations and continual observance of jurisdictional boundaries—fairly summarize the nearly 50-year history of FBI criminal investigation under Hoover. The history has had its share of exciting events, of course, but the impact of FBI effort is told more by some mundane facts.

Perhaps foremost of these is the fingerprint system established by the FBI. An idea of its importance to law enforcement can be derived from a look at its work in 1971. In that year, the FBI Identification Division received over six million fingerprint cards, processing more than 26,000 each day. Fingerprint data had been pouring into the FBI files at similar rates ever since 1930, and at the end of 1971, the bureau had 196 million sets of fingerprints.*

The impact of this identification system is told by another statistic. In 1971, searches of these millions of fingerprints resulted in the identification of more than 43,000 fugitives. Included in this figure are arrested individuals whose identities are reliably established by comparing fingerprints with those on file. In some of these cases, the fugitives may have attempted to hide their identities; and in others the police may not have known the arrestees were fugitives. Fingerprints do not lie, however.

This is an even more important aspect of the work of the Identification Division's Latent Fingerprint Section. Fingerprints left on weapons, glasses, desk tops, and other places at the scene of crimes do not lie either, and these latent prints when checked against prints on file at the FBI were used by police to identify nearly 5,000 suspects and subjects in 1971. The FBI received 33,000 latent fingerprint cases in that year alone.

The importance to law enforcement of this identification system was realized by J. Edgar Hoover at the time of his appointment in 1924. The bureau then had nearly a million identification records, most of them fingerprints, but they were not usable. Piled in storage, there was no way to search the records quickly and reliably for establishing identities with fingerprints.** These records had existed in other places—at Leavenworth Prison, and at the Washington headquarters of the International Association of Chiefs of Police. When the records were turned over to the bureau, no central system was yet established and Hoover took office in the midst of a tug-of-war among parties interested in controlling the central system which everybody agreed was necessary.

Congress seemed to have settled the question in July, 1924

*FBI Release, January 6, 1972.
**Whitehead, p. 135.

by appropriating the funds necessary for Hoover to render the bureau's system operable. Within two months, the new director had an identification service operating,* and in 1930 the Congress approved permanent establishment of the FBI's Identification Division. Police agencies across the country quickly learned the usefulness of the system and by 1932 nearly 5,000 of them were cooperating by sending fingerprint cards and using identification services.**

This effective law enforcement tool could immensely increase in potential by computerization. The FBI conducted a feasibility study in 1971, and at this writing is developing the programming techniques and system designs to implement a computer system.

While this is being accomplished, computer technology has been utilized by the FBI to keep pace with crime problems in other ways. On November 30, 1971 the bureau put in operation a national computerized criminal data bank. Into this system goes the arrest records of thousands of criminals. Personal identification information, arrest charges, case dispositions, sentences and custody or supervision status of serious offenders are programmed into the computer from the records of state and federal agencies. This information is immediately available to cooperating agencies via connecting computer outlets.

The primary booster of scientific crime detection in the bureau has been the FBI Laboratory, established in 1932. From an original collection of a few science books and a small assortment of instruments and equipment, the bureau lab grew into a well-equipped scientific crime detection center with experts ready to service the needs of local law enforcement agencies without charge. Of course, its own agents find constant use for the technical assistance provided by the laboratory.

FBI experts in firearms, explosives, electronics, handwriting,

*Ibid.
**FBI Report, 1932

blood and hair, materials as varied as ink and paper, soil, fibers and metals, chemistry, and languages, apply their skills to evidence of crime sent in from around the country. In 1973, to illustrate the importance of this work, over 338,800 specimens of evidence were examined at the Laboratory.* Many of these required extensive use of massive reference files which contain samples of type from nearly every American-made typewriter, thousands of paper types and watermarks, photographic copies of forged checks, soils, paints, hairs, tire prints, and other items which may be clues in a crime.

Tales are numerous of how this type of scientific law enforcement has processed seemingly impossible clues to solve crimes. For one example, in 1970, an enterprising criminal twice sent hand-printed extortion notes to separate airline companies. The first note demanded $35,000 for the continued safety of the passengers on the company's airplanes. The second demanded $30,000. The extortionist knew how vulnerable the airlines were to such attempts, but he never figured that the notes would lead to his identification. The notes were sent to the FBI Laboratory, and it was found that the reference files happened to have samples of this extortionist's work, samples which had been developed through previous investigations. Laboratory comparisons resulted in his identification. He was arrested and ultimately convicted in June, 1971 on the basis of this evidence, gleaned from the only available clue.

Criminals would step lightly if they knew how scientific crime detection worked. In July, 1963 a hardware store was burglarized and the tools stolen were used for several other burglaries that night. Police found shoe sole impressions outside the hardware store, including one which appeared to be a double print made by two different kinds of shoes. This double print was copied in a plaster cast and the copy was sent to the FBI Laboratory. The lab examination disclosed that the shoes belonged

*Fiscal 1973—see FBI reports.

to two persons suspected by the police. This, and expert testimony by the examining FBI agent, helped convict the suspects.

Small bits of evidence, examined by experts, can catch the violent criminal as well. In April, 1963, a young British woman, an Olympic skier, was raped, murdered, and mutilated. An 18-year-old man was suspected. He had sold a camera missing from the victim's home, and signed a bill of sale which led to his arrest.

Police sent the bill of sale, clothing from the suspect, a piece of twine found in his possession and thought to have been used to strangle the young woman, and a shred of twine found on the woman's camera. FBI examiners established that the signature was the suspect's, that human blood remained on his clothing, and that the twine was the same as the garrote he had used. This scientific evidence convicted the suspect, and he was sentenced to be executed.

Of course, this type of success of the FBI's scientific methods has involved expert police work by local law enforcement personnel—the police who gather such shreds of evidence. The complexity of this work requires training, and the FBI has not been a laggard in this regard.

Police training was a pet project of J. Edgar Hoover, who prided himself in the professional work of his own agents, and continuously prodded the law enforcement establishment on the subject. He repeatedly propounded the need for professional, career policemen. In 1934-1935 his idea became a more concrete proposal, and a national training school for police was established at bureau headquarters. This school became the FBI National Academy at Quantico, Virginia, which Hoover and many law enforcement officials thought of as the West Point of law enforcement.

Since 1934, the 12-week training course at the academy has helped educate thousands of policemen in the newest techniques and police procedures. Many of the nation's top policemen received advanced training there. Yet, this training is not the school's greatest accomplishment, albeit helpful toward proper law enforcement.

It is the advancement of the concept of professional police work which has been the major benefit of the FBI National Academy. If nothing else is impressed on the police who study there, it is the dedication and respect which the good peace officer must have. No one other institution has done so much to instill that concept into America's lawmen, and the graduates of the academy promote the same in police ranks everywhere.

The professional law enforcement man, in the FBI view, does not employ tactics which brutalize the accused or violate his civil rights. This rule is not just FBI Academy pontification; it is the practice expected of FBI agents, and it is a rule the bureau insists on in its dealings with other law enforcement agencies. Here is how J. Edgar Hoover explained it in a 1952 article:

> Here is the very heart of the problem: the vital necessity of having men and women in law enforcement who hold inner allegiance to the principles of democracy and perform their duties in a completely legal manner. There have been abuses—that cannot be denied. But these are the symptoms of a dying school in law enforcement, of the poorly trained officer who lacks the technical know-how to compete with the criminal. Year after year these abuses are decreasing; the modern-day officer feels no need to stoop to dishonorable methods. He is better trained. He is utilizing up-to-date scientific techniques of crime detection to win his battles.
>
> I have fought, during my 27 years as director of the FBI, for the development of law enforcement as a profession. I have worked for better training programs, modern equipment, adequate salaries, and, above all, a personal integrity which scorns the temptations of graft, bribery and corruption. Time after time I have seen law enforcement betrayed and civil liberties violated by one of these factors: by a poorly trained officer who thinks brute strength and sadistic cruelty will bring a confession; by the resignation of intelligent, fearless and honest police officers who simply could not and would not make law enforcement a career at such low wages and long hours; by poor morale caused by lack of civic respect and the treatment of the

police department as the "lost duckling" of government, deprived of funds, equipment and interest; by police officers who, for a piece of silver, betray their sacred calling to the lust, greed and vice of the crooked politican or gang leader.*

Insistence on professionalism has not always earned friends for the bureau. Sometimes local law enforcement agencies have found FBI agents to be what the local officers thought was uncooperative. They found that FBI agents sometimes viewed exchange of information with locals as a one-way street—in the bureau's direction. Bureau files are closed even to cooperating police agencies, although FBI agents have easy access to most of the other agencies' materials. There also may have been irritations at times about the special treatment FBI agents reserved for the National Academy graduates in the ranks. And some police departments find that the FBI agents do not trust their honesty or ability.

These none-too-frequent irritations are not so much the result of interagency rivalry as the result of conscious policy at FBI headquarters and rules of operation in the field offices. The bureau is insistent that its operations be professional, and will not give way even for the sake of cooperation. For one, files are not opened to anybody. To do so could, no doubt, assist local police; but it would also be in violation of the bureau's rules intended to protect the confidential nature of the derogatory data it stacks up. This is a protection for the subjects of those files and the innocents who may have their names included. So, too, the other irritants pop up due to the FBI's rigid adherence of its own procedures—procedures which have served well to protect the rights of citizens.

The FBI has this policy for itself, and its cooperation with local police depends on it. J. Edgar Hoover's ground rules for cooperating with other agencies were that: 1) their officers must not be corrupt and the agency must not be controlled by politicians who protect corruption; 2) the agency must be able to maintain confidences and otherwise be trustworthy; and

*37 *Iowa Law Review,* pp. 175, 178.

3) they must be competent enough to assist the FBI effort. These are reasonable standards. There have been obvious cases where the bureau's cooperation with another police agency would have been ruled out.

However, cooperation has been generally excellent between the FBI and other agencies. Many criminal informants report to bureau agents, and more often than not, their tips relate to matters outside the jurisdiction of the FBI. In such cases the bureau will relay this information to the authority which has jurisdiction, and the cooperation results in thousands of arrests each year.

Police who work cases with FBI agents are nearly always impressed with the agents' work, and they safely assume the G-men are trustworthy. They are impressed as well with the agents' observance of jurisdictional and practical lines of demarcation between the agencies. The FBI does not muscle into the local police investigations; nor do the federal agents highhandedly attempt to control cooperative investigations.

There are, of course, the rivalries which one would expect between the gentleman's police force which is the FBI, and the local cops who so often have performed the dirty work of law enforcement. Not that the federal investigators refuse to take on undesirable jobs (try staking out a fugitive's home for 30 hours on a New Year's holiday); but the FBI is not a patrol force as are the local police departments. The *modus operandi* is different. Rather than sudden calls over the police radio, furious chases of suspects, and snap judgments to arrest or search suspects, the FBI has the luxury of *preparing* most of its cases. For this reason, it has an easier time avoiding the rough treatment and mistakes which mark unprofessional police work—easier in the sense that FBI agents can get results and still act as gentlemen. Most police sense this distinction, fueling the rivalry; but most are aware of the broader outlook and the "high class" FBI is not really resented by most police.

The opportunity for an extended case preparation results from the nature of the FBI's jurisdiction in large part. Not having general jurisdiction, the bureau does not have to protect the streets day and night. It can select its targets, usually.

In fugitive cases, where the agents cannot always select the time and place of the arrests, the case is still one step further along than in many arrests by local police. Charges have, necessarily, already been brought; otherwise the bureau does not have jurisdiction.

The advantage of case preparation is made clear in the prosecution record of FBI cases. Repeatedly, J. Edgar Hoover reported 95 percent and higher conviction rates of those brought to trial as a result of FBI investigations. In 1964, to choose a year, the bureau's investigations led to 12,921 convictions representing 96.5 percent of those cases tried.* A large percentage of the convictions are secured by guilty pleas—further testimony to the FBI's thorough preparation of the cases.

But the best evidence of the FBI's excellence in investigation is the testimony of those who must rely on the investigations to prove cases beyond a reasonable doubt in court. These are the U.S. attorneys and their assistants, who handle prosecutions.

Thomas Foran, formerly U.S. attorney for the Northern District of Illinois, worked closely with FBI agents in an investigation of events at the Democratic Convention of 1968. Violations of the law by both police and demonstrators were the subject of about 2,400 FBI interviews. Persons interviewed were thought to have information concerning incitement to riot allegations, police brutality allegations, and allegations of illegal electronic bugging and wiretapping of Democratic Party committee meetings at the Conrad Hilton Hotel.

After the proceedings, Foran, in a letter to a research assistant of the editors, wrote his impressions of the FBI's work:

> The FBI's participation in the trial was consistent with its participation in all matters which I conducted while I was United

*1964 Annual Report of the Attorney General of the United States.

States attorney. I found the FBI to be an able, careful, highly motivated, and totally honorable investigative agency. I found it totally conscious of the rights of defendants and totally objective in its dealings with my office. I feel that the type of criticism their activity has been subjected to in recent years is irresponsible since they are so obviously the best law enforcement agency available to us.

Other attorneys in similar capacities have dealt with the FBI, and they echo Mr. Foran's sentiments. They know the bureau investigations provide good preparation for their cases.

These things were known by J. Edgar Hoover, and they were a primary reason he resisted many and continuing efforts to broaden the bureau's scope of responsibility. By keeping jurisdiction as narrow as possible and by limiting its police function mainly to that of investigation, Hoover was able to keep the bureau on course, performing aggressively and thoroughly in its field.

These characteristics also permitted the FBI to concentrate on the important investigations, which the agent calls "major cases." Major cases have earned a good reputation for the bureau; and it is in these cases that the flexibility of the FBI operation has proved its worth. The bureau seems to have a unique capability to concentrate its agents' work on important cases—rarely does the big one get away.

This was precisely the nature of the FBI campaign against the gangland crime, the bank robbers and the kidnappers of the 1930s. A wave of violent lawlessness seemed to be sweeping the land. The public was worried, and at times outraged. Congress responded by sending the FBI into the action.

At the time, federal crime laws did not provide the jurisdiction and power the bureau needed for a campaign. Its agents did not even have the full police authority to make arrests, and could carry weapons only in special circumstances.

But the crime wave seemed to require strengthening the federal crime laws and the FBI's law enforcement powers. Bank robberies, in 1933, were occurring at a rate of nearly 2 per day.* The Dillinger gang terrorized the Midwest in 1933 and 1934, and the Machine Gun Kelly, Pretty Boy Floyd, Frank Nash, Baby Face Nelson, and Ma Barker hoodlums and gangs robbed and killed and spread fear among law-abiding citizens.

On March 1, 1932, Bruno Richard Hauptmann kidnapped the Lindbergh's twenty-month-old son, Charles, Jr., for $50,000 ransom. He murdered and buried the boy. The nation was overcome by grief and shock.

In response, on June 22, 1932 Congress enacted the Lindbergh Kidnap Law, making kidnapping a person across state lines a federal crime. Previously, kidnapping was strictly a state and local law enforcement concern.

The New Jersey authorities and the FBI formed special investigative teams on the case—an early demonstration of the bureau's ability to apply itself to a major case.

The concentrated effort paid off, finally, in 1934, when one of the Lindbergh ransom notes was identified by a teller at the Corn Exchange Bank and Trust Company, which had received the note from a gas station attendant who was suspicious of the note. The attendant had noted the license number of the auto driven by his customer. The owner of the note happened to have been Hauptmann, the FBI determined.

He was arrested, tried, convicted, and executed for his crime. Yet, while the Lindbergh Law was now in effect, kidnappings were on the increase. The kidnappers had not yet found out what it was like to be chased by a determined FBI.

Machine Gun Kelly, Albert Bates, and family were soon to find out, however. On July 23, 1933 they kidnapped and held for ransom Charles Urschel and Walter Jarrett.

Hoover, however, had his agency on a regular anti-kidnapping campaign. A special line for kidnap calls was established at FBI headquarters. Mrs. Urschel called to Hoover's kidnap line, and gave the details directly to the chief of the bureau. Moments later, FBI agents were at the Urschel home.

*Whitehead, p. 96.

It was the decision of the family to pay the ransom demanded. Jarrett had been turned loose, and Mr. Urschel was also freed, unharmed, after the ransom was received.

Urschel recounted in detail what he had experienced, although he had been blindfolded. He guessed that the area near the place he was held had been experiencing drought, and that he was held at a farm. One thing he remembered is that an airplane passed over the house every morning at about 9:45, but that on one day, when it was raining, the plane did not appear.

This information was enough for the FBI. Systematic checks of weather and airline schedules and flight paths revealed that on July 30 an American Airways flight had avoided a thunderstorm over an area previously stricken by drought.

A house in that area was owned by Machine Gun Kelly's in-laws. Knowing now the identities of the kidnappers, a relentless nationwide search was conducted by FBI agents. They tracked Bates to Denver and arrested him, and in Memphis, special agents caught Kelly and his wife without a machine gun. "Don't shoot, G-men!" the once-bold crook is said to have exclaimed.

As Bates and the Kellys found, kidnapping was becoming a dangerous occupation for hoodlums. Indeed, with such tenacious investigations by a federal force, it was soon to become a field of criminal activity dealt in by amateurs. The professionals would find less risky ventures.

But the FBI applied the same concentrated effort in the less frequent but equally appalling kidnappings by the amateurs. The most famous case in point is the Weinberger baby kidnapping.

Hardly one month old, Peter Weinberger was stolen on July 4, 1956 from a baby carriage resting on the Weinberger's patio at their Westbury, Long Island home. The kidnapper demanded $2,000 ransom, which was dropped for the kidnapper but never picked up.

After waiting the seven days then required by the Lindbergh Law, the FBI entered the case. All the bureau had were two handwritten ransom notes. More than a hundred agents began screening handwriting specimens contained in every conceivable government or institutional file, as well as FBI files. Comparable specimens were sent to a special operation headquarters for examination by bureau handwriting experts.

Finally, more than a month later on August 22, an agent found a strikingly similar handwriting sample in an arrest file of Angelo LaMarca. Experts positively identified LaMarca as author of the kidnap notes from a comparison of the samples. LaMarca was arrested and confessed. The body of Peter Weinberger was found the next day.

The public anger over this kidnapping, and the good impression of the painstaking effort by the FBI, resulted in Congress' amending the kidnapping law to permit FBI entry into the cases after 24 hours rather than the seven days which the old law required.

Bank robbery was soon to join kidnapping as an amateur's crime. The FBI was sent to battle again by Congress. Tired of the daily reports of bank holdups, Congress enacted Public Law 73-235 on May 18, 1934 which provided that bank robbery would be a federal offense (generally).

The FBI went to work. The Barker-Karpis gang, the Dillinger-Gillis gang and others were all wanted on federal charges now, and no longer could they elude the police by escaping across a state line to "hole up" and plan their next crime. Dillinger and "Baby Face" Nelson were chased relentlessly and both shot dead. "Ma" Barker and her son Fred were killed in a 1935 gun battle with FBI agents, and Alvin Karpis was taken in a celebrated arrest by J. Edgar Hoover himself.

The professionals were being forced out of the field and most of them faced prison. By 1936, 79 bank robbers were convicted as the result of FBI investigations. This was having its effect.

In 1933, there were 519 bank robberies reported. This number started to go down after the FBI got into the act in 1934. In 1935, only 229 were reported and in 1936, the number declined again to 161. A good part of the reason for this success was that the FBI had apprehended and the courts had sent to jail nearly 160 bank robbers.*

However, as crime rose in the late 1950s, bank robberies and bank burglaries became more frequent. In a record year, 1960, 764 robberies, burglaries and larcenies were reported in banks within the bureau's jurisdiction. But the perpetrators were amateurs, and they had a penchant for getting caught. In the same year 420 of them were convicted, among these a young veterinarian and a young man who had acted while armed only with a razor. The criminals in this field were a new breed, and while more numerous, considerably less of a threat than the Dillinger-Barker type desperados.

The capabilities of the FBI were noticed in Washington and in the state governments during those formative years of the 1930s. Comment was not merely favorable—it tended to go overboard, and Director Hoover was aware of danger ahead.

Hoover fought the tendency to broaden the scope of the FBI in a manner which would alter the character of the agency. In 1933, for instance, President Roosevelt ordered the combining of the Justice Department's Prohibition Enforcement Unit with the FBI. This meant that the 1200 Prohibition agents, some of whom were tainted by corruption, would be mingled with 326 dedicated FBI agents.

Hoover went to Attorney General Homer Cummings, arguing that the FBI would be dealt a death blow by this move. He won his argument; the Prohibition Unit remained separate.

At about the same time, the Director fought off a proposal to have FBI-trained men serve with "roving commissions." These agents would have worked in the states to enforce federal and state laws. Hoover protested again to Cummings, who agreed and later told Congress that it was "not the duty of the federal government generally to preserve peace and order in the various communities of our nation."

*1936 Report of the Director of the Federal Bureau of Investigation.

Hoover was fearful that centralized control over his forces would be lost, but he was fearful also of a national police force. Perhaps the best statement of his opinion on the latter is found in a 1952 *Iowa Law Review* article he wrote, in which he addressed the role of the FBI and civil liberties:

> Moreover, as I have repeatedly reiterated, the United States has no need for a national police agency. The present system of law enforcement, local, state, and national, working together in voluntary and fraternal cooperation, can fulfill its responsibilities. What is needed is not a new structure of law enforcement, but strengthening, improving, and making more efficient the present arrangement. That is what intelligent law enforcement officers are now attempting to do, and with the aid of America's citizenry, it can be done.*

Critics such as William Turner have scored Hoover for his intransigence on this subject. They claim that the director employed the national police bugaboo as an excuse for FBI inactivity in "important" areas of crime while the bureau energetically applied itself to the easy jobs which piled up a statistical record of excellence. Turner bases his attack on the fugitive arrests, return of stolen property, and auto theft cases—all of which appear as statistical proof of successful FBI action in the annual reports. When the critics start complaining about *success* instead of failure, one can assume they have no serious criticism to make.

Nonetheless, the matter of a national police cannot be dealt with lightly. It seems that critics like Turner cannot take seriously anyone who professes concern about overreaching federal power. But to many thoughtful persons, it is not at all healthy to have law enforcement increasingly becoming a federal power as against a state and local function. Neither is it healthy for any law enforcement agency, local or federal, to accumulate too much power—more than the minimum needed to perform its rightful duties. Hoover worried about the problem in all earnestness, and it says something about these critics'

*37 *Iowa Law Review* 175, p. 194.

own reputations as "civil libertarians" if they cannot see the problem and believe the director meant what he said.*

The critics' argument that the FBI emphasizes the less important but statistically more productive areas of law enforcement falls flat. First, it ignores once again the simple fact that the bureau is bound to investigate as directed by the people's representatives in Congress. It is for the latter to decide whether FBI agents are to recover stolen property and chase car thieves. And since interstate car theft rings are involved in a good part of the more than one-half million cars stolen each year, the Congress has not seen fit to take the FBI off the chase.

Actually, many of the nearly 30,000 vehicles reported as recovered in each recent annual FBI report are spotted by local police and other authorities. The FBI takes part in the recoveries because it is responsible for the return of the vehicles. There is good reason for continuing this task as an FBI assignment: the recoveries can and do lead to interstate theft rings. In 1971 the FBI had under investigation more than 120 major interstate auto theft rings. In one case the network extended from New York to Miami and San Juan, Puerto Rico. Stolen cars from New York were being transported to other Eastern states and to Florida and the Caribbean. The FBI ended the activities of this ring on August 9, 1971 with arrests of 33 persons in Miami, Newark, and San Juan.**

The same considerations apply to stolen property recovery statistics. However, the usual statement in the FBI reports that this figure amounts to about 150 percent return on the tax dollar each year is an obvious public relations gimmick. Surely the public is not measuring the worth of law enforcement in terms of tax dollar returns.

Similarly, fugitive arrests by the FBI now amount to more than 35,000 per year and make a nice statistic for the annual

*See M. Stanton Evans' article in Chapter 3 for libertarian views on the dangers of a national police agency.
**FBI Release, op. cit.

reports. The figure can be misleading, but in this case that is no fault of the bureau.

The word "fugitive" is one which, in the public minds, is almost synonymous with "desperado." To a public whose knowledge of law enforcement comes more from television, motion pictures, and paperback novels than from first-hand association, the term conjures up a vision of the fleeing felon—tough, perhaps frightened, actively seeking to escape the clutches of the law and, like an animal, dangerous when cornered. Because of this popularized view, the FBI's statistics on fugitive apprehensions have been cited by critics of the bureau to hint that the bureau seeks to mislead Congress and the public. This is not a reasonable criticism.

In the legally precise FBI terminology, a fugitive is any person whose whereabouts are unknown and for whom proper legal process for an arrest has been issued in a case in which the FBI has jurisdiction. An FBI arrest made without a warrant occurs only in exceptional instances and is made within the circumstances clearly permitted by law. The average working FBI agent is something of an expert on the law of arrest. When an agent feels he has obtained enough evidence to identify his subject and to provide probable cause for arrest, he presents the facts to an assistant United States attorney who may, if he deems the case sufficient, authorize prosecution. The United States attorney, accompanied by the agent as the complaining witness, goes before a federal magistrate who may issue an arrest warrant. In some cases the warrant may be issued after an indictment is returned by a federal grand jury. When the warrant is issued, the subject of the warrant becomes a "fugitive" in the eyes of the FBI, in the event the agent working the case finds that the location of the subject of the warrant is unknown at the time. However, the term "fugitive" is *not* independently applied by the bureau as a convenience or as a statistic-building device. In many cases, such as those of deserters, parole and probation violators, and a few others, the legal processes required for arrest are virtually automatic and have been issued even before the case is referred to the FBI. But in no case does the bureau create the "fugitive" designation itself.

So it is that many "fugitive" apprehensions as recorded by the FBI are of a strictly routine nature (because of the possible danger, FBI agents are taught to treat none as "routine"). As an example, we may use Selective Service cases, particularly before these violations became comingled with anti-war protest. The mission of the Selective Service System, the Department of Justice, and, hence, the FBI in these cases has been to gain compliance with the Selective Service Act rather than to seek prosecutions and convictions. Many individuals who became delinquent under Selective Service became so through ignorance or carelessness, simply neglecting to maintain contact with their local draft board. Many young people registered under false names in order to obtain identification which would prove they were at least age 18. Many "violators" were already in the armed services. Relatively few were those cases in which the United States attorney's office sought prosecution of an active, motivated draft evader. Even in these, the opportunity to escape penalty by entering the service was normally afforded the subject. Many Selective Service cases became fugitive cases when the agent in charge found evidence that the subject might be deliberately evading service or that he might prove to be difficult to handle when located. In these cases it was normal for the agent to seek a warrant and for the United States attorney to authorize one, primarily for the protection of both the subject and the agents who would have to locate the subject. The arrest might be made within hours, or even minutes, after the warrant was issued but was, nonetheless, recorded as a "fugitive" apprehension.* The working FBI agent who seeks a warrant in a Selective Service case is not prettying up the statistics. He is a trained law enforcement officer who has conducted an investigation and has found good reason to believe

---

*All deserters are considered fugitives by the Armed Services and are recorded as "fugitive" arrests.

that the arrest of his subject is the surest and safest way of handling the case.

From the bureau's point of view, sound management and administrative practice dictates that FBI headquarters learn promptly of the issuance of legal process authorizing the arrest of a subject, hence the designation "fugitive." The arrest of fugitives makes a nice statistic, obviously, but the figure is not fabricated to glorify the agency.

In any event, objective observers would have to agree that the Federal Bureau of Investigation does deserve a measure of glory in the criminal investigative field. No matter how much the critics pooh-pooh the bureau's record, the fact remains that the agency has performed excellently in the areas to which it has been directed by proper authority.

16. Civil Rights: Doing the Job
Andrew Seamans
with the Editors

An Impartial Effort / Editors
The concentration of effort by the FBI which has so handsome-
ly rewarded the nation in certain areas of criminal justice is
less obvious in the civil rights field. This chapter is devoted
largely to an exploration of one concentrated FBI effort, its
war against the Ku Klux Klan, in which the bureau's famous
abilities were so thoroughly applied.

   This is not to condemn the FBI record in the civil rights
struggle. One must be careful not to transfer one's own civil
rights zeal and frustration over snail-like progress toward racial
equality to either the federal government or the FBI. The civil
rights struggle has not enjoyed the unanimity of support, politically and socially, which the crime fighters have enjoyed; and
for the most part the political governors of the nation have
been cautious to avoid similar ramrod techniques, which would

have alienated even more severely their constituencies. Some have thought this the wisest approach to racial justice, others have been more impatient, but, once again, it must be pointed out that the Federal Bureau of Investigation can only follow the elected government's lead. The bureau cannot expand its own jurisdiction to do a job it thinks must be done. The question which ought to be asked is: has the FBI done the job it was supposed to do?

In Chapter 2 it was demonstrated that the FBI had until the 1960s relatively little jurisdiction, due to limited statutory law and limiting court interpretations, in the civil rights area. This situation has changed, now, and the field of civil rights itself has expanded, in practical terms and in terms of society's conception of the problem. What effect has this had on the FBI's role?

It should be noted that neither the bureau officials nor its force of special agents resisted the expanded role given it by its superiors. Liberal critics of the bureau do not wish to believe this, it being more convenient to their own prejudices to think the agency is populated with something like the stereotyped Southern cops. But the fact of the matter is, the FBI performs practically every investigation of civil rights matters with which the federal government is concerned. The bureau has no choice. Complaints are filed, and complaints must be investigated. Moreover, there is no evidence that the bureau does not apply itself in these investigations with the same thoroughness and neutrality it employs in other jurisdictions.

Perhaps it is this neutral posture in these investigations which bother the liberal detractors of the bureau. They would, in their enthusiasm, have a much more heavy-handed approach. Similarly, they might expect the FBI to adopt the liberal bias, and presume beforehand that, because of the racial prejudice which permeates certain segments of the country, the civil rights complainant is correct, and the violator is guilty. But the FBI cannot operate in that manner.

The bureau must, and does, leave to others the judgment

as to the validity of civil rights complaints, and what should be done about them. The FBI field offices and the U.S. attorney's offices receive the complaints. In the more routine cases, the bureau can investigate on its own initiative. In other cases the Justice Department decides whether it merits a preliminary investigation, and, if so, the FBI is so instructed. The results of the FBI investigation are then reported to the Civil Rights Division, which decides whether the case warrants prosecution. In those cases that do, the bureau is ordered to make a full investigation leading to eventual prosecution. In these cases, the decisions are made by the Civil Rights Division attorneys, not the FBI.

It should be noted, parenthetically, that general continuing investigations, such as that employed against organized crime and subversive organizations would be unproductive in the civil rights jurisdiction. The Justice Department and the FBI, except in certain campaigns, have been compelled to wait for the violations to surface and then willingly participate in prosecuting the cases. The civil rights violations seldom involve organizations (the KKK is the primary exception) whose substantial purpose is violation of the law or threatening national security. Quite often, government institutions, public accommodations and services, and similar establishments are the violators. Continuing FBI intelligence within these institutions would be impossible. Thus, the civil rights laws are enforced most often without the sort of continuing campaigns that have marked other areas of the FBI's jurisdiction.

Besides the war on the organized racists, there are two civil rights "crusades" which have involved the bureau. The one, discussed in Chapter 2, was Attorney General Robert Kennedy's voter rights campaign in the South. The FBI carried a heavy investigative workload throughout this effort, which was designed to prove general patterns of discrimination.

The second crusade is actually the FBI's own, and perhaps its most important. This has been in the area of police training. The FBI, through its academy, and through independent seminars, and schools has done yeoman service in raising the level of local law enforcement regard for civil liberties.

With this we turn to an article by Andrew Seamans on one of the FBI's most heartening civil rights efforts; the war against the KKK. It is in this battle that the FBI applied itself in the manner which has long been its hallmark.

War on the Klan/Andrew Seamans
The history of the Ku Klux Klan (or more correctly, Klans) is a veritable register of hotheads, malcontents, con artists, and rabblerousers. Its name and original membership were for amusement in 1865, but the joke has since been lost in periods of reorganization, inactivity, and resurgence.

In the recent past, from 1944 to 1954, the Klans were chiefly autonomous localized groups with such regional names as the Association of Georgia Klans, which had the dubious distinction of conducting the first public cross burning since Pearl Harbor, the Ku Klux Klan of Florida, Inc., Alabama's Federated Ku Klux Klans, Inc., the Southern Knights of the Ku Klux Klan, the Association of Carolina Klans, the Original Ku Klux Klan of the Confederacy, and on and on.

But it took the Supreme Court decision of May 17, 1954, to put some starch in the sheets of the Klansmen. This court ruling in *Brown* vs. *Board of Education* not only upset the segregated school systems in some 17 Southern and Border states, along with the District of Columbia, but it touched off repercussions that led to violence against blacks, bitterness between races, flare-ups within races, and a host of other side effects that have continued to the present.

A resurgence of Klan activity was bred by the decision, and at the same time a new civil rights movement was born. It was not until these occurrences that the FBI obtained the tools to fight the Invisible Empire—tools it lacked in the prior century of Klan activity. It is in this context that the story of the FBI's war against the Klan begins.

It cannot be a total war. Neither the Congress nor any other agency is capable of eliminating bigotry or establishing morality. But we can and should legislate against overt and violent acts by hate groups, and if such are a substantial purpose of an organization, then the group ought to be "repressed" severely. This the FBI has accomplished, even if the KKK can never be eliminated entirely.

Many of the cruel and malicious acts of the Klan are now within the jurisdiction of the Federal Bureau of Investigation. They were not until recent years. Flogging, dynamiting, burning, raping and those other reprehensible actions of the Klansmen were violations of state law not within the purview of the FBI.*

The stepped-up activism of the various Klans began to die in the late '50s as it appeared that the desegregation of the affected school systems did not herald the end of the world. But then with the turn of the decade, civil rights activities increased sharply with 1960's lunch counter sit-ins and 1961's invasion of the South with the "freedom" bus rides.

Only eight Klans of the myriad Klans of the previous ten years were then still in some semblance of existence, and by the time of a House Committee on Un-American Activities investigation in 1965, only five of these remained—the U.S. Klans, Knights of the Ku Klux Klan, Inc., "reduced to a single klavern with a steadily dwindling membership," the Association of South Carolina Klans, the Dixie Knights and the Association of Arkansas Klans. They were anemic groups at best.

But due to the resilience of racist hatred and in reaction to the passage of the Civil Rights Act of 1964, some of the wildest and most vicious of the Klan units began their ascent in the

---

*It stands to reason that a large majority of the Klansmen are not a part of the violence, or there would have been a great deal more mayhem. The majority therefore must be inactive bigots practicing their racial prejudice on an individual, mostly passive, plane.

mid-60s. In 1966 there were 15 or more groups. The membership rolls rose with every civil rights demonstration that got out of hand. For every American who accepted integration, there were others who became more hard-nosed or more redneck. But now the FBI was getting authority to take action. Finally the FBI, castigated by some for an alleged inaction against the hate-mongers despite a lack of jurisdiction, was able to move against the Klans.

Tracing the history of the bureau in civil rights cases is difficult, just as it is sometimes hard to define what constitutes a "civil rights" violation and what falls under the listing of just plain crime.

For example, there was a case in the Roaring Twenties involving the brutal murders of several American Indians in Osage County, Oklahoma carried out by one William K. Hale, a banker who was methodically wiping out wealthy members of the Osage Indians to rob their heirs of their inheritance. Federal agents, called in by the Tribal Council, spent a frustrating three years trying to prove their case against Hale under the only law which gave them jurisdiction—killing Henry Roan Horse on federal land. Was this a civil rights case? Or was it merely a criminal case that happened to involve Indians as victims? One would at first thought say the latter, but it must be taken into consideration that the American Indian has a unique position under federal laws. Had it not been for the Indians' special status, the FBI could not have entered the case. In this instance the FBI, under Director Hoover, did thoroughly investigate, and did bring William K. Hale to justice. Hale served approximately 18 and a half years of a life sentence before being granted a parole.

Although the crimes perpetrated in the name of the Klan, like Hale's murder spree, were appalling to the bureau and its director, there was little that could be done by the federal government to stop the hooded henchmen because of legal restraints, except in a few isolated cases where Klansmen stepped over that dividing line into the jurisdiction of the FBI. On these rare occasions there was federal action, though often this was an exercise in futility since many of those areas were virtually controlled by Klansmen and their fellow travelers.

Take, for example, the case of the vicious mob killing of accused murderer Willie Earle in 1947. Earle was arrested in Pickens County, South Carolina, as a suspect in the fatal stabbing of a cab driver. Fellow cabbies assembled and forcibly removed Earle from the county jail, forced a "confession" from him, and completed the job by beating, knifing, carving "chunks of flesh from his body," and finally shooting him with a shotgun.* The Criminal Division of the U.S. Department of Justice instructed the bureau to investigate under the federal statute permitting such where a law officer or official of any state is accused of a possible civil rights violation. Despite evidence amassed by the FBI in tandem with local lawmen, the identification of 28 persons in the mob, the confessions of 26 of the defendants, the appointment by then Governor Strom Thurmond of a special prosecutor, and the refusal of the defense to offer any testimony, all 28 were found innocent.

In his 1956 testimony before the House Appropriations Subcommittee, Hoover commented: "In civil rights cases the bureau is in a situation that if it obtains facts which result in prosecution it is unpopular, and if it doesn't obtain facts it is unpopular. Our sole purpose is to do our job objectively."

With the most recent rebirth of the Klan organizations, which has been met with FBI investigative activity, there has been divided opinion about what kind of job the FBI has done. Another of Don Whitehead's books, *Attack on Terror,*** is dedicated almost entirely to the bureau's work against the Mississippi Klans. He loads his pages with a veritable ledger of credits for the success of the G-men. On the other hand, some civil rights activists give the bureau low marks for not sufficiently preventing attacks on civil rights workers. In fact, J. Edgar

*Don Whitehead, *The FBI Story* (New York, 1963), p. 313.
**Funk & Wagnalls (New York, 1970).

Hoover and Martin Luther King had quite a verbal duel going in the news media in 1964 over statements attributed to King. The origin of the flap was a clipping from the *Chicago Defender,* a black newspaper, quoting King—in an outburst of his own brand of prejudice—warning blacks not to report civil rights violations to the Albany, Georgia FBI office, because it was staffed by Southerners. The FBI director opened fire on King at an informal press conference with a group of distaff Washington news gatherers. Hoover told the women that he had checked the FBI records and found that of five agents in the strife-torn town of Albany, one agent was from New York, one from Massachusetts, one hailed from Indiana, one from Minnesota, and only one was a native of Georgia. Then, in one of the most controversial moments of his long, distinguished career as a lawman, an angry Hoover concluded: "He [King] is the most notorious liar in the country." Civil rights leaders immediately jumped on Hoover with the able assistance of the liberal editorial writers and broadcast commentators, while conservatives generally applauded the director.

King fired off a telegram to the FBI chief: "I was appalled and surprised at your reported statement maligning my integrity. What motivated such an irresponsible accusation is a mystery to me. I have sincerely questioned the effectiveness of the FBI in racial incidents, particularly where bombings and brutalities against Negroes are at issue, but I have never attributed this merely to the presence of Southerners in the FBI." King's wire, then, indicated his dissatisfaction with the FBI's "effectiveness" at the same time Klansmen were labeling the bureau the "Federal Bureau of Integration."

Many civil rights activists still criticize the FBI, tearing it down at every opportunity. Some comment on these attacks must of necessity be touched on, albeit briefly, but first one note should be added to the Hoover-King story. When Martin Luther King was killed by a sniper in Memphis, Tennessee, 3,500 FBI agents conducted a feverish two-month investigation, costing over one million dollars, and reaching into 12 countries. These efforts resulted in the apprehension and con- viction of James Earl Ray who entered a plea of guilty to the murder. Ironic? No, dutiful would better describe it. Yet, not even one year later, the Reverend Jesse Jackson of the same organization called Hoover "one of the greatest threats to our national security" heading "what is very nearly a secret po- lice."*

Mayor Charles Evers of Fayette, Mississippi using a misguid- ed logic or lack of information, also gives the bureau low marks. Evers, whose brother Medgar was murdered while heading the Mississippi NAACP branch in 1963, blasted the FBI both for tapping King's phone, and for not preventing King's death. Like so many Americans, Evers simply disregard- ed the distinction between a national police force and a federal bureau of *investigation*. Even most liberals will agree that Hoover was consistent in restricting the bureau's activities to the investigative end of federal law enforcement and the bounds of federal jurisdiction. Evers' critique of the FBI seems simply ignorant of the legalities, criticizing the FBI for "failure" to do something it had no legal right to do, and again for doing something well within its jurisdiction. But Evers' personal feel- ings may well have outweighed his logic in this case.

The complaints of Jackson and Evers and other newsworthy civil rights figures are not universally supported by black Americans. This writer has found several contrary opinions among blacks—both liberal and conservative. One quite obvi- ous example is Jay Parker, the head of a citizens group which supports the bureau, the Friends of the FBI (FOF). Parker is an articulate young conservative who has dedicated his life to defending the free enterprise system and opposing the spread of communism. He has headed the FOF since its inception, and sees it as a necessary force *against* those who would have the FBI assume greater powers in those areas of law best left to

---

*Arthur Kretchmer, "Playboy Interviews Jesse Jackson," *Playboy* (November, 1969), p. 90.

state officers. The very fact of his leadership of FOF shows his feelings about the bureau. And while there is no doubt Parker would like to see the KKK eliminated as much as Evers would, unlike Evers he feels the bureau is doing a creditable job.

What of other Negroes? During a demonstration in front of the Soviet Embassy in Washington, this writer met a black Metropolitan Police plainclothesman. This law officer, in his early twenties, sees his future in the FBI. It is his lifelong ambition to join the bureau as a special agent, and he intends to take the necessary tests as soon as he picks up "a little more" education. He ignores the barbs thrown by some in the news media indicating there is no future in the FBI for blacks.

But Parker and the police officer are both in positions that would tend to sway them toward sympathy for the FBI. What about the civil rights groups? Are these activists universally critical of the federal investigative agency?

To find out, this writer interviewed Clarence Mitchell, a liberal who heads the Washington Bureau of the National Association for the Advancement of Colored People. The 61-year-old Mitchell's liberal credentials are not to be doubted. In the Senate hearings into the qualifications of now Associate Supreme Court Justice William Rehnquist, even liberal Indiana Democratic Senator Birch Bayh thought that the NAACP leader went too far in his attack on the former assistant attorney general by trying to brand him as a former John Birch Society member. Though conservatives will cite Mitchell in many cases as being overzealous there is no questioning his sincerity and dedication to civil rights. Thus his opinions on the FBI in the battle against the Ku Kluxers must be given a hearing.

Mitchell said he believes the bureau has done "an excellent job" investigating the KKK. "In fact," said Mitchell, "I think that we would have seen a much worse kind of violence in this country if the bureau, the FBI, had not done such a good job."

The 40-year veteran of civil rights activity agreed the bureau has not always been able to win convictions in cases of violence against members of minority races by terrorists, but he said this has not always been the FBI's fault. He said its very presence has often been sufficient in curbing the radicals' violence. Mitchell recognizes the necessity for the FBI to protect its confidential sources, although this sometimes means having evidence—proof positive—that cannot be introduced in a court of law. "When I said that evidence that can't be used in court is available to the FBI," he said, "I have several cases in mind. But one that happened very close to this area occurred up in Maryland where a person who was connected with the Klan dynamited a dwelling, and was in the act of getting ready to dynamite something else . . . the FBI gave the information to the state police, and they, in turn, apprehended him before he was able to carry out his second act. When the case came up in court, the accused man's lawyer wanted to cross-examine the person who had furnished the FBI with the information . . . but the FBI decided that it would be unwise to introduce that testimony, because it would destroy a source of information. And I'm reasonably certain cases of that kind occur from time to time."

Another point Mitchell brought up was that of whether or not Department of Justice attorneys feel they will be able to win a case in court considering "the problem it has with juries in certain parts of the country."

Mitchell would not get into a debate with Charles Evers over the effectiveness of the FBI in the case of the KKK, but stuck to his own personal experience in dealing with the agency, saying, "I can only say my assessment is based on my own firsthand observation on the matters with which I dealt. And I do know that there are people in the South who feel that the FBI has not done all that it could have done in many matters. I also know there are people who feel that the FBI uses too many Southern investigators to investigate Southern problems . . . . My personal feeling is that it is a lot more complicated than those explanations would seem to indicate."

One incident personally observed by the NAACP official took place in the course of an FBI investigation of a Mississippi lynching. Relating this story, Mitchell said, "The FBI made an investigation into the lynching. It showed that the victim was in jail. That the sheriff had left the keys to the jail and to the cell at a place where they were picked up by the people who committed the crime. Apparently this was by prearrangement. The victim was taken across a bridge from a point in Mississippi to a point in Louisiana, and this, of course, established jurisdiction of the Federal Bureau of Investigation under the kidnapping statute."

Mitchell stated that the FBI turned the evidence over to the state which failed to conduct an aggressive prosecution. Defending the FBI action, he continued, "The bureau in that case was so upset, and I think quite rightly, that they didn't make any bones about indicating that they had the goods on the accused and that it was because of the way in which it was handled by the state authorities that the whole thing blew up. I think that it would be fair to say that a lot of things the FBI uncovers run into that same kind of problem."

Civil rights cases, more than most other federal crimes in which the FBI has jurisdiction, require a high degree of local law enforcement involvement. Because of the nature of civil rights violation charges, this often becomes a sticky problem for the local lawmen. They must live in the area and do their jobs after the Feds have long since gone on their way. Given the problems, there nonetheless has been a considerable change in the conduct of law enforcement, most noticeably in the South. To no small degree this can often be traced back to the FBI and the FBI National Academy.

One of the most interesting facets of the FBI has been its contribution in protecting civil rights through its FBI National Academy and the thousands of police training schools operated on the local level since 1945. The FBI launched a countrywide program of Civil Rights Training Schools early in 1956, and 420 schools were held in the first six months. These schools have been well received and supported by local, county, and state authorities. The officers who attend them do not get mixed up in violations of the civil rights of citizens.

FBI investigations into the murders of the three civil rights activists in Mississippi in 1964—Michael Schwerner, Andrew Goodman, and James Chaney—were conducted with assistance of the Mississippi state police. One of the FBI's informants who helped to crack the case was a local law officer-Klansman, who broke with the KKK when it came to differentiating between personal bigotry, which is a private matter, and violence bred from racial prejudice. Police Sgt. Wallace Miller of Meridian, Mississippi, was no rank-and-file KKK member. He was a Kleagle, an organizer for the Invisible Empire. The law officer bitterly opposed integration and went so far as to have his picture taken holding a charred cross while displaying the secret sign of the KKK for all the brotherhood to see. But Miller was a policeman first and Klansman second. He had not participated in the murders of the three civil rights activists but he knew who had done it and told FBI agents everything he knew, breaking the case.

This was one of the instances—the arrest of 21 men on charges of crimes connected with these tragic murders—when civil rights chieftains publicly praised the bureau's work. Whitehead, in *Attack on Terror,* includes some of the comments from Martin Luther King of the Southern Christian Leadership Conference: "I must commend the Federal Bureau of Investigation for the work they have done in uncovering the perpetrators of this dastardly act. It renews again my faith in democracy." The National Urban League's Whitney Young said: "This is the kind of outstanding effort to protect the civil liberties and freedom of American citizens which one expects of the FBI. The agency and all its officials who worked to bring the accused to the bar of justice deserve the congratulations of the entire nation." Roy Wilkins of the NAACP said: "The FBI has done its job gathering the evidence, detecting and arresting the suspects. It is up to Mississippi to do the rest."*

*Whitehead, p.202.

Bigotry, whether it is hatred aimed at a particular race or religion or hatred of a particular cause (wars against would-be oppressors), readily leads to extremism. Individual passions may never go beyond the stage of name-calling or demonstrating. At some stage hatred can poison the thinking of the individual or the group to the point of inciting violence. But when? How? No one can say with any guarantee of accuracy. And that is the problem faced by the FBI and state and local investigative agencies. It is doubtful that all the weight of evidence one might amass would convince "anti-war" advocates that gathering intelligence about their organizations is justifiable; the same is true of the racist organizations, both black and white, from the Black Panthers to the Ku Klux Klan, from the Black Liberation Army to the National States Rights Party. Yet the evidence does justify government surveillance of these groups.

An example of this was cited by Clarence Mitchell. The NAACP held a convention in Jackson, Mississippi a few years ago. Mitchell was in charge of security for the gathering, working with the FBI and the state police. By coincidence, the father of a man involved in an attempted bombing which resulted in Klanswoman Kathy Ainsworth's death was also in Jackson to visit his son and ended up in the midst of the NAACP conventioneers, reportedly making some volatile and potentially trouble-making remarks. "We were forewarned about that by the Federal Bureau of Investigation," said Mitchell, "and I received information from the Mississippi State Police. . . . And I must say it was handled in a way that only those who were in the immediate vicinity of this individual know what was going on. It was never a big issue."

It may never have struck home with Mitchell that here indeed was a prime example of intelligence work. Apparently the incident could easily have gotten out of hand were it not for the presence of the FBI and the Jackson and Mississippi lawmen. This was definitely a case of the proximity of the law officers and their watchfulness bringing about a "chilling" effect.

Now let's look at the fear the FBI has thrown into the Klan. Following the exchange in the press between Martin Luther King and J. Edgar Hoover, the strong-willed pair met to discuss the controversy. James Phelan discussed this conference in an article in the *Saturday Evening Post* in 1965.* In the report, Phelan claimed to have inside information concerning what transpired during that face-to-face encounter. According to his account, King praised the bureau for its "strong restraining influence on violence down there [in the South]." The definition of a "strong restraining influence" could only be translated as "chilling effect."

"King told Hoover," writes Phelan, "that any criticism of either Hoover or the FBI attributed to him had been a misquotation. He praised the role of the FBI in Mississippi, and said the bureau had a strong restraining influence on violence down there. He denied he had ever advised Negroes not to report violations to the FBI, and said he encouraged them to cooperate with the bureau, and would continue to do so.

"The only complaint he had, King went on, was that sometimes Negroes would report grievances to FBI agents, and the following day they might see the agents apparently fraternizing with the police officers who had brutalized them. 'We are sometimes on the verge of temporary despair,' King said. When King finished, Hoover assured King that the FBI is in full sympathy with the 'sincere aspects of the civil rights movement.' He said that much of the difficulty arose out of the great misunderstanding by the general public, and particularly Negroes, on what the FBI can and cannot do. He pointed out that the bureau cannot recommend prosecution, provide protection to individuals, or make on-the-spot arrests, that it can only investigate and turn its findings over to the Justice Department.

"Hoover told King that the FBI had 'put the fear of God in the Ku Klux Klan' in the South, and dismissed the Klan as

---

*James Phelan, "Hoover of the FBI," *Saturday Evening Post* (September 25, 1965), p.32.

'white trash' and 'yellow cowards.' Hoover said his agents 'have interviewed every Klan member in Mississippi and put them on notice that if trouble comes, the FBI plans to look into the Klan first.' Hoover boasted that the FBI often knows what the Klan plans to do in advance, and that Klan members now suspect each other of informing and are fighting among themselves."

Hoover's definition of the Klansmen as "yellow cowards" is demonstrated in Whitehead's book *Attack on Terror* in several instances. Two of these were almost amusing. In one a Klansman threatened to kill any federal agent who set foot on his property. The next morning two FBI agents were there to accept the challenge. Confronted by the red-necked braggart holding a shotgun, the pair quietly told him they were there to talk, but if he made a move with the gun "we'll shoot to kill." The showdown ended with the Klan member in tears, dropping the gun. His brother later told the agents: "I don't believe it. Nobody ever faced down my brother."*

In another confrontation, a storeowner boasted of the thrashing he would give any FBI man who entered the shop. Word leaked and the following day he, too, received a visit from an agent who called his bluff successfully.**

These cases and others like them point up one of the chief dangers in a Klan-like organization that engages in terrorism. Individually the members would probably live out their lives without committing an act of viciousness. But put them together into a mob situation or a conspiratorial gathering and you have a violent crime looking for a place to happen. The explosion can come at any instant. This is the problem law officers face, whether from KKKs, SDS, Weatherman, rioters, American Nazis, or whatever.

Just a few years back, there were many who thought they were seeing the end of the Klan, but this assessment may yet

---

*Whitehead, *Attack on Terror,* p. 105-106.
**Ibid., p. 107.

prove premature. There still exists an Invisible Empire. And a good deal of the action seems to be in the North rather than the South.

In June of 1971, Frank F. Converse, Grand Dragon of the Houston chapter of the United Klans of America, Knights of the Ku Klux Klan (UKA), was quoted by *Los Angeles Times* newsman Nicholas C. Chriss as saying: "Everything that's ever been done to gain what's decent in the world, I guess, started out with violence. I guess that's why we have wars."* Houston has been the scene of some violence in the past few years, including bombings, shootings, arson, and malicious mischief, much of which has been attributed to members of Converse's group, according to Chriss. Converse denied that any of this was Klan action.

In 1969, an alleged Klansman was arrested in Fayette, Mississippi on charges of planning to murder Mayor Evers. When picked up by local police the suspect was driving a car containing two shotguns, a rifle, a carbine, and a .38-caliber pistol.

In 1971 UKA adherents were charged with dynamiting ten school buses in Pontiac, Michigan. The group, uncovered by an FBI informant, also plotted to knock out a power station as a diversionary tactic in order to cover their prime goal—a mortar attack on the school bus depot. The unpaid informant had been a member of the United Klans of America for four years preceding the school bus assault and in that period had been feeding back information to the Detroit FBI office.

Although these incidents flare up from time to time, there is much contrary information showing the decline of support for the Invisible Empire. As Rep. John Buchanan (R.-Ala.) stated, following reports that top Alabama officials had participated in a United Klans gathering, "It is difficult for me to believe that any responsible public official would lend any kind of aid and comfort to the Ku Klux Klan." Buchanan summed up what many believe is true of the KKK: "It is a tiny unrepre-

*Washington Post, June 20, 1971.

sentative group of misguided people who have brought so much shame upon themselves and those associated with them." In the January 1966 issue of the *Reader's Digest,* John Barron wrote that Klan membership was "well past 10,000 and is growing." But by 1970, J. Edgar Hoover was able to report to Congress that the 18 Klan-type organizations had a combined membership of "some 5,300."* In his last report released on May 16, 1972, two weeks after his death, Hoover set the membership of the various Klans at "approximately 4,500 at present."** He did warn, however, that "in addition to the membership, many thousands of sympathizers lend their support to Klan programs and activities."

The propaganda issued by these "hate-type" groups is yet another facet of their dissemination of bigotry that has not been disregarded by the bureau. In the earlier appropriations report cited, the late director noted: "Indicative of how the propaganda from these groups reaches far beyond the membership, the National States Rights Party, dedicated to white supremacy and highly anti-Negro and anti-Semitic, has an ever-changing active membership of 75 to 200 persons, but the subscription list to its hate-filled tabloid, *The Thunderbolt,* has reached as high as 10,000."*** Just as the bureau should carefully observe those who join radicals in their gatherings, lending moral support on Earth Days or to Free Angela Davis activities or "peace" marches, so, also, should those who subscribe to hate sheets be observed. At the very least their names should be cross-referenced against those on other similar special interest groups' lists. There is little if any doubt this is actually done.

Due to space limitations this report on the FBI vs. the KKK cannot touch on all of the varied aspects of the bureau's work in this area. But one must at least note the fact that the Klans

*Testimony of John Edgar Hoover before the House Subcommittee on Appropriations, *FBI 1971 Appropriation* (Washington, 1970), p. 73.
**Testimony of John Edgar Hoover before the House Subcommittee on Appropriations, *FBI 1973 Appropriation* (Washington, 1972), p. 66.
***Hoover, *FBI 1971 Appropriation,* p. 73.

are not the only purveyors of race hatred in the nation. There are equally dangerous race-mongering organizations spreading their poison among black Americans, yellow Americans, Spanish-speaking Americans, Indians, and possibly every single segment of our society. To go into all of these would not only run into encyclopedic volumes; it would cloud the message— the FBI has been given the task of protecting the victims of violence borne of class hatred.

That the Federal Bureau of Investigation under the late Director Hoover often opposed being bridled with new powers and duties is at this point immaterial. We cannot live in the past, though we must learn from it. The point is: the bureau now has this added duty, and it has, as in every instance in which the agency has been given jurisdiction, performed its work admirably, the views of its critics notwithstanding.

For the Bureau of Investigation in the dawning decades of the twentieth century, there was no category dealing with "civil rights." In the 1925 *Annual Report of the Attorney General of the United States,* civil rights was lumped under "miscellaneous" along with Alaskan affairs, interstate commerce, immigration, customs and smuggling, "and numerous others." No longer is this the case. Not only is civil rights work now a distinct category of the bureau's annual case work, it is an ever-increasing one. In 1960, the FBI handled a total of 1,398 civil rights cases. Three years later the figure had risen to 2,692. This increase was not due to an increased awareness by the bureau that there were people being victimized because of their heritage, it was due to the FBI being placed in charge of these investigations by such legislation as the civil rights acts of 1960 and 1964. Prior to this the agency was not authorized to take action in most cases.

The final figures for 1967 were double those of 1963—5,366. And the later statistics (1972) show yet another all-time high in civil rights cases handled—7,163. We can hope that this action on the part of the FBI men will have a "chilling effect" on would-be hate merchants.

There is much yet to be done, but it has begun. As he so often did, J. Edgar Hoover said it well in January of 1964: "We have conscientiously carried out our responsibilities in the area of civil rights and I have always insisted that every civil rights complaint be given thorough, prompt, and impartial attention. . . . It is known throughout all law enforcement circles that alleged civil rights violations are investigated by the FBI. Many allegations have been referred to the bureau by enlightened police officials who realize that the most effective method of resolving complaints against their departments is to have the true facts developed through impartial investigation by the FBI. . . . Our work in the civil rights field includes far more than unbiased, prompt, objective, and thorough investigations. We took the initiative years ago in providing civil rights training to law enforcement agencies in all parts of the nation. Hundreds of special civil rights schools were conducted during the mid-1950s at the specific request of police officials. These dealt with the Constitution; the Bill of Rights; rulings pertaining to arrests, searches, and seizures; and other matters having a direct bearing on the civil rights field.

"Along the same lines, since January 1957, FBI instructors have lectured on the topic of civil rights at over 1,200 police training schools throughout the country which were attended by over 51,000 police officers.

"In addition, over the years our fingerprint identification and scientific laboratory facilities have been at the disposal of the police departments at all levels, aiding them in establishing the guilty.

"All of these items serve to illustrate the longstanding efforts of the FBI to devote its resources and facilities to the preservation of those rights guaranteed by the Constitution and the laws of the United States."*

How best to conclude a brief report on the FBI vs. the KKK? Perhaps one would just repeat the words of that young black Washington, D.C. police officer: "I want to be an FBI agent."

*Testimony of John Edgar Hoover before the House Subcommittee on Appropriations, *FBI 1965 Appropriation* (Washington, 1964), pp. 57-59.

17. Crime and Civil Rights —A New Federal War
Editors

It is difficult at this juncture, but necessary, to urge a measure of caution in the expanding federal battle against crime and discrimination. In the midst of a straining effort to combat crime in America, it is rather like complaining about the costs of fire fighting to the man whose home is ablaze. Who will listen? The problem is severe; people are concerned, at times angry, about rampant crime that threatens safety; no wonder the public turns for its defense to the government which seems to have most resources, the federal government. But increasing federal police powers is decidedly a mixed blessing. It should not be our first recourse but our last resort. It must be most carefully weighed.

In the case of both crime and civil rights, the federal government, initially through its elected officials, has responded to demands for action. But there are differences, of course, between the federal battle against crime and its war on racial discrimination. Except for some intellectual dissenters, the support for strong measures against crime has been nearly unanimous. Civil rights, while a popular cause in some parts of the country, was prompted more by an elite and a racial minority than by the general public. Nevertheless a similar federal emphasis on both problems blossomed in the 1960s.

Actually, the government in Washington, D.C. went much further toward preempting the civil rights cause than it did the battle against crime. There is a simple reason for this. The civil rights crusade was resisted by states and local communities. But the same communities were very willing to participate in nearly any effort against crime, one exception being in the area of organized crime.

It was in the early 1960s that the civil rights movement began expanding in the South. At that time, FBI jurisdiction was confined almost exclusively to investigating the denial of civil rights "under color of law." This brought the bureau into occasional conflict with Southern law enforcement officials with whom agents needed to cooperate in the performance of their daily duties. At about the same time, in the cities of the North, Midwest, and Far West, organized crime was being recognized as a problem, and it was growing—feeding primarily upon revenue from gambling and prostitution, which were not federal offenses. This crime flourished partly because of general public apathy, but also because in all too many cases local political officials profited from sluggish enforcement. To the extent that the FBI had any jurisdiction in these cases they were again on occasion brought into conflict with local and state officers.

It can be argued that Congress believed that both civil rights matters and organized crime matters were properly the tasks of local law enforcement and, where this broke down, the responsibility of the states. As has often been the case, however, when local communities or states hesitated in moving toward solutions, public demand increased for a federal solution. Congress responded with the civil rights acts in 1957, 1960,

1964, 1965 and 1968, broadly expanding FBI jurisdiction. Moreover, the court decisions and Justice Department policy further widened the bureau's work under older statutes. In the same period, Congress began to study expanded federal jurisdiction in crime areas, enacting the Crime Control and Safe Streets Act of 1968 and the Organized Crime Control Act of 1970. The greatest impetus to the war against organized crime was the congressional authorization of FBI electronic surveillance.

With these tools, the FBI has responded with the same sort of vigor it has displayed in other investigative areas into which it has been thrust by congressional measures, and the results are beginning to show just as was the case in its anti-subversive work of the '40s and '50s. In the most recently reported five-year period the FBI handled a yearly average of nearly 6,000 civil rights cases per year, and it has had some well-publicized successes. It has virtually destroyed the rebuilding Ku Klux Klan and other violence-prone groups fueled by race hatred. The net result has been that the violence and wholesale resistance that marked the most extreme reaction to progress in civil rights efforts has become more and more rare. No one would suggest that violence and resistance to civil rights have disappeared any more than has kidnapping or the Communist Party; but it is no longer a predictable response to civil rights activism in either the South or the North. In addition, the FBI's activity in cases of urban terrorist groups, white and black, in anti-riot cases and in bombings aimed at educational and religious buildings can be said to fall within the broad category of "civil rights" cases and, under the pressure of FBI activity, these too have been sharply reduced.

The same kind of result seems to be in the process of fulfillment in organized crime matters. For many years, the law enforcement community believed that it was necessary to get the "top dogs" in the crime syndicate in order to stifle it effectively. However, armed with new statutory authority, court-sanctioned wiretaps and the experience of the Bureau of Narcotics and

Dangerous Drugs, the FBI has engaged in numerous raids against syndicate gambling operations. The working bookmakers, numbers runners, and *bolita* operators as well as some of their loan shark partners have been arrested and sent to prison rather than receiving the once-common $25.00 fine. In his March 1, 1972 testimony before the House Appropriations Committee, Director Hoover announced that 631 syndicate figures had been convicted of various crimes during the previous fiscal year and that there were an additional 2,361 persons whose cases were in various stages of prosecution.

This is not the text in which to argue the pros and cons of the federal government's civil rights programs. We must note, nevertheless, that law enforcement as it regards civil rights has become nearly exclusively a federal jurisdiction. Violations of state laws, of course, are handled by state authorities; but most current law enforcement seems to deal with violations of U.S. civil rights provisions. It cannot be denied that this has had a tremendous impact on society, and federal police power has grown considerably in the process.

The same is true in the federal campaign against organized crime—and make no mistake about it, somebody *must* campaign against that criminal element, all agree. The scourge is threatened as never before, primarily as the result of the impetus of federal forces—the U.S. Treasury, Justice Department, and the Bureau of Narcotics and Dangerous Drugs, as well as the FBI.

Consider, however, what this trend, if caution is not exercised, means to the nature of American law enforcement. Civil rights and freedom from the power of organized crime are laudable causes, but it should be asked now, before the nation becomes too accustomed to federal law enforcement campaigns, how far do we want to go in this direction? Particularly regarding the FBI, how much power of law enforcement can we afford to put in a national force?

Caution is necessary here; for the real danger of reaching the "police state" is not the FBI as it has been administered, but in the overexpansion of its jurisdiction and power in the course of laudable law enforcement campaigns. As long as a J. Edgar Hoover directs the bureau, overweening power will not be accumulated by the FBI by its own request. But it could happen—it is likely to happen—by a piecemeal federal aggrandizement of new powers, always, of course, for good causes. That adds up to trouble, in the long run.

This is not to say that the nation has gone too far already. There is obviously a place for federal law enforcement and law enforcement assistance. Certain criminal conduct cannot be adequately dealt with as a state and local problem, and so far the FBI's jurisdiction has been restricted to those situations. Organized crime has its interstate operations,* for instance, and certainly the Fugitive Felon Act, as another example, establishes a legitimate law enforcement concern of the federal government. The FBI has not supplanted the local police in the area of street crime and other criminal conduct which troubles our communities.

The FBI is *not* the primary law enforcement agency in the nation. It should never be. Both its record of success (the result of its being a small flexible force) and the checks on its power would deteriorate alarmingly if, one day, the bureau were looked on as our great savior from crime. Its limitations must be observed, for neither the FBI nor any other federal agency can be a panacea. It could, however, become our oppressor.

The division of powers set forth in the United States Constitution is one guideline for avoiding this eventuality. But saying this today is akin to the proverbial woeful cry in the wilderness. Measures are passed in Washington today without mention, let alone serious consideration, of limitations on federal power.

To date, law enforcement has not been preempted over-extensively by congressional grants of power to the FBI. But the one man who realized as did no other the proper limitations

---

*The October, 1972 "mass" investigations of hundreds of the New York City Mafia illustrates that local authorities continue to have a vital input in this field.

of federal law enforcement is gone. It was J. Edgar Hoover who was responsible over 40 years for educating congressmen to the bureau's limitations. With his passing, will the lesson be remembered?

It is this problem with which those who think themselves civil libertarians and the guardians against a police state ought to concern themselves.

18. A Beacon for the Future
Editors

John Edgar Hoover passed away during the course of the study which resulted in this book. Death thus succeeded, where so many critics had failed: the director was replaced. Now is the time for sober assessment of the FBI which was so much the reflection of J. Edgar Hoover, and our guess is that the honest critics, many of whom breathed fire at the longtime director will learn to miss him.

The nation will learn that the FBI which he successfully guided wove the threads of justice and lawful authority with the twine of America's cherished liberties and constitutional rights. It was that same doggedness for which his critics at the time damned him that protected the FBI from misuse. It was that same independence which, again, his critics bemoaned that is being demanded of the FBI without him.

Perhaps the critics see the point already. They seemed to

when they were concerned about L. Patrick Gray's nomination as director. The position was denied Gray on the basis of his *lack* of independence of his chief, the President. Whether or not this was the proper view of Gray is beside the point (it would have been nearly impossible for him to be too independent as an acting director hoping to be nominated as the director); the fact remains that Director Hoover had often been attacked for having been sometimes less than responsive to his political superiors.

If one-time critics of Hoover now find it easier to see the worth of Hoover's sort of independence, so be it. We must be careful not to lose sight of the principle. Just as important, we must not let it be carried to extremes. Independence of political authority can be as dangerous to our liberties as dependence.

The middle ground, fortunately, is lighted by the principles of operation which J. Edgar Hoover left within the bureau which survives him. The FBI is his widow, and she holds the beacon for the proper guidance of the future FBI.

Respect for law is the light from this beacon, and the late director embedded this principle deep into the heart of the bureau. J. Edgar Hoover knew well what the FBI could and could not do properly. He resisted attempts to use his force politically, and he resisted suggestions from whatever source that the FBI undertake illegal operations. In this regard he was independent of his political superiors: he listened to a higher authority—the law.

Just as Hoover was resolute in his regard to his highest authority, his ultimate superior, the law, the FBI which goes on must be resolute. Of course, the agency must be responsible to its political superiors. But even as Hoover had to weigh these two principles in the few instances where they conflicted, the new FBI officials must make their stand first for the higher authority of law.

Admittedly, this will not be so easy for the new director. Hoover, because of his earned respect, had a trump card which he was not afraid to play—he would resign rather than not do his duty as he saw fit. A new director, as Pat Gray no doubt learned, does not have that effective option. He must resolve to use it in any case. He must be ready, foremost, to decline improper orders from his political superiors, and resign if they persist.

In this connection, it makes little difference *which* political body, the presidency or the Congress, controls the bureau most directly. Both are political, and both are capable of misdirecting the FBI. The agency cannot be overly responsive to either.

Nor will it be so easy, with Hoover's passing, for the country to avoid the mistake the late director so often cautioned against. His opponents refused to take his cautions seriously, ascribing to him the worst of motives, but his record was consistent in lobbying against broadened jurisdictions for the FBI. Law enforcement is not constitutionally, nor ought it be, primarily the concern of the national government. The FBI must continue as a limited agency, concerning itself with police functions which are truly those of the national government. We have no need of a national police, or at least the objections to such a force are of more importance than its possible accomplishments.

So, too, we ought to heed the FBI's historic refusal to entertain the passions of the moment. The agency should be directed only to those tasks necessarily requiring the use of the national government's police powers. Within the bureau, we must hope that the corps of special agents continue to dispatch its duties with the same "lack of enthusiasm" which its zealous critics often bemoaned when Hoover was around. What was to some "lack of enthusiasm" was in actuality the FBI's dedication to neutral law enforcement, neutral in the sense that the law was enforced without the passionate anger which sometimes characterized the proponents of the law, no matter whether against organized crime, civil rights violations, or revolutionist conspiracies. The FBI without Hoover must continue in its dispassionate, neutral mode.

Some thought will be given in the near future to fashioning new controls on the FBI, and to reconstituting its basis of authority. A new congressional watchdog is being mentioned. Safeguards against misuse of the FBI ought to be often reassessed, but no watchdog is sufficient once the FBI strays from its highest authority, the law. This could happen under political guidance from the Congress as well as the presidency.

There is danger, too, in the possible mutations which could result from ill-considered changes in the bureau and its functions. For one, the bureau's own built-in safeguards for the rights of the investigated (e. g., the confidentiality of FBI files) are jeopardized when a political body attempts to gain access to the inner workings of the FBI. Also, we risk endangering the public by hamstringing the bureau's methods in the course of protecting the rights of the accused.

No responsible person would advocate abolition of the FBI. It has a function in a free society; and accepting this, we must grant it the agency powers necessary to fulfill that function. Electronic eavesdropping and intelligence activities have obviously been misused of late—but by private parties, not by the FBI. In protecting against such misuse, we must be careful not to destroy the legitimate and necessary uses. Sweeping broadly with the reformer's broom in this area would only destroy the protections against criminal acts and disorder which the average citizen needs and expects. Balancing this consideration with the constitutional liberties of the accused is no easy task, but not one impossible of achievement by a reasonable, freedom-loving people.

Again, the guiding light should be the Federal Bureau of Investigation which J. Edgar Hoover left with us. Changes that are needed or advisable should be in accordance with his main principle, the rule of law which protects and preserves a free America.

INDEX